HOW TO CONVERT ORDINARY GARAGES INTO EXCITING FAMILY ROOMS

Dedication

To Monica and Bill, Betty and Pete, Kay and Joe, Jeanette and Dennis, Betty and Byron, and Liz and their wonderfully convertible garages.

No. 1210
$18.95

HOW TO CONVERT ORDINARY GARAGES INTO EXCITING FAMILY ROOMS

BY RUTH & MIKE WOLVERTON

 TAB BOOKS Inc.

BLUE RIDGE SUMMIT, PA. 17214

FIRST EDITION

FIRST PRINTING

JANUARY 1981

Copyright © 1981 by TAB BOOKS Inc.

Printed in the United States of America

Library of Congress Cataloging in Publication Data

Wolverton, Ruth.
    How to convert ordinary garages into exciting
family rooms.

        Includes index.
        1. Dwellings—Remodeling—Amateurs' manuals.
2. Garages—Remodeling for other use—Amateurs' manuals.
3. Recreation rooms—Design and construction—Amateurs'
manuals. I. Wolverton, Mike, joint author. II. Title.
TH4816.W62   643'.55   80-23572
ISBN 0-8306-9682-2
ISBN 0-8306-1210-6 (pbk.)

Cover photo courtesy of Armstrong Corp.

Contents

Introduction

You maneuver around your daughter sprawled on the living room floor with every one of her 500 jigsaw puzzle pieces spread around her, push aside the spaceship model drying on the dining table and try to find some space for your bookwork between the airplane glue and the wool spilling out of the knitting basket. For the hundredth time you wish that the builder had thought to leave some extra space somewhere in your house—space that, with some work on your part, could become the kind of room of which you and your family dream. A room in which everyone can pursue hobbies, play games, do homework, munch popcorn, watch TV and still have room enough to walk around. If only there *were* such space—

Stop. There is no need for "if only." Your kind of fairy godmother, otherwise known as your builder, has done just that for you. Under your roof, right now, is a large room, which has a roof, a slab floor, and more than likely finished or semi-finished walls and ceiling, probably a door into the kitchen, an outside door, and if you're lucky a window or two. Quite a good start on that great family room you are dreaming about, don't you think?

As you've undoubtedly guessed, that hidden bonus room is your garage, be it single, double, attached or detached. We've all been so conditioned to look upon garages as rooms for cars, bicycles, lawn furniture and all sorts of odds and ends, that we tend to forget that all that lovely space can be put to other use. We don't dispute that it's nice to have a garage for cars and the etc., and we are certainly fond of our cars, may they run forever on little drops of gas, but when it comes to precious living space, our family has definite priority. And so, we are sure, has yours.

The beauty of garage-into-family room conversion is that no expensive new construction is required. No foundation needs to be laid, no roof erected. Even the utilities are already installed. All that needs to be built is one wall. The rest is basically finishing work which can be done a little at a time, indoors, in comfort.

If you think we are sold on garage-to-family room conversions, you are absolutely right. We have done quite a few, one for every house we've lived in and we've moved quite a lot. In fact, when we buy a house we take a good look at the garage to see how well it will convert into that great family room we have come to expect—a room custom made to fit us and our diverse interests and hobbies.

We have tried to put the experience of our many conversions, plus what we could learn from other people and books on a great number of related topics, into the most handy form for you. Chapters 1 through 11 cover all the things you need to know before you drive your first nail: how to plan, how to estimate costs, how to finance, what tools and materials you need, and what the basic techniques are. Chapters 12 through 23 contain actual, step-by-step conversions. You may follow one of these by the numbers, so to speak, if it happens to fit your space and your family.

The space, incidentally, is easier to match than the family interests, since most garages are more or less standard size. However, few families have standard interests, whatever the statistical norm might be. You can easily borrow those features that would make your family happy from another conversion and incorporate them into the basic conversion you are following.

For instance, your wife is longing for a pottery area and you pine for a home office, but the conversion you've chosen talks about sewing centers and potting benches. Simply substitute the pottery area from another conversion for the sewing center in your plans and follow the instructions on how to build a pottery area. Ditto with the home office. All you have to do is to make sure that the alterations are properly incorporated in your plan so they'll fit the available space. We'll show you how to do this in the chapter on planning.

The best was to use this book is to read the first half thoroughly. Then study the chapters containing plans and select the conversion that best suits your space and tastes, incorporating extras if you wish and deleting what doesn't suit. And then you're ready to start.

Warning: Garage conversions can become addictive. It may happen to you.

Ruth and Mike Wolverton

Chapter 1
Climbing the
Financial Jungle Gym

The need for extra family living space seldom, if ever, coincides with times of prosperity when there's extra money in the bank to cover the cost of materials and services necessary to bring about that added family room. As a matter of fact, in our own experience, every time we most desperately needed a family room was the very time when our family finances were at low tide. But not to worry. There is a way to finance your extra room even though your financial tide at the moment is exposing acres of embarrassing monetary mud flats.

HOW TO FINANCE YOUR NEW FAMILY ROOM

If you live in a state that allows "open end" mortgages or other types of mortgages than can be added on to, you may find it surprisingly easy to get a home improvement loan from your mortgage company. Once, when we lived in Missouri, we went this quick, painless route. In a couple of hours one afternoon we had the cost of our planned improvements added to our 20-year mortgage, our monthly payments increased by a few dollars and the cash in hand to carry out our plans. By all means follow this route if you can. A call to your mortgage company will tell you if it is possible. Let's hope it is. If, however, your inquiry gets a negative response, then a credit union is your next best option.

Credit Union Loans, A Preferred Route

One of the best places to obtain a loan for any purpose is from a credit union—if you are a member, that is. Most credit unions offer low-interest loans for home improvements. Furthermore, their officers are not likely to give you the third degree about your competency if you plan to do the home improvements yourself, as indeed you are. You can often make personal unsecured loans up to $10,000 at half the interest rate charged by finance companies and at even less interest than that charged by commercial banks.

We recently checked a local credit union, a commercial bank and a small loan company on the same day, shopping for interest rates on personal loans (which will be higher than any other type of loan). We were quoted 12.1 percent by the credit union, 14.7 percent by the bank, and a whooping 22.6 percent by the friendly finance company.

If you do not belong to a credit union you will find it's now possible to join one thanks to liberalized federal and state regulations governing the charters of financial cooperatives.

Anyone in New York City can join the 58-year-old Melrose Credit Union, for example, and in Washington, D.C., nearly anyone can become a member of the Greenbelt Federal Credit Union by joining Consumer's Co-op, which operates inflation fighting shopping centers around the area. The states of New York, Wisconsin, Michigan and Texas, among others, allow open membership in credit unions as long as a member lives and works in the state or city where the cooperative is located.

For information on credit unions near you and what it takes to join one, contact your state's credit union association (it may go be "league") or write the Credit Union National Association, Box 431 Madison, WI 53701.

Overdraft Checking Account: A Neat Way To Finance Your Family Room

If you think an overdraft (or "reserve") checking account is just a convenient way to avoid bounced checks, we have great news for you. A revolution in American banking during the 1970's gave rise to the idea that banks could offer a *line of credit* to customers through their regular checking accounts. The typical line of credit around the country usually ranges between $500 and $5,000. However, we've come across some that allow you take out an unsecured loan of $25,000 or more by simply writing a check.

Using the overdraft checking account method to borrow money for a garage-to-family room conversion is ideal if you plan to do most of the work yourself. You'll never borrow more than you need and you won't borrow until you do need the money, so you'll save yourself a bundle on interest.

You can hunt for a bargain in a sliding glass door, for instance, and take your time in doing so, without any borrowed money steadily adding up interest in the meantime. When you do find just the door you're looking for at the price you want to pay, you'll write a check which will take a few days to pass through your bank. The bank will not start charging you interest on the money until the day they debit your overdraft account. Which means you have several days free use of the bank's money.

How's that? Interest rates on money borrowed from your bank by legally overdrawing your checking account are usually less than interest rates for other type loans, too. In the spring of 1980, for instance, finance charges were about 12½—slightly less than the going rate for new home mortgages! Most banks were giving customers up to five years to repay these loans—some required 1/20 of the amount overdrawn to be repaid each month, plus interest.

One word of warning if you do decide to open one of these checking accounts to finance your home improvements. Shop around for the best deal. And be leary of traps. Some banks will let you overdraw your checking account by the amount you have in your savings account. That's great for the bank but costly for you. What happens in effect you wind up paying the bank interest for using your own money. So make sure you're not paying interest unless you're using the *bank's* money.

We recommend that you call several banks in your area and ask them to send you information and an application for their overdraft accounts. When you receive the information, look for the bank that offers you the most liberal credit line with lowest interest rate and most flexible repayment schedule—and the lowest cost credit life insurance, if you want that. In all likelihood you can set up the account entirely by mail, without setting foot inside the bank at all.

Banks and Savings and Loan Associations, the Traditional Route

Commercial banks, savings banks, and savings and loan associations offer specific loans for home improvement and for energy-saving improvements. These loans tend to be more rigid than over-draft loans but, on the bright side, interest charges are often lower. Special discounts are sometimes offered, so you might find a bargain—a 9-10% annual interest rate. These loans are a great way to go if you are the kind of person who thrives on a rigid repayment schedule.

The very lowest interest rates can be had by taking out a "passbook loan" — only 7-9% at times. But beware—the bank is actually loaning you your own money! They will charge you in essence from 1-5% more to use an amount of money equal to what you have in your savings account than what they are paying you in interest on your savings. And if, God forbid, you default on your payments, the bank will confiscate your savings account to pay off the loan. Definitely not a recommended route.

Second Mortgages, a So-So Proposition for Family Room Conversions

In some states it is easy to get a few thousand dollars together by taking out a second mortgage on your home. In this case you are borrowing on your equity in the property. Interest rates for second mortgages run high—16-18% in most places as of early 1980. And still rising, naturally. You may find that you can refinance a new mortgage at a higher interest rate and have money left over for your project. This, again, is a good deal for the mortgage company, but can be very expensive for you in the long run. Just think of all that interest you'll be paying for those long, long years. A second mortgage is a last resort option and not used unless all else fails. In some states, such as Kansas and Texas, where they have Homestead Laws, it is very difficult to come by second mortgages and impossible to refinance an existing mortgage while you use the property as your home.

Finance Companies

Although there are plenty of local and national finance companies who will generously offer to give you "easy" loans for your project, we cannot recommend this method of getting funds for garage conversions as a viable alternative. Interest rates are simply exorbitant. We found interest rates of up to 40% for loans under $300.00, sliding down to 20% for loans over $2,500.

Executive Loans By Mail

If you want to pay up to 20% for a hassle-free, unsecured loan you can borrow up to about $15,000 from any one of several large consumer finance companies. The only catch is that you must have an annual income of no lower than $18,000 and a good standing at your local retail merchants credit bureau. These loans are handled in confidence by mail and require no interviews, co-signers or witnesses. It takes only about two weeks to finalize such loans and most companies give you up to five years to repay. If you're interested in going this route to finance your new family room, you might write to any of the following companies for information:

Beneficial Executive Loan Service
2858 Steven Creek Blvd.
San Jose, CA 95128 (Toll-free 800-538-6811)

Nationwide Finance Corp.
1660 S. Albion Street (Suite 927)
Denver, CL 80222 (Toll-free 800-525-2131)

Postal Thrift Loans
703 Douglas Street
Sioux City, IA 51102

If you have a Diners Club Card, or other executive credit card, you can arrange personal loans by mail up to $25,000, also through the above agencies.

Still Another Way To Go If You Have Collateral

You don't have to live in New York City to cash in on a unique loan service offered by the Provident Loan Society, 346 Park Avenue South, New York, NY 10010. You can put up almost anything of value as collateral—jewelry, furs, stamps, coins, whatever—and send it to them by mail. They make no investigation into your finances, your employment, or purpose of the loan. Why should they, with all that lovely collateral in their hot flippers? Of course, you pay a price for all that confidentiality—an interest rate computed daily that amounts to 19-20% annually on loans up to $3,000. That's pretty steep for a secured loan.

THERE IS A WAY

The point is, don't just sit there and stare longingly at that immense garage space because you don't happen to have the cash in the bank to pay for the conversion. A familyroom/garage conversion will increase the value of your home by much more than it will cost even if you use expensive borrowed money. In any case—it's only money and with the way inflation is going you'll be paying it back with cheaper and cheaper dollars anyway. So pick the method to finance your conversion that suits you best and go to it.

Chapter 2
The Joys of
Space Planning

When you go through all the hassle and expense of converting your garage into a family room, you deserve to come out with an outstanding addition to your family living space: a room that is multi-purpose and provides the space and equipment needed by you and your family to pursue your interests and hobbies. In order to come up with such an extraordinary room you have to do some sleuthing and planning. Your first task will be to make an inventory of the wants and needs of your family.

MAKING A SPACE INVENTORY FOR YOUR FAMILY

You'll need a pen and sheet of paper for each member of your family. Let those old enough to write their name acoss the top of the page and then list all of the activities they hope to have room for in the new family room. For those not yet able to write you'll have to perform this chore. And don't forget those members of the family who can't speak for themselves—the fish in the aquarium you've always wanted, the house plants that need a home, even the special cushion for good old Rex.

As for you, you'll not only list your wants and needs, but also try to cover those activities that members of the family engage in as a group: game playing, TV watching and such.

Your completed inventory sheets will probably resemble these which started off our latest family room conversion.

David (age 12)

- A good place to draw and paint.
- Lots of room to let my models dry.
- A place where I can listen to the stereo while I work.
- A place for model building and storing the stuff.
- Room to play games.

Alyson (age 9)

- A place to do my jigsaw puzzles where they can stay put.
- A place for coloring and painting where I also can see the TV.
- A place where I can do my home work so I won't have to be alone upstairs.
- A place where I can practice my dance steps.
- A place to play games with other people.

Ruth

- A place for my sewing machine and sewing stuff.
- Room for my craft stuff and space to spread it out.
- A place to play games with the kids.
- Lots of room for my plants.
- A place for listening to music while working with craft materials and sewing.
- A place to watch TV while doing more of the above.

Mike

- A place for hand building pottery.
- A place to make drawings.
- A place to play games.
- A place to listen to music.
- A place to play my guitar and sing.

In addition to the inventory lists watch your family at work and play for a few days. You might notice another, unverbalized need or two. We found out that one thing our proposed family room needed, which nobody mentioned and that the present arrangements sadly lacked, was some sort of snack facility and simple food preparation area.

Our kitchen is small and neither one of us likes to cook in there by ourselves except for the day-by-day, regular meal preparation which we've streamlined as much as possible. Our fun cooking—treats for the family or special dishes we prepare ahead for weekends or company, we like to whip up while talking, playing games or listening to music. Also, since we are nibblers and avid fans of PBS and pay-TV, we find it quite difficult to make the popcorn or hot chocolate everyone is craving without missing part of the TV program. So we added a simple food preparation to our inventory list of wants and needs.

If, by this time, you feel that even your converted double garage with the extra alcove will only be a drop in the bucket of your space needs and what is really needed would equal the size of your local air terminal, don't worry. We all go through this. Rest assured that your garage conversion can and will provide all the space you need. The answer is overlapping and multi-use.

OVERLAPPING AND MULTI-USE OF SPACE AND EQUIPMENT

The real secret of designing an extra-ordinary familyroom is learning to apply the tricks of overlapping and multi-use of space. Multi-use is a fine art which the designers of RV vehicles and small recreational cruisers have perfected to an amazing degree. We recommend that you "window shop" these vehicles, as well as some of the smaller mobile homes and campers for ideas on how small areas can be used for large activities.

The first step in multi-use and/or overlapping is to make a list of the equipment you need for each of the wants on your lists. While this may seem tedious and elementary we beg you not to omit this step. It is much better to be a bit simple and even redundant now than to remember much later that you left out something vital which you may or may not be able to fit in. So—going back to our sample lists we could then have the following lists of needed equipment:

David

1. A work table or counter with a large washable surface for painting and drawing. Also storage for paints, pencils, brushes, paper. Room to let paintings dry. Storage for work in progress and finished work.

2. A table for model building and shelves for the models to dry on.

3. Stereo for listening to music and the records and tapes plus storage for the latter.

4. Floor cushions for TV watching.

5. Room for TV set.

6. A game table and chairs.

Alyson

1. Table, counter or other surface for her jigsaw puzzles, also storage for work in progress and boxes of puzzles.

2. Work table or counter for drawing and painting, storage for crayons, paints, coloring books, paper, work in progress and finished work.

3. Game table and chairs.

4. Desk or table for homework.

5. Open space for dancing.

6. Stereo and records, tapes.

7. TV.

We're sure you can see how this multi-use game works, but just for practice let's finish the lists and then go on to the next step.

Ruth

1. Sewing center including table or counter for sewing machine, storage for patterns, materials, findings. Cutting table, room for ironing board which she finds indispensable while sewing.

2. Work table or counter for craft work, storage for craft materials.

3. Game table and chairs.

4. Stereo.

5. TV.

6. Comfortable chair for listening and watching the above.

7. Shelves, tables or floor garden for houseplants.

Mike

1. Counter for pottery making and easy clean-up area, clay storage, tool storage and room for drying work.

2. Drawing table and storage for drawing materials.

3. Game table and chairs.

4. Music stand and storage for music books and sheet music plus special place for guitar.

5. Stereo plus tapes and records.

6. TV and comfortable chair.

In addition we needed a counter/work center for our cooking and snacking. Which reminded us that we also had to make room for books: cook books for our culinary activities, reference books for homework, current books we were reading, a permanent central location for all our library books so that we no longer supported the local library with our fines alone, and space for magazines and newspapers. So we added shelves to our lists, lots of them.

Now we are ready for the next step. Take a fresh sheet of paper. Write "MASTER LIST" across the top. Now, going back over your inventory lists one by one, transfer each item to the master list. When you come to a duplication, cross it out on the inventory list. Enter each item only once on the master list.

Our master list looked like this:

SAMPLE MASTER LIST

1. A work table or counter for painting and drawing with washable surface. Storage for drawing and painting materials, also for work in progress and finished work. Drying space.

2. A work table for model building with storage and shelves for drying and display.

3. Counter and/or table for sewing plus storage.

4. Counter and/or table for craft work plus storage.

5. Counter or work table for hand building pottery and storage.

6. Plant center for display and care of plants.

7. Desk or table for home work.

8. Game table and four chairs.

9. TV.

10. Stereo and storage for records and tapes.

11. Book shelves.

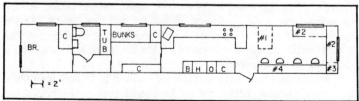

Fig. 2-1. Five of us lived, worked and played in this 8×58 marvel.

12. Snackbar/food preparation center.
13. Comfortable chairs.
14. Couch and floor cushions.

As we were making our master list we noticed that the drawing and/or painting counter are among the top priority items. They are so much in demand that they might be used by more than one person at a time since David, Alyson and Mike all asked for them. In order to accomodate a multi-use of the drawing area we could use any of five options: we could use a drop leaf on a counter to accomodate two people intent on drawing or painting, we could build a special drawing board which could be set on the game table or on a counter, we could make room for an easel or even a double easel, or we could use a large fold-down table. Any of these solutions would be quite satisfactory and take in an area of about 2×5-feet. Storage could be above and below the work surfaces, except for the easels, which are part of a counter/storage system.

The next major item on the list is a craft center. Since Ruth requested it as a sewing center as well, it is highly unlikely that she would use both at the same time, so the centers could be combined. However, Mike wanted a work center for his pottery, David asked for space for model building activities, and Alyson likes to work with clay and dabble in crafts, too. So, since all members of the family engage in craft work at some time or other we decided that it would probably be best to build a large, well equipped craft center for all to enjoy. This would take a good deal of room, we realized, an area of about 4×6 feet or more. But if we made the craft center adjacent to the drawing/painting area we would have additional work space and storage space for supplies. Also, since craft work tends to be messy, the floor and wall area in that part of the room could be finished in a way that makes clean up easy. Which made us think of our house plants.

House plants, as those who raise them know, also tends to be messy, what with dropping leaves, spilled water, traces of sand and soil and so forth. At least ours are. Since our plants tend to be on the untidy side we thought it would be great to incorporate the plant center in the easy clean-up area, adjacent to the craft center. And, since both craft work and plants need good lighting this works from that angle, too. We had a number of options on how to do this as shown in Fig. 2-2.

Next was the sewing center. We decided to make it part of a storage wall which would house records, tapes, games, books, as well as sewing accessories, patterns, magazines and newspapers. As we looked more closely at our plans for the sewing center we noticed that it could easily double as a home office and also provide Alyson with a neat place to do homework.

We checked back and found that we still had to account for a place for Alyson's jigsaw puzzles and the food/snack center. We thought we could provide Alyson with a board on casters that would slide under the

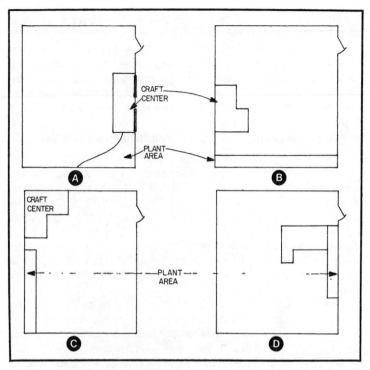

Fig. 2-2. Trying out positions for proposed plant area and craft Center.

couch for safe keeping, or we could equip a drawer with a set-in top, or we could have a pull-up or fold-down shelf for her, or we could settle for a plain board and a place for it on a shelf.

As we discussed our proposed food snack preparation center we came to the conclusion that to be of most use and of greatest efficiency the center would have to be movable. We could have loved to build one of those great serving carts with flip-up sides but our kitchen was so tiny we never could have gotten the cart into it and that made the whole cart idea worthless. Instead we settled on a simple three-shelved serving cart with a built-in electrical outlet built that could be rolled from frig to family room, use borrowed counter space from the craft center and then back to the kitchen for cleaning and garbage disposal.

And that, my friend, is the way to go about making a master list. Your lot is much easier than ours, since we had to design from among the options offered in the conversions in this book.

We had a crash course in this some years ago when we and our three oldest children spent several months in a mobile home designed for traveling. Not only did we have to provide play and recreational space in this narrow 58-foot wonder for the kids and us, but the living room/dinette/kitchen also had to serve as our temporary office. How we did it can be seen in Fig. 2-1.

While the results were far from ideal, we managed to enjoy our time in the mobile home and still cherish fond memories of cooking sprees that included making jam and vast batches of cookies for Christmas presents; a wild week of sewing Easter clothes; carpentry projects and a bit of extra whittling thrown in for the fun. And, believe it or not, we met our deadlines.

DRAWING A PRELIMINARY SKETCH OF YOUR FUTURE FAMILY ROOM

Before you go any further, it is a good idea to hunt up paper and pencil again and to make a preliminary sketch of all the goodies you're going to build. We like to use a tablet of 4×4 quad ruled paper (our favorite is the "Executive Planning Pad" by Stuart Hall, K.C. Mo.). A plastic T-square, ruler and triangle set from your friendly supermarket will set you up in the sketching business. The hard back of the afore-mentioned Executive Planning Pad can serve as a portable drawing board against which you can work your T-square. Not quite in accordance with the latest from the drafting profession but adequate for the job.

For your preliminary sketch, simply draw the rough outline of your garage on the paper and indicate with lines where you are going to put what project. Don't worry about proportions and measurements right now, that comes later. Just be sure to get everything on the sketch. And please, don't forget any existing windows and doors which you indicate by using the symbols shown in (Fig. 2-3). When you're finished, take your master plan to the garage and compare what's there to what you have drawn. Next get out your trusty power tape rule and sharpen your pencils—the time has come for a scale drawing and the first step is measuring your space.

Measuring Space

Starting in one corner of your garage use your power tape rule to measure the entire length of each wall from corner to corner where the walls meet the floor. Jot down the measurements along the corresponding lines of your sketch on the *outside* of the rectangle. Next measure each wall again, this time at the heigh of any window openings and note down the widths of the oepnings separately as well as the distances from windows to windows and from windows to the corners of the room. Do the same for the door openings and record all the new measurements on the *inside* of the rectangle in the proper places (Fig. 2-4). Lastly measure the height of the walls. Now you're ready to make a floor plan of your garage.

How To Make A Floor Plan To Scale

Get out a fresh piece of your 4×4 quad ruled paper. Now you have to decide how big a sketch or plan you want. We find it easy to use a

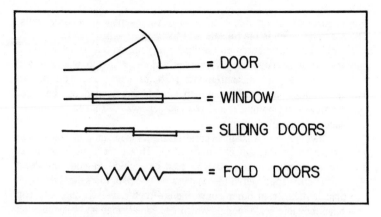

Fig. 2-3. Architectural symbols for marking windows and doors.

scale of 1 square (¼-inch = 1 foot). If you prefer a bigger sketch you can use a 2 square, (½-inch = 1 foot ratio), or, if you really like to work large, a 4 square, (1-inch =1 foot).

For the moment we'll go with the 1 inch = 1foot scale. Take the complete measurement of one of your garage walls, the number you've recorded on the outside of your sketch, draw a line on your paper and count off the required number of squares to come up with the requisite length. Do the same with the other walls. You have now a scale plan of the inside of your garage. With your T-square draw another rectangle

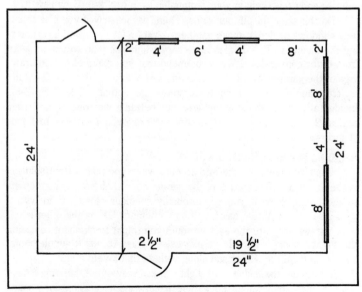

Fig. 2-4. Noting measurements on a plan.

half a square to the outside of the first to represent your outside walls. The space between is the thickness of the wall, roughly 6 inches.

Next, take the figures on the inside of your sketch, translate them into the scale by counting off squares and draw in the windows and doors. Compare your measurements with the conversion you plan to use and indicate any adjustments that might be needed on the plan. Usually that won't be much, and you can get away with a little more or less space around the projects.

If, however, you want incorporate projects from another conversion you'll have to go through one more step. This time on a fresh sheet draw to scale all the projects you plan to include in your proposed room—the ones specified in the conversion you plan to use and the ones you plan to take from other conversions—then cut each one out. You now have movable scale models which you can arrange and rearrange on your floor plan until you find just the right place for them. When you do, trace your models onto your scaled floor plan and you have a complete plan of your proposed family room.

How To Make An Elevation Drawing To Scale

Making an elevation drawing to scale can be quite helpful when planning any conversions. Here's how its done: Make a rectangle using the height and length of a wall. You'll have to dash back out to the garage and record some vertical facts—the height from floor to window bottom, and from top of window to ceiling, also from top of doors to ceiling. Back at your pad, translate your measurements into scale squares and draw them in your rectangles as in Fig. 2-5. Easy isn't it?

Do the same for all four walls. Then, particularly if you plan to cut new windows or doors, make another elevation for each wall incorporating the changes. This is also necessary when you plan to use projects from other conversions. We recommend that you make elevation drawings of the garage door wall both inside and outside nothing such details as trim and facing boards to simplify the actual work (Fig. 2-5). Incidentally, when drawing elevation it's better to use one of the larger scales: 2 squares to 1 foot (½-inch=1foot) or even 4 squares to 1 foot (1-inch=1-foot).

DECIDING THE BEST FRONT SOLUTION

What you need to take into account when you plan a front solution is the directional orientation of the garage door(s). If your garage opens to the north or west you will probably consider closing it in with a well-insulated wall that has few if any, openings. If, on the other hand, your garage opens to the east or south you might think about replacing the garage doors with a large expanse of glass to admit supplemental solar heat from the winter sun along with all that lovely light.

While on the subject of light, more residential building codes require that your converted garage have window and/or door space admitting natural light equal to 1/10th its floor space. In other words, a

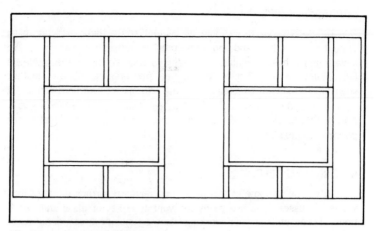

Fig. 2-5. A front elevation drawing.

20×20-foot garage (400 square feet) conversion will require at least 40 square feet of transparent or translucent window and/or door space. A skylight will qualify as a window in this case. Forty square feet isn't all that much, so it's no problem to conform to that rule. Actually you'll in all likelihood opt for more than the basic light requirements as all our conversions do.

CHOOSING DOORS, WINDOWS AND SKYLIGHTS

Window and door placement will be determined to some extent by the ways in which you plan to use your new room. Your particular climate, the exposure of your building and the immediate environment (i.e.) busy streets, blank walls, or close neighbors, will also have a lot to do with your final decision of how many openings to put where. Cross ventilation is still another consideration.

Sliding glass doors, the simplest solution, work well if they lead out onto a patio or garden, but are rather grim and uninspiring when the view is your old driveway. Your car may be the latest model and kept in immaculate condition but for a steady view it leaves much to be desired.

In any case, be sure that your sliding doors are well insulated. More about that in the chapter on insulation. There is no law that says your new family room has to have an outside door, so if you want to keep the through traffic down or if you already have several outside doors in your home, omit another entrance altogether. This goes for security reasons, too.

Skylights are usually installed when windows or doors not practical or desirable for any of the above reasons or because it would be too difficult to break through brick or masonry walls. Also, skylights can bring desired light just where you want it, right in the middle of the room or in a corner, which is a great boon for plants and such.

OUTSIDE FINISHING.

Unless you go the sliding glass door route there will be space around new windows and doors that must be finished in some way. We have found it best to match the original siding which, on the whole, is fairly easy to do. Painted or stained plywood panels are another solution. But stay away from brick work. No matter how hard you try, it won't match the original brick until it has weathered for several years. And don't attempt to tackle stucco unless you are a professional or can get professional help.

GETTING IT ALL TOGETHER

After you've come to satisfactory decisions regarding the questions we've discussed, you are ready for your final set of plans and elevations. These will be your working plans so include every detail carefully. Don't be afraid to change something here or there after a day or so. Make absolutely sure that the plans depict exactly what you want in your future family room. In fact, it is a good idea to put the plans aside for a few days and then study them once more. It's amazing how often we find a flaw or mistake, or discover something we haven't thought of when we follow this routine. But, on the other hand, don't draw out this process too long either. There has to be a point at which you say, "This is It," and begin the actual work.

However, before you swing that hammer and tote that crowbar you'll have to consider the question of permits and other such bureaucratic red tape.

When You Do and Do Not Need Permits

Generally speaking you do not need a building permit unless you are planning to alter the exterior of your home or build onto it. However, there are exceptions and these exceptions vary from place to place. Contact your local city or county planning department to learn the rules that apply in your area. You may well be pleasantly surprised at the help you can get from this source.

At any rate you will profit from getting acquainted with your local building codes whether permits are required of you or not. These codes, which regulate such things as insulation, wiring, plumbing, heating and air conditioning, are set up for your protection. If you follow the recommendations of the building codes in your locality you can be assured that what you build will be safe and secure for your family. Even if some of the regulations seem bothersome and unnecessary, it is always good insurance for the future to go along. If you do come across a requirement you simply can't live with, you have recourse. Variations to building codes are granted quite frequently if you can show good cause.

How To Move Smoothly Through City Hall

After you've done your homework with your local building codes and finalized your plans or converting your garage into a family room, double check your plans and material lists to be sure they conform with all your community's building requirements. Take them to your city or county Planning Department and ask for someone to go over them with you. If you need to make something in your plans at variance with one of the code regulations, this is the time to bring it up. Simply ask the person helping you for his/her suggestions and assistance. Most of the time the problem can be solved on the spot by adopting a suggested acceptable alternative. If not, you will have a "friend in court" when it is necessary to go before the Planning Commission for a formal variance.

If you follow the family room conversions we have outlined later in the book, you most probably will not encounter any problems since all of our plans conform to the Uniform Building Codes in use in most parts of the country.

With all these preliminaries out of the way we can now turn our attention to the tools we'll need for the job.

Chapter 3
The Tools You'll Need

Turning your garage into a familyroom will be an enjoyable, satisfying experience if you choose the proper tools for the job and learn to use them efficiently. That means becoming thoroughly familiar with each of your tools, knowing its capabilities as well as its limitations. Nothing is quite so frustrating as using the wrong tool for a job. A little practice with your tools will give you the feel of the work—in this case a little experience in hand is worth a thousand words on a page. And if, in addition to the above, you will faithfully promise to keep your tools sharp, clean and well organized, you're well on your way to becoming a professional garage converter. The basic rule is to respect your tools, know them well and take your time when you use them. Patience is a much neglected virtue, here as well as elsewhere.

BASIC TOOLS

Two hammers will be necessary for the variety of work you'll encounter when you convert your garage. A good quality nail or claw hammer is essential for driving the bucketfuls of common and finishing nails you'll be using. You'll also need a medium weight ball peen hammer for driving hardened masonry nails into concrete, for striking cold chisels and for hammering metal.

When you use your hammer hold it where it feels most comfortable when you swing it and strike squarely, with the hammer face parallel to the surface being nailed. Never strike with the cheek of the hammer. Don't ever use a hammer with a loose or damaged handle. That could be quite a pain—literally. Nor should you work with a hammer that has a chipped striking face, a worn face or one that looks like a mushroom. (No prejudice against mushrooms or other fungi intended).

When it comes to cutting windows and doors, a multi-purpose saw made by Wells Manufacturing Corp., Three Rivers, MI, and available at most hardware stores is a joy to use. It also does a fine job cutting beams, posts and notches without undercutting. And the saw has both front and rear handles to keep your work steady. A ¼-horsepower saber saw with an assortment of blades will do most of what's left of your sawing chores. More about that versatile favorite of ours later.

You won't need a circular saw, which is good because they are rather expensive. Of course, if you already own one use it whenever you feel the time is right. If you don't have one, but on rare occasions want to use a circular saw, you can use our own solution which works quite well. We use an inexpensive attachment for our portable electric drill available from Sears. It's a circular saw blade in an aluminum-cast housing which mounts to the arbor on the drill chuck. The base will tilt to 45 degrees and the circular saw attachment fits the ¼- and the ⅜-inch drill as well.

When it comes to drills, opt for a good one. It should be double insulated so you can plug it into any 115-volt outlet without grounding. It should also be capable of drilling through most materials: wood, masonry, plastic and ceramics. A good drill should have a trigger that lets you change speed by varying the pressure on it, a speed lock and reversible drilling action for easy removal of screws. Our pet is one sold by Montgomery Ward which has a plastic housing that doesn't rust, chip, peel, crack or dent.

Dull drill bits can not only ruin your work but they can be injurious to you. So—get yourself a drill sharpener. We find the one made by Black & Decker most useful. It works like an electric pencil sharpener (what could be easier?) and keep your bits sharp at the correct relief angle.

If you have trouble with your bit skittering and marring the surface of the material you are working on, you can get help if you invest a few bucks in a drill guide made by The Stanley Works. That little gadget makes it possible to drill perfect right angles without any innate talent in that direction on your part. The guide holds the bit while you do the drilling and will accomodate 13 different bits—from 1/16- to ¼-inch.

"Less is More" With Tools

The hammers, saws and drills suggested above are all the basic tools you'll need to acquire. You should get some helper and hand tools, too, and we'll discuss these in a minute. But as far as other tools are concerned, they are used so seldom that it's much more economical to rent them when needed. You can actually use more tools in the long run if you don't invest in expensive welders, circular and chain saws, drill presses, paint sprayers, sandblasters and so forth, but instead set a fraction of the money aside to rent exactly what you need when you need it. It's amazing how many tools you can get your hands on by *not* buying. Not to mention the considerable savings in work space.

A Few of the Best Helper Tools

If you truly want to enjoy your conversion projects you'll need to treat yourself to some extras. They'll make the work go easier and faster and, in addition, act as a growth hormone to your timidly sprouting gut feeling of competency. Here is our tried and true list of these extras, starting with what we consider to be "basic essential extras" namely sawhorses.

Sawhorses. By all means get some of these super helpers. You'll never regret it. We didn't own any for quite some time, and didn't know what we were missing until a kind friend brought his set over when we were starting on a new project.

We wouldn't be without them now—ever. So get yourself a couple, four if you can. There are kits available at building supply stores and lumberyards and we recommend that you get one or two and build your own. If you have a storage problem, it might be better to get some of the sturdy steel sawhorses made by Porta-Horse Corp. These nifty things fold quite compactly for storage and carrying.

Hand Tools. There's a four-in-one tool made by Diamond Tool and Horseshoe Co., which combines an adjustable wrench, pliers, screwdriver pry and wire cutter. Its called the "Handyboy" and for once the name fits the kid. Get one.

The Brookstone Company makes a dandy pair of pliers with especially designed tip and jaws to grasp a wide range of nut sizes. No matter how many wrenches you accumulate you never have the right size handy. (At least we never do, you might be luckier). Regular pliers have a nasty habit of slipping and barking knuckles—or stripping the nut so it can't be worked. The above jewel won't do either.

On the more mundane side, you'll need to acquire two sets of four to six screwdrivers, one with conventional and the other with Phillips head drivers.

An item which will be handy even though it lacks in excitment is a large adjustable wrench. Together with the smaller one on your Handyboy, it should cover all your "wrenching" needs.

A mechanical stapler is another hand tool we'd hate to be without and always mention in our "When We Convert Our Next Garage" list. The trusty staple gun can do a long list of jobs quite efficiently. Sears has a heavy duty stapler with two settings for extra driving force when needed. It drives ¼-inch to 9/16-inch long staples which will take you all the way from light upholstering to roofing.

Two sizes of wood chisels (½-inch and 1-inch blades) and one larger sized cold chisel (1½-inch blade) are rather necessary, too. And, of course, you'll have to have at least a half dozen C-clamps in three different sizes. And these, friend, are your nifty helpers.

We do have a couple more favorites—not exactly necessary but so helpful we can't resist mentioning them. We find frequent use for an adjustable locking plier/wrench and C-clamps. The thing is a joy to use—when you pick it up you actually have about seven different tools in your hand all at once. Yes—seven. You get a clamp, pliers, gripping tool, adjustable wrench, portable vise, pipe wrench, and locking wrench. The C-clamp works the same way—with a ten inch deep throat, yet. We call the plier wrench our Woodward/Bernstein tool. The C-clamp is, naturally, Deep Throat. These "Watergate" tools come to our rescue when we are in deep trouble. The plier/wrench has a fingertip release and the ten-inch, straight-jaw model gives more than two tons of positive grip. All that can be had for roughly $5.00 at Sears.

To Measure And Mark. The most important tools for coming up with an extraordinary family room from an ordinary garage are your measuring tools. It took us several years to learn that our projects did not turn out well because of shoddy measuring. It took some more time, trial and error to come up with the proper measuring tools to do a craftsman-like job. Believe us, the simple skill of measuring materials accurately and properly marking lines where cuts are to be made is the key to having your projects turn out the way you want them.

While less is more when it comes to regular tools, more is better—as far as accuracy is concerned—when considering measuring tools. These days we wouldn't think of beginning the simplest project without all the following handily available:

- Steel rule
- Bench rule
- Yardstick
- Zigzag folding rule with extension
- Power tape rule
- Tape
- Calipers
- Slip-stick
- Carpenter's steel square
- Try square
- Sliding T-bevel
- Protractor
- Dividers
- Plumb bob
- Chalk line tool
- Carpenter's level
- Pocket level
- Scriber
- Assortment of well sharpened pencils

There are also various kinds of gauges that come in handy from time to time when you need specialized measurement, but those can be borrowed or bought when actually needed. The tools on the list above will keep you from the fatal temptation, that nemesis of all amateur craftpersons, the tendency to "guess-timation." Brandish any one of them and that evil will be exorcised for a while, brandish all and it will be gone for good.

Acquiring all the necessary tools plus the extras is only half the battle, keeping the tools well organized and easily accessible is the other. There are many ways to accomplish the latter and everyone swears by his/her own method. As far as we are concerned, workbenches aren't necessary.

In the many home improvement and remodeling projects we have carried out over the past twenty years or so we've never needed one. We differ, however, somewhat on what we do need. Mike prefers to hang his tools on a peg board. Ruth, on the other hand, abhors peg boards and prefers tool-totes and tool boxes. In fact, one of her favorites is an cavernous old satchel reminiscent of the famous baby-bag of the Victorian era, which can be filled to the brim with hand tools and transported anywhere. You're on your own with that decision. Just as long as you know where everything is and can get to it without a hassle that's all that's necessary.

Buying and organizing your tools is the beginning of a long and hopefully happy, relationship between you and them. As we mentioned before, the next vital step is to become thoroughly familiar with your tools and learn the most effective ways to use them. That applies to each and every tool, from the simplest rule to the most complex power drill with millions of accessories. So here we go—starting with your measuring tools because they are the key tools that insure the success of your projects.

MEASURING AND MARKING TOOLS

In our world today there are two systems of measurements. Most of the world uses the metric system. The United States, however, still uses the U.S. Customary System (U.S.C.S.) although we are involved in the hesitant process of conversion to metric. In effect, both systems are presently in use, though metric users are by far the minority in the U.S.

Each system converts quite easily to the other so actually there is no problem, except one of custom and habit. We like metric because the arithmetic is so easy you can do it in your head. The conversion from U.S.C.S. isn't difficult either if you keep two sets of figures in your mind: 1 meter=39.37 inches, and 1 inch = 25.4 millimeters. As you can see it's a bit easier to go from inches into millimeters than the other way around.

Most of the linear measuring devices made in the U.S.A. now carry both the metric and U.S.C.S. scales. U.S.C.S. rules offer a large variety of both fractional and decimal increments down to 1/100 (0.01) of an inch—almost the limit of the resolving power of the human eye.

Metric scales are usually graduated by millimeters and half-millimeters which goes down to 0.0254 inch. All of your rules and tapes should be read down to the 1/64 the of an inch or to ½ millimeter at all times.

Steel rules, bench rules and *yard sticks* should not be too thick. Thin rulers measure more accurately because their division marks are closer to the work. Always hold the rule with its *edge* on the surface of the object to be measured and you'll eliminate errors due to the thickness of the rule. Read the measurement and reduce the fractions to their lowest terms, (i.e.) a measurement of 12 16/64 would be stated as 12¼-inch. And write it down, don't trust your memory. Make a note on a pad, write it directly on the board and don't forget to indicate to what the measurement refers. Nothing is more exasperating than a measurement in search of an object. By the way, the hook at the end of the rule or the eye at the end of the tape, is included as part of the first inch measured.

A *zigzag folding rule* with a 6-inch sliding extension is by far the best tool for taking inside measurements. Unfold the rule to the approximate dimension then extend the end of the rule to the full distance to be measured. Add together the length of the main body of the rule and the length the extender is extended.

We like to drill tiny holes (1/16-inch) in our folding rule centered exactly at the 1, 2, 3, and 4-inch lines. This gives us a scribing tool we can use by butting the folded part of the rule against the board edge and then inserting a sharp pencil in one of the holes. Your folding rule can also be converted into a circle scriber by boring a hole at a more distant section through which you can slip a pin or tack and anchor it to a table top.

You can also use your folding rule to mark accurate angles. Some folding rules are even equipped with the proper markings for this trick. In case yours isn't, all you have to do is bend the rule down at the 6-inch and 12-inch joints, until the metal end tip touches the reading you need for the particular angle you want. At the 6-inch end of the rule there will be a small angle of 60 degrees if you touch the metal tip to 17¾ inches. If you'd like to mark you own rule, here is the placement table for some common angles you'll be using from time to time:

> 14 13/16 inches make a 30 degree angle.
> 16 ⅜ inches make a 45 degree angle.
> 17 ¾ inches make a 60 degree angle.
> 18 9/16 inches make a 70 degree angle.
> 20 ¼ inches make a 90 degree angle.

Your folding rule should be handled carefully. Never strike its edge with a hard object which might nick it. That goes for all straight edge rules, incidentally. Also, keep the hinges on your folding rule lightly oiled to prevent them from rusting and to assure free movement.

Your *tape rule* is best used for measuring outside dimensions and for measuring across and along lumber stock. If you do use it for inside measurements, extend the rule between the two inside surfaces between which you are measuring and take a reading at the point on the scale where the rule enters the case. *Then add the width of the case.* This is *usually 2 inches*, but *not always*. We have one that measures 2½ inches! So help us. And it came in a box with a set of direction that said in neat, black print, "add 2 inches". Which we did a few times, with dire results. It took us a bit to catch on to that crazy tape. But now we measure the case of each new tape personally. No more blind faith in directions. Let that be a lesson to you. Measure!

To measure outside dimensions with your tape rule, anchor the hook over the edge where your measurement starts and pull the tape out of the case until you can just read the exact distance being measured. The hook is designed so that your measurement begins from "zero." Read the rule at the exact edge of the stock or object to be measured.

Reel tapes are most useful for making long measurements. Hook one end on some sort of anchor—drive a small nail or tack if you have to—and walk in the direction to be measured. You'll be pulling the tape from the case as you walk. Be sure to stretch the slack out of the tape and to keep it parallel to the edge or surface to be measured.

Cloth or *plastic tape measures* are used for measuring the perimeter or circumference of things. To keep errors to a minimum when doing this kind of measuring, hold the tape firmly and bring it around to the 2-inch mark as your beginning point of reference instead of the front edge of the tape. Be sure not to stretch the tape as you work. And remember to subtract 2-inches from the total amount of inches to arrive at the correct measurement.

Simple *spring calipers*, non-calibrated, are beautiful tools for measuring diameters. You may want two pair. One "bowlegged" pair for measuring outside diameters and thicknesses and one with feet turned outward for inside measurements.

To measure accurately with an outside caliper, adjust the instrument so that you feel a slight drag as you move the caliper back and forth. To measure with an inside caliper approximate the distance to be measured and set the caliper accordingly. Now hold the caliper with one leg in contact with one of the surfaces then open up the instrument, moving it back and forth, until you feel a slight drag. That will be the proper setting. You must, of course, measure the caliper setting against a tape or other rule to get your final measurement which you will record. When reading the measurement be sure the caliper is set squarely with its face to the rule and you sight over the leg to read the result.

Never use calipers for anything but taking measurements. They do make tempting pry bars or screwdrivers but that is a definite no-no if you want to keep the calipers measuring correctly. Keep them clean and lightly oiled—very lightly, for you want them to stay firm at the joint.

A *slip-stick* is a kind of sliding caliper which you can make yourself from two long narrow strips of wood and a C-clamp. One stick slips up and down over the other inside the jaws of a loosened C-clamp for measuring ceiling heights and distances between top and bottom plates for cutting studs. Once the sticks are firmly touching top and bottom, tighten the C-clamp and carry the slip-stick to your work or to a rule for exact measurment.

The problems that can be solved with a *carpenter's steel square* are so many and varied that a book could be written solely on that subject and we've been tempted to do just that. For now, let's just say that this tool is indispensable for laying out stringers and risers when construction calls for making steps and stairways. It can also be used as a calculator for painless extraction of square roots. How's *that* for versatility? The steel square also comes in handy when you solve such basic problems as the length of roof rafters, or braces or any kind when the two sides of a right triangle are known and the hypotenuse of that triangle is the length of the brace you need to cut. Fig. 3-1 shows how simple this calculation is and how it can be accomplished with that great steel square. Fig. 3-2 shows the steps involved when you lay out stringers and risers.

A *try square* is needed to test the squareness of things—like ends and edges of lumber stock, and the trueness of a right angle. (We can't

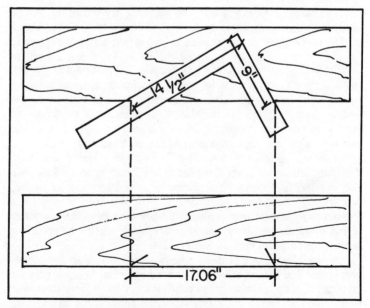

Fig.3-1. Using the carpenter's square as a calculator.

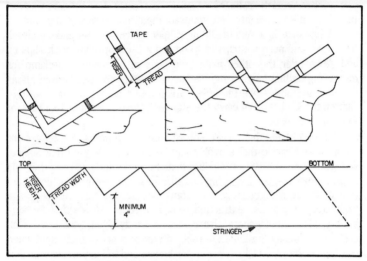

Fig. 3-2. Laying out threads and risers for stairway.

have any fibbing right angles now, can we?) Hold the try square upside down on a flat surface and you can check the surface for warp. (Handy when you're buying lumber.) We also like to use the try square for measuring and scribing straight lines for sawing boards less than 12-inches wide.

The *sliding T-bevel* is actually an adjustable try square that can be used for laying out any angle at all. It is not limited to 90 degree angles as is the try square. It can be used in conjunction with a protractor to set the desired angle by loosening the blade screw just enough to permit the blade to rotate with a little friction. In the same way, you can set it for a 45 degree angle by holding the handle against your steel square and adjusting the blade to intersect equal gradations on the tongue (short member) and the blade (long member) of the square. It can, in the same way, be set to match the angles formed by your folding rule—or "copy" any angle from any piece of work you may have.

There is simply no substitute for *dividers* when it comes to matching wall panels to the irregular edge of brick or stone walls. We also like to use dividers for scribing circles and arcs and, of course, dividers are unsurpassed for accuracy when you need to step off a measurement several times. When the work goes beyond the capacity of our dividers, we use trammel points along a stick to make our home-made king-size version. See Fig. 3-4.

A *plumb bob* is one of those precision tools that is so deceptively simple that you tend to take it for granted and often forget to care for properly. The tip of the weighted bob is the key and if it becomes even slightly bent or damaged the line above the bob will not be true. We recommend that you get the kind of bob that has a detachable tip so that the entire instrument won't have to be replaced if the tip becomes damaged, something that happens to the most careful users, too.

To locate a point which is directly below another point in space in order to set in vertical uprights, corner posts and such, fasten the plumb bob string to the top point. When the bob comes to rest it will point to the point in space directly below the top point. Keep your plumb bob in a box with a sheath to protect that all important point and do wind the string. It's such a nuisance when you find it all twisted and tangled.

A *chalk line tool* is handy because the chalked line can be reeled up inside a case and you don't have to stop to rechalk for every line. To get a striaght line between any two points up to 20 feet apart, stretch your

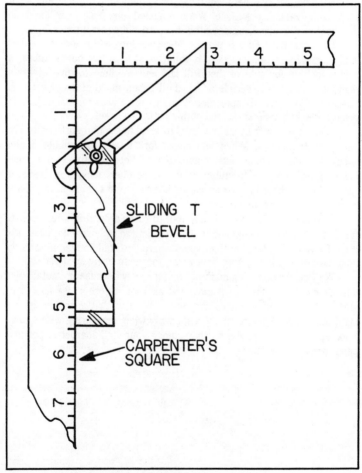

Fig. 3-3. How to set angles on a T-bevel.

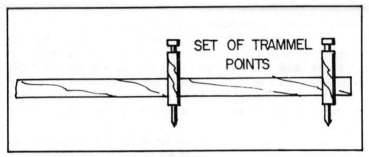

Fig. 3-4. Dividers using trammel points.

chalked string or line between these two points, lift the line and let it snap down against the surface. When you need to rechalk your line, hold the chalk in your hand and draw the line across it several times.

The *carpenter's level* is usually 24-inches long and made of wood or is of I-beam metal construction. It will have at least two bubble tubes. If you're looking for a level that will last and continue to give accurate readings for the next decade or so, the I-beam, made of magnesium, is the best. Wood and cheaper metal tend to warp with time and that, as you can easily guess, is the end of that particular level.

You'll use your carpenter's level to level horizontal surfaces and to plumb vertical ones. When you check for "level" the bubble in the horizontal bubble tube must come to rest between the two scratch marks in the center of the tube. By the same token, when you check for "plumb" the bubble in the vertical tube must come to rest in the space between the two scratch marks.

A *pocket level* is a very handy tool to carry around in your pocket. It's just a few inches long and though it's limited to horizontal uses, it's great for checking level in tight spots where you could never squeeze in your carpenter's level. And, believe us, there are many such places.

We like a *scriber* as a marking tool, not only because its metal point doesn't need constant sharpening, but also for its other use as awl to start holes for screws, nails and brads. We find that a scriber is just right for making lines on metal, especially when measuring with a rule. So keep a couple of scribers handy among your well-sharpened pencils, pens, crayons and chalk.

Chapter 4
Portable Power Tools

Once you have your lumber stock or other material measured and marked you are usually ready to apply a power tool to the material. Power tools are a great blessing especially for the do-it-yourselfer with limited time. Portable power tools, which we prefer and use ourselves, are quite friendly and non-threatening even to a novice and can be of tremendous help once you have established an effective, safe and lasting relationship with them. Speed is the key ingredient you have to take into account in your relationship—it is speed that gives you such a boost in your work and speed that makes your portable power tools potentially so much more dangerous than your hand tools.

For instance: a power saw can cut wood ten times faster than a hand saw. An electric drill turns up to 2,000 times per minute. You have to be an absolute whiz with a hand-drill if you can turn 120 times per minute. All that extra speed not only means that you can do your work ever so much faster, it also implies that you can make mistakes at a mighty good clip! On the other hand, let us reassure you, that with some instruction, practice and careful observation of the rules we are providing, you and your power tools can turn out accurate, professional looking work safely and at a good rate.

THE ELECTRIC DRILL

If we had to face the old dilemma of what tool you would take with you if you were only allowed one power tool and were expecting to be marooned on a deserted island (with an adequate power supply— natch—) our vote would go to the power drill. That loveable grand-daddy of all power tools is still the most helpful of all, at least in our opinion. While a drill is originally designed for drilling holes, as we all know, a power drill can do many other things as well. Its talents extend to buffing, brushing, grinding, hedge trimming, paint mixing, polishing, sanding, sawing and driving screws—to mention just a few—with the aid of readily available attachments. In fact, over the years, we have delighted in finding new uses for our power drill. One of the most unique is our potters' wheel which has seen a lot of use over the past ten years and is powered by—guess what? Right.

Using an electric drill effectively for whatever purpose is a matter of knowing the tool's limitations and staying within them. Home-use drills come in three sizes: ¼; ⅜; and ½-inch sizes. These fractions refer to the maximum size of the straight-shank drills the chuck will hold. That is, a ½-inch drill will take any size up to and including a ½-inch shank, whereas the ¼-- and ⅜-inch drill chucks will take only shanks up to ¼ to ⅜ inches respectively.

A ½-inch drill is built to handle tougher jobs. As a result it runs relatively slowly but delivers considerable power (torque). Seven hundred r.p.m. (revolutions per minute) is the top speed for a ½-inch drill, while your ¼-inch model (much less torque) will free-run at about 2,000 r.p.m.

The ⅜-inch size is a good compromise, delivering enough torque for most drilling jobs and accessories at a top speed of 1,000 r.p.m. With a ⅜-inch power drill, if you take the time to let it do its work at its own rate, you can do almost anything. All you have to remember is to try not to do a big job too fast.

Many electric drills are available with a trigger switch that lets you control the speed of the drill according to how hard you pull the trigger. We simply love that feature. For instance, you can start slowly when drilling into hard material and so prevent your drill from jumping around. You can also use that same slow speed to drive screws and tighten nuts and bolts.

Another feature we like is *reversing*. This will let you use your drill to loosen nuts and bolts and extract screws as well as drive them. Neat, don't you think?

Unless you are really into the fine points of electric motors we suggest you ignore all the literature and particularily the salesperson's chatter about the power rating of electric drill motors, usually given in "amperes" though at times they mention horsepower. Both are meaningless for comparisons because manufacturers have different methods of arriving at their "ratings." But most manufacturers do offer a "Good," "Better" and "Best" model. Buy the best if your budget will allow.

When you buy a drill make sure to look for a "double-insulated" or so-called shock-proof drill. (This goes for other power tools, too. Look for double insulation and don't settle for anything else.) This safety feature will protect you no matter what goes wrong inside the case. Shock-proof drills have cases made out of plastic which, as you know, is a non-conductor of electricity and that's great. So is the fact that the plastic has high impact strength which will protect the drill if it is dropped. In addition, it's much nicer to handle a plastic case than one made out of metal. However, be careful about cleaning it. Household detergents that contain ammonia can dissolve the plastic. It's best to stick to ethyl alcohol or kerosene. **Do not** use gasoline, gasohol, or any chlorinated cleaning agents.

The *chuck* we mentioned earlier is a feature of all electric drills. It holds the tools to be driven by the drill motor. The chuck is tightened around the tool either by hand, with an Allen wrench or key, or with a geared key. The latter, called a "jacob's chuck," is the one we recommend. We'd like to urge you to tape the key for tightening and opening the chuck to the power cord, near the plug. This will not only keep the key from getting lost, which wastes a lot of time and patience, but it forces you to unplug the tool when changing bits. It also insures that the key is removed from the chuck before the drill is plugged in and started. Failure to do this will cause the key to be expelled with considerable force when the drill is started up and that can result in serious injury to you or someone else.

Know Your Bits

The bits most often used in electric drills are the ones called "*twist drills.*" You can buy a drill bit to make holes in anything—ceramic, glass, masonry, and stone materials as well as plastic, metal or wood. These "anything" bits are twist drills made from "high-speed" steel (alloyed with tungsten, chromium and vanadium) or from carbon-steel alloys. High-speed drills are expensive but they can work without any coolant. The carbon-steel drills are soft and inexpensive, but work fine on wood, plastic of soft metal. On soft metal, though, they do require a coolant to keep them from burning. Water, light machine oil or kerosene may be used. If it is not possible to keep the coolant flowing into the hole while drilling, then the drill bit needs to be withdrawn from the work frequently and dipped into a cold water bath.

Twist drills come in all kinds of sizes and you will have no trouble fitting bit size to required hole size. Three different systems of notation for twist drill sizes will take you from a needle's eye (0.0135 inch) to ½-inch. Beyond the ½-inch is a range of *spade bits* up to 1 ½-inch. Actually the spade bits start at about ⅜-inch—for those who like exactness in these matters.

Holes larger than 1½ inches should be cut with a *hole saw*—which is literally a saw blade bent into circle. Although hole saw blades (or are they bits? a fine point in semantics which can be disputed) are available in sized up to 6 inches the larger sizes are strictly for use with heayv-duty, industrial drills, not your dainty home model. Your ½-inch drill will cut holes up to 4 inches. But don't, whatever the temptation, go beyond a 2½-inch hole with your ⅜-inch drill, or beyond 1 ½ with a ¼-inch drill. They simply can't take it. Leave the larger holes to your portable jig or saber saw if you have only a few to cut. If you need a large number of big holes drilled you might rent a heavy-duty industrial drill or a hole saw.

There is a circle maker available called a *fly-cutter*, which some craftspeople have used successfully in conjunction with their ordinary drills. It is a tricky device since the load on you, and your drill, too, is off-center. This sets up a lot of disturbing vibrations and gives one the sensation of riding an unbroken stallion. Not for the cautious or people who need to feel "in control" at all times. It can, though, be thrilling for adventuresome, daring persons who like that sort of challenge. The secret to "breaking" the device seems to be to have your work firmly clamped to a solid surface, use to be to have your work firmly clamped to a solid surface, use a slow cutting speed, then cut the hole only about half way through from one side, turn the work over and finish cutting the hole from the opposite face of the work. This is what we gathered from research and observation. We, individually and together, get our kicks from different kinds of adventures. However, we have found that clamping and turning your work is a good idea no matter what size hole you are making.

If you do not, or can not, reverse your work and drill your holes from both sides, splintering can be kept to a minimum by reducing the pressure on the drill and easing the bit through the last part of the hole. If possible, clamp a piece of scrap to the back face of the work and continue the hole part way into the scrap.

Drilling Techniques

Don't hesitate to use both hands on the drill. It will help you hold the tool firmly at the correct drilling angle. Turn on the drill only after you have placed the point of the bit into a punched layout hole. Feed the bit into the work with a gentle pressure applied in a straight line right along the shank of the bit. Brace yourself against the twisting motion of the drill. If you push too hard you may deflect the bit or stall the motor. If the drill motor stalls it is telling you that it is overloaded. Stop the drill, remove the bit from the work and find out the cause of the overload so you can correct it. Most often it will be cuttings jamming the bit. When drilling deep holes you will need to withdraw the drill several times, while you keep the motor running, so you can clear out the cuttings. Sometimes you will overload your drill motor by being impatient and applying too much pressure to get the work done more quickly. Ease up. Let the tool do its work in its own good time. It'll save you time in th end.

Finally, be sure to work with sharp bits at all times. This is why we wouldn't be without our pet, the drill-bit sharpener. Do you know that it takes only from one to four *seconds*, yes, seconds, to sharpen a bit to its proper angle, thanks to the properly angled grinding wheel in the drill bit sharpener? The variation in time is related to the size of the drill. So why would you ever want to struggle along with a dull bit?

POWER SAWS

The wisdom of keeping your tools sharp applies to saws as well as to drills. You can buy your own sharpener if you wish for your saw blades, but the sharpener is expensive and requires extra skill to use. Our own solution is to keep several sharpened blades on hand and leave the actual sharpening in the hands of the professional. He knows his job and the service is inexpensive.

Circular Saws

If you have followed our advice and selected the circular saw attachment for your portable electric drill, do not expect it to be the work horse that an expensive portable circular saw would be. You'll find it just as versatile since there are quickly interchangeable blades for cutting all kinds of material as well as for all manner of different cuts. But your attachment will work slower, and on occasion not cut as smoothly as would a regular circular saw. A regular circular saw turns the blade at 4400 to 7000 r.p.m., where as your drill-adapted circular saw blade will run at no more than 2,000 r.p.m. If you keep this in mind and adapt yourself to the slower cutting speed, you will be able to straight-cut or bevel-cut through 2×4's with ease. You'll even pick up any dadoing and rabbeting work your saber saw can't do.

Saber Saws

The saber saw has much greater versatility than the circular saw, though one must admit that the circular saw is faster. In fact, that's what the circular saw excells in—fast cutting, and that's about it. A good saber saw can handle almost any cutting job exceptionally well, with the above mentioned exceptions: (i.e.) dadoing and reabbeting. Your saber saw simply loves to rip, crosscut, miter and bevel and also enjoys doing a masterful job of making plunge cuts, arcs, circles, scrolls—you name it. So you see, between your drill and your saber saw you've got itfar as power tools are concerned. We have lived and worked with only those two and have done a good many jobs satisfactorily and quickly.

If you, too, limit yourself to only these two power tools we would advise you to buy or otherwise acquire a large, variable speed saber saw. If you opt for the multi-purpose saw we suggested earlier, on the other hand, one of the less expensive, one-speed models will do your work most satisfactorily. As with all other power equipment, we recommend the double insulated type which frees you from any grounding problems.

Getting Acquainted With Your Sabers. Blades for saber saws come in four general types: wood-cutting, metal-cutting, knife, and toothless. The knife and toothless blades will slice through such materials as cork, insulation board, rubber and leather. Toothless blades are the most versatile since they will cut through formica, ceramic tile, stainless steel, brick, slate and even asbestos and cement. We like to use a coarse metal-cutting blade for rough cutting wood, especially when there's a danger of running into nails.

Blade lengths will vary from 2 ½ to 6 inches. Saber saw blades should be treated as "disposable." Never use worn or dull blades. Even though tungsten-carbide blades are more expensive and might seem to cost too much to be "disposable" they are the ones we prefer. What we found, by close study, is that you can get ten hours of sawing service out of any one of these blades for every single hour of service from your standard toothed blade. There's quite a savings in the long run.

In the course of the garage conversions we'll be discussing, we will be using the saber saw more than any other tool. So we might as well give you the gist of how to use that marvelous tool most effectively.

Why Saber Sawing Demands Attention And Thought. If you're relatively inexperienced in using a saber saw, the first thing you do is clamp your work down firmly with C-clamps so you can be free to concentrate on using the saw. Saber sawing demands attention. Even if you're an experienced pro, you wouldn't try to hold small work pieces by hand. Anything shorter than 18 inches must be laid across blocks that leave plenty of blade clearance below.

Not only does the saber saw, like a spoiled child, clamor for your attention, it also requires considerable forethought. When cutting long pieces or panels there'll be a considerable weight shift when an unsupported segment is cut off. That's why, unless precautions are taken, ends of boards tend to sag and even to break off before they are cut free. So always support the cut-off part with your free hand as you move the saw along until the blade cuts it entirely free. By the way, two supports may not be enough for a plywood panel since the middle will sag more and more as the cutting proceeds. Soon the blade will bind and refuse to be fed. What you must do is support the work close to the cutting line on both sides, but — more trouble. Now your outer sections are flapping free and are in danger of breaking off. What you need then is extra support, out near the edges of the panel. You can also get more control on the work by clamping a block across the start of the cut and inserting a small triangular shaped wedge into the cut to keep it open behind the saw blade to avoid binding.

Your Working Habits And Your Saber Saw. If you make a habit of picking up a saber saw with your thumb and three fingers leaving your index finger straight and off the switch, you will save yourself the scary surprise of having your saw take off before you're set to control it. And believe us, that's one surprise you can well do without. Also, please, as an article of faith if need be—just as the old soldier was taught to keep his powder dry—so train yourself to swing the electric cord behind the saw. Always. *You must keep it out of the line of the projected cut.*

You should have a firm grip on the handle of the saw before you switch it on. Set the front of the saw base on the edge of you work with the blade almost, but not quite, touching the cutting line. Now switch on your motor and move the blade into the work edge right on the cutting line. Keep the base (shoe) parallel to the work surface. Once you have the shoe firmly on the work surface, keep it that way with a steady hand and the help of good old gravity itself. While you may have an inclination to tilt the shoe up in front or back, suppress it and instead exert a steady downward pressure which makes it possible to get the most help from gravity. So there you are—co-operating with gravity— and getting quite a boost out of it, too. If you use a good sharp blade your saw will do its job and require only very light forward pressure. And remember: Steady as she goes, let the blade cut at its own pace. If you tend to push or shove at this stage of the work you'll actually get very little increase in forward speed but a much rougher cut and maybe even an overloaded blade and saw motor. And you don't need that.

Your cutting speed is going to vary with the kind of material and its individual thickness, as well as with variations within the materials. Train yourself to maintain just enough pressure to keep the saw moving at its own pace and let the saw blade and material continually interact without outside interference, and you will get the best possible cut with the least effort on your part. Don't, however, get so carried away with this symbiosis of moving blade and static material, that you fail to notice the cause of a sudden slow down such as the electric cord behind you getting hung up on something, or the blade having encountered the hidden edge of your supporting structure. (This is heartfelt advice and comes from one of us who has done just such dumb things, not once, but many times over).

Why Clamp Down Is The Solution For Neat Cutting. If you find that your work vibrates or flutters around while you're cutting, you can take that as a direct request for better clamping. Always try to clamp or otherwise secure your work quite close to the line of cut. It makes life with your saw much simpler.

By the way, don't forget to turn off your saw immediately when you've completed a cut and then to lay it down in a safe place before unclamping your work. Never, never, try holding a running saw in one hand while doing something else with the free one. That's asking for trouble.

A long rip cut can be made straight and true by clamping or tacking a straight edged piece of wood onto the upper surface of the work exactly a half a shoe width from the cut line. Make the cut with the side of the shoe riding firmly against the straight edge. Be sure to keep your eyes on the shoe edge and straight edge, not the saw blade. And make certain to have the guide strip longer than the cut line or the work. You can actually dispense with a cut line if you like. If you're worrying about the tacks used to hold down the guide strip marring the work surface, cheer up. You've forgotten that we always saw back side up. As you know, the top of the work tends to splinter so we work with the "good side" down at all times. When you tack down that guide strip let the tacks barely penetrate the work and leave enough head protruding above the strip to make pulling them out an easy job.

Your saber saw is ideal for cutting uneven edges that must fit closely against a wall or ceiling that is not straight. (As most of them are not, unfortunately). When you mark such a cutting edge, hold the panel to be fitted alongside the surface it is to match. Use your dividers, set at whatever spacing is most convenient, to trace the cutting line. During the actual cutting, go slow and easy and keep the blade right on the cutting line.

Inside cutting can also be done with your saber saw. You don't even have to drill a pilot hole, just make a plunge cut through the work. Here's how it's done. First mark your work for the inside cut and clamp it down. Next put your saw into a nose dive by placing the front end of the shoe firmly on the work with the blade directly above and nearly parallel to the cut line—with the motor *turned off*, naturally. Hang on to the saw with both hands (it'll act like a bucking bronco when it first contacts the work) turn on the motor with your thumb, and level off the saw by bringing the back edge of the shoe down onto the work. Make sure you are flying straight and level with the shoe flat against the work before you begin the forward cut.

Two-hands-on-the-saw is also a necessity when making bevel cuts. Keep the shoe flat, absolutely so, on the work. If it lifts even a little bit, the bevel will not be true. Expect your saw to move more slowly when you cut at an angle of less than 90 degrees because the blade has to cut through a greater thickness of material. Also, because the blade thrust is not vertical, the saw will have a greater tendency to wander around, which makes going slowly a good idea. Your saw comes, of course, with a set of directions for tilting the base or for mounting a separate tilt shoe in place of the standard one. Your saw, most likely, will also come with a circle cutting attachment which you'll love if you go in for cutting ornamental curves and such.

SAWING METAL

Sawing metal with a saber saw is as easy as sawing wood if you use the proper blade and follow a few simple tips. Blades for cutting metal are finer than those for cutting wood. For thin metal (3/32-inch or thinner) a cutting blade with no fewer than 24 teeth should be used. A 14 tooth blade can be used on metal thicker than 3/32-inch.

You can make cutting through metal easier if you first lubricate the blade with candle wax. Also, stop often to brush chips out of the blade. Remember to support the work as close to the cutting line as you can and feed the blade very slowly. For a really nice job clamp your sheet metal stock between two sheets of thin plywood, mark your cutting line on top of the "sandwich" and cut through the whole thing at once. If you clamp the work tightly there is no possibility of bending or tearing your metal.

You should also use your metal cutting blades and techniques when you work with asphalt-asbestos tile. You can and should use the knife blade on most other kinds of tile—especially vinyl and rubber. Soft leather, canvas, and cloth are best cut with the knife, but in a sandwich of cardboard, similar to the one we described for thin sheet metal. In this case, tape or staple your leather or fabric sandwich together. You can cut up to about a 1-inch thick pile of cardboard-plus-whatever at one time, so you can stack the sandwiches in a multiple layer if you like. Always keep your knife blade honed to a sharp edge (sharpen it like any other knife blade) and keep in mind while you work with it that it is a lot more dangerous than the fine-toothed saw blades. *Warning: Overheating May Be Hazardous.*

Any good saber saw will last you for years if you do not allow it to overheat. When it gets hot—not just warm—let it run free for a few minutes. That will cool it down much quicker than stopping it. And be sure to keep the cooling vents clear by cleaning them thoroughly and often with a stiff bristle brush. Oh, and just one more thing. If blue smoke, smelling like burning wood rises from your work, don't panic. Your saw *is not*, repeat, *is not* about to blow up. The blue smoke is a signal for a new saw blade. The one in the saw is hopelessly dull. So replace it immediately and proceed full speed ahead.

SAFETY TIPS

Safety is very important in using tools effectively, particularly power tools. The threat of electrical shock can be easily prevented by grounding all power tools that are not clearly marked, "double insulated." Never, never remove the third (ground) prong from the plug of a power tool so it'll fit into a two-hole electrical receptacle. Instead make it a rule to use an adapter plug with a pigtail connected to a known ground such as the face plate screw on the electric receptacle or a water pipe that goes underground.

Don't stand in a wet area when working with power tools, or work outside when it's raining—under any circumstances whatsoever. That's asking for it and there are simpler ways of committing suicide if that's what you have in mind. The only possible exception to the above are *battery operated* tools, but we frown even on that. So, please just wait until the rain stops or the floor dries, okay?

Keep your work area clean as well as dry at all times. It really pays to spend a few minutes cleaning up quite frequently. An do work within the limit of your reach. Over-reaching makes you loose your balance, often your footing and at times your health. (This comes from one of us who bears bodily scars of just such over-reaches. In one case an effort to save a few seconds in moving the work caused a fall and sprained ankle that took weeks of pain, inconvenience and expense to heal.)

Besides being hazardous to your health, over-reaching causes sloppy, inaccurate work. Horrors.

Here's a simple tip—but one that's all too often violated. When your work needs to be held down for cutting or drilling, don't use your free hand just because it's so readily available. Use your trusty C-clamps instead. It's a lot safer for your paw and helps your work to be more accurate.

If you don't need to wear glasses to see better, you do need glasses to work with. Get yourself a pair of safety glasses that fit comfortably and wear them all the time. No matter what you are working with there's always all kinds of stuff flying through the air that you'd just as soon keep out of your eyes.

Before you start to work, make it a habit to remove rings, watches, bracelets, necklaces and all else that could get caught in your work. If in doubt, remove it anyway. The same goes for wide sleeves and pantlegs, dangling ties and ribbons. Not so long ago there was an ad for jeans in which a contractor made the point that his jeans were part of his work equipment. That's truer than most of the guff from Madison Avenue— your clothes should fit comfortably and snugly, with no loose ends to get caught.

THE TOOLS, YOU AND THE WORK

There is always a right tool for the job at hand. But not necessarily in hand. It's a good idea to match job and tool as closely as you can. Don't worry along with an under-powered tool or makeshift attachment for heavy-duty work. Don't ever try to force a tool into work.

Once, for instance, when we put our little 1½ horsepower circular saw to a wall that we thought was plaster board on 2 " 4 studs, the poor saw smoked and choked and spluttered and nearly died. When we finally caught on that the poor thing wasn't just being onery we ripped off some of the wallpaper and discovered that what we were trying to do was cut through the two layers of shiplap wood constructions that made up our "little" partition. No wonder the saw protested.

Of course, we could have been bull-headed and worried our little saw along, forced it to do what it wasn't designed for and it might even have survived the whole affair, though it would have taken years off its working life. Besides, the job would have been long and frustrating for us as well as for the saw. So instead, we went out and rented a big Skil Saw with worm drive gearing. That saw purred happily through both sides of the shiplap at once and cut our wall down to the size we wanted in a few minutes without a single huff or puff.

CARE OF TOOLS

It not only pays to be considerate of the capacity of your tools, but to be aware of and tend to their need for cleaning, adjusting, lubricating and sharpening, too. Sharp tools, contrary to what you might think, are far less dangerous than dull tools. And they do more professional work, of course.

Never use a tool you are not happy with. To love your work requires that you be happy with your tools and the way that they help you work your material. If you feel frustrated while using a tool or working a material, look at it as invitation to learn more about your tools, your materials, or the process you are using.

Frustration is often a funny way of expressing a desire for growth. Take a break, study your instructions, then take a turn around the yard, jog around the block, or run to the store for whatever you might need next. By the time you get back to your work you'll be surprised by how often you've found a new way of holding the tool, or handling the material, or otherwise discovered a new means to deal with the frustration.

And above all, make a conscious effort to relax while you work. Operations like sawing, drilling and hammering tend to tense you up. The tensions usually build up around the jaw, and across the top of your chest. Make a conscious effort to keep your jaw relaxed by jutting it from side to side, clenching and unclenching your teeth and letting it hang slack every once in a while. Move your shoulders in circles, backwards and frontwards and rotate your head. Do this every hour or so and you'll find that you can cut a straighter line, drill a better hole and swing a hammer with greater ease. Best of all, you'll find that physical work can be truly recreational.

Chapter 5
Insulation

Our love affair with insulation is of long standing. It much precedes the present energy crunch. Insulation has been, and is, our way of keeping our house and converted garage more comforatable, winter or summer, up north or down here in Texas. And when we consider the savings in heating and cooling costs over the years we are doubly sold. The house we live in right now is seventeen years old and rather a rarity. Even though it is located in central Texas, a mild climate by any standards, it was bundled in a blanket of insulation that equals the recommendations for insulation in the energy starved 1980s. The house has undergone a garage-to-family-room conversion, naturally, and we carried on the tradition of generous insulation. We enjoy the comfort and the savings in utility bills.

Now, more than ever, you can profit from using insulation because Uncle Sam has offered to foot the bill. Yes, indeed—you may take the cost of insulation, storm doors, thermal windows and so forth right off the bottom line of your tax return. You get a credit for 15 percent of the first $2,000 spent on improving the energy efficiency of your home if it was built prior to April 20, 1977. So, as long as you are converting your garage into a family room, you might as well do it in such a way as to qualify for this generous tax credit. And you'll also wind up with a family room that is comfortable winter, summer and in between and quite economical to heat and cool. In some climates you may even be able to come up with a conversion that results in a family room heated and cooled by sun and air alone.

PLANNING FOR GREATEST ENERGY CONSERVATION

Before you can plan for energy conservation, great or otherwise, you will need to learn about R-values and U-values. All insulating materials should have their R value stamped on them. R is a measure of heat resistance—a high R means good insulating qualities. R varies according to the quality and thickness of the product.

A U-value, on the other hand, clues you in on the ability of the insulating material to transfer heat. U-values can be determined for any kind of material. You can talk about the U-value of an entire wall, for example. In that case you'll be speaking about the insulation characteristics of siding, sheathing, insulation, air space and wallboard in combination. If you talk about a low U-value you will be referring to good structural insulation. So you should *use materials of a low U-value plus insulation of a high R-value in your wall and roof construction* to come up with the best over all energy saving.

Even though you have walls, floor and roof already in place in most garage conversions, you can still improve the structural insulation by paying attention to the U-values of your new wall and of the finishing materials in the existing structure. Remember, U=1/R, it's a most useful conversion formula.

Even if some insulation is already in place in your garage you may want to add more. If your builder has finished your garage with wallboard, and you don't want to take it down, which we don't recommend in any case, you can still get extra insulation by having loose fill insulation blown in between the studs, siding and finished wall. We do recommend that you have this done by a professional, since the needed equipment is not readily available for do-it-yourselfers.

In many cases you will have accessible construction in which case it's easy to do the insulation job yourself. To guide you here are some good insulation values:

● **For ceilings:** R-19
If you choose fiber glass insulation it will be 6 inches thick.
● **For Walls:** R-11
The thickness of fiber glass with this R-value is 3½ inches.
● **For Interior Walls:** R-7
These walls are ones which separate heated from unheated rooms. If you live in an exceptionally cold or extremely hot climate you might do well to increase these R-values by two or three. Here are some other ideas for energy conservation before we go into the nitty-gritty of insulation:

● Reroof your garage with light colored shingles to reflect sunlight.
● Leave all the trees around the garage in place for their great summer cooling effect.
● Use solid core doors with storm doors for all exterior openings.
● Install thermal windows and sky lights.

● Use a small heat pump for heating and cooling the new family room independently from the rest of the house.

● Caulk cracks around all existing door and window trim.

● If you are adding a fireplace, make sure the damper (plate to control the draft) fits tightly.

TYPES OF INSULATION

Insulation products differ a bit from one manufacturer to the next, but entrapped or dead air space is the basis of them all. The more small air pockets there are in a given material the better the insulating qualities, (i.e.) the higher the R-value. That's why most insulation is "fluffy" and can be easily compressed. However, and this is the rub, when compressed the number of air pockets is reduced and some of the insulation efficiency is lost. So—don't compress insulation. Most insulation is also capable of absorbing and holding water vapor in its air pockets. That, too, reduces the resisitance, or R-value, of the material. This is why a vapor barrier is always used in tandem with insulating material.

Foil-faced fiberglass insulation in rolls and batts faced with an aluminum foil vapor barrier is the most popular insulation material used. Another popular insulating material is mineral wool which can be made from rock, slag or glass fiber. It, too, comes in the three basic forms: batts, blankets (rolled), and loose fill (the blow-in stuff).

Batts usually come in four foot lengths and in 16-inch and 24-inch widths. Standard thicknesses are 3⅝-inch and 6-inch. Batts come with or without vapor barriers and are used primarily where there is a ceiling to support the batts. Batts can be easily cut to size by compressing them along the line to be cut and then making the cut with scissors or a knife. Batts are sometimes useful for insulating between wall framing, but generally speaking blanket insulation is better for this kind of job.

Blankets come in rolls rather than short lengths but are otherwise very much like the batts. Seven inch thick blankets with an R-26 value come in 10 foot rolls. As blankets get thinner the rolls get longer, so that the R-19 and R-11 value rolls (3-inch and 5-inch thick) come in rolls that are from 24 to 56 feet long. The 1⅛-inch insulation which is usually used between furring, comes in giant 100-foot rolls.

Blankets usually have stapling flanges and can be easily installed by one person. You can buy blanket insulation with or without a kraft paper or foil barrier. The unfaced type must be covered over with a vapor barrier so don't use it unless there is a vapor barrier already in existence. The blankets are held in place between the studding by friction. Blankets, we find, work well for any kind of insulation work in any place.

Plastic Foam Boards were originally used for perimeter insulation. Of late they find their way into more and more general insulation work.

The boards come in standard 8×2 foot sections and are from ½-inch to over 4 inches thick. They are made from polyurethane or polystyrene foam and come with square or tongue-and-groove edges. Plastic foam boards are light and a joy to handle. They go into place with mastic adhesive and can be cut and shaped with ordinary wood working tools. A 2-inch thick board will have a value of at least R-16—a very efficient insulator.

Loose fill, which consists of nodules of slag or mineral wool, is used mainly by contractors who have the equipment needed to blow the stuff into existing walls and attics. *Vermiculite*, a loose fill material made of expanded mica, is nearly twice as expensive as mineral wool nodules but is sometimes used to fill areas by hand that can't be reached with any other kind of insulation. It flows nicely and is easy to handle.

There is also another type of insulation on the market, or at least was, which we strongly *warn* you against. This is *urea-formaldehyde* insulation, very popular with contractors who loved the way the foam could be blown into walls. While the urea-formaldehyde insulation has not been officially included in the list of government-encouraged energy-savers, it is at present still eligible for tax credit. However, the Consumer Product Safety Commission is questioning the safety of urea-formaldehyde insulation as far as health is concerned. There is reason to believe that in addition to unpleasant side effects such as skin irritations, headaches, dizziness and vomiting, the formaldehyde gas, which escapes in small constant doses from the insulation, might be a cancer producing substance.

While we have been warned against more and more cancer producing substances which are not easily avoidable, urea-formaldehyde we can do without nicely, thank you. Besides, the effect of a carcinogen which is built right into your house and surrounds you day and night is potentially so much greater that only a fool would be willing to expose himself to it voluntarily. So beware of the urea-formaldehyde or any other insulation combo in which formaldehyde is included. It is an other case when reading labels and knowing what they mean can save you and yours untold misery.

Foil or reflective insulation is not very effective when used alone. Since it doesn't depend on trapped air for its heat flow, all it does is simply reflect heat back toward its source. It works, if reflective insulation is used together with other insulating materials. To give credit where it's due, reflective insulation makes an excellent vapor barrier, and effectively reduces heat loss or gain from radiation. That is the great advantage of using batts or blankets with foil, rather than paper vapor barriers. Foil-backed gypsum board over plastic foam board (as long as the foam isn't you know what) makes a wall that has excellent U-value.

Many garages built recently use foil backed gypsum board for insulation and "finishing" at the same time. As we've just said, this isn't very helpful. However, if you use it for a starter you can gain more effective insulation by nailing heavy furring strips to the wall, putting up blanket insulation in between and then paneling over the whole thing. (You'll need spacers to bring out window or door casings flush with the new wall). One of our friends did just that and then had loose fill insulation blown into the air space in the original walls for a "coup de grace." Which seemed a bit excessive even to us, but then if insulation is your thing—go to it baby.

INSULATION INSTALLATION TECHNIQUES

Batt and blanket insulation is simple to install. All you do is staple the paper flanges to the inside faces of studs, joints or rafters. Pretty easy, don't you think? There are a few things you've got to remember, though. One is that the vapor barrier should face *inside* the room. Water vapor tends to flow from the warm side to the cool side of a wall. It then condenses on the outside wall and causes such horrible things as wood rot and paint blistering along with lowering the efficiency of the insulating material. Which is what you don't want. The idea is to place your vapor barrier in a position where it can function to prevent moisture vapor from reaching the cold surface so it can't condense. So—vapor barrier to the inside, always.

When you staple your insulation keep your staples close together, less than five inches apart and be sure the edges to be stapled fit tightly against the stud, joist or rafter. When stapling insulation on walls, start from the top and work your way down. The ends of the insulation must be stapled tightly against framing members at the top and bottom of the wall—that is against the top and bottom "plates."

Incidentally, when you insulate a ceiling you'll want to put your vapor barrier face *downward*. And if, for some reason you ever want to insulate a floor you'll put it how? Face up, that's right.

Always fit your insulation behind obstructions—wall outlets, pipes, electrical cables and such. If you have to cut the insulation material to make it fit, remember to patch your vapor barrier with a piece of scrap vapor barrier and contact adhesive. Vapor barriers must be continuous.

If the full width of the insulating material cannot be used around doors and windows, you'll have to stuff small pieces of the insulating material into the left-over spaces, then cover them with vapor barrier and tape the whole thing securely.

If you want to insulate a floor, which is most unusual in a garage/family room conversion (in fact, the only possibility we can see is if the garage is over a basement or crawl space which happens once in a light year)—but just in case so you'll be prepared—here's how. You'll fit the insulation behind the floor bridging if possible. And you'll remember, of course, to put your vapor barrier face up, against the floor. If the insulation can't be installed behind the floor bridging you'll have to fit it against the bridging. And be sure to cover any gaps in the vapor barrier and keep the insulation as continuous as possible.

When you insulate a ceiling, which, in contrast to the above, is one of the most common insulating tasks in older garage/family room conversions, you'll want to fit the insulation to the outside framing members. You can easily form a stapling edge or flange on your insulation by peeling back the insulation from the vapor barrier. Be sure your insulation material fits tightly and staple it down at least every five inches. For reflective insulation you will want to allow about an inch of air space between the ceiling and the insulation.

In garages where you have a mini-attic, start by insulating across the collar beams that tie the rafters together, and then go on to the spaces between the wall studs. Cut and fit the insulation for each space. This is no time for a continuous blanket. Cover the splices in the insulation with vapor barrier material and be sure to leave ventilation space above the collar beams.

Plastic foam boards are fitted into wall surfaces between the framing members and glued in place with mastic. Again, make sure your insulation is continuous. It doesn't matter how tight the boat is, if there's a gap somewhere the craft will become water logged. (We are trying to use as many different analogies as possible to impress this important fact indelibly in your mind). As before, cut and fit bits of plastic foam board into small areas. Some types of plastic foam board are natural moisture barriers in and of themselves and can be used under most conditions without the addition of vapor barriers. Ask your building materials supplier about this when you buy the boards. If he is not sure or in case you opt to use styrofoam, you'll want to use sheets of 2-mil polyethylene film or reflective foil vapor barrier over the rigid insulation and studs or furring strips.

Heed these words of wisdom: wear safety glasses, leather gloves and a long sleeved shirt or blouse when you work with insulation. And keep your jeans rolled down and sneakers on your feet. This comes from the bitter experience of one of us who insisted on doing the work in shorts, sleeveless top and barefoot. Even the memory brings on uncontrolled fits of itching. And the itching is the least serious complication of getting fiberglass directly on your skin. The blasted stuff works itself right into the pores and can cause infections and allergic rashes. So keep covered. Also, if you work with loose fill insulation make sure the room is well ventilated. It's dusty work and again can lead to allergic reactions.

THERMOPANES AND STORM WINDOWS

Thermopanes (multi-glazed windows), storm windows and storm doors are all declared energy efficient and therefore, joy of joys, tax deductible. On the other hand, your conventional singled glazed windows and sliding glass patio doors are not. So it's pretty easy to make a choice even without this quote from the U.S. Housing and Urban Development Department: "Almost 70% of a typical single-family dwelling heating and cooling load is traceable to windows (and outer doors)." Translated into everyday language: your greatest heat or cooling loss comes from windows (or outer doors).

You'll have to consider your window and outer door carefully when you convert your garage to an extraordinary family room. Because of the energy robbing characteristics of conventional windows and outer doors there's a lot of advice around which tells you to keep these areas down to a minimum, or even better, eliminate them all together. That's great if energy efficiency is your only consideration and your family exhibits mole-like tendencies. We have found that said advice leads to rooms that are more claustrophobic than cozy and are quickly shunned by most people. Which is not what you have in mind when you labor by the sweat of your brow and your checkbook to create additional living space for your loved ones. However, you don't have to choose between being energy efficient and having a pleasant room. Here are some special design considerations we highly recommend, that will let you have the light and easy access to the out-of-doors you want for a family room, while allowing you to reap the benefits of energy saving and tax deductions.

First, have your large window areas face the south and/or east and eliminate, if possible, large expanses of glass to the west and north. Large windows and sliding glass doors should admit the sun in winter to take advantage of the considerable amount of passive solar heat available from "Old Sol." You should have some means of closing off these large glass areas at night in order to hold the captured "greenhouse effect" heat. Roof overhangs and/or special awning arrangements will keep the sun out of the room in the summertime.

All windows in the sun's path should be shaded in summer, preferably with trees or shrubs which themselves contribute to further cooling by transpiration. If you keep these thoughts in mind, your windows or sliding glass doors can be energy gainers instead of energy squanderers. So keep your windows oriented with the sun's winter path in mind. Your south windows will develop the largest gain. But, you'll still have to install double-glazed or triple-glazed units to hold the heat gain, and you'll need to have good insulation around window and door frames.

Facts About Windows You Need To Know

The basics of window knowledge can be summed up like this: (1) all windows are either single, double or triple glazed, and (2) the designation of single, double or triple refers to the number of panes (or "lites") in each window.

There are also two basic kinds of double-glazed windows. In the first, the window is made of two panes sealed to an aluminum spacer of about ¼-inch width. A chemical desiccant is sealed between these two panes to absorb any moisture that might seep in.

The second type of double-glazed window has the two pa[nes] together at the edges (still maintaining a ¼-inch air space) a[nd] space itself is evacuated so that there's little air left between the sh[eets] of glass—in fact, it's almost a vacuum. This kind of window is ofte[n] referred to in the singular—it's called "insulating glass."

There are also two major kinds of triple-glazed windows. Most common is a storm window used with either kind of double-glazed window we have just discussed.

A second type of triple-glazed unit is a double glazed window mounted in a frame designed to permit a third pane of glass to be inserted about 1 inch out from the double pane, and removed at will. This particular feature was considered very valuable back in the days when storm windows were unattractive and ill fitting. As far as energy efficiency is concerned it's about the same for both kinds of triple-glazed windows.

The Special Case Of Storm Windows

Most current storm windows are of the "self-storing" variety a blessing only those of us can appreciate who have struggled in the blast of the first blizzard of the year to put the pesky things up (we never thought of it earlier in the season) and wrestled them down when the summer sun beckoned us to the nearest swimming pool. Now, of course, storm windows are kept up in the summer for energy saving, to keep out the heat.

Storm windows are designed to fit outside windows and are available in three types: half-hung (lower part opens vertically), sliding glass (slides open horizontally) and the so-called picture window (which usually doesn't open at all).

If you want to get the full benefits from your storm windows, both for heat and sound insulation, you've got to make sure the units are installed properly so you'll have a very tight seal with the existing window. For an added touch use weather-stripping whenever possible.

Temporary "Storms" And Other Such Window Insulation Ideas

If your budget currently doesn't run to storm windows, you can convert your screens into energy saving storm windows at a fraction of the cost. But you'll have to do a neat, careful job and use weather-stripping to get a perfect fit for your new storm window/screen conversion. Here's how:

Cover your screen with 2-mil polyethylene film by stapling the film to the screen at least every four inches all along the frame. You'll have to work slowly and keep the film taut so that it doesn't pucker or gap. Be careful not to stretch it, though. Seal your converted storm window with caulking compound. Don't forget to wash and dry the side of your window that faces the new storm window first or you'll be stuck with a a long time. If you want to take out the storm window, ...ly if you first remove the caulking.

...ood-Framed Windows

...es to the insulating properties of wood-framed win-
...ybody sell them short. The thermal conductivity of
aluminum is downright alarming. Aluminum will pass heat at 1,700 times the rate of most woods. (That is according to Van Nostrand's Scientific Encyclopedia, 5th Edition). This means that your heavily promoted aluminum window frames can slurp up your expensively generated heat energy in the winter and use it to heat up the great outdoors. And in the summer, in the same spirit, those aluminum frames can conduct the outside heat inside your house at a rate you wouldn't believe.

By the way, this is something your building material supplier isn't likely to expound upon. In fact, he may not even be aware of the facts himself. Also, they don't often stock the type of aluminum frame designed to overcome the energy robbing trait of the run-of-the-mill kind—the one made with a "thermal break." The thermal break is a piece of plastic fitted into the frame of either windows or doors so that the inside pieces of the aluminum frame do not touch the outside pieces. This helps prevent the heat from passing through at the fantastic rate associated with aluminum. It also aids in the prevention of the "sweating" that tends to occur with aluminum frames due to their propensity for being as cold on the inside as on the outside.

Wood framing, on the other hand, will never show signs of condensation due to its high resistance to heat transfer. The major disadvantage of wood-frame windows has always been that they are considerably more expensive than those made from aluminum. But with the tax advantages available to you, this may not be a major factor right now. In any case, we recommend wood-frame windows and sliding glass doors, too, over aluminum framed ones wherever and whenever possible.

If you do opt for aluminum for whatever reason, and your supplier doesn't stock thermal break frames, insist that they be ordered for you. Their cost is almost the same as the "standard" aluminum framed units but extra cost you might encounter will be paid back in energy saving and comfort. That's worth a little effort and even some waiting around.

Shades And Reflectors And How They Can Help Save Energy

When we were growing up roller shades were staple items of window dressing for comfort control in many homes. The folk wisdom of using roller shades has recently been vindicated by no less than the Illinois Institute of Technology. In the summer, a drawn roller shade will pass through only about half the heat that would enter through an unshaded window. And the same shade can prevent nearly one third of the heat loss through that same window in the winter. Venetian blinds and white lined draperies are less efficient. To be at its most effective best the roller shades must be installed within the window frames and not on top of them.

The Illinois Institute of Technology study also proved the value of other window shading devices you can still see in older homes—the wide roof overhangs, the wrap-around porches, the use of awnings and large shrubs and trees planted close to the house. Personally, we agree with the IIT and recommend any or all of these good old-fashioned ideas to conserve energy and increase the comfort in your new family room. In fact, it can serve as a test model for improving the energy efficiency of the remainder of your house.

In our own experience the old-fashioned ideas just mentioned are far better than the so-called "solar-energy reflectors" recently marketed—some with remarkably exaggerated claims about possible energy savings. These reflectors are made of screen and film materials. The screens are mounted on the outside of the window, while the film is used on the inside of the window.

The film material is generally about 3 mils thick, plastic, with a reflective film coating on one side. This material is hard to clean and, if used on double-glazed or tinted windows, liable to crack them. If that's not enough, the reflector material also prevents introduction of solar heat into your room in the winter, and since the material acts as a mirror, the glare from it may be quite annoying to your neighbors.

The screen material has all of the above drawbacks—except for the neat trick of cracking window panes. To keep up with the other one, however, it has a defect all of its own: it restricts the flow of air and makes it impossible to use natural air ventilation to cool your room.

We vote for old-fashioned wood-framed storm windows on the outside and white, opaque roller shades on the inside of extraordinary family room windows, just in case you haven't guessed from the above!

Chapter 6
Understanding
Lumberyard Jargon

Now that you are all ready to traipse to the nearest lumberyard or building supply house to buy your materials, it's time to acquaint you with the jargon of that particular industry. Not only are you suddenly confronted with a number of boards which look very similar except for price, but when you try to figure out how much lumber you get for how much money, you end up in a state of hopeless confusion...until you learn the language. And that, friend, is what we are about to do for you.

HARD AND SOFT WOODS

The first thing we learned was that wood is divided into hardwood and softwood. Now just because a wood is called a softwood doesn't necessarily mean that it is indeed softer than another wood which is called a hardwood. Never, never could things be so simple. Take the case of Douglas fir or yew-both firmly anchored in the category of softwoods, yet both actually much harder than some so-called hardwoods, like poplar, aspen or Philippine mahogany. Believe it or not, balsa, the softest of all woods is technically a hardwood.

Why all this confusion? Well, the terms hardwood and softwood refer to the trees that the lumber comes from, not the hardness or softness of the wood itself. So that you'll have the entire story just remember woods come from broadleafed deciduous trees while softwoods are derived from evergreens.

Since hardwoods are usually more expensive and harder to work than softwoods we prefer the use of the latter whenever possible. Take nailing...almost all softwoods are easy to nail while most hardwoods are too tough to drive a nail through and require special fastening techniques, something you can happily do without.

SEASONED AND UNSEASONED WOOD

Now that we have the name game settled, let us introduce some more terms--seasoned and unseasoned wood. You can actually distinguish between these by appearance: dried wood is white, unseasoned wood is green. Unseasoned lumber is usually quite a bit cheaper, but we don't recommend you buy it. Eventually, the unseasoned lumber has to dry out and if you use it as is, it will do the drying in your house, inside your laborious construction and can cause all kind of sagging, warping, squeaking, groaning and more. Contractors buy this unseasoned stuff cause they save a bundle on it and who's to know what's inside those walls until it's too late? But we ask you to desist.

Which brings us directly to the next hurdle in the mastering of lumberyard jargon grading. To begin with grading standards for hardwood and softwood differ.

Let us assure you mostly you'll be dealing with three grades: *Clear Wood*—no visible defects no knots, splits or other such; *Number Two*, which has knots which may interfere structually with load carrying, and *Construction Grade* the lowliest and least expensive of the three, which, of course, has the most flaws.

So much for the general knowledge for the moment. Let's get down to cases. If you're looking for a softwood for structural work that's easy to live with and fun to work you'll want to check out cedar, spruce, redwood and white pine. All of the above will resist shrinking, swelling and warping as will cypress wood. As if that wasn't enough, they all hold finish well. Equally well mannered and compatible are fir, hemlock and yellow pine though usually harder to come by. If you need lumber with unusual structual strength you can't do better than Douglas fir, with western larch and yellow pine close seconds. For resistance to our decay you can't beat good old cedar and redwood. These are our favorites. Study the charts and you may find a bargain on one of the less well known woods that you can cash in on.

You won't be using much hardwood in your garage/family room conversion, just for some build-ins and inside trim. The ones that are easiest to work are mahogany, gum, poplar and walnut. Of these, mahogany and walnut are most resistant to shrinking, warping and swelling. If you're looking for unusual strength try ash, hickory and oak. And if you want the nicest finish, gum, mahogany, oak and maple lead the pack. Again, for details study your chart. You might find something that suits your particular case better than any of the above.

LUMBER GRADES

As we said before, sooner or later in your lumberyard odyssey you'll be confronted by the dilemma of graded wood. Like graded milk or eggs, lumber grading is based on rather arbitrary standards of quality. Grading varies somewhat from place to place and grading methods change now and again, but what you are bound to run into in your local lumberyard is this:

A- and B-select, or Number 1 and Number 2 Clear as they are sometimes called are the highest quality lumber you can buy. It's virtually perfect though a bit weaker at times than other lumber. It takes finishes perfectly. But you won't need it except if you're in the market for wood for the finest cabinet work.

C-select, also called "custom," may have fine knots and some other minor imperfections, usually only on one side.

D-select is the lowest of the "finishing" grades and is about as high a grade as we have ever used for any of our work. What few knots and other blemishes can easily be covered with putty and finishing work or made into an asset by the use of a "knotty pine" finish.

The next grade is Number 1 "common", the first of the "board" grades. Actually it's almost as good as D-Select and we have found it to be the grade of lumber most economical to use for finishing work. It may have small imperfections, but the knots are small and sound, it will take finish well and you should have almost no waste when you use Number 1 "common."

Number 2 common is an all around grade of wood you can use almost anywhere. It's the best utility grade and can be used in finishing work, for instance as knotty pine paneling or flooring. It will have plenty of knots and some of these may be less than sound, but usually that can be fixed with a bit of glue. On the positive side you have very little waste when you work with Number 2 grade lumber.

When you get down to Number 3 Common, you are getting into weaker lumber. It won't be as strong as Number 2 and may also have pitch pockets, seasonal checking and larger knots. You'll be okay if you use this grade for non-structural work that does not show.

Number 4 and Number 5 Common are the poorest quality you'll find. Relatively cheap to buy but entailing lots of waste, too. It's a good grade to use for temporary structures, or in those cases where you don't need either beauty or much strength. One thing else in its favor, the wasted ends decay quickly and make excellent fire wood.

PLYWOOD

The next acquaintance we must urge you to make in your lumberyard sojourn is plywood. Plywood is man-made product—a sandwich made from an odd number of thin sheets of wood, with the grain running in alternate directions, bonded together under pressure, usually with glues, and rarely with heat. Again we have to take you by the hand and explain the plywood grading system bit by bit.

Plywood, too, is graded by quality, much the same as other lumber. However, in plywood, the designation always starts with "A" for top quality and goes down to "D" which is bottom quality. A word of warning: quality standards in the plywood industry are constantly changing—for the better, usually. It's still wise to be on the alert. But to give the industry its due, the difference between a sheet of plywood today compared with one manufactured 20 years ago is astounding.

In plywood talk, generally, "A" means a clean, smooth side. "B" is still smooth but will have some minor flaws. "C" will show a greater number of more obvious flaws, and "D" will be a rough side with splits and knotholes. Since plywood is made up of multiple layers of veneer, so to speak, the face and back of a piece of plywood will each bear a specific grade. So you'll find combination of A-A, A-B, B-B, A-C, B-C, C-C, A-D, B-D, C-D, and D-D. To add to the confusion, plywood also comes in exterior and interior grades which indicate whether the lumber should be used indoors or out. And, last but not least, plywood comes in a great variety of thicknesses from ¼-inch through ¾-inch to 1 inch...on rare occasions you can find a 7-ply 1½-inch panel.

We find a B-D grade plywood panel very useful when we need a good, all purpose grade which will have only one side that shows. Even the lowest and least expensive grade of plywood, a C-D panel, is still quite strong and will not split, because of its cross lamination construction so we use it whenever we need strength and can do without beauty for the time.

As a matter of fact, we're quite fond of plywood for a good number of reasons: plywood is strong and resists warping and cracking; plywood comes in handy large panels; it lets you use beautiful and rare woods which would be otherwise inaffordable and much more.

HARDBOARD

Hardboard is another man-made newcomer to the lumberyard. Hardboard is made from wood chips, reduced to the basic wood fibers and then re-united under heat and pressure to form a panel. Hardboard panels are grainless, dense, durable and you can use them for many purposes. There are no knots or imperfections and since the panels are grainless, the strength runs in either direction, which makes life simpler in many cases. You can work hardboard with regular lumber tools but watch out for dulling—hardboard is harder and more abrasive and requires that you sharpen your tools more often.

Hardboard, too, is grade. (What isn't, in these days of standards?) And so we have "standard" hardboard which is used a lot in construction and "tempered" hardboard, which, because of additional treatments is even harder, stiffer, stronger and more resistant to moisture than the "standard."

Hardboard is also graded with capital letters—S1S, or S2S which means—hardboard with 1 smooth side, or hardboard with 2 smooth sides. Clever, isn't it?

If you're looking for something with a rough finish, hardboard may still be your thing. You can get it with a serrated side, or grooved, embossed, or tiled. How's that for variety? And, of course, there's perforated hardboard more familiarily known as pegboard.

Hardboard comes in nice large panels most commonly 4 by 8 feet, though you can get panels up to 5 feet wide and 16 feet long. We don't advise these sizes, a 4 by 8 foot panel is big enough to handle not to mention transport. The thickness of hardboard varies from ⅛-inch to ¾-inch, but what you see mostly is the ⅛-inch, 3/16-inch and ¼-inch thicknesses.

We find many uses for hardboard in our garage/family room conversions as you will see when you study the material lists. Fortunately, hardboard is economical to use. Which, come to think of it, is probably why we find so many uses for it, including closet shelving, drawer bottoms, backs of build-ons, sliding doors and so on and so forth.

PARTICLEBOARD

Relatively new, this man-made building material also goes by the names of chipboard, flakeboard, or pressboard. In other words, a particleboard by any other name is made the same—by mixing wood chips and sawdust with an adhesive and then forming panels under intense heat and pressure. The result are grainless, extremely stable panels or boards. They don't warp easily but they are heavy, but inexpensive. Yes, at last there's something in all those endless aisles in your lumberyard that you can readily afford. Therefore, we love particleboard and use it whenever we can. (You should see our muscles!) Again, watch for dullness in your tools, particularly saw blades. Particleboard is quite hard on them.

Particleboard comes in boards in various widths, and also in panels up to 4 by 8 feet, in thicknesses from ¼-inch to 1⅞-inch.

Now that you've made the acquaintance of all the various materials available in your lumberyard you still need to make the final decision of what to buy for what purpose. And that's the operant word—purpose. As far as we are concerned we go a lot with..."when in doubt use Number 2 or B-D grade," depending on whether you're thinking of lumber or plywood. We rather suspect that you will seldom be tempted to pay the price for Clear wood, roughly twice as much as Number 2, and 4 times that of Number 4 and 5.

Even when you consider the price of Number 2 pine you may find that plywood is more economical. Besides, plywood is stronger, and you might prefer to go to the trouble of ripping plywood into strips for shelves rather than pay the price for the pine boards. Between you and us—hear this—a strip of ½-inch plywood, properly supported, to keep it from sagging, will hold more books than a ¾-inch pine board, also supported. So there! And if you are going to paint your boards anyway, you might as well go in for real savings and get particleboard. But you still have another hurdle to overcome before you approach the check-out counter. You've got to learn how they sell all the stuff you've just learned about.

HOW YOU BUY LUMBER

What we are getting into now are the matters of actual vs. quoted lumber sizes and the hocus-pocus of board feet. These two oddities are related and are among the most infuriating aspects ever encountered by consumers. So far, there seems no relief in sight and you might as well learn how to deal with these things without screaming, foot stamping and worse. (It wasn't easy, believe us, and one of us still tends to get shrill when confronted with either of the above.)

Nominal Size And Actual Size

When you go in a store and ask for typing paper you have your choice between regular or letter size which is 8½×11 inches, or legal size, 8½×14 inches. Now, if you get out your trusty rule and measure either paper you'll find that it conforms exactly to what it says it measures, i.e. 8½×11, or 8½×14. Which is what one expects.

Not so with lumber. When people in the lumber yard talk to you about 2×4's, 1×8's and 2×10's you will not get boards which measure 2 inches by 4 inches, or 1 inch by 8 inches, or even 2 inches by 10 inches. Never. Instead when you are handed a 2×4 you'll get a piece of lumber that measures 1½ by 3½ inches—while a 2×10 board will be 1½ by 9¼. So there. That, friend, is the way it is.

Tracing back the whys and wherefores, for strictly academic reasons, we have found the following explanation for the prevailing misnomers. What the quoted numbers refer to, the 2×4, for instance, is the *nominal* size, or rough-cut size. That means that when a 2×4 is cut out from the lot it will be exactly what it proclaims to be—a piece of lumber 2 inches by 4 inches and of varying length. But, alas, it doesn't remain there long. By the time it's milled and dried the actual dimensions of the piece of lumber will have shrunk down to the aforementioned 1½ x 3½-inch size. And so it goes with all the rest. All you can do is keep in mind the difference between nominal or quoted size and the actual size of what you get. To help you, we'll include a chart which spells out the difference for each and every one of the popular lumber sizes. Take it along whenever you go shopping. And most importantly, consult it religiously when you do your planning and ordering of materials. See Table 6-1.

Adding Board Feet To The Above Confusion

When it actually comes to buying lumber you'll find that the prices are quoted in something called *board foot*. What that stands for is a piece of wood 1 foot wide × 1 foot long × 1 inch thick. This alone can cause you untold confusion and orders of much more lumber than you need if you confuse board feet with linear feet. A linear foot is just the length of a piece of lumber and doesn't pay any heed to any other dimension thereof.

Table 6-1. Chart Showing Nominal and Dressed Sizes of Lumber and Boards.

NOMINAL AND DRESSED SIZES OF BOARDS AND LUMBER		
	NOMINAL	ACTUAL
BOARDS (UP TO 12" WIDE)	1"	3/4"
	11/4"	1"
	11/2"	11/4"
LUMBER (THICKNESS, 2", 3", 4",	2	11/2
WIDTH UP TO 12" AND OVER)	3	21/2
	4	31/2
	6	51/2
	8	71/4
	10	91/4
	12	11 1/4
	OVER 12	SUBTRACT 3/4"

But—a board that is 10 linear feet long and 6 inches wide and 1 inch thick will "measure" only 5 board feet! Now you see why the gnashing of teeth.

And of course, there's the other catch—that board we just mentioned will not measure 1-inch thick at all, it will be about ¾-inches thick out here in the real world. As we've stated before, the 1-inch refers to the dim, dark, distant past of said board which is no longer relevant—except in its name. Ditto with the width of that 6-inch board that'll measure 5½ inches in the here and now. But there's one dimension that is as quoted—just to make things more interesting—and that is the length of the board. If you ask for a 10-foot long (linear length) board, that's what you'll get, exactly 10 feet, no more or less.

To help you in ordering here's a formula to guide you:

$$\frac{T'' \times W'' \times L''}{12} = \text{Board Feet} \quad T=\text{Thickness, } W=\text{Width, } L=\text{Length}$$

Remember to use the *nominal* size in these computations. So—if you want to figure out the board feet involved in a piece of 2×4 that's 8 feet long you'd have your equation set up like this:

$$\frac{2 \text{ (T)} \times \text{(W)} \times 8 \text{ (L)}}{12} = \frac{64}{12}$$

= 5.33 or 5 1/3 board feet.

Here's another thing you must remember: Boards and other lumber up to 6 inches in width drops a ½ inch between nominal and actual measurements. But boards 8 inches wide and over will drop a full ¾ inches. Nothing is simple or uniform in this business. So if you want your board to actually be 1-inch thick you will need to order and pay for the next size up, which in turn will be about 1¼ inches. In other words, you can't win, and there aren't any short cuts.

It is an excellent idea to learn the jargon and to speak and think it fluently before you make any major purchases. Also learn to use the terms in your notes when you make up your lumber shopping list. The best way we've found—one that has saved us from making a lot of mistakes—is to write down the number of pieces needed first, their respective thicknesses next, then the width, length, grade, species, and finally whether you want the lumber rough cut or smooth.

If you figure, for instance that you'll need four pieces of Number 2 white oak, 1-inch thick (knowing fully well you'll get only ¾-inch) 8 inches wide (7½-inches actually) and 10 feet long, smooth on both sides you'll note down something like the following: four-1×8×10-#2 Wh Oak-S2S which any self respecting lumber dealer will instantly translate into four pieces of 1-inch × 8-inch × 10 feet long, Number 2 white oak, surfaced on two sides. In the end, it's all a matter of semantics or language. And you better learn theirs, because, nine times out of ten they won't bother to learn yours.

Things are much easier when you buy other types of building supplies. Plywood, hardboard and wallboard are all figured by the square foot or, even simpler, by the panel. So if you want a 4×8 foot plywood panel ½-inch thick, all you need to do is ask for same and you will get it, exactly as specified. These items are usually also priced that way—if you see a price sticker it will be for the panel, not a board foot.

PANELING

Sooner or later you'll have to find out about paneling and since we're on the subject we might as well make it sooner. The most gorgeous, and, of course, expensive type of paneling is board paneling, that uses actual boards from ⅜ to ¾-inches thick. You do the bit with the board feet to find out how much you need and put your boards one by one until you've covered your wall. Frankly, this is not our way, for a number of reasons which we won't go into now.

When we talk about paneling we refer to the building material which comes in the aforementioned panels of ⅛- to ½-inch thick. Usually the 4 × 8 panels foot size is best and most manageable. Plywood panels make it possible for you to have real, beautiful hardwood on your walls at a price that doesn't shock you into apoplexy. The work itself goes quickly and easily. In fact, some of the plywood panels are prefinished.

If you want something even less expensive investigate the wood-grained hardboard panels. They are suitable for both walls and ceiling, come in a variety of panel sizes, (again we prefer the 4×8 panels) and are ¼-inch thick.

Lately, there are also panels backed with particleboard which are even less expensive. We've used some and find they go up easily and look as well as any. The drawbacks are that they tend to crumble a bit along cut edges but with proper precautions that can be avoided. (See working with particleboard Chapter 8). All woodgrain panels are pre-finished and easy to clean. And, if at some future date you get tired of the color or grain of your paneling you can easily paint them with any latex paint. As a matter of fact we live with such painted paneling at the moment—they were that lachrymose blue that is absolutely guaranteed to produce deep depression—which we transformed into a lovely vanilla white three years ago. Incidentally, that bit about painting goes for all paneling. Some lovely effects can be achieved with a light color wash over the wood surface.

A bit of warning before you buy out all that gorgeous dark paneling that looks so rich on the showroom floor. Keep in mind that in most garage-to-family room conversions the resulting room tends to be a bit on the dark side, even if you've installed extra windows or skylights. That's because your room is large and the main source of light comes from the front end. So go easy on dark paneling. One wall of it might look great, but four may bring on instant claustraphobia. Also, watch out for panels that show a lot of grain pattern. Again, a little can look stunning—a lot overwhelming. Remember that just because it's wood, or looks like wood, doesn't mean that it automatically "blends in" with your floor pattern, your draperies, and upholstered furniture covers. A little restraint pays off well here.

Other materials that can be used for paneling are Malamine finished panels (great for hard use craft areas), Vinyl-covered and textured panels.

ACCESSORIES AVAILABLE AT LUMBERYARDS

When you buy other materials at the lumberyard you'll have to deal with different ways of classifying units. For instances, if you buy shingles, you'll be buying them in bundles and the same holds true of laths. Molding, trim, closet poles, stair railings and dowels on the other hand are sold by linear foot.

Windows and doors, and other ready made units are priced according to size and type. Usually the larger will be the more expensive, though not always. Metal and glass are mostly priced by the square foot and the "gauge" or thickness, as well as the manufacturing process.

STANDARD AND SPECIAL SIZES

Lumberyards and building supply places offer their stock lumber in standard sizes, (i.e.) most often used sizes, which usually start with 8-foot lengths and go up, in 2-foot increments, to a 20-foot length and sometimes even a 24-foot length. If you want to buy an odd length, your friendly dealer will gladly cut it to your specified length but—he will also charge you for the length he cut off—that is you'll pay for the next largest standard size. Therefore it is best to take the next standard size, up from the one you need, and cut it yourself. This way you not only save the price of the cutting, but you have the extra length to use when you need a short piece. Best of all, try to plan your projects so that you can use standard sizes as much as possible and will have only a minimum of waste. We also recommend that you buy the lowest grade or quality that will be suitable for your purpose. Most often a good material in a lower grade will do well for your purpose if you don't have a perfect natural finish in mind.

In fact, now that you know the jargon of the lumberyard we'd like to introduce you into the world of bargain hunting for lumber as well as for all other materials you will need in your garage/family room conversions.

Chapter 7
Bargain Hunting Lumber

Some sage or other once remarked that if you have the right materials and the proper tools for a job the results will be a natural symbiosis between the materials and the tools which will result in a beautiful product and give you much joy. While we dare not dispute a sage, we feel there was something left out of the formula. And that is the matter of price. Our formula then reads like this "Proper Tools + Proper Materials + Proper Price = Great Product + Good Cheer."

Now whether you believe in this kind of symbiosis or not, you'll have to agree that acquiring the right materials for the right price is of utmost importance. We've clued you in on the jargon of the lumberyard in the last chapter. Now we'll show you how to hunt for bargains in building materials. And believe us—you'll need to. Building materials, even more than other commodities, are skyrocketing on inflation propellant. The future doesn't seem to hold much hope of this trend reversing in spite of the old folk wisdom that "what goes up has to come down." The best we found is to learn the ins and outs of bargain hunting.

HOW TO SAVE MONEY IN THE LUMBERYARD

Saving money begins with being aware of the current prices for the article you propose to buy. That sounds simplistic and as if we were talking down to you, but we aren't. The catch in this truism is that prices vary—not only from one section of the country to another but from your friendly lumberyard across the road to your less well known lumberyard across town. And quite considerably so. This means regular, every day prices, not sales or specials which we'll discuss a little farther down the line.

We have no specific explanation why that is so, but we know, and you can prove it to yourself, that ten lumberyards in your community on one given day will have 10 different prices for a specified piece of wood. That price may vary as little as a penny or as much as five dollars a panel. The only way to beat the racket is to get on the phone. We find this a tremendous help in bargain hunting.

This is the way we get a grip on the going rate and locate bargains in a preliminary survey.

After you have made out your material shopping list in great detail, make a chart listing the biggest lumberyards, building supply houses and discount houses that carry building materials. Then, after looking in the newspaper to check on specials, start with any place on your list and ask for prices for the stuff you need which you duly enter in the specified column. You proceed the same way until you've covered at least a half dozen places. By that time you'll notice that certain items vary considerably, while others are fairly constant. Still, even a 5 cent difference per linear foot in molding can add up if you need a large number of said linear feet. The most interesting thing about this method is what we term "fall-out of bargain information."

Let's say you are on the look-out for 2×4's, plywood panels and a pre-hung door. You might very well discover a source for unbelievably cheap folding doors during the course of your research. In fact, you might even decide to replan and use folding doors instead of pre-hung ones. Or, you may discover a bonanza of shelving boards. Or whatever. Quite an interesting phenomenon, and most helpful.

But back to your chart. After you've entered all of the above, including the fall-out, you will have a clear picture of what is cheapest where and can proceed from there.

If you're really on a quite limited budget and the prices you've gathered together are in no way compatible with it, don't give up the project in despair. We've just begun out initiation into the nether world of bargain hunting.

First re-consider the lumber you've specified on your shopping list. Often you can save a bundle by buying the least expensive grade that will serve your purpose. For example, don't buy finishing grade lumber if you don't plan to use it where a good wood finish will show to advantage.

Second, look for "overs and seconds." This requires your very own presence and means foraging around building supply houses and lumberyards, investigating dark corners and hidden crannies. You can leave discount places, such as K-Mart and other such, out of your snooping tour since they will advertise any of these bargains if they have them as "Specials." However, don't overlook small lumberyards or lumber discount places. Be sure you know the going rate of everything. Take your trusty info sheet along. We have found that some of these "Extra Special Lumber Discount Places" so advertised, had prices on a lot of items that act higher than the ones in ordinary building supply houses, re were some honest-to-goodness bargains, too.

...rs are materials bought by the dealer which for some reason he can't move. They may also be items he ordered for a contractor and that were returned. In any case, these overs take up room and tend to get weathered. Also, as in the case of pre-hung doors and windows, or folding doors, they may be of sizes that are a bit unusual. But—you can often pick up these overs for a fraction of the going rate. Particularly doors and windows of all kinds. And while we're on the subject, if you happen to run into a real bargain on slab doors you might consider using them as table or desk tops, too.

Seconds are materials that are a bit less than perfect. With lumber it's often easy (though often time consuming) to fix up the defects. You can repair such things as loose knots, warping or twisting if it's not severe, cupping or checking. And you can use lumber that's weathered or stained to good advantage if you seal it before finishing.

THINK RE-CYCLING

Good sources of cheap building materials of all kinds, like lumber, windows, doors, brick, glass, and even ceramic tile, are buildings to be torn down to make room for new expressways, shopping centers, apartment complexes or other such innovations. Often there's a sign telling you that materials are for sale on the premises. Classified ads in the newspaper under Building Materials or the equivalent often carry announcements of sales of secondhand goods and you'll find so-called lumber salvage yards in a few communities.

In any of the above the prices are usually negotiable. In a way it's a great opportunity—it allows you to try your skill at horse trading and you might pick up a priceless bargain like hand-carved doors, finely-turned stair rails or intricate fretwork, for a pittance. Often you can make a deal with the owner of a small building who'll let you have everything within it for a small sum, provided you do your own wrecking and carting away. We warn you though, do not attempt a big or even medium size building unless you're an expert. Even a small building will give you most of what you need for your conversion and some left-overs which you can sell or trade at a used lumber dealer for whatever you still need.

Used lumber or salvage yards often are good sources for building materials. You'll find the lumber stacked according to use—that is, studding in one place, siding in another and flooring a third. We've found this the most convenient if not the least expensive or most exciting way to obtain inexpensive building materials. We recommend this route particularly for your garage conversion since you will need only a relatively small amount of materials and be limited, as most of us are, by a dire lack of time. If you enjoy the excitement of pawing through condemned buildings and hugh piles of odds and ends, by all means indulge yourself and go the direct route.

74

In any case you will need to be extra careful in your inspecti[on]
lumber since there is no grading and you can't return your purcha[se]
should change your mind. And, remember, you pull out your own _____.

Recycled Lumber

Of utmost importance in all bargain building materials is soundness
and workability. Ask yourself if the material needs repair or restoring, if
that can be done by you, and if, taking the time involved into consideration,
this will make the material still inexpensive, and, most importantly, as
durable as required. In a way, it's easier to list what you don't want.

For instance, you definitely don't want lumber that has decayed or is
riddled with insects. You can test for this with your pocket knife. If the
blade penetrates into the wood easily you don't want that piece of lumber.

If a piece of wood seems unusually light for its size, don't buy it.

If you're considering an intact wall that you might want to demolish for
materials and you notice what looks like saw dust around the base of the
wall, forget that particular lumber. Leave it to the termites already in
residence.

If, however you find some old lumber with a coat of paint or varnish
that's intact, you can almost be certain that the wood hidden underneath
will be in excellent condition. And that great coat of paint can be easily
removed with paint remover so don't fret about that.

Nail holes and other small holes, scratches and mars are no problem
either because they can easily be repaired with wood putty or other filler
material. Or, you can feature the imperfections and use an antique finish
for your second-hand wood. If you want to go all the way, take a chain and
help those imperfections along towards a "distressed" finish as they do
with all high-priced "reproductions" or what we call "assembly-belt-
antiques."

Salvaging Techniques

Whatever method you use to obtain lumber at a bargain price, always
inspect the ends of the lumber you are about to buy, scrounge or salvage. If
it's new lumber that's the place where you'll find the grade marking. New
or used, the ends are the place that will reveal any cupping and the depth of
checks if present. Cupping and checks, along with loose knots, bowed or
twisted boards, can be overcome rather simply so don't reject lumber with
such flaws if the price is right.

Checks. Unless checks—cracks in the ends of lumber—are deep
enough to weaken the wood seriously, you can obliterate them with a
commercial "plastic wood" or you can make your own filler from glue and
sawdust. Fill in the checks and let the filler harden, then sand for a smooth
finish.

Cupping. Cupping is that gutter-like hollow that forms from one end
of the board to the other when the grain of wood straightened out after
milling. Simply wet the concave side with damp rags and leave the rags in

place for about 12 hours. If you do this in a warm room the board will swell and flatten out.

Warps or Bows. A straightening grain pattern can also warp or bow a board along its length. If the board is to be nailed to a rigid framework that will hold it flat, just force it into place and use some extra nails to hold it straight and true. However, if the board needs straightening before you can nail it into place, support the board by both ends and then place weights on the up bow at the center. Use plenty of weights and give the board a lot of time to straighten itself out. Usually this takes a day or two.

Loose Knots. Loose knots should be pushed out of the board and coated around the rim with a clear cellulose cement. Put the knot back in its hole and wipe away any extra cement immediately. If you want a super job that can be varnished over smoothly, fill in every crack or depression with putty, let the putty and cement dry, then sand smooth being sure to go in the direction of the grain in the wood. If you forget and go across the grain you'll get scratches, cursed things which have been known to show up even under several coats of varnish and, yes, under a coat of paint. (That was because one of us doubted the rule).

Removing Nails and Such. If anything can try your patience, even if you're a natural saint, removing nails from salvage lumber is among the top ten. It also can break your hammer handle, cause you to pitch things across the room, kick the dog and scream at your spouse. To avoid these disasters here are a few tips:

● A gooseneck wrecking bar is a fantastic tool for pulling spikes out that your hammer wouldn't even budge. If you're going to do a bit of scrounging and salvaging, borrow or buy one. It's the extra leverage you get that does the trick here.

● If you do use a hammer to pull long nails, draw them just a little way—about an inch—then slip a scrap of block of wood under the hammer to finish the pull. This not only multiplies your leverage but also protects the wood.

● If you can't get at a nail head in a tightly nailed joint, open the joint slightly by hammering on the back side of the member that forms the top of the joint. Use a scrap block to protect the lumber from the hammer blows. Once the joint opens up a little, turn the work, and proceed from the other side. Tap the top board back in place leaving all nail heads elevated for easy pulling. Neat, isn't it? One of our professional carpenter friends taught us that one.

● To unclench nails for pulling without damaging you or your wood, raise the clenched points by inserting a cold chisel under the points. Drive the chisel between the nail and the wood to pry up the points. Finish straightening the nails with your hammer. Tap the points with your hammer to raise the heads on the other side, then pull.

● If you find split ends on a board nailed to another, you can save quite a bit of time and patience by simply sawing off the board near the joint. Pry off the split scrap and toss it.

Nuts and Bolts. A cold chisel will come in handy if you're trying to remove a nut that won't turn without damage to the lumber and you want to save the bolt. Back up to the nut with the face of the hammer. Clamp the board down, if necessary, and cut the nut off by driving the chisel into the side of the nut.

Often you can loosen nuts with a few swift applications of a light oil or DW-40 compound with several hours of soaking in between. We would rather be caught without a new ribbon for our typewriter than without the good old DW-40 that has saved the day for us many a time. After the DW-40 applications, administer the death blow by striking the nut a sharp blow with your hammer.

You'll find lots of carriage bolts—the round headed kind with the square shoulders, in old lumber. They are beastly things—there to stay for good because the wood around the shoulder has usually loosened so they simply spin round and round with their nut firmly attached while you go up and up toward the ceiling in rage. Before you hit—there's hope. If you can pry up the head a bit to hold it with a pipe wrench while you unscrew the nut on the other end, you can always cut a slot in the carriage bolt with a locksaw or an old file. Then hold the head with a screwdriver while you turn the nut off. Sometimes you can use the locksaw to cut through the bolt between the nut and the wood which simplifies operations.

Machinery and stone bolts are usually easy to remove by holding them with a screwdriver or wrench.

When it comes to rusted-in screws you might try clamping a crescent wrench onto a screwdriver blade. Or you might use an offset screwdriver which is especially neat for getting stuck screws out of old hinges and for working in hard to reach place. (This is an inexpensive tool which, like the regular screwdriver, comes in a variety of sizes).

A more original way to remove rusted-in screws is to heat them with a soldering iron. They expand, of course when heated and cut a slightly larger hole into the wood. Then, when they have cooled down, they shrink back to normal size and so are looser and can be turned out easily. This doesn't always work in practice, but the theory is so neat and so little actual work is involved that it certainly impresses onlookers no end.

HOW TO GET BUILDING MATERIALS FREE

The best bargain you can get, natch, is a freebie. With some building materials this is still to a limited extent possible. Often retail dealers of large goods have only limited space and considerable trouble in disposing of the containers in which their goods were shipped to them. Wooden crates and boxes can pose a problem to such dealer since most cities have ordinances which forbid burning trash. These people will often gladly give you their old crates and boxes provided you promise to pick them up promptly at a given time. Even if they usually have the crates or boxes picked up by a trash collector, you might be able to persuade them to let you do the picking up a time or two.

Just go in and talk to the person in charge. We find they are usually very amenable to reason and a little persuasion. And it certainly is worth your while to try a number of places if needed. Shipping crates and boxes usually contain very sound lumber free from knots and other blemishes. It's usually rough cut and needs light planing and sanding but if you can get it for free that's worth it. And don't forget your local liquor stores, which are sure to abound in any area. Their medium sized and small grates are very good and usually quite readily available. Large appliance dealers and dealers in medium goods which come from overseas are excellent sources for the large size crates.

Well, that's the story of how to hunt bargains in lumberyards and other such places. But that's not the only bargains you need to find for your garage/family room conversion. So we will go on to—How to buy everything else you need at a bargain.

Chapter 8
Bargain Hunting, Once More

Although you've surmounted the biggest hurdle of your bargain hunting/shopping for your garage/family room conversion when you've acquired the necessary building materials, you are still faced with the necessity of buying your finishing materials. And paying for them through the nose, if you're not in the know. So, here we are again, ready to give you the inside story of the finishing material scene.

FLOOR COVERINGS

Floor covering will be your next major expense and therefore worthy of a little time spent on the subject. The natural tendency when buying floor covering is to cope with the hassle of color, texture and pattern and leave all other considerations for that unpleasant moment at the cash register. However, that unpleasant moment at the check out and other unpleasant moments later when flooring doesn't seem to do quite what you expected, can be avoided if you will bear with us through this chapter.

Flooring comes in so-called hard covering which includes vinyl, linoleum and asbestos, both in sheet or seamless covering, and tiles. Soft covering—carpeting to you—has a number of different classifications which are nice to know but won't concern us here. For do-it-yourselfers we recommend that you stick to carpet tiles which come only in a limited array of pile and nomenclature. If you want to use carpet samples we will talk about that later. Indoor/outdoor carpeting is the one exception in roll carpeting for non-professional installation, but even that can get quite unwieldy and cause you a lot of trouble.

Hard Covering: The Tiles Have It

Let's go with the hard covering first. Our earnest recommendation is that you use tile and forget all about the sheet stuff. It is lovely, no seams to worry about, no matching, it comes in gorgeous patterns and colors, and so on, and so forth. Yes—we know. We've been there. But what the ads don't tell you is that a roll of hard flooring is heavy—really, truly heavy. Also, it is liable to crack, peel, tear and otherwise mutilate itself along the edges. We found it takes at least three people to lay sheet flooring successfully— two with lots of previous experience with that kind of flooring. Otherwise forget it.

The trouble is that no room is ever exactly so many feet long or x-number of feet wide. Nor is there such a thing in existence as a perfectly square or oblong room. A 90 degree angle is an unreachable goal of perfection in building. However, your vinyl sheeting comes in exact 6- or 12-foot widths and its ends are cut in nice right angles. So—in order to fit the vinyl to your room it has to be trimmed along the long edges, rolled out, and the short edges kept aligned with short walls all at the same time. Not to mention spreading adhesives, measuring and marking. Now if you still insist on tackling the job, that's your problem. We won't take any responsibility. We're still suffering from the trauma of our try.

That leads us directly to tiles, which have none of the problems of the sheet linoleum. Each tile is small and easily handled, though they, too, have the unfortunate tendency to crack and crumble around the corners. But with tiles you can avoid most of the mishaps and the ones that do happen are not critical because you can simply discard damaged tiles.

You can buy vinyl, vinyl-asbestos, linoleum, and asbestos tiles. Vinyl is considered the best: it's the hardest wearing and at the same time the most pliable. It does have some drawbacks. The floor underneath must be perfectly smooth and you might have to put down underlay if it isn't. Also, the vinyl will indent easily so you have to be careful with moving heavy furniture, high heels and furniture without big glides on the bottom.

Vinyl-asbestos tile is the most popular in use. It has most of the good qualities of the pure vinyl plus a greater thickness that hides slight uneven spots on the floor below and it is less likely to dent. Linoleum tile, once a favorite but of late becoming rare, is in about the same class as the vinyl-asbestos.

Low man on the totem pole is the pure asbestos tile which is usually used only in below grade installations where no other tile can be used.

If you think you know all about hard flooring tiles by now you're sorely mistaken, because there are many grades of vinyl and many, many combinations of vinyl-asbestos. You don't need to know them all, you just have to be aware of the fact that they exist and that one vinyl-asbestos tile is not necessarily of the same composition as another. A little judicious nosing around in the floorcovering stores will give you a broadened viewpoint. This is a case where a picture is worth 1000 words, even if we got paid by the word.

One word of warning that applies to pure vinyl, vinyl-asbestos or linoleum tiles. The deep textures embossed in the tile to make it like stone, brick, mosaic or whatever may have lines as deep as ½-inch below the surface of the tile. Which means you've got yourself a dirt catcher par excellence. It will require a periodic going over with a tooth pick if you're of the house proud breed, or else you'll have to settle for an antique effect of dark dirt lines which will eventually level out the surface. Neither alternative is quite our thing and if they aren't your idea of fun either, watch out for deep texture, not only in brick or stone patterns but in all patterns.

As long as we are talking about easy maintenance we feel a great love for no-wax tiles. There is something really endearing about a floor that will shine, and shine and shine without a drop of wax. And one that will never, never, never have to be stripped to get rid of the wax build-up that one has laboriously applied over the year. We ask you, what more can you want? Eggs in your beer?

Another pitfall in the tile buying department we feel necessary to mention is the matter of pattern. Designers, particularly of vinyl tiles for some reason, have a tendency to go berserk and design floors which look superb when four tiles are laid out as a sample in a store but which become overwhelming when the first four-tile pattern gets combined with four other four-tile patterns. Why? Because those other four-tile patterns will form extra patterns between them, so that you'll end up looking at a kaleidescope which can make you seasick if you're susceptible. Always insist that several four-tile patterns be laid out for you on the showroom floor before you even consider taking them home to avoid this problem.

The Economics of Hard Tiles

The next question on the agenda is whether to use ready-stick or the orthodox variety of floor tile. This is entirely up to you and your budget. While the ready-stick variety used to be of questionable stickiness, this fault seems to have been overcome satisfactorily by the industry. In addition, the possibility of being able to remove and replace individual tiles is really very tempting and practical. It also used to be true, and to a certain degree still is, that ready-stick tiles cost more.

As a matter of fact, they do run from 6 cents a tile to up to 50 cents higher. Strangely enough though, it goes in an inverse ratio—the more expensive the tile, the smaller the cost difference between ready-stick and ordinary tile. For instance, we priced tile at a discount store—plain vanilla-colored vinyl-asbestos, at 17 cents a tile (a bargain). The same tile with a sticky backing costs 29 cents. In the same store we found another kind of vinyl-asbestos tile that cost 83 cents plain and 89 cents ready-stick. To prove that the inverse ratio doesn't always apply we must mention the tile we found for 99 cents and ready-stick for $1.29. The last was in a regular flooring store where the fluctuations of price are at times without visible or reasonable cause.

While you consider the price differential between ready-stick and plain you must keep in mind that you will have to buy mastic for your ordinary tiles which, even at a discount store can run you around $13.00 a gallon, for enough to cover about 180 to 200 square feet. In other words, since most of your tiles are 1-foot square you'll have to add the cost of the mastic per tile (i.e. 1300-200 = 2.5) to the tile.

In order to get really good adherence from plain or ready-stick, you'll have to seal the floor. Sealer will cost from $14.95 per gallon for 440 square feet to somewhere around $11.95 per gallon for 220 square feet. This, of course, raises the cost per ready-stick tile.

So the whole problem is one of economics. You might think it's a lot of talk about a few cents, but remember these few cents are per single tile. In the case of the family room, you'll be using quite a few—around 288 if you have a single garage to about 580 if you have a large double. And that means that if the difference per tile is only 20 cents, the total cost of your floor can vary from $57.60 to $120.00 for tiles of the same basic quality.

There is no doubt that ready-stick goes on faster. You also eliminate any clean-up which can be messy when you use mastic and tend to be a bit sloppy like one of us. Before you definitely opt for the ready-stick, we must bring up one more consideration that might outweigh the convenience of the ready-stick: these handy tiles require a perfectly smooth floor for good adherence. If your garage floor is pitted or has some small holes, you can fill them. But unless you have this done professionally, we would advise you to go the mastic route.

Mastic, as you know, has a certain thickness, which as you spread tends to be self-leveling and so will easily compensate for any irregularities on your slab surface.

Soft Coverings Or The Case For Carpet Tiles

As we said before, only professionals should attempt sheet floor products and that goes for carpeting as well as hard surfaced materials. With carpeting, it's the sheer weight of the stuff that makes installation of wall-to-wall coverings a nightmare for the non-professional. The only possible exception is indoor/outdoor carpeting and even that can be hazardous. Believe us. We know—we have done it. And because of our personal experience and that of the others we heartily recommend that you limit your carpet laying activities to carpet tiles and carpet samples.

Tiles are almost all ready stick and the same rules for proper installation...a smooth surface and two coats of sealer...apply here. There's a wide range of patterns available and a comparable range in price. So, suit your taste and your wallet.

Speaking of the latter, whether you're in the market for hard or soft floor-covering materials, do take the time to shop around. We have had prices quoted that varied as much as *$1.00 per tile* for the same kind of tile on the same day in the same town. We've found that stores that specialize in discount floor coverings—and there are such in most cities—will be your best bet. You might have to visit two or three of them, or re-visit the same one a couple of times and you may find a little less selection in the over-all choice of patterns, but your total savings will make these inconveniences pretty insignificant. You'll also save a lot on mastic or sealer if you purchase it in one of these places. The discount floor-covering stores usually carry a full line of tiles: asbestos, vinyl-asbestos and pure vinyl tiles of several different grades, so you can see the practical, esthetic and economic differences for yourself.

If you can't find what you want in one of these stores, which hasn't happened to us yet, your next best bet will be your trusty Sears or Wards store. In this case, you'd be better off to wait for a sale to help keep the over-all cost down. As a last resort, tour building supply places. They often have tile on sale at pretty good prices. We mention them as a last resort because they are usually quite limited in color and pattern selection.

Incidentally—a tip worth remembering—if you can avoid solid color tiles, do so. Not only do they show more dirt a lot faster than any other kind, they might run you from 50 cents to 80 cents more per tile than their equivalent in quality in a pattern. (We are trying to find out why.)

A Road Less Traveled By But Just As Soft

There is yet another way to get a lovely carpeted floor. Our sister-in-law went that path on her garage conversion and we have her permission to tell you about her experience. What our smart relative did was to buy carpet samples. Hers came from J.C. Penney's but you can get them at most places that sell carpeting, or, better yet, at places that sell roll ends and short lengths of carpeting. Samples usually come in pieces of 18 × 36 inches. In other words, what you get are pieces about 3 to 6 square feet in dimension. These pieces will sell in different places for prices ranging from 50 cents to 2 dollars. Which, my friend, isn't bad at all, believe us.

What you end up with is a mix-and-match floor with any kind of nap your heart desires in any of the shades you like. Quite distinct and interesting patterns can be worked out.

We also experimented with a random effect—selecting only colors we liked and putting the pieces down in the order we unpacked them—with very pleasing results. In either case, planned or random, the carpet pieces are attached to the floor with double-faced carpet tape which you apply in wall-to-wall strips.

BARGAIN HUNTING FOR PAINT

A paint store is a bewildering place for a novice, not quite as bad as a lumberyard but a close second. And deciding what kind of paint to use for what can be quite agonizing. In the average paint store you'll find countless cans of paint with all kinds of fascinating labels promising a myriad of good things if you use the product. You then have to figure out what will do the job you want done best. And therein lies the trick.

What you need to know are the basics—the categories of paint and what they can do. And while it is not our intention to turn you into a professional painter (which we couldn't do in any case because that takes a lot more than "book knowledge") we thought it wise to give you a few general guidelines before we discuss the actual buying of paint or varnish. By the way—these guidelines are gleaned from research among professional house painters. We are happy to count many of them among our friends, and we have remained friends after trying out their advice. That surely means a lot.

Guideline 1. Paint has to suit the job it's intended for and expensive isn't necessarily best. For instance: the most expensive interior paint will do a lousy job outdoors. And the most highly rated latex-based paint will not cover a tiled surface. And a flat Latex paint will never work on your serving counter that needs frequent scrubbing.

Guideline 2. Convenience and fast application are great but remember that paint stays, or should stay in place a long time. Sometimes it pays to go to more trouble for a better, longer lasting result. For instance: you can now buy acrylic enamel which, as the label states, will dry in a couple of hours, is easy to apply and can be cleaned off hands and brushes with soap and water. Oil based enamel on the other hand, according to the can, requires several hours drying time, doesn't promise effortless brushing on, and requires paint thinner for clean-up. Also the oil based enamel is several dollars cheaper than the acrylic. What to do? That depends on what you're going to paint.

Let's say you are going to paint the home office in your garage conversion. You also plan to use the home office space for occasional bouts with the sewing machine, and the kids will do homework there. What you need is a good hard surface that won't scratch or mar and is easily cleaned. Personally our vote would go to the oil based enamel. It will take a bit more doing—you'll have to work more carefully, keep your brush from getting too full and use long even strokes going first one way then the other. You'll also have to put up with the nuisance of paint thinner clean-up. But if you allow the home office to dry overnight, or better yet for 24 hours undisturbed, you'll have a super surface that you can scrub time and again and that will, when the time comes, take a new coat of paint without any problems.

If you go the acrylic route, you'll have less hassle with the painting, and the drying time is shorter. Or so they say. Actually, if you read the fine print on the can, you will find out that the acrylic enamel is "dry to the touch" after two hours. And friend, therein lies half the trouble with that enamel. Because though it feels dry it isn't ready for use. It takes a week or more to harden. Acrylic, is soft—that's why it brushes on easier, but it takes forever to harden. And if you should touch it before it has had its hardening time, it'll peel and chip like crazy. In fact, we have found that the acrylic enamel you buy for furniture and such will not stand hard use, however long you let it dry, as well as the oil based variety. So again, it is a matter of where you want to apply the enamel. The acrylic would do great as an accent color or in areas where there is little wear and tear.

Guideline 3 (The Most Important). The way you prepare the surface to be painted or varnished, and the manner of application is at least as important as the kind of paint you use. For instance: if you apply paint over new wood you won't get good results. Although some people will tell you that Latex paint acts as a primer, most of our professional friends say that a good sealer used before you apply the first coat of paint will save you all kinds of possible problems like peeling and blistering and will insure a good, lasting finish. Likewise, if you try to cover an already painted surface without adequate preparation, or consideration, you can end up with an awful mess.

PAINT AND YOUR FAMILY ROOM

We found that for most of the painting you're going to do in garage/familyroom conversions you can use a good, semi-gloss latex based paint if you prepare the surface properly. That means that all new lumber gets a coat of sealer and that goes double for plywood and particleboard.

Most clerks in your paint stores will look you straight in the eye and say haughtily, "Sealer? You don't really need to use that—our best modern latex paints can go right on the surface. They seal themselves!" Well, latex paint does seal, after a fashion. It takes a lot of paint and the result isn't too good. In fact, often the paint peels right off in long, fat ribbons right back down to the bare wood. And, with particle board or plywood it'll take at least two, but more often three or more, coats of paint for even adequate coverage. Which, by any reckoning is a heck of a lot of coats and quite a paint build-up—and the reason why it tends to do the strip-tease number.

Our advice is to use a good sealer/primer. As an excellent, although a little more expensive and not quite so fashionable primer, particularly for outdoor jobs, you can't beat aluminum paint. We got this bit of advice from an old painter who got it in turn from the man who taught him to paint way back at the turn of the century. We tried it when we were faced with acres of hideous mahogany stained woodwork, the kind that is guaranteed to bleed through any paint. But when we covered it with a coat of aluminum paint as a primer/sealer and two coats of bargain, semi-gloss, off-white, latex paint, we never had a stain or chip in the next four years. (We moved after that so we can't vouch for how long it held up—we would guess indefinitely as far as the stain was concerned.) So we're sold on aluminum paint. Have it well shaken at the store and remember to stir it up often. That's all it takes.

Once you have a good, sealed surface—which has been sanded smooth and is free of dust—you can use any decent semi-gloss latex paint with excellent results, if you remember to have the paint well shaken when you buy it. That goes double for bargain paint, which tends to be on in years and so usually has settled out a bit. In fact, a double shaking is what's called for and you can often get it by having the paint shaken before you take it home, then storing it upside down for a few days and trundling it back to the store mumbling about having forgotten to have it shaken. Or, if you're more direct, just ask the clerk to shake it again or do it yourself. Those shakers are very simple to run. If you use one with authority nobody is going to question your right to do so.

While we're on the subject of shaking and stirring, we'd like to impress on you the importance of keeping your paint well-stirred. We stir out paint every ten minutes or so while we're working, in addition to a good thorough stirring before we start each time. The paint stirrer attachment for your drill is great for those of you who don't want to use too much muscle power. Just remember to hold your stirrer low in the can so that the very bottom, where the heavy particles tend to settle out, gets its bit of stirring, too. For those of a more rugged persuasion, the paint stirrer usually available gratis in the place where you buy paint, or a clean narrow board, wooden spoon or paddle will do the job as well. But meanwhile, back at the paint store we still haven't solved all the questions on how to buy paint.

Bargains Need Hunting

First of all, keep in mind what you need—what you want to paint. As we've said before, for most of the indoor painting you'll do in your garage/family room conversion—the walls, woodwork, ceiling and such, any good latex based, semi-gloss paint will do well. If you prefer the more vibrant shiny quality of enamel or need surfaces that will stand up to hard use and scrubbing use good oil-based enamel. If you want the enamel for accent or for small pieces which won't get much wear you might opt for latex enamel, if you can find it or even acrylic enamel. Just be sure and let it harden for a couple of weeks or more.

If you look around you can usually find white, off-white, ivory or cream colored paint on sale at any time you get ready to paint. The trick is in the operant words—look around. Avoid the regular paint stores—your local Sherwin Williams, or Mautz or fancy "Home Decorating" sort of places. Even if they do have a sale, their paint will still be more expensive than if you bought it somewhere else. And not any better, either. At least we don't think so. Hardware stores should also be avoided when you go paint shopping. There the paint has more mark-up than anywhere else.

That leaves you with the discount stores, building supply stores and the good old standbys Sears, and Wards. Strangely enough we've never used Ward's paint, or Penney's for that matter. This is probably due to the fact that somehow we always managed to be nearer to a Sears store. So we can only speak with real authority about Sears paint—though we are sure the other two stores have paint of equal quality. We really like Sears paint though there are those who don't. But we refuse to buy it unless it happens to be on sale, which fortunately happens quite frequently.

When it comes to buying paint at discount places look for the kind of store that also carries building materials. They have a greater volume of paint sales. K-Mart is great. We've bought a lot of paint there.

Also be sure to keep an eye out for paint bargains when you're shopping for other materials at your building supply stores. Quite often you can pick up some paint that's on sale because it's an "over," ordered by a builder or contractor—4 or 5 gallons of something or other he had no use for, or the paint might be stock that needs to move to make room for seasonal stuff like patio blocks and flowerbed fencing in the spring.

Price the kind of paint you need in several places: regular price and sale price. And be sure to find out about how much square footage a can will cover. It says so on the label, albeit often in small print. If you think you might have to waste a lot of that precious black stuff that made our Arab brethren so rich, you needn't. Let your fingers do the walking. Actually between you and the yellow pages you can have a quick paint bargain hunt, or any other kind of bargain hunt for that matter, without wasting an ounce, oops, mili-liter of gas.

Once you have the prices, check out the labels. That is an art all by itself, reminiscent of the lumberyard logic. Here are some things to look out for: Guaranteed one coat coverage. Baloney we say, pure and simple. While we won't argue that it can be done, (i.e.) it is possible to cover one wall with one coat of paint, we seriously question the advisability of doing so. First, you use a lot more paint because the paint, in order to have all that coverage, will be thicker than ordinary paint. Which leads to such painting no-nos as runs and globs, plus tiny bare or thinly covered spots you'll find here and there after the paint has dried. So you'll have to do some touch up work anyway. Unless you're a professional painter, in which case you don't need my advice and won't read this section, you're much better off with a paint that doesn't promise the near impossible and you can save money besides.

Next, compare the area of coverage promised on different brands of paint within a comparable price range. Less money may mean less square footage of coverage which means no saving at all.

Third, study the special features promised such as cleanability. This is of great importance to you and yours if you have chosen a light color, if you have kids, lots of company, pets or any or all of the above. The labels will have such words as "cleanable," "washable" (usually followed with the phrase—with care—) and "scrubbable." That's what you want— scrubbable. It's well worth paying a little extra for. Otherwise you might run the risk of washing off those finger prints and the paint at the same time.

Lastly, we always look for ease in cleaning-up. That's because one of us is the world's messiest painter. A good, quick, almost professional painter, but definitely, absolutely messy. You know—the paint in the hair, on arms, face, you name it. Not to mention the floor though that's usually adequately protected. Also, we've found to our sorrow that turpentine does sting and the odor definitely lacks the appeal of Chanel No. 5 though it is by far more penetrating and long lasting.

This is how we arrived at out distinct preference for semi-gloss = scrubbable, latex = water clean-up paint. You can also use this great paint on your walls and woodwork both. If you also use the same color you not only save on buying extra paint, but you'll save time since your work will go much faster and look more professional without worrying about splattering and smearing.

Incidentally, do wipe up any splatters instantly, even though they may be white on white, or blue on blue. You don't want any blobs that might peel off later.

Paint and The Outdoor Scene

The same rules apply for outdoor paint as for indoor. Preparation of the surface and application are at least equally important. Since you'll be using a relatively small amount of paint and because, in all likelihood, you'll need to match your new paint to the paint now on your outside walls or trim, you won't be looking for bargains. Unless, of course, you can use white paint which might be on sale. And who in these days of inflation can turn up their nose at even a five dollar savings.

Odds and Ends of Paint Bargains

Bargains in enamel paint are harder to find. But sometimes if you're willing to go with the primary colors on the paint chart, or willing to pick up a lot mixed for someone who didn't like it after all (sometimes those colors are lush, other times the veritable pits) you might luck out. And be sure to buy plenty of turpentine when you buy the enamel. It gives you a lovely sense of security when it comes to cleaning up. (Bigger cans are a good deal cheaper.)

Just a thought, if you have any of that great aluminum paint you used as a primer left over you may use it for some glamour touches—a neat, shiny, metallic finish.

BRUSHES AND ROLLERS

When it comes to paint rollers and paint brushes you'll need to exercise good judgement. Don't buy the cheapest rollers. They are no bargain. The inside of these roller heads is made of some thin cardboard stuff, similar to toilet paper rolls, which slowly dissolves when it gets wet with paint. The tacky thing gives no indication of its disintegration until you suddenly find yourself wielding a squashed mess which drips paint all over you and everything else and is absolute hell to get off the roller arm. Buy a medium priced roller and cover. And in spite of what's written on the packages, you really need only one kind of covering for walls and wood-work. Whatever else they offer is just a come-on for your cash. The only exception is when you use texture paint.

An extension arm that lets you get at the ceiling or high places (particularly for shorties like one of us) is a good investment. So are small cut-in rollers which we prefer to brushes. You can use the small roller on woodwork, too, if you have a narrow brush handy for corners and such.

As for paint brushes, we prefer the cheap kind since it's such a hassle to keep them clean from one job to the next. Nine times out of ten they get hard anyway and you've got to start the brush cleaner/softener routine which we loathe. There is one exception, though. And that is when we use enamel paint. For that kind of painting buy a good brush because a) you don't want any brush shedding into your enamel job, and b) you'll want a brush which will let the paint flow on evenly. And that takes a good brush.

Don't buy brushes that are too big. We know the temptation is great, with the bigger the brush the quicker the job rationale. But big brushes get awfully heavy when they are loaded with paint and unless you have your wrists developed to handle all that weight, you'll soon be in utter misery. If you're a tennis player you have a definite advantage here, though don't overdo it. The movement, and therefore, the muscle development, is not exactly the same.

By the same token, don't use a brush that's too narrow or you'll be painting for twice as long a time. Two and one half inches to three inches is a good general size for most uses plus a 1" or 1½" brush for narrow places and corners.

Incidentally, you don't have to clean out your brush each time you stop on the job, even if you use oil based paint. Just wrap your brush, (after you've got most of the paint out by painting on some newspaper) tightly in aluminum foil, two layers preferably, and secure with a rubber band around the bottom of the handle. This will keep your brush moist and soft for as long as a couple of days. You can use the same trick for rollers, too.

About Those Odds And Ends You'll Need

Let us consider the matter of masking tape next. This is something we have done many times and so far we've reached no agreement—so we'll present both sides. One of us is very fond of masking tape and spends a lot of time masking windows, etc. neatly and efficiently. That one swears that masking saves time and work. The other one, the anti-masking-tape faction, holds that soaping windows or applying petroleum jelly around the edges of the panes is a lot faster. The only use for masking tape that this person finds valid is to deliniate stripes, which doesn't happen very frequently. It's up to you entirely. Which ever works for you.

Paint Shields, those plastic gimmicks that are supposed to keep the brush from touching where it's not supposed to, sometimes work. You are supposed to hold the shield at an angle against the wall. The problem is keeping the shield clean so it won't smear paint as you move it from one place to the next. You must keep a rag handy and wipe the paint shield every few minutes. Personally, we prefer to use pieces of cardboard which are rather absorbent and tend to soak up paint rather than smear it. We discard the pieces quite frequently. In addition, we do a good clean up as soon as we get done with one wall.

Drop Cloths are a joy and a necessity. If you have some old shower curtains or heavy plastic sheeting you can use that, too. We usually supplement this drop cloth layer with a top layer of newspaper, that we change as often as necessary. (That depends on who is painting and how much dripping and splattering has been going on). Be sure to secure your drop cloth around the edges, either with weights or masking tape. Use fairly wide tape all the way around to give you a secure edge which is practically paint proof.

Liquid Sander or other chemical products that promise the same paint removing effect are great and we wouldn't be without them. While you don't need them as much when you paint new wood, they are most valuable for wiping down any unpainted wood surface before you start to get rid of any grease, oil, or dust which may have collected there. If you paint over an old paint job, the liquid sander will take off any remaining gloss and rough up the surface sufficiently to make the new paint adhere properly.

A BRIEF WORD ABOUT VARNISHES

On the whole we don't often use varnish of any kind. When we are in the market for a natural wood finish we prefer to use linseed oil. In our garage/family room conversions we usually have found it better to use paint than varnish because paint allowed us to use a more economical grade of lumber. Paint is also better because we use our family room for all kinds of activities—craft work, sewing, horticulture, what have you, and painted surfaces can take a lot more wear and tear. However, when we are in the market for varnish we like to use a polyurethane type which gives a really hard surface. In fact, we have used the polyurethane varnish over paint with great success.

You'll get a really tough antique finish, better than with any kit, but it also makes tables and countertops practically impervious to all kinds of abuses. It does, however, like any kind of varnish tend to yellow the surface.

HINTS ON CONSERVING PAINT, ENERGY AND TEMPER

While this does not strictly fit into the chapter heading we have decided to stretch a point and include it anyway. It helps conserve your bargains and your energy, too.

Hint 1: Always keep your paint cans tightly covered. If you don't, scum will form on top and you may have to throw out some perfectly good paint unless you want to spend hours with cheesecloth and sieve.

Hint 2: Store your paint cans upside down before they are opened. That'll keep the heavy particles from settling out at the bottom.

Hint 3: Always make a row of little holes along the inside rim of your paint can. You can do this with a big nail and a hammer. This allows the paint that comes from your brush (as you press it against the can to get rid of the excess) to run back into the can. Otherwise the paint forms a crust in the rim and that keeps the can from closing tightly and leads to the formation of scum and skin. This applies, too, if you pour the paint into a roller pan and aren't using a brush.

Hint 4: Never paint directly out of your paint can, because of the above. Pour some paint, after stirring, of course, into a clean can of some sort, and paint out of it. An ordinary #2 can does very nicely.

Hint 5: If you affix your smaller can to a plastic coated paper plate (or two—which are much better than one in this case) with a bit of paint or glue, you will have a handy rest for your brush, less drips on the floor, and cleaner, less slippery hands. This in turn, will lessen the chance of dropping the can of paint, one of our favorite tricks until we learned about hint 5.

Hint 6: If you're fanatic about clean roller pans (and that's nothing to be ashamed of, we all have our quirks) you might like to try those foil liners you can buy for roller pans. Or more cheaply, you can line your own pan with foil from your kitchen and discard it after the job is finished.

Hint 7: Wear gloves when you paint even if you hate to wear them at any other time. You'll have a better grip on your brush and your paint can, particularly when it's warm and your hands get sweaty. Also, you'll bless us when the phone rings or some other unavoidable interruption looms. You won't have to go in for a major clean-up—just slip off your gloves.

Hint 8: Wear comfortable old clothes. But no sneakers, unless they are ready for the junk heap. It is impossible to get paint off sneakers. However, it'll come off nicely if you wear leather or plastic shoes, particularly if you have been foresighted enough to coat the shoes with a little petroleum jelly.

By now you should be able to hold your own, bargain-wise, in any paint store or floor covering establishment. And that, plus your expertise in the lumberyard, will help you get the best stuff you need for your conversion at the best price. Before we move on to some of the basic techniques you'll need to know we want to add a word about buying wire and fixtures.

ELECTRIC BARGAIN KNOW-HOW

There usually isn't too much variation in price when you're out buying wire for your electrical projects. There is, though a mighty difference in the kind of wire you can buy. The best way to decide is to buy only the kind of wire approved by your city code. In most cases this is sufficient protection. The exception is the aluminum wire controversy. There are still many communities who approve aluminum wire for electrical installation. We definitely advise against the use of any aluminum wire anywhere. We feel it is dangerous to use aluminum wire and that the possible bad effects more than outweigh any "savings" in the initial purchase.

Buying Electric Light Fixtures

While you can get your wire anywhere, in the local hardware store or at a discount house, you'll have to look pretty hard to find a bargain in light fixtures. Strangely enough, there seems to be no such animal as medium priced light fixtures, we usually find inexpensive ones and very expensive ones with nothing in between. Our taste runs to simple lines and materials. In fact, we strictly believe in the "form follows function" dictum first pronounced by the famous Bauhause School of Design. Which is great because you usually can find good, simple designs in cheap light fixtures, while expensive models tend toward the over-elaborate.

But whatever your taste, before you buy a light fixture make sure that it will produce enough light for the job you want it to do. That goes double for craft and sewing areas where good lighting is of the utmost importance. So if you're in love with a Tiffany-type lamp by all means get it and hang it where it'll get a lot of attention, but don't expect it to give you enough light for serious sewing. And don't feel that track lighting is the only other alternative, either. You can get some rather handsome work lights, the kind architects and draftspersons use, for relatively little money. They do a fine job of casting light where you need it, whether onto a drafting board, a sewing machine, or a weaving loom. You can also rig up your own work lights, which, while not elaborate can be good looking and even stylish, from the components readily available in the electrical parts department in your hardware, discount or building supply stores.

It's time to stop shopping and find out how to use what you have. So upward and onward to the basic techniques you'll need to learn.

Chapter 9
Basic Building Techniques

While we will lead you by the hand, step by step through the actual work of converting your garage into that extra-ordinary family room we promised, we thought it wise to give you a quick overview of the techniques you will encounter and the rationale behind them—for instance, why do professionals insist on working a certain way when you can so obviously see a simpler or quicker version. And also why we have developed our own techniques and what our rationales are for those.

PARTITION BASICS

When we first started building walls and partitions we followed the hallowed tradition of most professional carpenters without deviation. We started, as we had been taught, at the ceiling and worked down. First we installed a top plate which we nailed to the ceiling joists. Then we added the framing for the new wall or partition, the studs, and hung them from the top plate, installed a bottom plate on the floor and finally attached the studs to that bottom plate. It worked fine and was strictly accordingly to Hoyle, but—and there was a but—our arms, necks and backs, unaccustomed to that particular kind of labor that requires over-head toe-nailing, protested mightily and slowed down production considerably.

So, we took a trip through a factory where entire homes were built on an assembly line. We studied their methods and found that we could adapt the modular building technique for our walls and partition. It not only worked, it worked better! We could do the job in less time with less effort, and pain in most cases. We found that if you have the necessary space, most of the frame of your new wall can be assembled flat on the floor. To erect the wall, you nail the sole plate to floor first, then lift the preassembled wall, complete with top plate on top of the sole plate and nail it in place, top and sides. Finally, toe-nail the studs into the sole plate to complete the wall framing. (That is, drive the nails into sole plate at an angle.)

Toe-nailing can be tough. We're not against toe-nailing overhead for those who have had the practice, but if you haven't done it before it's a boon to nail down through your top plate into the studs as you do when you construct your wall flat on the floor.

Toe-nailing a stud to a sole plate is easy after you've had some practice. If you're new at this, however, we suggest you make a path for the nail by drilling starter holes at a 45 degree angle through the stud into the plate. Make the hole slightly smaller than your nail. Should you get stuck, for any reason, with having to tow-nail your studs into the top plate, these pre-drilled starter holes will save you a lot of grief and pain.

You'll always try, of course, to put your new wall under a single joist or across the ceiling joints, so that the top plate can be nailed directly onto the joists. If, for some reason you must run a wall between joists, nail short lengths of wood between the joists to serve as nailing blocks.

If the space above the new wall is an unfloored attic as it will be in most garage conversions, these nailing boards or blocks should be put in from above. If not, you'll need to cut a strip of ceiling board about 4 feet wide and the length of the new wall in order to nail in the blocks from below. Cut the strip at the joists, flanking the ones you need to work on, and you can patch the strip with all new wall board.

In the same way, the end stud of a new wall should ideally butt up directly to a stud in an existing wall. If you can't arrange that, (and you really should try to do so in your planning), you'll have to again resort to nailing blocks between the studs of the existing wall. Cut two holes in the wall so you can install nailing blocks about 1/3 and 2/3 of the distance between the floor and the ceiling.

It's important to have the top plate and sole plate level. In older structures ceiling joists may sag and the slab foundation be uneven. If that happens to you, insert short lengths of thin wood, called shims, between the plate and the ceiling or the plate and the slab, whatever the case may be. Or at both ends, if need be.

WIRING FOR LIGHT: PRELIMINARIES

If you want to have electrical wiring in the new wall you'll do better to put it in the open frame before you sheath it up on both sides. Mount your outlet boxes on the studs wherever you'd like to have them. The flange mounted type are simply nailed in place.

Drill ¾-inch holes in the studs along the sole plate for running cables through. Install the cable in each box by securing it with clamps, then strip the ends of the cable wires. *Do not* please, connect your cable into the power outlet box until the receptacles have been installed in the boxes and all the bare wires properly connected. It could be dangerous to your health.

Don't install outlet boxes back to back so that they open on opposite sides of the wall. Why? Because this results in a conduit through which sound passes most readily. That you don't need. You'll be happier if you stagger the boxes with at least one stud between them.

PUTTING UP MORE SOUND BARRIER

Sound transmission through walls is something you are trying to avoid. You can actually suppress sound surprisingly well by using thicker than usual sheathing material.   An additional ⅛-inch thickness of gypsum wallboard, for example, will cut sound transmission by nearly 20 percent. This kind of soundproofing is of real value to you, if, you plan to do a lot of work in your home office which is divided from the main family room by a partition. The use of ⅝-inch rather than ½-inch wallboard may be well worth the extra cost. The same holds true of other sheathing materials, too.

BRINGING IN THE SHEATHS

Even if your garage conversion does not call for a new wall, it may well call for sheathing. Especially if you're stuck with the unfinished walls and ceiling your builder was too chintzy to do something about. The most often used sheathing for interior use is a wallboard that is called sheetrock (actually a trade name) dry wall, plaster board, or gypsum board.

Wallboard by any names is a paper and plaster sandwich, ½-inch and ⅝-inches in thickness. It usually comes in panels 4 feet wide and 8 feet high. Wallboard has a lot of little idiosyncrasies—for instance, it's not strong at all but it is quite heavy. If you stand it on one corner that corner will crumble away to powder. If you bend it, it'll break. But, and here is finally a plus, it will break neatly along a scored line and can be sawed through quickly with any wood cutting blade. Another plus is that you can patch any damaged wallboard back to its original smoothness and that you can smooth out joints between wallboard panels with a filling of plaster of Paris topped by glue-backed paper tape.

If your walls are higher than usual, you can buy wallboards panels in 10-foot, 12-foot, 14-foot and even 16-foot height. Or, if you'd rather, you can apply the standard 8-foot ones horizontally. By the way, if you go in for horizontal installation, remember to always work from the top down. Start at the ceiling and end up at the floor. Since the panels are so heavy—60 to 70 pounds a piece—start out by driving nails into studs 4 feet down from the ceiling. Eight-penny nails will do nicely. You will also need a helper to lift the wallboard so that it butts up against the ceiling and rests on the nails. Before you give the old heave-ho though, be sure to mark the position of the studs on the ceiling and floor. Make a line to connect these points so you'll have a guide for the next panel. After the first panel is nailed in place, remove the nails at the bottom that provided the "rest."

Before you put up the bottom panel measure from the edge of the top panel to the floor in at least six places. Though you may never have suspected it, the floor and ceiling in any structure are seldom parallel. This is why you must make your six measurements on the bottom panel and do a juggling job to fit it exactly.

To nail wallboard to studs you'll need special drywall nails. Hammer them in, in pairs, about 2 inches apart, allowing about 1-foot between pairs. On the edge, where your seam will be, nail in about ½-inch from the edge of the wallboard. Drive the nails flush and then set (with a nail set or an additional *careful* hammer tap) a fraction of an inch below the paper surface. This allows the nails to be hidden by covering them with joint compound (that plaster of Paris mix we mentioned earlier) when you are taping the seams.

If you're going to use your wallboard vertically, you may be able to do without a helper. You can get those panels up all by yourself if you learn the following trick. Shove a piece of wood shingle under the bottom of the panel after leaning it in place. Put a scrap of wood under that shingle and step on the shingle. This will push the panel up against the ceiling and hold it there while you nail it in place. How's that?

Align the edges of the panels along the center line of the studs. Use your ceiling and floor marks again to help you located the studs hidden by the panel. Drive one drywall nail into each stud about 1 foot down from the ceiling. This will now hold the panel in place for the final nailing and relieve you from keeping pressure on your shingle-and-block foot lever.

To fit wallboard around a window, always measure down from the ceiling to the top of the window jamb on both sides. Do the same for the bottom, measuring from the ceiling. Now measure across from the last sheet you installed to the edge of the nearest side jamb. If the panel will surround a window, you should also measure to the edge of the farthest side jamb. After you've transferred your measurements to the drywall panel and drawn your cutting line, make a plunge cut with your saber saw and cut out three sides. The fourth side can be broken out cleanly if you score the line well. If your panel will enclose only three sides of the window you can do a similar bit—cut the two parallel lines, score and snap off the remaining line.

For paneling around a door you will need only to mark the distance from the ceiling to the top jamb and from the last installed panel to the edge of the side jamb.

BUILD-IN FUNDAMENTALS

Build-ins come in different sizes, shapes and forms. There are true build-ins, the kind that are built into the walls, the usual kind of build-ins which are attached to a wall or ceiling and the pseudo build-ins which look like either of the above but are really free standing, or only attached loosely and can be easily moved to a different location. Besides these categories build-ins can be divided also by function—build-in closets, cabinets, shelves, bookcases, beds, tables, what have you. Let's take a closer look at cabinets first.

Cabinets

Actually cabinets include such things as bookcases (which are really cabinets without doors), built/in beds, and tables. Cabinets are hung from the ceiling or from a wall. There are about five different choices for doing this:

Angle Irons. You can support your cabinet from underneath with several small angle irons and use an equal number and size of them on top. They will be quite unobtrusive. If you have a yen for those decorative, angle irons that come all dolled up with fancy curves and curliques, we recommend that you still attach some small ordinary angles irons up on top. Why? Because the decorative numbers have a lot of "spring" in them, which means that your cabinet tends to bounce about a bit.

Rails. A simple way to hang a backless cabinet is to make a rail from a 1×2-inch strip, attach the strip to the wall and hang your cabinet from there. This makes a very solid attachment—you might even call it a lasting relationship.

Directly to the Wall. If you like a no-nonsense, direct approach you may prefer to hang your cabinet directly from the studs in your wall. You can do that easily and well if, and there's an if, your cabinet has a good solid back. all you do is nail and screw your cabinet back onto the studs. If you have drywall construction behind your cabinet use molly bolts, if you have a masonry wall, lead plugs will do well. By the way, what we mean by a strong back (on a cabinet, not you) is one that's ⅝-inch or ¾-inch thick.

Joist Hung. If you opt for joist hung cabinets, which are quite sturdy and attractive, be sure you attach your hanging chains, straps, or rods to the side of the joists, not the bottom edge.

Tracks And Supports. Those tracks and support rods you can buy for shelving will support some types of cabinets. You can get track supports up to 18 inches long, so a reasonably deep cabinet can be placed on them.

Closets

When you think about it, closets are really just small rooms built into larger rooms and you should remember that when it comes to constructing them. You can "furnish" your little room with all kinds of cabinets, shelves, racks, and drawers which will hang nicely from the studs in the walls and give you a variety of storage possibilities that should take care of the largest collection of odds and ends.

Another thing to remember is that closets need some ventilation and lots of light so you can locate what you're looking for. Ventilation can come from louvered doors at their most elegant or simply a small louver placed in a side wall. If your closet has daily use then you can forget about the ventilation problem because the opening and shutting of doors will do the trick. As far as lights in closets are concerned, we love the door frame mounted battery operated kind. It has a plunger type switch that turns the light on automatically when you open the door, and turns it off when you close it. You can readily see the advantages of this over regular lighting— you don't have to go to the hassle of installing wiring, there's no possible fire hazard from bulbs dangling from extension cords, and the light won't be left on to burn all day.

Wardrobes

Wardrobes are either super cabinets or free-standing closets, whichever definition suits you best. Both are correct. Wardrobes were originally used for clothes storage, for everything that could come under that heading from hats to cuff links. Therefore wardrobes were among the first pieces of furniture to be multi-modular with a variety of shelves, drawers, cabinets and such incorporated into the wardrobe structure.

One more fact about build-ins—in addition to storing all your stuff, a row of build-ins along an outside wall will help insulate your room and a row of same against an inside wall will effectively cut your noise transmission. Hurrah for build-ins!

For details see the conversions in Chapters 12 through 23.

Chapter 10
A Mini-Course
In Healthy Wiring

Since in the course of your garage/familyroom conversion you will, sooner or later, boldly go where no non-professional electrician has gone before, we thought it might be wise to acquaint or re-acquaint you with your home electrical system and how it works.

Believe it or not, your electric system is somewhat like your home's plumbing system: in the plumbing system water flows through the pipes, in the electrical system electrons flow through wires. And like water, electricity needs a circuit to flow around and some sort of "pump" to keep the flow going and the pressure up.

ELECTRICITY BASICS

The electric "pump" in your home electric system is the generator at the power company where the waves of electrons are pumped through high-tension wires to a service line that leads into your home—the service entrance cable. The line goes through your electric meter (naturally, how else would they know how much you've used?) and continues on to your fuse box or circuit breaker panel. From there it flows through your several house circuits to the different fixtures and receptacles where your electrical devices are fed by it. There has to be complete circuit, or closed loop, between these devices—your frig, water heater, TV, toaster, coffee maker, or whatever else you plug into the outlets—and the generator at the power station or nothing will work.

The pressure exerted on the waves of the electrons, which we likened to water pressure, is called the "voltage" and may be either 120 or 240 volts. A black wire (called the "hot leg") carries the current to the appliance or fixture and a white wire carries it away, completing the loop back to the power station. (In this case the black hats and the white hats have no emotional or sociological implications.)

On your 240 volts circuits there will be still another hot wire which is appropriately colorcoded red. This adds another 120 volts to the usual black and white circuit and makes a total of 240 volts which is needed for many major appliances. A white wire "returns" the current and so you have a three wire circuit when you are working with 240 volts of electric pressure.

In case you're wondering why all that bit about 240 volts when you've always heard and referred to that voltage as 220 it's because there is a drop of 20 volts between you and the source. So go right ahead and call it 220 which, after all, is what you actually get. And we, now that the technicalities are out of the way, will also refer to it in this way. 220 volts it is.

By the way, a third wire, a green one, may be added to your ordinary 120 volt circuits for grounding purposes. The 120 volt circuits are the ones we'll work with and therefore study more closely.

GROUNDING ELECTRICAL CIRCUITS

All electrical systems must be grounded, or connected to the earth. That's for reasons of safety. Because, though much poorer than metal, the human body will serve as a conductor of electricity and then you get what we call a shock. If the shock is large enough it can kill you.

A ground or grounding device is simply a metallic path to the earth in case an electrical device springs a leak and sprays electrons around over its metallic case or other parts. The case will then become electrified and if you touch it, you'll get the above mentioned shock. When you ground the appliance, the electricity will take the path of least resistance, which is the metallic ground path and drain off leaks into the ground instead of through you. So ground—ground—ground.

Different electrical circuits are grounded in many different ways. All of them are good as long as they provide a metallic path to the earth. And, of course, you never, never circumvent or fail to make ground connections when you do electrical wiring work.

AMPS AND WATTS AND OTHER TERMS

A few of the terms you will have to deal with in addition to "voltage" and "grounding" include:

Amps, or amperage, describing the rate at which electrical current flows. Your circuits are rated in amps just like your water pipes are rated by their diameters. And just as a 2-inch pipe will carry more water than a 1-inch pipe, so a 20-amp circuit will carry more electricity than a 15-amp circuit.

A *watt* is a unit of measurement for electricity. Appliances are often rated in watts rather than amps. It's easy to go back and forth between amps and watts if you remember this formula: watts = amps × volts. An appliance rated at 5-amps, for example, operating on a 120 volt circuit will consume 600 watts. (5×120=600).

A device that consumes 100 watts, on the other hand will require .833 amps to operate properly. (amps = watts ÷ volts) (100 ÷ 120 = 0.833 amps). Your friendly utility company charges you according to the number of watts of power you use per hour—usually termed as per 1000 watt or kilowatt, hour.

A *circuit breaker* is a safety device that, like a fuse, shuts off the current if too much current flows through. Unlike a fuse, however, a circuit breaker can be reset to restore current to the circuit, and does not have to be replaced. Just as an overloaded water system would cause burst pipes and flooding, an overloaded electrical system causes burned up wires and fires. So respect your fuses and circuit breakers. They are there to protect you and your property. And never, never try to go around those life and property saving devices.

An *electric service panel* is the name given to the use box or circuit breaker panel normally located close to the electric meter in your home.

Alternating current, or "AC" is the type of power used in almost all home wiring systems.

A *short circuit* is caused when for some reason the circuit the electricity takes is shorter than it should be and so raises the amount of current (amps) to a dangerously high level. Fuses will "blow" and circuit breakers "trip" in most instances before any damage is done.

KNOW YOUR CIRCUIT'S CAPACITY

Now is as good a time as any to calculate the capacities of all your electrical circuits so that you can use your electrical devices present and future without overloading any of the circuits.

This is how you do it:

● Turn on all the lights in your house and plug lamps in all outlets that you use regularly—like for your coffee maker, toaster, etc. If you don't have enough lamps do this one room at a time.

● Turn off your circuit breakers or unscrew your fuses one at a time. Each time, check to see which lights go off and mark down the wattage of each light and device you use in the circuit. Be sure to mark down the wattage of the *appliance* used on the wall plug, not the wattage of the lamp you just plugged in. The lamp only helps you to tell which plug-in is on what circuit, by going out when you throw the proper circuit breaker or unscrew the right fuse. The wattage is usually marked somewhere on the appliance casing. If amps are listed instead of the wattage all you have to do is multiply by 120 to get the wattage.

● When you've added up all the wattages on the first circuit breaker or fuse, write this figure down and call it circuit #1. If it's a 15 amp circuit, i.e. the figure marked on the circuit breaker or fuse, you can use up to 1800 watts (15 × 120 = 1,800) without overloading. If it's a 20-amp circuit you can use up to 2,400 watts.

● Repeat this procedure for every circuit in your home.

● When you come to the garage circuit subtract the wattage you use normally on the circuit from the total capacity of the circuit. Let's say you use about 800 watts there and your circuit is a 15-amp or 1800-watt circuit. So by subtracting your use wattage from the circuit wattage (1800 − 800 = 1,000) you will come up with excess capacity you may put to new use in your family room without overloading your circuit. In other words, you'll know how many appliances or devices of one sort or another you can operate at one time.

Wire Sizes

The amp rating of your garage circuit will also tell you what size wire you must use when adding on to that circuit. We really should say *conductor*, not *wire*, but that surely would sound strange. The wire, which is bare metal covered with plastic insulation, should be called a conductor because that's what it does—conduct electricity.

Conductors, or wires come in either copper or aluminum. We recommend copper. There's a great deal of controversy at this time about the safety of aluminum wire and we feel it takes the judgement of a very experienced electrician to decide what wiring applications can be safely done with aluminum wire. And since our motto has always been—"when in doubt don't," we ask you not to use aluminum. Just go the copper route.

Conductors are designated by numbers which in turn refer to the diameter of the wire in the conductor. The *smaller* the number the *larger* the wire. Another of those irrationalities that seem to plague the building materials industry more than others. Anyway, a number 40 wire is about as thick as a hair on your head. A number 0 wire on the other hand is thicker than a pencil. So there.

Actually you won't need to worry about either extreme. You'll be using either 12 or 14, these numbers are commonly installed in houses to handle the current—#14 for the current in 15-amp circuits, #12 for 20-amp circuits.

Wire Cable

You'll be buying your conductor in cable form, that is with all the wires grouped together. For use in places where conductors never get wet you'll buy non-metallic sheather (NM) cable. Romex is the most popular trade name for this type cable. We found Romex is easy to cut and use. It's lightweight and flexible, but still stiff enough to snake easily through walls. It comes in 250-foot rolls but you can get it cut to any length you need. If you're in the market for large quantities you'll save money by buying directly from an electrical supply house. Otherwise just run to your favorite hardware or building supply dealer. If you have any technical questions, however, take the time to trot down to the electrical supply house. Usually you'll find the staff quite knowledgeable and most helpful in answering your questions and finding solutions for any special needs you may have.

WIRING RECEPTACLES AND SWITCHES

First thing to do when you're about to wire a receptacle or switch is to use your trusty wire stripper and cut off the insulation at an angle—not square. You can use a simple pocket knife as a wire stripper. Remove a little less than 1 inch of the insulation and then wrap the bare wire around the shank screw in a *clockwise* direction. That is the direction the screw goes when it is tightened and so the wire will tend to tighten also. (Just for fun, try to do it the other way and you'll find out for yourself that in doing so the wire will slip out every time you tighten the screw!)

For joining wires together always use wire nuts. These solderless connectors come in various sizes to match the size of the wire you have. They are usually color coded according to the size of wire they accept. When you join wires don't twist them together. Instead, hold them side by side and insert them together into the wire nut. Then turn the nut down over them to clamp them tightly together. If you want to have a super secure connection, wrap some electrical tape around the wires. You can join three or four wires securely with a single wire nut if the nut is the proper size.

The number one rule to remember when you make an electrical connection is that a loose connection is probably the most frequent cause of malfunction. Therefore—check and double check to make sure all your electrical connections are as tight as you can make them. That should keep your new wiring in top working condition.

When you fasten a Romex cable to your receptacle and switch boxes, you'll have to cut back the insulation about 8 inches. Then you can slip the wires through the knockout and secure the cable by turning down the set screws on the built-in clamp.

The Romex bare ground wire must be connected either to the metal outlet box or to the green grounding screw on the receptacle or switch.

The black, or hot wire, will go to the copper or brass colored screw on the receptacle and the white, or neutral, wire to the silver screw.

Follow same procedure when wiring in the switch. The switch should always break the circuit on the black or hot side of the line, never on the white or neutral side.

WIRING LIGHT FIXTURES

Those wire leads coming out of your new outside or inside, light fixture will be color coded, thank the Lord, and you'll be using those aforementioned wire nuts again to connect black to black and white to white on your cable.

When you want to replace the overhead garage light fixture—that porcelain ceiling horror—with a new fluorescent, or incandescent fixture if you prefer, you'll need to turn the current off at the circuit breaker or remove a fuse. Be sure though to turn on the overhead light before you trip the circuit breaker or remove the fuse so that you can be sure that you switched off the right circuit. Electricity, as we all know, can be as dangerous as a power saw if applied to the human body. We can't tell you often enough to be certain to observe all the proper precautions when working with it.

Here's a brief safety review:

1. Always turn off the current at the fuse box or circuit breaker panel no matter what you are working on in the electrical line.

2. If you are working on a portable device unplug it.

3. Before you trip the circuit breaker or loosen the fuse, always have the light burning or the device working so you'll know for certain you've tripped the right circuit or loosened the proper fuse. That's when the light goes out or the device stops working.

Chapter 11
Your Introduction To Conversions

The time has come for action. Arm yourself with your sketch and compare it to the conversions we've collected for you in this part of the book. Look for the one that comes closest in physical features, (doors and windows), and in size. If you've lived right it may turn out that our twin to your garage also contains the essentials of your own space needs and wants. In that case you're home free. All you have to do is follow the conversion from A-to-Z and you'll get exactly what you want.

But life is seldom that simple—Murphy's law rears its head again. Most likely, what will happen is that you will see a conversion that in size and layout matches your garage and which also contains some of the features that you want. But—and here is the rub—it also contains a plant center and a sewing center which you don't need, while there's no provision for your much longed for home, office or craft center, not to speak of the area you've planned especially for your fish.

Actually, there's no great problem. Go with the conversion and substitute the home office you'll find in another conversion for the sewing center. These two are usually easily exchangeable. In fact, home offices normally take less space so you might be able to squeeze in a home for your fish there, too. Then take another look at the plant center area and compare its size with craft centers in other conversions. You'll be sure to find one that'll fit or can be made to fit easily. So—there you are.

A third way to use the conversions in this book to make your special space needs and wants a reality is to be completely eclectic about it. It's a bit more trouble in the planning stage but does not make the actual work any harder at all. And it's a lot of fun if you happen to be that kind of person.

The way to do this is to consider the conversions as a smorgasbord of features from which you can pick and choose what suits you and your family. In order to avoid pitfalls, and there can be many, we advise that you plan this type of conversion very thoroughly on paper. We also strongly recommend that you stick to one single conversion as far as the actual conversion of the space is concerned: the new wall, new windows, doors, skylight, what have you, that have all been carefully planned to work together. Find the conversion that best fits your garage and go with it. As far as the projects are concerned, you are free to take your pick, as long as you keep in mind that moderation is the key and that it's easier to add a feature later than to take out one because the place is too crowded. And double check with chapter 2 on planning, particularly the section on multi-use of space.

Next make a careful sketch, then a scale drawing of your ideas as explained in Chapter 2. If you still like the result make a work sheet listing the projects in order in which they will be completed as we have done for each of our conversions. See Table 11-1. As you do this try to be as efficient and farsighted as you can. Put the list aside for a day, while you browse through the first section of this book again, read a couple of the worksheets in our conversions and do a bit of thinking. Finally, look over your work sheet once more. Five will get you ten if there's not a single thing that needs to be rearranged.

Now add your list to the work list of the conversion you've chosen for the garage proper and you are ready for the next step: figuring out what we'll need to materialize our ideas and how much we'll have to fork over to do so.

HOW TO MAKE A COST ESTIMATE AND SHOPPING LIST

Once your plans are more or less finalized (and we say more or less advisedly because to us finalized means when the thing is finished, complete, a 3-D reality) and you've done your homework of looking and pricing all kinds of materials, it's time to sit down and figure out exactly what you need and then try to square that need with your available funds.

If you plan to borrow the money you'll have to have a complete, down-to-the-last-cent, estimate of what materials it will take to complete your project. In an estimate which you are going to submit to a lending institution it is wise to work in a pad factor or, more politely, a contingency fund.

This contingency column has saved us from dire consequences many a time when unexpected expenses or snags we hadn't anticipated made their appearance. So be sure to include such in your estimate. It's not only wise but perfectly legitimate and quite businesslike. If you're making the cost estimate for yourself, include this book too.

Back to the original cost estimate. The first thing you'll have to figure out is how much you need of each material. For this you can follow our material list up to a point. As we've said before, no two garages are exactly alike in size and layout and therefore material lists have to be adjusted. In addition you have the options of substituting, including or deleting any

Table 11-1. Materials Check List.

MATERIALS	PLANT CENTER	BOOK SHELVES	STORAGE WALL	NEW WALL INTERIOR	NEW WALL EXTERIOR	PAINTING	FLOOR	FINISHING
PLYWOOD 1/4"								
PLYWOOD 1/2"								
PLYWOOD 3/4"								
HARD BOARD								
DRY WALL								
LUMBER 1 X 2s								
2 X 2s								
2 X 4s								
1 X 4s								
1 X 10s								
2 X 12s								
MOLDING								
BASEBOARD								
NAILS 2d								
4d								
6d								
8d								
10d								
16d								
LAG SCREWS								
CARRIAGE BOLTS								
SCREWS WOOD								
METAL								
PAINT INTERIOR								
EXTERIOR								
PARTICLE BOARD								
TILES CARPET								
CERAMIC								
MASTIC								
SEALER								
WINDOWS								
DOORS								
BRICK								
MORTAR MIX								
SPECIALTY H-WARE								
MISC H-WARE								
OTHER								

feature or changing the dimensions of same, which may make a difference. Furthermore—so that you can do this substituting, deleting and adding, we have worked up separate material lists for each project. Now as you very well know, though two can't live as cheaply as one, you can save quite a bit in tandem. That goes for materials, too. In any project there will be some left-overs. We've tried to keep them to a minimum but left-overs are inevitable. You'll have those extra nails, glue, screws and so forth left from each project. You'll also have a bit of scrap lumber: ends of 2 × 4's which you can use quite well for spacers or as corner posts for small cabinets, pieces of plywood that might do for shelves, and ends of paneling that might fit in somewhere else.

For instance: If you are covering a 21-foot long wall with paneling, and lots of garages are precisely that length, you'll have a 3 × 8-foot piece of paneling left over whatever way you try to finagle. But, using that same finagling factor, that same 3 × 8 piece might be just the thing for that three foot space you'll have on another wall after you've incorporated the home office from another conversion. Ergo—you save the price of a panel.

On the other side of the coin is the sad fact that some things have to be bought in bulk, regardless of whether you need that many or not. If you want floor tiles or carpet tiles they usually have to be bought by the carton, (i.e.) 45 tiles at a clip, sometimes less for carpet tiles. Now—if you have a single garage and it happens to be 12×20 feet in size, you'll need 240 tiles right? (the average tile is 1 square foot). So you'll buy 240 tiles or maybe 245 to have the margin of safety? No—sorry about that. If you try to divide 240 by 45 you run into a problem. You'll be 25 tiles short if you buy five boxes and 30 tiles long if you buy six boxes. Obviously, you have no choice but to go with the six boxes. In your cost estimate you'll have to enter cost of six boxes of tiles, not five, which can make a difference of $50.00 or more. (We hope you'll be ingenious to find a good use for those extra 30 tiles, maybe on a counter or even in another room).

ADAPTING CONVERSIONS

Here is a rule of thumb that'll make all this cost estimating as easy as possible.

● If you use a complete conversion and your space is the same or smaller than the one we use, simply add up all the materials of all the projects, add a column of cost per, and total at the end (Table 11-1). This will give you a total cost which is a bit padded—you'll have some of your contingency fund already built in—because, as we pointed out previously, there will be left-overs from each project. Even though, be sure to add a bit on the top for your contingency fund.

● If you're planning to use a conversion but your garage is bigger, you'll have to sit down with your measurements and do some arithmetic. Better use your trusty calculator to make sure it's correct. Usually the number of 2 × 4's will remain the same unless you have a drastic size change. Your board-feet of shelves will differ, however, and so will the area for panels of plywood or other wall coverings. Your closets and cabinets will often vary, and so may the size of doors. So you'll have to add an extra sheet of plywood or two, some extra paneling, plus the extra length in planks for shelves which can make quite a cost difference.

If you like, you can use one of our single car garage conversions and turn it into a double one. In that case you'll have to do some extra figuring to account for the double width of your space.

It is more difficult if you go the other way, that is from double to single. You may use the same kind of windows and doors, sky lights are all right, too, but you have to be careful to keep it all in proportion. A 10-foot window might look good in a double garage conversion and not so great in the slimmer one-car garage version. Ditto for doors.

You have to be most careful about adapting the projects of a double conversion to your single garage. You can probably get them all in—on paper. Maybe in reality, too. But you'll still have to maneuver around them, and who wants to live in a sort of shrunken-aisled supermarket? The best rule is to leave a project out entirely. Or, if you can't bear to do that, scale the projects down—instead of a four closet storage will make do with a two closet one, or use a 5-foot craft center instead of a 7-foot job.

● If you are planning to substitute a project from one conversion for another, simply omit the one you delete from your list of materials needed and instead enter the material list for the project you plan to include.

● If you plan to include an extra project in a complete conversion, simply add the materials for that project to the total for the conversion.

● If you've gone the road less traveled, and been eclectic, simply add up all your projects' material lists plus the material list for the conversion of the garage proper you've chosen. Your work sheet will be a big help in this.

What follows frequently at this point are cries of anguish and much gnashing of teeth. The final sum is *always* higher than one expects. Unclench your jaws, take some deep breaths and go back to chapter 7 which tells you how to get materials at a price you can afford. Re-read carefully. Consider your options. Remember—you always have options, more than you think. In this case, could you substitute a less costly material such as plastic wood grain paneling for real wood paneling, or asbestos/vinyl tiles for pure vinyl? Can you follow some of the avenues suggested for using recycled materials? Can you scrounge some?

If you really put your mind to it, you can probably cut quite a bit off that first estimate. But remember, too, and this is quite important—what might at first glance seem a large sum isn't really. Think of what you'll get for that sum—a room of a size that in new homes would be touted as a "Great Room" which the developers say is big enough in which to relax, eat, entertain and play. A single living area for a lot of people. For you this will be all lovely extra space. You're adding a goodly number of livable square footage to your home, somewhere between 230 and 550 depending on your garage size. So, to make you feel better and give you a different perspective on the cost factor, divide your total cost by the new square footage you gain. Now compare this figure with its equivalent in new construction costs. We're sure you'll be quite elated.

Lastly, don't forget that in adding a custom-designed room to your house for you and your family to enjoy, you've also made a substantial contribution to your major investment/your home. In these times only real estate keeps up with inflationary trends and your investment, the adding of a family room, will appreciate along with the rest of the house, at the same rate. Which, as you well know, is quite considerable.

Chapter 12
Garage Conversion

This garage was a great one and if you have one similar to it you're lucky. As you can see from the plans (Fig. 12-1A-B) it was attached on one short side and one long side to the main part of the house. It shared the house's facade and had two large windows which matched the living room windows. The ceiling and walls of the garage were finished, but not painted. Along the short wall to the south were two enclosures: a large storage closet which had been used for garden furniture, tools, and whatever else accumulated plus a small laundry just big enough to include a washer, dryer, hot water heater and mini-sink. Both enclosures had louvered fold doors.

The garage had one door which connected with the hall in the house and gave access to the bathroom and kitchen, as well as one of the children's bedrooms without any traipsing through the rest of the place. The only negative feature of the garage was a 3-foot wide strip of raised floor along the south wall which projected out from the enclosed areas and then dropped down to the main garage floor level. The drop in our garage was somewhat higher than usual, about 5 inches. (In the conversion we used the more usual measurement of 3-4 inches).

We decided to make lemonade out of that lemon by widening the elevated aisle to five feet and adding a divider-railing which would do double duty as an indoor plant center, complete with over-head lighting. The center is located conveniently close to the sink in the laundry area for water and to the big storage closet, now slated to hold all the necessary and bulky supplies for indoor horticulture. We also figured that the dampness from the laundry was good for the plants, and that the plants in turn, in sort of a symbiosis, helped dry out the air. As a bonus, the plant center made an

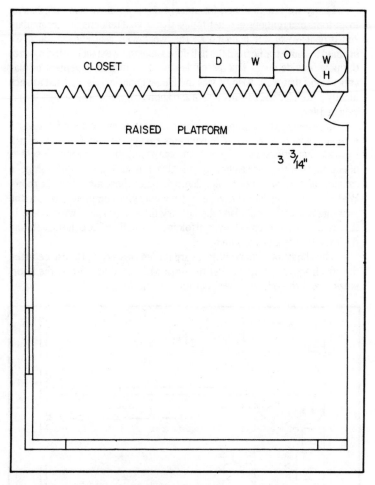

Fig. 12-1A. Floor plan showing before view of Conversion I.

attractive division between the more utilitarian area and the recreational one and kept the traffic routed along one side of the room.

The next decision concerned what to do with the garage door wall. Since we were going to continue to use the driveway for our cars and had plans to eventually build a carport further up the drive (Fig. 12-1B) we wanted an outside door because there was no other entrance on that side of the house. We also felt that an additional source of natural light would be welcome. So we planned a window to match the others and a solid door. Later we added a glass storm door that we used in all but the extremes of hot and cold weather and which gave us additional light. Though the main house was built out of brick there was siding along the gables and we decided to match the siding in enclosing the garage door opening.

Lastly we felt the need for storage space to stow away the books, toys, tools and millions of other things that have a tendency to accumulate and propagate in our household. The west wall was chosen since we planned to route traffic from the hall door along the west side of the room to the new outside door. This precluded any furniture arrangement or play areas along that wall. Also, it was the longest continuous wall and as such ideally suited for the row of closets and shelves our storage-hungry hearts yearned for.

In planning the storage, we chose closets over cabinets for several reasons: closets accomodate bulky items easily; they offer more versatility in storing different sized items; one can change the interior of closets as needs change; they are easier to build than the same amount of storage in cabinets and we could use folding doors to match those already in the room. We do love folding doors because they not only give complete access to the contents of a closet but also take up very little floor space when open. In this case, where we used louvered folding doors, they keep the closets and their content fresh-smelling and dry.

The choice of indoor/outdoor carpet tiles was a compromise between the two fractions of the family: the ones who voted for carpet, the floor-sitters; and the one who held out for hard flooring for easy cleaning.

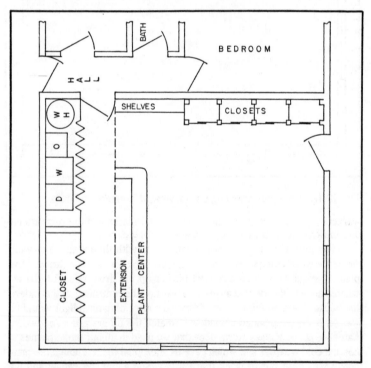

Fig. 12-1B. Floor plan showing after view of Conversion I.

With all these major decisions duly made and noted down on a pad to forstall future arguments of the "...but you said we'd have a..." or "I never in a million years agreed to have a.." kind, it's time to draw a plan incorporating the proposed changes solutions and decisions. This is the final plan. No more changes. If you can carve it in stone, do so. If not, act as if it were. As the good book says, there is a time for everything. A time for change and a time to stand firm. That time, friend, has arrived. Be firm. Or your family room will remain in limbo forever.

Your next step is the work list which we mentioned in the introduction to this section. In other words a list of what comes first, second and so on. In this conversion the approach was relatively straightforward and simple. (That is a euphimism meaning that there was little argument between the partner who goes from step A-to-step Z (Mike) and the one who constantly looks for and often finds short cuts, albeit frequently complicated and requiring odd protocol).

Our list of steps, or work list looked like this:
Project 1: Remove old garage door.
Project 2: Build new wall, insulate, hang door, window.
Project 3: Build storage wall.
Project 4: Build platform and plant center.
Project 5: Build shelves.
Project 6: Painting and varnishing.
Project 7: Finishing wiring.
Project 8: Floor covering and finishing.
Project 9: Finishing.

Note: Project 7, painting, is not strictly speaking a project, not in the sense that it is a self-contained unit. It is, however, a self-contained task and needs to be incorporated into the projects at the right time to avoid time and trouble.

If you follow our conversion exactly, you can simply go by this and the more detailed breakdowns that follow. Actually you'll be doing it strictly by the numbers. Except for one thing. Most garages are about the same size, yes, but notice the operant word in the sentence—*about*. They can vary 2 or 3 feet in either direction, or in both on a double garage and 2 in width and 3 or 4 in length on a single. So be sure you measure your own space and compare it with our plans. The adjustments are simple at this stage, not so simple later.

If you plan to include some feature from another conversion, now is the time to do so on your project list/work sheet. Do so at the logical point. For example, it would be tempting to put down the carpeting on the platform after we'd finished the plant center, but it would have been a nuisance to be careful of the new carpeting when painting the railing and the rest of the room.

Simply take the project breakdown of the feature you want to incorporate and add it to the others needed for the conversion. Sometimes a little reshuffling of projects will occur later when you notice that it might be easier to change the sequence of work. That's up to you. The step by step progression in which the projects are presented is tried and true. Follow it and you'll avoid the pitfalls we fell into many times before we developed the format.

Now study Project 1. Consult the tool list, get everything together and you are ready to start.

PROJECT 1: REMOVAL OF SPRING POWERED GARAGE DOORS

The first step in the transformation of your garage into that extraordinary familyroom is the removal of the garage door or doors. If you have the old-fashioned outward opening garage doors this is a simple matter. Alas, most of us are not so blessed. It must be another instance of Murphy's law or something like it. If you have one of those modern, spring-powered, sectional garage doors you have our heartfelt sympathy. Removing one can be a problem. We won't think any less of you if you opt to have it done by a professional. In fact, if you can find one that won't bankrupt you on the spot, send us his address.

If, however, you're stuck with doing the job yourself, as most of us are, be sure to line up a helper to two. Even if you have to hire someone. This is not a one-man job unless you happen to be four-handed, which we consider unlikely.

Releasing The Torsion Spring

Materials: None.
Tools: 2 strong metal winding rods, at least 1½ feet long made of cold rolled steel; wrenches, pliers, screwdriver.
Also needed: one or more assistants
Instructions:

1. Lower the door so you can get at the spring.

2. Insert a rod into one of the holes in the winding cone. It should fit snugly. (Fig. 12-2).

3. While you hang onto the rod with a firm, and we mean *firm*, grip to restrain the cone (the spring is at utmost tension with the door down so beware and exert all possible caution) have your helper loosen the cone's set screw with a pair of pliers.

4. This is the exciting part. You are ready to unwind that blasted spring. Have your helper insert the other rod in a cone hole and slowly unwind spring by alternating rods in the holes as the cone turns. Be sure you and your helper hold the rods near the ends for the best possible leverage on the spring. You'll need all the help you can get. Work slowly.

5. Success. When the spring is unwound the wire cable which connects it to the door will be slack. You can now unfasten the cable (Fig. 12-3).

6. If yours is a sectional door, start dismantling it from the top by removing first the hinges and fixtures from the top section, then the section itself. Keep this up till there's no more door left. (Fig. 12-4).

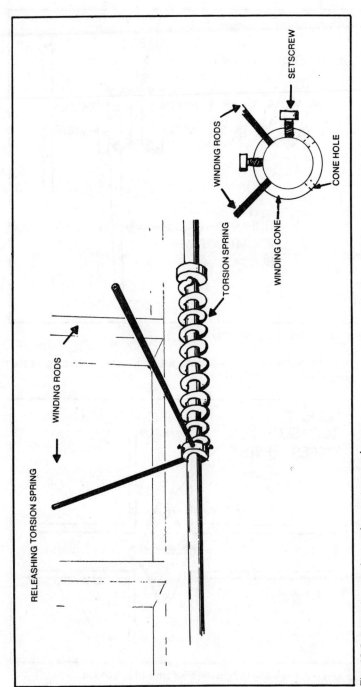

SETSCREW

WINDING RODS

CONE HOLE

WINDING CONE

RELEASHING TORSION SPRING

WINDING RODS

TORSION SPRING

Fig. 12-2. Releasing torsion spring on garage door.

115

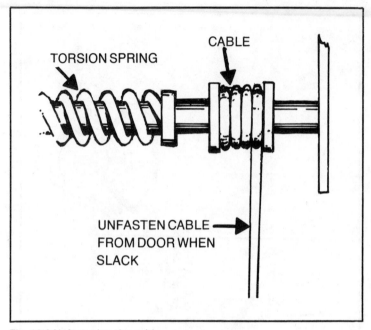

Fig. 12-3 Unfastening the cable.

7. To remove the torsion shaft, unbolt it from the framing of the garage door.

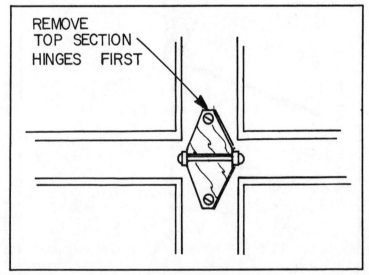

Fig. 12-4 · Dismantling the garage door section by section.

8. To remove the track, start at the back of the garage and work forward. Begin by unbolting the horizontal tracks. (Fig. 12-5).

9. Unscrew the vertical tracks from the door jamb.

10. Optional—find a cool place and an iced drink and collapse.

Extension Spring Garage Doors

Materials: None.

Tools: Wrenches, pliers, screwdrivers, couple of 2×4's.

Instructions:

1. Open garage door or doors to decrease spring tension.

2. Brace door open with a couple of 2×4's or such.

3. Carefully remove the "S" hook which anchors one end of one of one of the wire cables (Fig. 12-6).

4. Let the cable pass through the pulley at the end of the spring, then detach the other end of the cable from the door.

5. Remove the other cable in the same way.

6. Take out bracing and lower door.

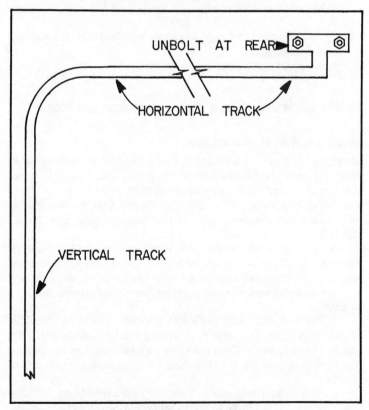

Fig. 12-5. Removing the door tracks from the garage.

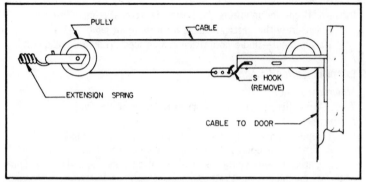

Fig. 12-6. Dismantling a door with extension spring.

7. If the door is sectional start dismantling it from the top, beginning by removing hinges and fixtures from top section, and then taking out the top panel. Proceed this way until there's no more door left.

8. Remove hardware of extension spring from framing with screwdriver.

9. Take out track in the same way as we described in steps 8 and 9 for the torsion spring door.

10. Optional, same as in torsion spring door.

PROJECT 2: BUILDING THE NEW WALL, PLUS WINDOW AND DOOR

Roughing In Wall, Window and Door

Materials: two 2×4's, 16 feet long; 13 2×4's, 8 feet long; ½-inch lag bolts; nails: eight-penny, ten-penny and sixteen-penny, (8d, 10d, 16d), wood preservative, (small can); lockwashers; mending plates.

Tools: Wrecking bar, claw hammer, electric drill with masonry bit and wood bits, crescent wrench, saber saw, carpenter's apron, paint brush, slipstick.

Note: While a carpenter's apron is not exactly a tool, at least by dictionary definition, it is one of the biggest savers of time and patience that we know. If you can't buy one or find one follow directions for making one (or have your friend make you one). See instructions at end of chapter.

Instructions:

1. Treat one of the long 2×4's with wood preservative. It should be slightly longer than the garage door opening usually about 16 feet. This will be your sole plate. If you have to go with shorter lumber, treat as above and make your sole plate in sections. Be sure that sections fit tightly together.

2. Remove trim and jambs with wrecking bar and hammer. Carefully insert the tapered end of the wrecking bar behind the piece of lumber you want to pry off. Don't try to pry off too much at one time. Loosen a bit at the

bottom or at one end, then go on up or over and loosen that side. If you pull the lumber away a little at a time over its entire length, it will come off all in one piece and you can re-cycle it later on.

3. You'll be uncovering the headers and side studs. There'll probably be two header beams across the top to support the wall above and transfer its weight to the side studs. This is eventually where you'll attach your new wall frame. But not for a while.

4. Place your slip-stick on the slab at the opening of the garage door and slip it out until it fits snugly against the existing sole plates on each side of the door or doors. Tighten the C-clamp on the slip-stick and use it to cut the preservative treated 2×4 exactly to size.

5. Bolt the sole plate in place, we beg. We've never had any luck in using the eight-penny masonry nails the do-it-yourself articles and books blithly advise. Ours either won't go in or, if they do, they come loose again in no time. So we bolt and it stays put. First drill holes for the ½-inch lag bolts every 30 inches along the length of your sole plate, using the wood bit on your electric drill. Next lay the sole plate in place and mark the positions of the holes to be drilled into the slab for the insertion of the lead shields your lag bolts will fasten into (Fig. 12-7).

6. Drill holes in the slab using your masonry bit, ⅛-inch larger in diameter than the holes in the sole plate and make them one inch deep. Insert the lead and put the sole plate back in place.

7. Insert the lag bolts and tighten them down firmly with a wrench. If you put a lock washer under the bolts it'll keep the bolt tight forever.

8. Use your slip-stick to measure the exact length of the top plate already in place and cut a 2×4 to this length. If you need to use two, tie them together with mending plates, one on each side (Fig. 12-8).

9. Measure and mark stud positions along the top plate. The very first stud will go at the very end of the top plate. Measure 16 inches from the center of this stud and mark the center of the next stud.

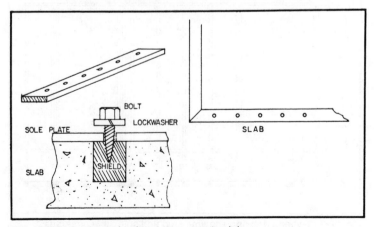

Fig. 12-7. Fastening sole plate to a concrete slab.

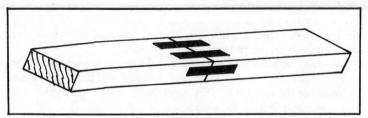

Fig. 12-8.Attaching two 2×4s to each other with mending plates.

10. Since the window will come all the way to the top of the wall, the next stud connected to the top plate will be 48 inches away from the second stud you just measured, measuring from center of stud to center. Next you will have four full length studs which again will be 16 inches on centers, one after the other until we come to the door opening.

11. Since we are using a pre-hung door in this conversion, we will let the door determine the position of the remaining stud. Then there will be one more end stud, butting up against the old door frame and that's the set.

12. To measure the exact length of each of these nine studs, mark their position on the sole plate and use your slip-stick to determine the exact distance for each individual stud. You can't use the short cut that one of us thought so neat, (i.e.) measure once and cut all, because the slightest warping or bowing in one of the studs will make a difference in length (Fig. 12-9).

13. When you cut your marked 2×4's cut them *1 ½ inches shorter* than your measurement to allow for the thickness of your new top plate.

14. Set the top plate on its side on the floor and nail eight of the nine studs into place as marked. Drive two 16d nails (16 penny) through the top plate into the top of each stud to tie it in securely (Fig. 12-10).

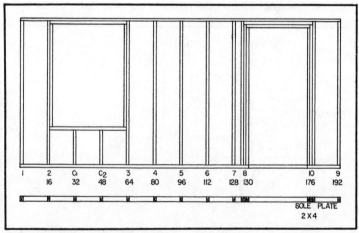

Fig. 12-9.Elevation drawing showing stud and sole plate markings.

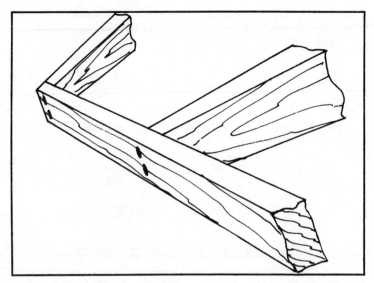

Fig. 12-10. Nailing studs to top plate.

15. When you frame in the door area, first measure the outside width of your pre-hung door, from outside of the jamb to outside of jamb at the top of the door.

16. To this measurement add 3½ inches: the width of the 2×4 header. Cut the header and lay it under the top plate with one end butted up against #7 stud, the other end against stud #8. Mark it and nail it in place, then secure it by driving several 16d nails into it through the outer studs and a few 8d nails into it through the outer studs and a few 8d nails into the top plate from the underneath side of the header (Fig. 12-11).

17. Two additional studs, called trimmers or jack studs, will be needed to finish the door frame. These will run inside the outer studs between the header and the sole plate.

18. Again use your slip-stick to measure carefully for a tight fit. Cut and secure the jack studs to the outer studs with 10 8d nails driven in pairs about every 16 inches along the length of the studs (Fig. 12-11).

19. Since the ends of the studs are unattached (for the moment) you'll need to brace your work for nailing by inserting 14½-inch lengths of 2×4's between the members to be nailed (Fig. 12-11).

20. If you build your wall in a corner so that the bottom and one side is braced by sole plates already in place, you won't have any problem nailing up the wall frame.

21. Rough in your window the same way as you did your door, that is, with a header on top, and trimmer studs on each side.

22. Your window will have a sill at the bottom and that will be supported by "crippled" or short studs, 16 inches on center between the sill and the sole plate (Fig. 12-12).

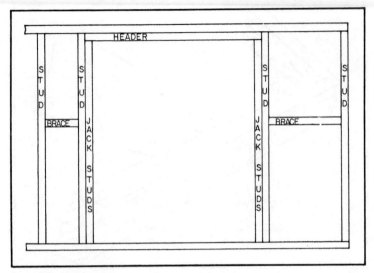

Fig. 12-11. Framing in for a door.

23. IMPORTANT. Buy your door and window (s) *before* you rough in the wall so you have exact measurements to work with. And don't forget to allow for the thickness of wall and or window inset.

24. Cut your rough window opening about ½-inch larger than the size of your window.

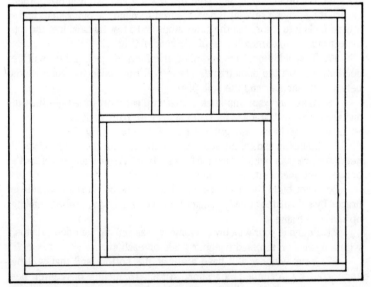

Fig.12-12. Roughing in the framing for a window.

25. MAKE SURE THAT THE OPENING IS SQUARE, PLUMB AND LEVEL!

26. Measure and cut your header, sill and trimmers very carefully and then lay them in place before doing any nailing. Use your carpenter's square to square the corners and tie the header to the top plate with a mending plate.

27. Square the top two corners again and tie the trimmers to the outer studs with mending plates. Position the mending plates in the center of the header and trimmers so that thin wood, or metal, known as shims in the trade, can be inserted a t the ends to "fine tune" the square if necessary.

28. Now you can nail the sill in place after you're sure the bottom window opening is square.

29. Back to square one and check all the four angles for square. Make final adjustments with shims if needed. Then you can nail all members firmly in place.

30. Cut and nail the crippled studs on to the sill.

31. On your sole plate draw in the rectangles at the exact place your studs will fasten, taking your measurements from the top plate and the window sill.

32. Now is the time for all good friends to come to the aid of the party, namely you. Get one or two helpers and raise the wall frame into place.

33. Make sure that your new and old sole and top plates line up exactly with one another, then drive 16d, nails through your new side studs and new top plate into the old studs and plate in pairs at approximately 16 inch intervals.

34. Now tap your studs into place on the position markings on the sole plate and toe-nail all except the door frame studs into place.

35. If you're not so great at toe-nailing, which is strictly an esoteric skill, you can use angle braces, one on each side of the stud, to secure the studs to the sole plate (Fig. 12-13).

36. Angle braces are a good idea in any case when you secure the door frame studs, since the door frame must be again as square, plumb and level as the window frame, and, unfortunately, it's easy for an inexperienced toe-nailer to knock the framing out of true with some clumsy hammering and you don't need that.

37. To square and level the door opening, first square the top two corners with your carpenter's square as you did for the window, and hold the studs in place temporarily by tacking on a diagonal brace between the outer studs (Fig. 12-14).

38. Square the bottom two corners one at a time and hold in place with angle irons on the outside of the studs.

39. The studs may then be toe-nailed down or you could use angle irons put in place beside the first one.

40. The jack stud is an exception, since the sole plate will have to be cut out for door clearance, in line with the inside of the jack studs. This, however, is done after all other studs are tied into the sole plate and the

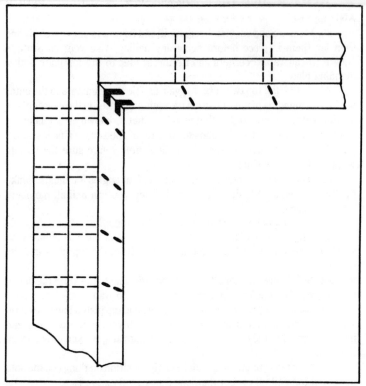

Fig.12-13. Nailing in studs when enclosing garage door opening.

window and door openings are square. The final product should resemble Fig. 12-15.

Finishing Off Exterior Wall

When it came to finishing off the exterior wall we naturally wanted to match it to the rest of the house, which happened to be brick veneer to the second floor and horizontal wood siding up to the roof lines. We chose to go with the siding instead of the brick because a) brick laying is tedious and takes time, and b) it takes years for the new brick to match the old brick exactly even if you start out with exactly the same kind of brick.

Since siding varies in width and since your door and window size will differ from the ones we used by a few inches, we will break our rule and not give you exact amounts of materials to purchase. Instead here is the rule to figure out how much sheathing and siding you'll need for the new all:

1. Amount of sheathing = square footage of total new wall minus door-square-footage plus window-square-footage or:
S= (length × height of wall − height × width of window− height × width of door).

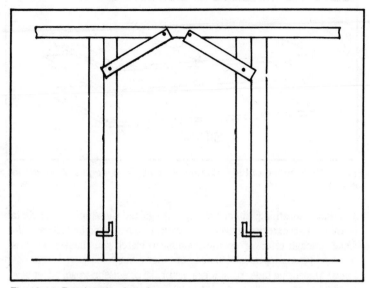

Fig. 12-14. Bracing the door frame.

2, You'll need the same square footage for your siding but there is the matter of overlap and the fact that siding is sold by the linear foot. So you'll have to measure the entire width of the new all first. That will give you the linear length of your siding boards—the longest ones. Then measure the height and divide that number by the widths of a siding board plus the amount of overlap. That'll give you the number of boards you need. Next you can figure out the exact length of each board by deducting the width of the window and door where needed. Confusing? Look at Fig. 12-16 and the formula.

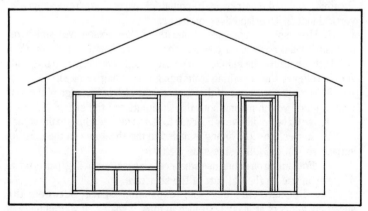

Fig. 12-15. Front elevation showing stud placement for garage door enclosures.

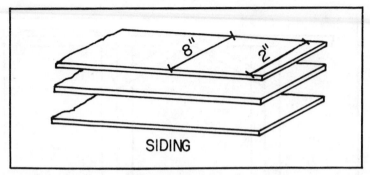

Fig.12-16. Figuring out the number of boards and lengths of boards for siding.

Materials: Sheathing: either asphalt impregnated sheathing for horizontal boards or C-D exterior plywood for vertical siding; 15-pound felt paper for same, enough to cover opening; siding to match your house; 6d nails; plywood panels (optional—instead of other siding).

Tools: Measuring tape, pencil, calculator, large scissors, pad, saber saw, wrecking bar, claw hammer, hammer.

Instructions:

1. Rip off some of the existing siding using a wrecking bar and claw hammer.

2. Take to building supply store to get perfect match.

3. Measure the thickness of the sheathing underneath the siding so you can match that, too.

4. Armed with pencil, pad, measuring tape and calculator figure out how much siding you'll need.

5. Ditto for sheathing.

6. Use C-D exterior plywood of the same thickness as the existing sheathing and nail on strips of 15-pound felt paper if you're dealing with vertical siding. Overlap edges on paper.

7. Use asphalt impregnated sheathing (less expensive) which requires no paper covering if you are working with horizontal siding. (You can do this because the siding in this case is nailed directly into the studs and so relieves the sheathing from being the nailing surface).

8. Mark the positions of the studs on the slab at the edge of the new wall to guide you in nailing both the sheathing and the siding.

9. Use 6d box nails every 6 inches to fasten the sheathing to the studs.

10. Inspect how the siding is nailed to the sheathing on the existing surface so you can follow the same pattern.

11. For nailing on siding use whatever size nail and nailing pattern you discover in use on the old part of the structure.

12. Be sure to leave an expansion space between the sheathing joints of at least 1/16-inch in most climates. If your climate is particularly humid leave ⅛-inch.

13. New siding is always nailed on from the bottom up. Begin with installing a starter strip, then add the bottom course. Sometimes you'll need 8d nails instead of 6d, it depends on the thickness of the siding.

14. If you're unable to match the siding on your house, contrast rather than match and use exterior plywood panels which can be painted the same color as the trim of the house itself.

15. Trim out your panels and decorate with molding of your choice if desired.

16. You can be sneaky and paint the plywood panels any color you fancy, repainting the trim on the house and matching the main house color with your molding.

17. If you use plywood panels, cut them and nail them so that the grain of each sections runs in the same direction as the rest.

18. Make sure the edges of the panels fall along the centers of the studs.

19. Set the edges 1/16 inch apart to allow for expansion and caulk the edges.

20. Use 8d casing nails and drive them every 16 inches along the edges of each panel.

21. Use 12 inch intervals on intermediate studs.

22. Lengths of 1×2 can be used as trim instead of molding. It is less expensive and looks great. Attach with 6d casing nails.

23. Caulk the bottom of the new wall for waterproofing.

24. Cut out the sole plate for the door opening.

25. Remove the temporary brace (diagonal) you tacked onto the outside studs of your door opening.

26. Depending on the weather, it might be a good idea to tack some plastic over the window and door opening while you do your bit with the inside wall—the wiring and covering with wallboard. This must be done before the pre-hung door and window units are installed.

Roughing In The Wiring

Materials: Flange mounted type of switch box; electric outlet receptacle box; 30-feet of Romex cable; outside light-fixture.
Tools: Drill, large wood bit, screwdriver, hammer.
Instructions:

1. Mount your switch box for your new outside light on the outside stud that frames the door (#11 stud) about 4 feet 6 inches from the floor (Fig. 12-17). This will put it behind and a little below the outside light fixture it will control.

2. Nail the flange mounted switch box directly to the stud.

3. Bore a ¾-inch hole through the outside wall at the place where the outside light fixture will go.

4. Run your Romex cable out of this hole, leaving 6-8 inches projecting outside to tie into the fixture.

5. Run the cable through the switch box, cut and leave two ends (at least 8 inches) of cable protruding from switch box (Fig. 12-18).

6. Mark where you want your electric outlets on your plan.

7. Mark position of receptacles on nearest studs. Nail in.

8. Drill ¾-inch holes through studs to run cable through.

9. At each receptacle cut cable and leave two ends of 8 inches each.

10. Don't install receptacles back to back because they will conduct noise as well as electricity. Install them at least one stud apart.

11. At the last receptacle you want to install, take the cable up through another ¾-inch hole drilled through the top plates into the space above the ceiling where you can tie into the house circuit later.

12. Measure off a couple of feet more than you you'll need to bring the cable from the top of your new wall to the overhead fixture.

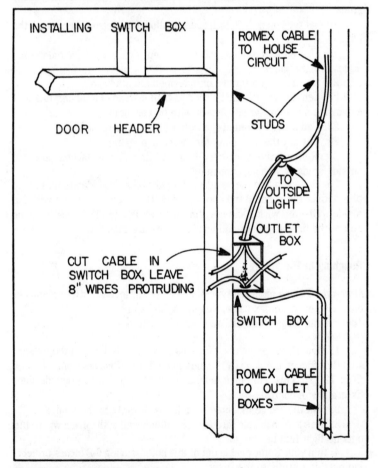

INSTALLING SWITCH BOX

ROMEX CABLE TO HOUSE CIRCUIT

DOOR HEADER

STUDS

TO OUTSIDE LIGHT

OUTLET BOX

CUT CABLE IN SWITCH BOX, LEAVE 8" WIRES PROTRUDING

SWITCH BOX

ROMEX CABLE TO OUTLET BOXES

Fig.12-17. Installing the switch box.

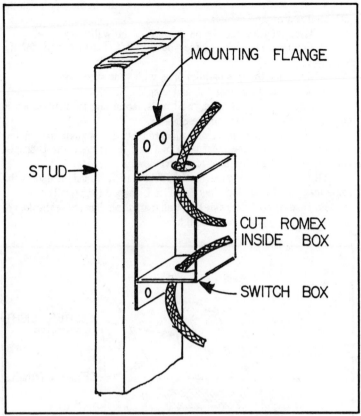

Fig. 12-18. Running the Romex cable through the switch box.

13. Cut a small hole into the ceiling panel.

14. Thread the Romex cable through the hole and push it in toward the overhead fixture above the ceiling panel. Since the cable is pretty stiff it's not hard to do (Fig. 12-19).

Finishing Inside Of New Wall

Materials: 4 sheets of 4×8 foot wallboard; 14 16×48-foot insulation bats; press-on drywall tape; joint compound.

Tools: Measuring tape, pencil, saber saw, putty knife, sand paper, staple gun, scissors, mask.

Instructions:

1. Staple insulation bats between studs, cut to fit where needed (Fig. 12-20).

2. For fitting wallboard around window, measure down from the ceiling to the bottom of the header.

3. Next measure on down to the top of the framing sill.

129

4. Measure from the corner of the room to the farthest point on the jack stud nearest the corner.

5. Mark theses distances on the face of the wall board.

6. Connect the lines to give you the "U" shaped cut-out for the window.

7. Cut along the two parallel lines with your saber saw.

8. Score the remaining line and snap the score.

9. Nail in place, using drywall nails, according to instructions in chapter 9 under "Bringing in the Sheaths."

10. For the second piece of wallboard that will complete the window enclosure, use the same measuring methods to arrive at the U-shaped cut-out around the other side of the window.

11. Cut the other two pieces of wallboard to fit around the door in the same manner. The cut-outs here will be L-shaped (Fig. 12-21).

12. On the floor, alongside the stud, mark the height above the floor of any outlets or switch boxes you'll have.

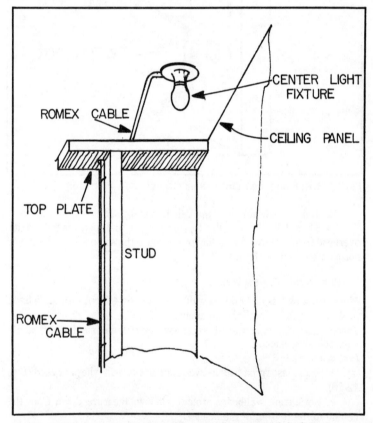

Fig.12-19. Bringing the Romex cable up to the central light fixture.

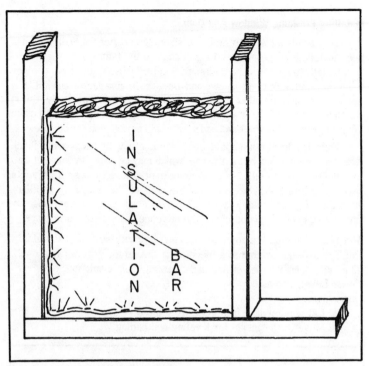

Fig. 12-20. Installing insulation bats.

13. After the wallboard is in place, measure up the wall and mark the position of the box (es) with an X

14. Make a plunge cut with your saber saw at that point and use the outside of the box itself to guide your saw to cut around the opening for the box.

15. When you need to put up only a few drywall or wallboard panels as you do in this case, use press-on drywall tape (EZT Drywall Tape by Minter Homes Corp., Huntington W. VA if you can get it) as a time saver.

16. You can also use it if you have a lot of joints to cover. There's no law against it, but it runs into money. Since it saves time and is easier to apply than paper tape, the money savings might be spurious to particularly if you figure in the extra joint compound you need to use with paper tape.

17. Also this pressure-sensitive tape has a center spine that fits between the panels and makes alignment perfect. The inside corner tapes, too, go up with a lot less nailing than is required with conventional metal strips.

18. Put a layer of joint compound over each strip with a putty knife.

19. Sand smooth and feather long edges to blend in with panels.

20. Wear mask when sanding. *Asbestos is dangerous* if particles are inhaled or swallowed.

Installing Pre-hung Window And Door

Your pre-hung window and door should go in after the wallboard has been installed but before anything is done to the floor.

Installing windows and doors are "couple" jobs. You'll need a helper to lift the window or door in place and, once there, one person can hold the unit steady while the other levels and finally tries it in. Incidentally, this is the time when you'll be grateful for all the time and care you took to make your rough openings was level and square. It'll pay off, you can be sure.

Your window unit should come complete with hardware. Check whether your window has a drip cap, which may be only a groove cut into the underside of the sill. This is an important groove because it prevents rain water being drawn back into the wall of the house by capillary attraction. If your window doesn't have drip cap, you can improvise by fitting a strip of hardwood under the sill once the window is in place.

Materials: Pre-hung window and door complete with hardware; shingles or thin scrap wood for shims; a piece of hardwood for drip cap (optional); aluminum or galvanized casing nails; tacking nails insulation.
Tools: Level, hammer.
Instructions:
1. Lift window unit into place from the outside.
2. Move to the inside for leveling and nailing.

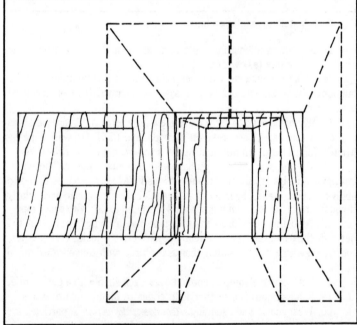

Fig. 12-21. Measuring and cutting drywall panels for door opening.

3. Helper stays outside to hold window in place.

4. If window checks out level at sill go directly to step 6 (you may collect your reward later).

5. If window isn't level use shims (wood or shingles wedged under the sill to bring the window to dead level). Shingles are best because they slope and so can be stacked in opposite directions to get various thicknesses (Fig. 12-22).

6. To tack in window, drive in a few holding nails but let them protrude at least ¼-inch each.

7. Open and close the window to make sure it's working properly.

8. Check sill with level once more.

9. If all is well, nail the window in permanently using your aluminum or galvanized casing nails. Space them about 16 inches apart.

10. Stuff insulation into any spaces left between the window unit and the rough opening. This will prevent heat loss and drafts.

Installing your pre-hung door is essentially the same as installing the window unit but we'll give you the the blow-by-blow for this installation, too.

Materials: Same as window.

Tools: Same as window, plumb bob.

Instructions:

1. Pull the two two halves of the jamb apart and push one side into each side of the door opening (Fig. 12-23).

2. Check the door for plumb on the hing side.

3. Be sure sill and door are flush.

4. Keep in mind that you'll have a wood or metal threshhold after you put in the flooring.

5. When the door is plumb, tack it in place.

6. Try the door, make sure it closes and opens well.

7. Nail the door down through the jamb and shims. *Never* through the doorstep.

8. Fill in any spaces between door unit and opening, with insulation.

Installing Lockset On Door

Materials: Lockset.

Tools: Chisel, screwdriver, electric drill, wood bits, pencil.

Note: Though lockset manufacturers always provide good instruction sheets for installing their locksets, we thought we might as well give you our breakdown for the job, too. Be sure to use the template included in your lockset directions to drill your door for the proper accomodation of the lockset if your door is not pre-drilled. It'll make your job a lot easier.

Instructions:

1. Insert the latch into the bored hole.

2. With a pencil mark the outline.

3. Remove latch and chisel out the area where the latch will be so that it will be flush with the door.

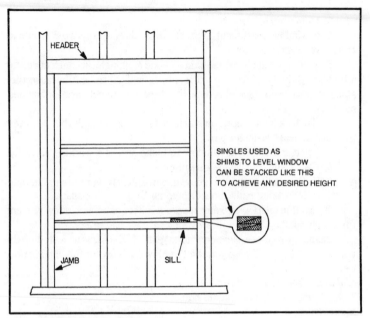

HEADER

SINGLES USED AS
SHIMS TO LEVEL WINDOW
CAN BE STACKED LIKE THIS
TO ACHIEVE ANY DESIRED HEIGHT

JAMB

SILL

Fig. 12-22. Leveling a window.

4. Put latch back in and tighten the screws down very firmly.

5. Use your template to find the location of the strike plate screws.

6. Mark on door jamb.

7. Drill the latch bolt hole.

8. Match the center line of the screw holes on the strike plate with the ones you have drawn on the door jamb and draw in the outline of the plate.

9. Chisel out the outlined area enough so that the strike plate will be flush with the door jamb.

10. Screw strike plate firmly in place.

11. Insert the knob attached to the spindle into the latch and push against the door.

12. Place the second knob onto the spindle of the first and again push against door.

13. Use the screws to tighten both knobs firmly.

14. For illustrations see instruction sheet.

PROJECT 3: THE STORAGE WALL SYSTEM
Enclosure and Shelves

Materials: 14 2×4's, 8 feet long; 3½ 4×8-foot plywood panels, ¼-inch thick; 10 1×4 facing boards, 8-feet long each; 1 1×4 facing board, 14-feet long; 18 particle-board shelves, 36×18 inches; 1 particle-board shelf, 12×36 inches; 1 wood dowel, 36 inches long, ½-inch diameter; 6 standards, 6-foot in length each; 4 36-inch double panel fold doors and required

134

hardware; 36 18-inch brackets; 2 12-inch utility brackets. Corner molding or quarter-round to trim out inside of closets([4×depth + 2× width + 4×height] × 4) (optional). Baseboard for inside (optional); molding for outside trim (optional); 40 corner plates, one box of 1-inch round-head screws; 12 toggle bolts; 4 lag screws.

Tools: Saber saw, hammer, drill, screwdriver, wrench, level, pencil.

Instructions;

1. Cut 10 of the 2×4's to ceiling height, roughly 7-feet each.

2. Fasten five 2×4's upright to the wall on 40-inch centers.

3. Since the first, third and fifth stud will probably be back-to-back with a stud in the wall, you can nail them in place after checking that this is so.

4. The second and fourth studs will not be back-to-back with a stud in the wall and must be secured to the wall with wall anchors or toggle bolts.

5. Should any other studs not line up with existing wall studs so that they can be nailed in place, secure them with toggle bolts, too. These members will carry very little load, so they will not put undue strain on the wallboard.

6. Cut the remaining 2×4's into 21-inch lengths.

7. Lay five of them on the floor at the base of the 2×4's you have fastened to the wall and secure with angle irons to the uprights.

8. Those secured to a stud nailed to a wall stud don't have to be tied into the floor with lag bolts, but it won't hurt.

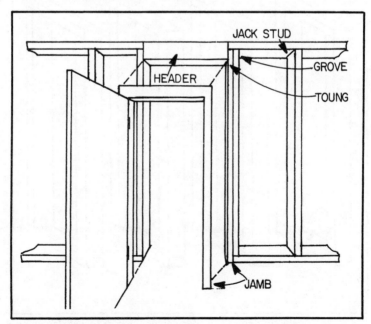

Fig.12-23.Installing a pre-hung door.

9. However, the short 2×4's tied into studs which have toggle bolts tying them into the wall, (i.e.) no studs behind them, must be secured to the floor with at least two lag bolts.

10. See all about lag bolts in Project 2, steps 5-7.

11. Tie in the remaining five short lengths of 2×4's to the top of the studs with angle irons.

12. Complete framing by fastening the five remaining long 2×4's to the front of the short 2×4's with nails and angles irons ending up with "U" shaped structures (Fig. 12-24).

13. Cut plywood panels to 2×7-feet or 2× ceiling height and nail onto each side of the 2×4 frames. You have now made a series of universal boxes, one of the strongest and simplest constructions you can make.

14. If your ceiling height equals the height of the door +3¾ inches you're in luck. We were. If not, consult note at end of this section.

15. Cut nine 1×4 facing boards to the length of floor to ceiling — 3¾ inches if you want your finished framing to look like Fig. 12-25A (unmitered).

16. If you want the corners mitered, proceed to steps 20 and 21.

Fig. 12-24. Framing in a storage wall-fastening uprights to wall; fastening sole plates to uprights; tying in top plates to uprights.

Fig.12-25. A Finishing the storage wall with 1×4 boards.

17. Cut the tenth facing board into two pieces 2-feet long each and attach to top of closet along short sides.

18. Attach your long (14 foot) facing board to the top of your closet enclosure, securing it to each 2 × 4.

19. Face each of the upright 2×4's with one of the shorter facing boards. Do the same along each side of side wall.

20. If you want to miter, use your two miter box for the six shorter facing boards and the long facing board, as well as the two short top/side facing boards.

21. If you really have a thing about mitering you can also miter four of your facing boards at the bottom and miter two more short pieces, 2-foot long each, to fit at the bottom of the side walls (Fig. 12-25B).

22. If you go the low or non-mitering route, cut the remaining piece of your facing board into two 17-inch lengths and nail them to the sides at the bottom.

23. If you want to use molding around the top of the closet outside and inside, top and bottom, that's fine. Simply buy the required amount, miter at corners with your miter box and tack in place.

24. Don't put in bottom molding until after the carpeting or flooring is installed. Personally, we can do without all that molding on the outside, we like the plain look. But that's a matter of choice.

Note: If your ceiling height is such that your door height plus your facing board (3½-inch) still needs 2 or 3 inches you'll have to drop a piece of paneling in the gap (Fig. 12-26). To do this:

A) Measure the distance from ceiling to top of door.

B) Cut enough paneling to make a strip 14-feet long and as wide as distance from ceiling to top of door minus three inches.

C) Attach strip to top of closet across front.

D) Attach facing board, overlapping paneling by ½-inch.

E) Miter or not as you choose.

Note: If you need more than 5-inches you'll have to go with a second top plate. Conversion IV, Project 5.

Now we are ready to install the fold-doors, the easiest of all doors to install provided you've been a good carpenter and made your openings nice and square. These fold-doors can be quite a hassle if your opening is not square.

Our design is such that you will not have to hang a double set of folding doors. And for that you may thank us. Even in a true plumb and square opening, double-folds require hours of installation time. Actually the first time we tried it in a not so square opening it took days—what with planing, rehinging, screwing and unscrewing, drilling and shimming (oh, that eternal shimming) before the damned things opened and closed properly.

The main problem, and one you don't think of at first, is the floor, which forms the fourth side of your door frame. Floors hardly ever make proper right angles with the walls and are never quite parallel to the ceiling. The trick then, we finally figured out, is to hang your fold-doors in single bi-fold sections so that the unevenness of the floor will make little if any difference.

Here are our tried and true, sweat-tested rules for the installation of hassle-free fold-door hanging.

Installation of Fold-Doors

Materials: Fold doors and hardware.
Tools: Plumb line, screwdriver, thin wrench (if not included in hardware kit with door), electric drill, wood bit.

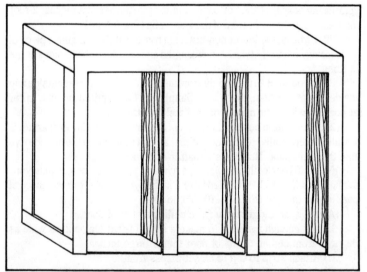

Fig. 12-25B. Finishing the storage wall with 1×4 boards mitered in corners.

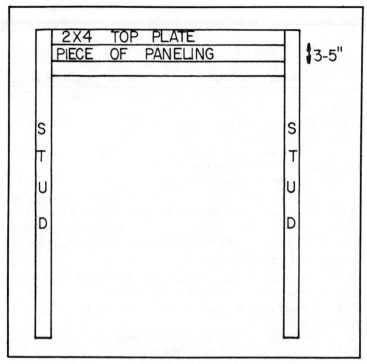

Fig. 12-26. Piecing in a strip of paneling.

Instructions:

1. Install the fold-door track on the underside edge of your 1×4 facing board at the top front of your storage unit.

2. Insert the top pivot bracket and slide it back against the edge of the facing board to your left.

3. Drop a plumb line from the center of the bracket to the floor.

4. Screw the bottom bracket to the bottom of the upright facing board and/or the 2 × 4 and anchor to the floor.

5. If your floor is concrete, which it will be in all likelihood, substitute a small lag screw for the ordinary screw that comes with the hardware and refresh your memory about lag screw installation if needed, Project 2-A, steps 5, 6, 7, this chapter.

6. Fold the door panels together and slip the door's bottom pivot into the bottom pivot socket.

7. Lean the top of the door to about the center of the opening and slide the top pivot bracket over the door so that you can slip the top pivot socket over the top pivot.

8. Now slip the spring mounted slide guide at the top of the door into the track as you push the door back to its final resting place alongside of your 1×4 facing board.

139

9. As part of your door hardware kit you will usually get a handy little thin wrench made to fit the bolts that lock the bottom and top pivot sockets in place.

10. Loosen these bolts and horizontally adjust the pivot sockets until the door folds and extends easily. Then tighten the bolts.

11. As a final hedge against uneven floors and slightly out of true framing, the door may be raised or lowered slightly by turning the vertical adjusting bolt on the door's bottom pivot.

12. Hang each of the four bi-fold doors the same way, reversing the hinged side every other door.

13. Bore holes for the knobs 36 inches from the bottom of doors and 8 inches in from the door's opening edge.

14. For illustrations see instruction sheet.

That's it as far as your storage wall enclosure and doors are concerned. You'll need to install your shelves and closet pole and here are directions. However, don't do this bit of work until after you've painted the inside of the closet. It's faster and easier that way—the painting that is.

Installation of Shelves and Pole

Materials: Shelves (see material list for Enclosure of Shelves;); standards, brackets, pole (also on above material list).
Tools: Screwdriver, measuring tape, drill, pencil, level.
Instructions:

1. Fasten the six standards to the back wall, two to each section. Make certain that each standard is anchored to a wall stud.

2. Install brackets.

3. Install pre-painted shelves making certain that shelves are level.

4. In the fourth cubicle install two utility brackets to hold the 12×36 inch shelf about 5½ feet from the floor and tie into studs.

5. Attach pre-painted shelf.

6. Attach two pieces of 1×4 along the side walls of the closet enclosure, nailing them into the studs front and back (Fig. 12-27) with the top edge about 3 inches below shelf.

7. If you're clear out of 1×4's you may use two scrap pieces of 2×4 though they are bit thicker. Cut to length, (i.e.) inside dimension of closet, side wall.

8. Attach hardware for closet pole about 10 inches to the front from back wall.

9. If you prefer, you can notch the top of the 1×4's at the 10-inch mark with a notch large and deep enough to accomodate the pole.

Finishing Storage Wall System

Instructions:

1. Countersink all nails on outside of structure.

2. Putty in with wood putty any cracks or uneveness.

3. Sand well, first with medium-coarse, then with medium-fine sand paper. Your storage wall is now ready for paint.

PROJECT 4: PLATFORM AND PLANT CENTER
Extension Platform, Railing, Planter Box

Materials: 4 14-foot 2×4's; 4 8-foot 1×2's; 1½ 4×8 foot ¾-inch thick plywood panels; 4 4×8 foot ⅜-inch thick plywood panels; Corner molding, 55 feet of your choice; baseboard, 35-feet (optional); and quarter-round; corrugated fasteners; polyethlene, 4mm; aluminum foil; corner braces, 2-inch size; 8 4-inch lag bolts; 4 d and 8 d finishing nails; screws; wood glue.

Tools: Saber saw, hammer, drill and masonry bit, carpenter's square, staple gun.

Instructions:

1. Lay one of the 14-foot 2×4's against the bumper (rise in the floor) starting at window wall. Lay 4-inch side down.

2. Attach 2×4 to bumper using lag bolts.

3. Cut two pieces of 2×4 to 29-inch length.

4. Attach one of these to each end of long 2×4 with corner braces on the inside edges and mending plates on top (Fig. 12-28).

5. Fasten second 14-foot 2×4 to front of structure by nailing in place.

6. Cut eight 1×2's, 36 inches long each, and nail across the top of frame work.

7. Cut two plywood panels from the ¾-inch thick plywood: one to be 3×8 feet, the other 3×6 feet.

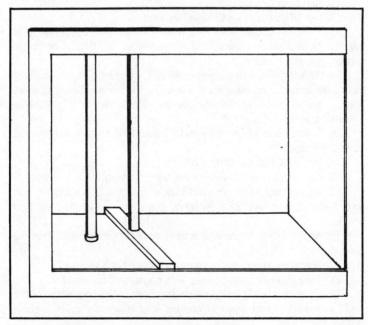

Fig. 12-27. Installing shelf and closet pole in closet.

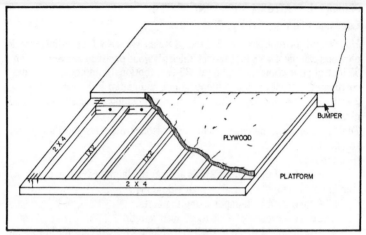

Fig.12-28. Building the platform extension for the plant center.

8. Nail plywood panels on top of 1×2's (Fig. 12-28).

9. Lay another 14-foot 2×4, 4-inch side down, on front edge of platform.

10. Cut a 32½-inch length of 2×4 and lay it along the other free edge of the platform.

11. Nail both 2×4's down.

12. Cut 15 pieces of 2×4, 30 inches long.

13. Fasten one to the side wall; make a corner post out of four as in Fig. 12-29. Fasten to corner; attach two pieces to the end or inside corner. Toe-nail in place.

14. Attach the remaining pieces in this way: seven across the long front edge about 20 inches apart and one piece in the middle of the short edge. Turn all 2×4's so that the narrow side faces out (Fig. 12-30). Toe-nail in place.

15. Lay out last 14-foot 2×4 and a 3-foot 2×4 section. Miter them along the four inch side.

16. Nail 2×4's on top of uprights.

17. Fasten mitered edges with corrugated fasteners.

18. Rip ⅜-thick, 4×8 plywood panels into two 3×8 sections; two 3×6 sections, and two 3×2 sections. From the scrap cut two 1×3 panels.

19. Apply plywood panels to both sides of 2×4 frame with finishing nails.

20. Miter one short side of 14-foot 1×12 and of 3-foot 1×2.

21. Tie mitered edges together with corrugated fasteners.

22. Glue and nail 14-foot 1×8's along each of the long edges of the 1×12 and short, 3-foot, pieces along the long edges of the 1×12 which is only 3 feet long.

23. Cut two pieces of 1×8 to 5¾-inch width.

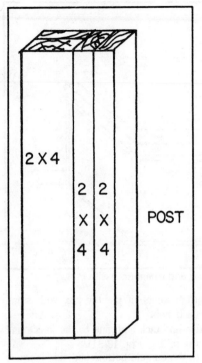

Fig.12-29. Building post out of 2×4's.

2 X 4

2 X 4   2 X 4   POST

24. Nail and glue across short open sides of planter box (Fig. 12-31).

25. Attach planter to center of 2×4 railing with screws.

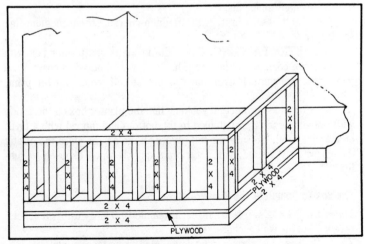

Fig.12-30. Constructing the railing.

143

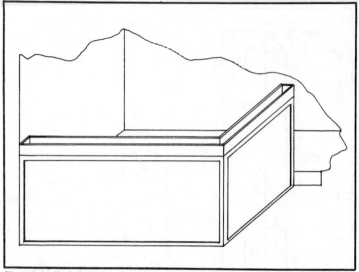

Fig. 12-31. Building the planter box and trimming it with molding.

26. Reinforce side and bottom joints of planter box with small corner braces every two feet on each side.

27. Cut corner molding strips and tack and glue to the inside and outside corners on both sides of the railing (Fig. 12-31).

28. Glue and tack molding to the outside bottom and side (corner) edges of the planter box.

29. Optional—nail baseboards along the bottom edge of planter on both sides.

30. Fill in seams with wood putty.

31. Countersink nails.

32. Sand well, first with medium-course, then medium-fine sandpaper.

33. AFTER PAINTING. Cover the inside of the planter box with two or three coats of marine varnish. Let dry well between coats. (You may apply the varnish over the raw but sealed wood or over paint, whichever you prefer.

34. For added protection you may line the planter box on the inside with polyethylene (4mm) stapled to the bottom and topped with a layer of aluminum foil. Be sure the foil covers all the plastic since the plastic though water resistant, will deteriorate quickly when exposed to sunlight.

Shelves To Complete The Planter Center

Materials: 2 1×12's, 6 feet long each, (painted); 8 fancy utility brackets; screws; hollow wall anchors.
Tools: Drill and bit, screwdriver, level, measuring tape, pencil.

144

Instructions:

    1. Measure and mark position for brackets.

    2. Pre-drill holes and mount brackets directly on the wall with screws driven into the studs if at all possible.

    3. If you can't mount them on the studs use hollow wall anchors.

    4. Be sure you're mounting the brackets at a height that will be convenient for the person watering the plants.

    5. You can use the utility brackets with the supporting arm up or down. (We prefer down, with the bracket supporting the shelf from underneath so that we can hang from the brackets, too (Fig. 12-32).

    6. To make sure the shelf is level, secure the first supporting bracket to the wall and lay the shelf on it and the second supporting

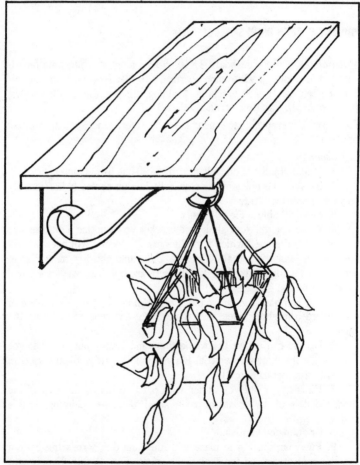

Fig. 12-32.Installing shelf with decorative support brackets that double as hangers for hanging baskets.

bracket which you hold in place by hand. (Unless you're three-handed a helper is very nice at this point.)

7. Put a carpenter's level on the shelf and push the hand-held bracket up and down until the shelf is dead level.

8. With your pencil make a dot for the screws that will hold the second supporting bracket.

9. Remove your shelf and make the starter holes for the screws.

10. Fasten second support bracket firmly in place.

11. Put additional supports in place, spaced evenly.

12. Fasten the shelf to supports from underneath with small screws.

13. Repeat for second shelf.

PROJECT 5: OPEN BOOK SHELVES

Materials: 1 white pine board 1×10, 6 feet long; 2 white pine boards 1×10, 4 feet long; 2 white pine boards 1×10, 3½ feet long; 3 standards 5 feet long; 12 10-inch brackets; Molding, 21 feet (optional); screws; glue (optional); Paint; or varnish.

Tools: Drill, measuring tape, pencil, screwdriver, sandpaper, paintbrush or roller.

Instructions:

1. Mount standards on wall after the wall has been painted.

2. Be sure the holes of the standards line up perfectly horizontally on your shelves will tilt.

3. Pre-drill holes. *Tie into studs.*

4. When you put your shelf on a bracket you'll notice a discrepancy in size, (i.e.) the shelf which is really only 9¼ inches will not quite fill the bracket which is a real 10 inches. Unfortunately this same discrepancy exists with all size boards and there are only two ways we found to deal with this:

5. You can glue and tack a piece of molding along the front edge of each board (the short sides, too, if you like) and that will take up the slack.

6. Or you can ignore the whole thing and simply put your shelves in and slide them forward a little. It's your choice. (If you come up with a new solution let us know!)

7. Finish your shelves either with paint to match the rest of the room (sand, seal, two coats of paint, see Project #6, painting, in this chapter.)

8. Or stain and varnish.

9. Put your shelves in place with the long one across the bottom and the rest staggered for a pleasant effect (Fig. 12-33). Experiment until you find the patter that pleases you, and that fits best what you plan to put on the shelves. Remember, form follows function.

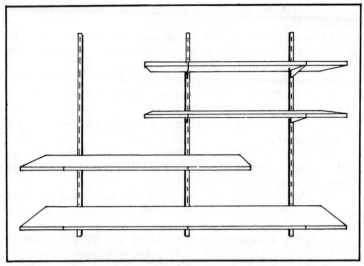

Fig. 12-33. Installing open book shelves with standards and brackets.

PROJECT 6: PAINT AND VARNISH
Painting Indoors

Since there's quite a bit of painting to do in this conversion we intend to treat the painting as a project though actually, you are painting the projects you finished earlier.

Materials: Latex-based sealer for all new wood and new or unpainted wallboard; semi-gloss latex-based paint for walls and ceiling; marine and polyurethane varnish or enamel for railing and plant center if desired; or latex based semi-gloss; paint thinner (optional); sand paper; plastic coated paper plates; clean empty cans; goggles (optional); brimmed cap; newspapers.

Tools: Paint rollers and trays (regular size); small roller for narrow places; 2½-inch paint brush; stirrers; screw-driver; nail; hammer; drop cloths; rags; 1-1½-inch sash brush.

Instructions:

1. Give all the new wood a good rub with fine-grade steel wool.
2. Dust off thoroughly.
3. Use vacuum on walls to be painted, also ceiling.
4. Spread drop cloths and/or newspaper.
5. Open can of sealer, punch several holes in rim with nail and hammer. Stir thoroughly.
6. Pour off into tray and roll on walls and new wood. Make sure everything is completely covered.
7. Start with ceiling. Use roller extension and wear a cap.
8. Use small roller to cut in the corners and cover narrow sections like the railing.

9. If you prefer (as one of us does) use your 2-inch brush instead of the small roller.

10. Since you are sealing, not painting, you don't have to worry about an even coverage. Just make sure everything is covered and that there are no runs or blobs. They will show through.

11. Wash brush and rollers in warm soapy water.

12. Most sealers dry quickly and you can start your actual painting by the time you have all your sealer applied.

13. Open your paint can and make drain holes the same way you did on the sealer can.

14. Take two paperplates and dab a bit of paint on them then set your paint can on the plates and stir. This will give you a place to put down a brush and prevent some spills.

15. When you think you've stirred enough, stir some more. Then pour off into tray and roll on ceiling using extension on paint roller. Wear cap. *Don't get roller too full* of paint.

16. Roll on walls next, make a big "M" or "W" and fill in, repeat.

17. Cut in with small roller and/or brush, on walls and ceiling.

18. Paint lightly and evenly; don't try to cover everything perfectly in one coat. That leads to minor disasters.

19. Cover brushes and rollers with aluminum foil while you wait for first coat to dry. Cover paint tray, too.

20. Apply second coat to ceiling and walls.

21. If you use the semi-gloss on the wood, too, you can give the wood in the plant center and storage unit, a first coat along with the walls. Start in one corner of the room and work around until you've covered everything.

22. If you use enamel, wait until the walls and ceiling are done, then tackle the job.

23. There is no short-cut when you paint louvered doors. Some people swear it's easier to spray paint them and it is if you have a professional sprayer and know how to use it. But most of us don't have on and using one is not easy. You'll need lots of patience, a narrow sash brush (1 inch or less), a small can for your paint sitting on a paper plate, and radio, stereo or good conversation.

24. Go slowly on your louvers so you won't get globs. Two coats are a must. *Don't forget to seal first.*

25. Paint all shelves before they are installed. Seal (use two coats of sealer on particle board if needed) first.

26. Paint shelves either leaning against a wall (not yet painted) by covering one big surface and one short edge and two long edges. Let dry, turn and flip upside down paint other side and remaining short edge. Repeat for second coat.

27. Or you can paint shelves by laying them flat on the floor, over newspaper or on saw horses. Paint one side and all four edges. Dry and flip and paint other side. Repeat for second coat.

28. By all means use your roller for painting shelves. You can use your little roller for edges if you wish or your narrow brush. Watch for drips when you paint edges and wipe up with brush so you won't get blobs on other side of shelf.

29. If you want to use enamel paint on part or all of the wood (or the walls, for that matter) you'll have to take a bit more time. Brush the paint on fairly thinly in *one* direction first, then go across.

30. You can use a roller to paint with enamel and it's a must if you plan to do walls that way. A short napped roller will do a nice job on wood, too, but it's a bit harder to do and the finish isn't quite as smooth as a brushed surface.

31. Stirring is even more important with enamel if that's possible, so stir, stir, stir.

32. Toward the bottom of the can you'll need to thin the enamel a bit, with a drop or two of thinner. But be careful, you can always add more thinner, but you can't take it out once it's been added to the paint.

33. If you don't want to use enamel but would like to have the paint on your plant center a bit more rugged, you can try the following: Proceed as indicated with the latex based paint. After is has thoroughly dried, cover paint with one or more coats of clear polyurethane varnish. This will produce an extra hard surface. However, the varnish tends to yellow the color a little bit, even though it is supposedly clear. (Only shows up if you have pure white, is okay with any of the creamy tones or yellows.)

34. Even if you don't use the varnish anywhere else you should put two coats in the planter top of the plan center: marine varnish directly on the wood; polyurethane over paint.

35. We also recommend that you give the shelves which will hold plants a couple of coats of polyurethane varnish for extra protection against the dampness. Helps with the cleaning, too. Wait till paint is cured, one week.

36. Allow enough time for drying between coats. This is important in all painting.

37. Some people advise light sanding between coats, but we don't, unless you're refinishing furniture.

38. Keep a damp rag handy and wipe up spills as they occur.

39. Keep dropcloths and/or newspapers clean. Change or clean when needed. This keeps your from tracking paint into other rooms on your shoes.

40. Wear gloves to paint, it makes it much more pleasant.

41. Wear your glasses or goggles when you paint ceilings or areas over your eyelevel. It might sound foolish and unnecessary but if you get a big glob of paint in your eye you'll know how unpleasant that can be.

42. If you loathe wearing either, you can get around that two ways: either wear a brimmed cap or paint up on a ladder or stool when you do

the top part of walls. For ceilings we stand by the glasses/goggles without flinching.

43. Clean up thoroughly but carefully after you've finished painting. Remember the painting is still wet and an energetic scrubbing of the spill on the floor can inadvertently smear the wall or wood above it.

44. Leave the last bit of clean up around the very edges until the paint is completely dry and scrape off carefully.

45. Allow enough time for drying before putting room to use. Wet, or damp paint is weak and doesn't adhere as well. Latex paint takes time to cure. (The labels all say don't wash before a month is up—that's why.) So treat gently at first.

46. Don't clean up your window glass area until at least a couple of days or your might scrape off more than you'd bargained for.

47. Wash brushes, rollers and trays thoroughly and dry outside if possible. Hose off drop clothes.

Painting Indoors

Basically, of course, painting is painting wherever you happen to swing the paint brush. But there are some small differences.

Materials: Exterior sealer or aluminum paint: exterior oil or water based paint.

Tools: Larger brushes or rollers.

Instructions:

1. Seal, seal, seal. This even more important outside where the weather plays havoc with your paint job.

2. Always use products designed for **exterior** use. The best interior paint won't stand up outside.

3. Choose the day you're going to paint wisely. Make sure it is reasonably dry and won't rain for a day or two. Don't paint when it's very hot or your paint will blister. Avoid windy days because of the dust in the air.

4. Okay, so you don't live in a perfect climate—do the best you can.

5. Don't paint if the weather is too cold, either, never near freezing.

6. Prepare surface as for indoor painting. Fill in any holes, cracks or such with putty.

7. Sand or use steel wool if you're a perfectionist.

8. Paint, using a larger brush. You can use a roller if you like but you'll cut in with a brush.

9. On siding use a brush, a roller is a hassel.

10. Allow enough time to dry between coats.

11. Remember that time is relative—on a damp and humid day or when there's a lot of dew, your paint will take a longer time to dry than on a clear, dry, sunny day.

12. Here's a bit of trick we learned from an old German painter friend: He swears that if you use aluminum paint as a sealer your paint job will last twice as long regardless of the quality of paint you put on top, and will withstand the weather beautifully.

Using Varnish As A Finish

Materials: Varnish (the synthetic kind, preferably); sealer-stain or stain/varnish; or shellac, (optional); alcohol (optional); turpentine; paste wax; small bowl.

Tools: New 2- or 2½-inch brush, tablespoon, paint stirrer, tack rag or similar thing.

Instructions:

1. Prepare surface as for painting. Sand, steel wool dust.

2. Wipe off with tacky rag. A tacky rag is a rag that has been moistened with a bit of varnish then squeezed out.

3. If you have hardwood (cherry, oak, walnut, birch, mahogany butternut or chestnut) you'll have to first apply a filler.

4. If you're using fir plywood it must be sealed.

5. You can apply sealer either by using an ordinary clear sealer or—

6. By using a stain sealer which stains the wood a different color as it does its sealing job—

7. Or by using shellac thinned with alcohol in a 1: 4 proportion. In other words, one part of shellac to four parts of alcohol.

8. Orange shellac is neat, you can use it to get an instant-old-pine look when you apply it to pine or fir plywood.

9. We prefer wipe-on stains to varnish stains because they are easier to handle. And remember it's a lot easier to apply more stain than to get off what you already put on.

10. To apply wipe-on stain simply pour some stain on a clean, lint-free rag and wipe with the grain onto the wood, a little at a time.

11. You can use a small brush if you like but the temptation to "paint on" the stain is great and stain *always* dries darker than you think it will.

12. In any case, whether you stain your wood or not, let the sealer dry thoroughly, then wipe again with tacky rag to get off any dust that might have settled there.

13. Open your can of varnish (which you have made sure is of the synthetic kind if you're going to use it to finish shelves the way we did. For outdoor use, too, but check the can for particulars as to which kind for what.) and pour off about one cup into a bowl.

14. Add three tablespoonfuls of turpentine to bowl and stir.

15. Cap your varnish instantly to protect it from dust and never put your brush directly into the can of varnish.

16. Now get your brush good and wet, or load it heavily as they say in the trade, and with shorty heavy strokes go back and forth on an area

about 2×3 feet and make sure you've covered every speck of wood evenly.

17. That'll raise a lot of foam and bubbles and, if you've ever listened to an "expert" on varnishing that's exactly what you should never do. But—don't worry, it'll be fine.

18. The reason we thinned the varnish with the turpentine was because of these same bubbles and foam. Thinned down you can make them disappear easily, with a method that's called the "tip-off". Hold your brush at an angle a bit less than 90 degrees or vertical, about 20 less if you need a figure, and gently brush the varnish off with strokes running from one end of the varnished surface to the other, in the same direction. That'll take care of the bubbles.

19. Since the varnish has been thinned, your brush marks will disappear, too.

20. Let the varnish dry as long as it says on the label. You can always trust your label to give you the right time if—and there is an if—you let the varnish dry in a warm dry place. If not, add time.

21. After the finish is thoroughly dry and hard, you may apply a coat of paste wax if you like.

Note: Never let anyone tell you that you can use spar varnish on shelves, build-ins or furniture. Spar varnish is designed to work great outdoors: to contract and expand with changing weather conditions. In essence, it doesn't get completely dry or hard—ever. Which is great when covering something exposed to blizzards and 100 degree sunshine, but it doesn't do so well in your house. In fact, what you get is a a sticky, gummy feeling finish which you don't need.

PROJECT 7: FINISHING WIRING

Whether you finish your wiring by installing your receptacles and new light fixtures before or after you paint is a matter of personal preference. Since we are divided down the middle on that question we leave the decision up to you. Do, however, leave off the switch and receptacle plates in case you do your wiring before the painting.

Wiring Receptacles and Switches

Materials: Romex cable (already threaded through wall); switch and receptacle boxes; wire nuts.
Tools: Wire stripper or pocket knife, screwdriver.
Instructions:

1. Cut back the insulation for about 8 inches on the Romex cable coming out of your receptacle and switch boxes.

2. Slip the wires through the knockout.

3. Secure the cable by turning down the set screws on the built-in clamp.

4. Connect the Romex bare ground wire to the metal outlet box.

5. Or connect the green grounding screw on the receptacle or switch (Fig. 12-34).

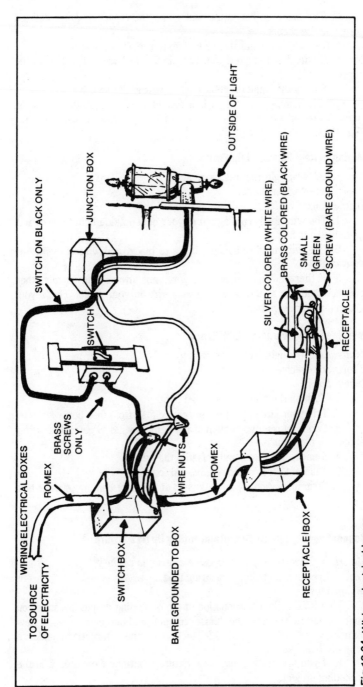

Fig. 12-34. Wiring electrical boxes.

WIRING ELECTRICAL BOXES

OUTSIDE OF LIGHT

JUNCTION BOX

SWITCH ON BLACK ONLY

SWITCH

SILVER COLORED (WHITE WIRE)

BRASS COLORED (BLACK WIRE)

SMALL GREEN SCREW (BARE GROUND WIRE)

RECEPTACLE

BRASS SCREWS ONLY

WIRE NUTS

ROMEX

ROMEX

TO SOURCE OF ELECTRICITY

SWITCH BOX

BARE GROUNDED TO BOX

RECEPTACLE BOX

153

6. The *black* or hot, wire will go to the *copper* or *brass* colored screw on the receptacle.

7. The *white* or neutral wire will go to the *silver screw.*

8. Remember to fasten your wire in a *clock-wise* direction to the screw.

9. Follow the same procedure when wiring the switch.

10. Remember that the switch should always break the circuit on the black or hot side of the line, never on the white or neutral side. See Fig. 12-34.

Wiring In New Outside Light Fixture

Materials: New light fixtures, wire nuts.
Tools: Screwdriver, knife.
Instructions:

1. The wire leads coming out of your new outside light fixtures will be color-coded.

2. Use wire nuts to connect black to black, and white to white on your cable.

3. If there is a green or bare wire, not always, but usually, then connect that one to the bare or green wire in your cable. That's your ground wire, remember?

Wiring In New Overhead Light Fixture

Materials: New light fixture, wire nuts.
Tools: Screwdriver, knife.
Instructions:

1. Turn on the present overhead light.

2. Trip your circuit breaker or *remove* fuse from fuse box.

3. Carefully remove enough of the ceiling panel to get at the wiring above the old fixture.

4. Remove wire nuts and unfasten the wiring.

5. Take out screws and remove old fixture.

6. Strip insulation off a few inches of the wire coming off your new fixture.

Connecting to the House Circuit and Putting Up New Fixture

Materials: New fixture, Romex cable already in ceiling.
Tools: Screwdriver, knife, measuring tape.
Instructions:

This is actually a continuation of the preceding project because you might want to tie into the house current without putting up a new fixture, we decided to put this section of the instructions under a separate heading.

1. If you are putting up a new fixture, continue from step 6 in the preceding project.

2. If you're just connecting to the house current, go the same route, but omit steps 5 and 6.

3. Now fish out that Romex cable that your threaded through the wall and space above the ceiling in Project 2-C, (Roughing in the wiring in the new wall, step 11) and bring it up to where the fixture hooks on to the electric circuit.

4. Strip insulation off your Romex cable for about eight inches.

5. If you'll observe closely you will now be the proud possessor of three black wires, three white wires and three green or bare wires—one set from the Romex cable, one set from your new fixture or the old one you took down temporarily and one set from the cable coming from your circuit breaker or fuse box.

6. Strip and place all three of the black wires together, side by side, and stick them into a wire nut. Turn down wire nut over them.

7. Then put all the white wires together into a wire nut and turn nut down over them.

8. Once more join all of the green or bare wires.

9. For extra security wrap some electrical tape around each of these connections (Fig. 12-35).

10. Now fasten new fixture in place, or replace old one.

11. Rush to your electric service panel and trip your circuit breaker or replace your fuse.

12. It works! Hurrah!

13. If needed, patch the ceiling around the fixture with some pressure sensitive joint tape and joint compound. Let dry thoroughly. Sand lightly, touch up with paint.

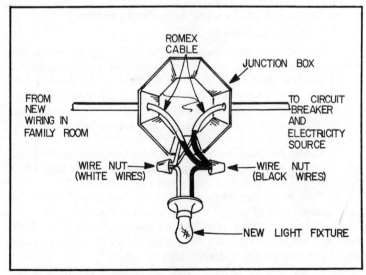

Fig. 12-35.Tying into the house circuit.

Installing Flourescent Work/Plant Lights Over Plant Center

Materials: two fluorescent worklights each containing two 40-watt tubes, 48 inches long, on chains; four decorative hooks that screw into the ceiling; No. 12 3-wire indoor cable; one heavy duty three-pronged male plug; insulated staples; switch (optional), four warm white bulbs.
Tools: Knife, screwdriver, drill measuring tape, staple gun.

Note: Two fluorescent light fixtures, the 48-inch variety that takes two 40 watt bulbs each, will give your planter box plenty of light for good plant growth as well as furnishing some cheery "daylight" in that section of the room. The warm white bulbs that come with the lights work just fine, both for the photosynthesis and the cheer, but the problem is those blasted 3-foot long cords which don't reach anywhere. So we have come up with two solutions—

Instructions: Solution #1:

1. Since the work lights come from the store only partly assembled it's easy matter to replace the short cord that comes with the fixture with a longer one of your choice.

2. Be sure to replace it with a white cord, too. The black cord can never be camouflaged properly.

3. Watch for bargains on these lights at your local K-Mart or other such discount store. They appear periodically for very little.

4. If you like, replace the cheap looking chain that comes with the fixture with some nice, decorative chain that you can buy at the hardware store.

5. Ditto with the hooks that the fixture hangs on.

6. The hooks should be fastened into the ceiling joists.

Solution #2: Wire your lights in tandem:

1. Measure from the nearest electrical outlet along the wall to the center of the planter box, up the wall about 6 feet, across another 6 feet. Then allow about 8 feet for wiring the fixtures. Buy that length of #123- wire indoor cable plus a heavy duty male (three prong) plug.

2. Fasten plug to one end of cable. Though there's a bewildering variety of male plugs available they all come with specific instructions about how to wire them in.

3. The light fixtures, too, come with wiring instructions which you will follow in toto, except for wiring in your own beautiful, long, white cord instead of that short black horror that came with the fixture.

4. When you are wiring your fixtures line them up on the floor the same distance apart (if any) they will be when hanging.

5. You have a choice as to how you want to arrange them. They could go 3 feet in from the side wall and hang 3 feet apart, or they could go in 2 feet from the side wall and hang 4 feet apart.

6. In any case the inner light should be positioned close to the planter's corner so that the light will fall on the short "L" as well.

7. Now feed your power cord through the knock-out hole in fixture #1.

8. Push it all the way through and knock out the hole on the other side.

9. Allow for the distance in cable and feed end into fixture #2 through its knock-out hole.

10. Wire your power cable into fixture #2 *first* just the way it says in the instructions.

11. When you reach the place in the instructions on fixture #1 where it says to tie it into the power cord, cut your new power cord.

12. Insert both ends into the wire nuts just as the instructions tell you—black wire goes with black wire, and white with white, ground with ground (Fig. 12-36).

13. Mark your places on the joists of the ceiling where your hooks are going to be. Center them above the planter box crosswise.

14. Use ornamental hooks, if you like. The ones that come with the fixtures will hold them up all right but they are not things of beauty.

15. Get some nice white chain to replace the chain that comes with the fixture if you like.

16. Remember though to keep your lights up pretty high for two reasons, 1) you get more light that way, and 2) the lights won't bang against your head when you water or otherwise tend the plants.

17. If you want a switch on your lights, which we think is a good idea because there is no such things on these fixtures, proceed thusly:

18. Buy a non-house wiring switch, we personally prefer the ones made by Gem, though there are other good ones.

19. The Gem switch is neat because it comes in two halves that are screwed together. These halves are unscrewed and the wire connected inside. No splicing of wires. When the switch is put back together, points inside pierce the insulation to make contact with the wires. See how neat it is?

20. To install your gem of a Gem cord switch on your cable you first carefully peel off the cable insulation exposing the insulated wires the exact same length of the switch.

21. Cut the black wire only and place the two ends along with the white wires into the switch (Fig. 12-37).

22. Let the ground wire run underneath the switch and don't try to put it inside. Don't scrape any insulation of that wire.

23. Press halves of the switch together.

24. Replace nut onto switch and replace the screw you unscrewed to take switch apart in the first place.

25. Other types of switches can be spliced in using wire nuts but it doesn't make as neat as installation.

26. What ever type of switch you use, remember to always break the "hot" or black side of the circuit for the switch. Also make sure the switch is rated to handle more current than the fixture consumes. In

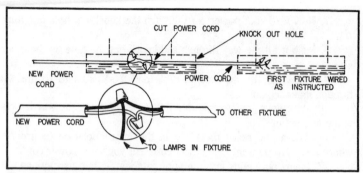

Fig. 12-36. Wiring work/plant lights.

this case it would be 4×40 watts=160 watts. At 110 volts that is about 1.5 amps.

27. You will probably want to staple the cable to the wall with insulated staples. It makes a neater picture.

28. Now hang your fixtures from the hooks and admire your handy work. (After you've turned them on and plugged them in, that is.)

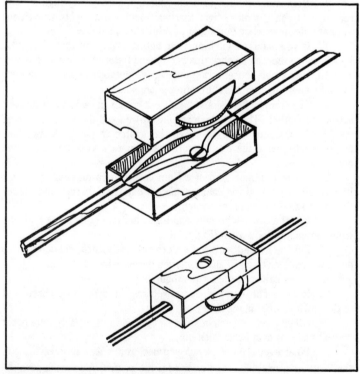

Fig. 12-37. Switch for plant light completed.

PROJECT 8: LAYING CARPET TILES

Materials: Self-stick carpet tiles, sealer.

Tools: Chalk-line, scissors, yard stick, long board or piece of 2×4, steel-edged rule and carpet knife (optional), large paint brush, sandpaper (very coarse) and block, vacuum sweeper.

Instructions:

1. Vacuum floor thoroughly.

2. Inspect floor for unevenness. If there are any bumps or paint blobs, sand them off with sand paper and block.

3. Don't worry about pitting, that can be filled in with the sealer.

4. Vacuum again.

5. Apply two coats of sealer. Let dry thoroughly between coats and after second coat.

6. Measure along the two long sides of your room and mark the center.

7. Do the same with the two short walls.

8. Snap a chalk line from center to center along both walls.

9. Now you have a center point from which you can start to lay the tiles if you want a perfect job (Fig. 12-38A).

10. If you are just as happy with a quicker and less perfect though quite workman-like version, omit steps 6-9 and lay out a course of tiles along your long window wall. Then along your short new wall where the garage door used to be (Fig. 12-38B).

11. If you go the A-1 route you will lay out tiles in this manner: Up along the chalkline from the center and again along the crossed line to mark out a square.

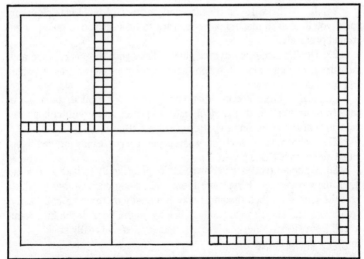

Fig. 12-38. Starting to lay tile in center of room (A); Starting to the tile laying in a corner, (B).

12. The reason we have two versions is that in the traditional or A-1, you usually have to trim tiles on all four sides. That makes sense if you have a lot of free standing furniture, but since we have a strong wall along one wall and have to piece the insides of that in any case, we found that going the other way was a lot faster and didn't detract from the whole effect at all.

13. Peel off the backing paper of the first tile and press in place, either in a corner or in the center of the room, with the center of the tile resting on the intersection of the chalk lines.

14. Be sure to press the tile down thoroughly—in the middle and along the edges, working from the middle out.

15. Peel off the next tile backing and press down.

16. Proceed in this manner until all tiles that don't need to be cut have been attached to the floor.

17. Check yourself occasionally with the long board to make sure you're still going perfectly straight once you've left the chalk lines far behind. Especially check if you're not using chalk lines at all.

18. To lay the border tiles, lay a tile, backing side up, without removing the backing on top of the last tile you've installed.

19. On top of this tile put a third tile and slide that one even until it touches the wall.

20. Use the edge of the top tile as guide, mark the tile underneath with a pencil line (Fig. 12-39).

21. Cut tile along that line either with scissors or with your carpet knife against a steel edged ruler.

22. Remove backing from cut tile and press in place.

23. Continue in this way all around the border.

24. If you have to fit tiles around corners of build-ins, pipes or such, you'll need to make a paper pattern to fit what you're going to go around precisely.

25. Don't proceed by eye or guess. Take your measuring tape and measure each dimension of the obstacle transfer measurements to paper and connect lines.

26. Cut out the section that you have to go around, then place pattern on top of tile (*tile is right side up*) fasten down with cellophane tape and cut tile according to pattern (Fig. 12-40).

27. Keep a large sack or wastepaper basket handy or you'll be inundated with backing paper.

28. When all the floor is down, invite your family to take a walk on it, in their bare feet. First have them walk along each course of tiles, first the long way, then the short way and finally on the diagonal. Lastly do a bit of exuberant dancing and frolicking on the floor. If the kids want to roll from side to side, that's great. Those tiles will really stick.

PROJECT 9: FINISHING

Materials: Threshold; stair nosing; quarter round (pre-painted); baseboard (pre-painted), (optional); glue.

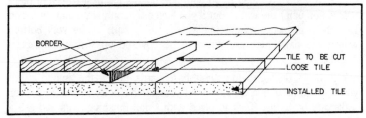

Fig.12-39. Making a tile sandwich for accurate cutting of tiles.

Tools: Hacksaw, screwdriver, hammer, measuring tape.
Instructions:

1. We should have settled the question of baseboards earlier perhaps, but better late than never.

> Pro-baseboard: Most rooms have them to keep the furniture away from the wall.

> Con-baseboards: Baseboards are expensive and they don't really do the job for which they are designed.

So—make your choice.

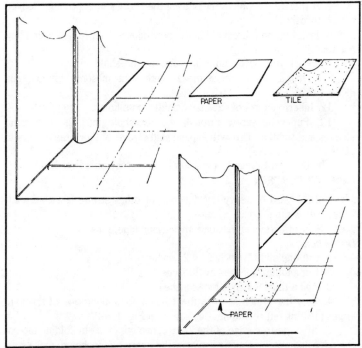

Fig. 12-40. Cutting a pattern for fitting carpet tiles around pipes and other protrusions.

2. If you've decided to go with baseboards it's best to install them before you paint the walls. But if you haven't, simply pre-paint them and glue them in place, reinforcing with finishing nails at the very bottom where the nail holes are going to be covered up with the quarter-rounds.

3. If you decide to do without baseboards, now is the time to install your pre-painted quarter-round all around the bottom edges of your walls and build-ins. Tack in place with small finishing nails and use a block when you hammer to protect the quarter-round from your hammer blows.

4. Installing the stair nosing is next. Isn't that a delightful word—stair nosing? And it is an accurate term, believe it or not. It'll go at the edge of your former bumper which is now covered over with carpet tile.

5. Measure the distance between the plant center and the wall and buy enough of the stair nosing to cover the distance.

6. The stuff comes in 39-inch lengths and you can cut it to size with the hacksaw blade on your saber saw.

7. Theoretically, you're supposed to affix the stair nosing with the screws that come with it. Which is fine and good if the masonry bit in your drill will work on your particular concrete in such a manner that the screws will remain in the holes.

8. If there's a problem try putting the screws in expansion sleeves for the threshold.

9. Installing the threshold in the new door is last. Measure and buy one that fits your opening.

10. Mark your screw holes through the threshold.

11. Drill holes in these places with your masonry bit on your electric drill.

12. Insert sleeves of expansion shields into holes.

13. Put your screw through the threshold into the expansion sleeves and tighten. This will expand said sleeve and lock the screws in place.

The finished Garage Conversion I should resemble Fig. 12-41.

CARPENTER'S APRON

Materials: 1 yard of heavy duck, denim or other strong fabric; thread; heavy cotton tape, 1-inch wide.

Tools: Scissors, sewing machine, measuring tape, pins.

Instructions:

1. Cut one strip 10 inches by 21 inches.

2. Cut another 7 inches by 26 inches.

3. And a third 5 inches by 22 inches.

4. Sew the 7-inch strip to the 10-inch strip along one of the long edges pleating out the fullness as shown in Fig. 12-42.

5. Bind the free edge of the 7-inch strip with tape by folding tape of the edge and stitching along it twice. Pin every two inches to make sure you'll catch all three thicknesses on the first stitching.

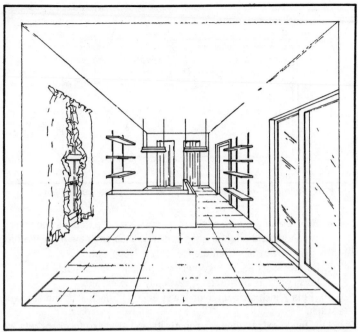

Fig. 12-41. Plant center complete with lights and shelves and view of book shelves and storage wall.

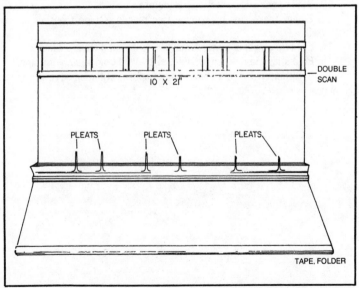

Fig. 12-42.Joining pocket to backing, taping edges and attaching pocket strip.

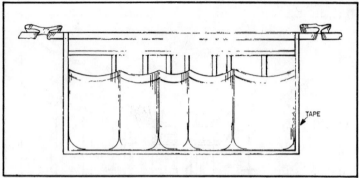
Fig. 12-43.Reinforcing seams with tape and complete view of apron.

6. Bind one of the long edges of your 5-inch strip in the same way.

7. Fold unbound edge of strip under ½-inch and sew it on the big 10-inch strip, 6½ inches from the free edge. Double stitch.

8. Pin the short edges together on both sides and stitch.

9. Form pockets by stitching vertically at intervals.

10. Fold 7-inch strip up over lower edge of 5-inch strip pin at sides and stitch.

11. Divide extra fullness over pleats and stitch to form pockets as in step 9.

12. Bind seams with tape, on the outside.

13. Bind upper edge with tape as before.

14. Either make ties by sewing two pieces of tape together as in Fig. 12-43.

15. Cut two strips of fabric 18 inches long and 3 inches wide.

16. Fold strips in half lengthwise, stitch and bind seam with tape.

17. In either case sew to each end of apron, stitching several times to secure.

Chapter 13
Garage Conversion II

This was the garage of some relatives of ours which required special thought in the layout as well as in the wants and needs of the owners.

The double-size garage was attached to the house. It had an extra "L" at the back that fitted into an enclosed open-to-the interior, utility room. The garage itself was twenty-two feet by twenty-three feet six inches and the "L" was twelve feet by six feet, six inches. It was attached to the house along one long wall and at the "L". There were neither windows nor an outside door except for garage door openings in front.

The structure was made of brick and the second long wall set within 3 feet of a tall hedge which belonged to the neighbors. Putting windows into that wall would have resulted in a lot of trouble for very little extra light and no view whatsoever. The rear wall of the "L", which would have been the next best choice for letting in light and air was an equal dud. It had an electric service panel smack in the middle and also had all kinds of ducts in it that led to the central heat and air compressor which had its home right behind it.

So there we were, and there they were, with a huge cavern of a room with virtually no light because the front of the lot, on either side of the driveway was shaded by big trees.

A skylight, in spite of the owners first objections, was the logical and least expensive answer. The next consideration was getting the most light through the front without having the feeling of sitting in a goldfish bowl, since house and grage were set close to a busy street. We finally solved that problem with sliding glass doors across the garage door openings and with the construction of a privacy screen 8 feet down the driveway.

This created a patio which we covered with the same indoor-outdoor carpeting that we used indoors, giving a feeling of visual continuity.

Since this garage conversion was done in San Antonio, Texas, we knew that the patio would be in use at least nine months out of the year and that even during the other three, the patio would provide enough shelter from the wind to keep some hardy plants there so that the view from the family room would be pleasant throughout the year.

The owners wanted the family room primarily as a second living area to take some of the load off the more formal room in the house. They looked forward to having extra space for big parties.

The owners also expressed the need for some extra storage, particularly for party and Christmas decorations and also for large tablecloths and games. Our solution was a storage platform that fills the need in a special way. Betsy had polio as a baby and has to use crutches so it is difficult for her to store fragile or bulky things on conventional shelves. The storage drawers, however, make it easy for her to get out or put in what she wants while sitting on the edge of the platform.

The platform also serves as a special conversation area—much like a conversation pit. It can also be used as a viewing area for giant screen TV. See Fig. 13-1 A-B "before" and "after."

PROJECT 1: SKYLIGHTS

As we've said in the introduction to this conversion, the only solution to getting light into this two-car garage was the addition of some skylights. Of course, we had heard all the horror stories about leaky skylights. In fact, we have some good friends who have a large skylight in their family room (no garage conversion, this) which not only brings in huge amounts of light but also quantities of Texas' famous torrential rains. And although this particular skylight was installed by a professional contractor who has come back time and again to patch leaks, the skylight can still double as a shower in heavy rains.

We also knew of dozens of skylight installations in commercial buildings which were completely successful, not giving in to even the very worst cloudbursts. So, we set out to find the secret of installing leakproof skylights before attempting to make our own first installation.

The first thing we learned was most surprising. Several manufacturers told us that they had much better success with their product when it was installed by do-it-yourselfers, than when experienced contractors and roofers did the job. The reason, they told us, was that inexperienced do-it-yourselfers will usually follow manufacturer's instructions to the letter. Experienced roofers and contractors, on the other hand, will seal in a skylight the same way they have always sealed in roof openings for chimneys, vent pipes and attic ventilators. They won't let some upstart skylight salesman or manufacturer tell them how to do the job.

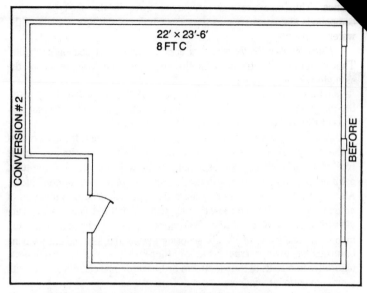

Fig. 13-1 A. Floor plan showing before view of Conversion II.

The conventional tar-type sealing compounds routinely used by professional roofers to seal the usual roof openings do not work for skylights because of two reasons—the larger area opened by a skylight and, especially, the excessive expansion and contraction of skylight

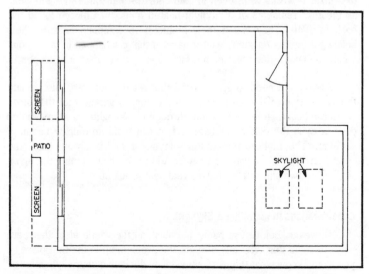

Fig. 13-1 B. Floor plan showing after view of Conversion II.

is stress causes cracks to form in the tar-type sealing
almost as soon as they dry. And these cracks are where the
in.

Rubber Roofing Mastics are the answer for sealing skylights.
ial will stretch with the expansion and contraction of the
skylight without cracking.

While stalking the elusive leak-proof skylight, we found out about
the many other things that need consideration before you take that saw
and cut the roof open to the sky and the elements.

Among the advantages of flooding a room with light from a skylight
is the new perspective everything in the room seems to acquire. This is
true of all furnishings but especially noticeable on plants, sculpture,
paintings and pottery. You will notice aspects you've never seen before.
Also, you may be astonished to learn that you will acquire quite a bit of
unique scenery when you install a skylight. You'll get your own private
view of a chunk of the Milky Way, a personalized glimpse of the full
moon, the spectacle of clouds scooting across the sky behind swaying
branches or even a true "you are there" exposure, in all comfort,
naturally, to a roaring thunderstorm or blizzard. You can't beat that with
your conventional windows.

One unapparent disadvantage of skylighting a room is the bleaching
that comes when direct sunlight reaches into the far corners of a room.
It can do all sorts of nasty things like fading the backs of books and
leaving streaks on rugs and upholstery. Another disadvantage is glare
and a third is heat build-up, which can be considerable. This last, heat
build-up, is the famous passive solar heat that architects are now trying
to utilize. It works well, even in cold climates and sometimes too well,
as the first residents of a skylight-heated house in Chicago found out
back in 1940. They called their architect to complain because their
house got too hot on sunny winter days. If that can happen in the famous
windy, and cold (think of the chill factor) city, it can certainly happen to
you, too.

So you will need to give careful thought to your local climate and
the orientation of the garage roof to the sun. A garage roof that faces
south can heat a large family room through its skylights on sunny winter
days in even the coldest climates. Heat can build up quickly behind a
skylight. The highest temperature in any room is always near the
ceiling anyway, since warm air rises. Add to this heat coming through a
skylight or two and you can have a real heat problem.

Considerations In Installing a Skylight.

However, before you panic and abandon the whole idea, there are
ways to solve this. We only brought the problem up in the first place so
you would know what things to consider in designing your skylights.

Here are some of the choices you have:

1. You can install a skylight that can be opened so you can vent the heat when it gets too warm.

2. You can shade your skylight permanently or, if you like, only part of the year.

3. You can put your skylight in a roof facing away from the sun, as we did, considering our mild climate and high summer cooling requirements. This garage roof faced north—which gives nice light, as all artists will attest to, and only a very little sunshine early in the morning and late in the afternoon in summer. That's why the skylight in Conversion II adds very little heat to the room.

4. You can use heat absorbing glass which cuts heat transmission by as much as 50 percent in your skylight.

5. You can use plastic bubbles that are translucent rather than clear and so help reflect the sunlight.

6. You can paint the skylight with white paint, the wash-off kind, in summer and then scrub it off when winter comes.

7. You could use a lattice frame over the skylight to shade the skylight from the direct sun in summer and remove same in winter.

One thing you must do, according to the Uniform Building Code and regardless of any of the above, is install a skylight which will support the weight of a man. Why? As protection for that hypothetical fireman who might one dark night be cavorting on your roof in an effort to save your home from fire and who, being a careless individual might mistake your skylight for an ordinary roof, step on same and fall through. You can see how farsighted the Universal Building Code is. This is clearly a case of obeying the letter of the law.

The last problem you have to take into consideration in deciding on your skylight is the possibility of a condensation problem, especially with a large skylight.

You have undoubtedly noticed that whenever there's a rather large difference between the indoor and outdoor temperatures and a high relative humidity, moisture collects on your windows. The same thing happens to skylights. However, moisture on skylights doesn't just stay on the glass, it is likely to drip down on heads, furniture or rugs below. So unless you situate an indoor garden or planter directly underneath your skylight, which is a valid solution and one that we admire, or by luck live in an exceptionally dry climate, you better do something to protect said heads, furniture and rugs. Again you have choices. You can get a well insulated skylight like a hollow glass block for your room or you can make sure that your skylight surface slopes so that water will run down into a condensation gutter. From there the said water will either evaporate or run outside through special weep holes. There—that's solved.

Before you trip off with your little basket over your arm to buy a skylight, beware. It is amazing how many different kinds of dangerous skylights there are just waiting to be snapped up by the unwary do-it-yourselfer.

The most often seen, and probably most responsible for the skylight's nasty reputation, is the kind which consists of a sheet metal frame with the glass set into it with putty. This type of skylight requires a lot of maintenance, wet-nursing you might say, if it is not to leak. The putty joint must be maintained with paint and fresh putty. But that's not all. Often, when the putty is maintained in leakproof condition by all that work, it holds the glass so tightly that the glass will crack under the stresses of heat expansion. This, of course, happens more frequently with large skylights than with small ones. So if you plan to use the smaller sizes and don't mind keeping them in top condition, you can take advantage of the fact that these types of skylights are least expensive to buy. Also, they are usually made to order so you can get the exact size and shape you want.

Types of Skylights

Those great leakproof skylights they use in public buildings and industrial plants are usually of the aluminum putty-less kind. In most areas of the country you can get these skylights in smaller sizes suitable for residential use. They work very well. The aluminum bars that hold the glass in place allow the glass to contract and expand without requiring any maintenance. Some manufacturers will give you a guarantee against leaks and thermal breakage.

Glass blocks, designed specifically for skylight use, are available in individual 1-foot squares set in metal frames. Glass bricks give a diffused prismatic effect to the light they transmit. Also, as very effective insulators, they transmit very little solar heat and hold back interior heat as well which is nice both summer and winter.

Plastic bubble skylights are rapidly gaining acceptance at this writing and by the time this book finds its way into your hands, those skylights may have overtaken the sheet metal framed types in popularity. The plastic bubble units are pre-fabricated in square, rectangular and circular metal frames. Stock sizes range from 14 square inches up to a 67-inch circular dome or a 57 by 89 inch rectangle. These skylights come in clear plastic, or tinted white, gray or bronze. More esoteric color tints are also available in some models.

In addition to all the above, it is also possible to order plastic bubbles of all sizes and/or shapes from plastics fabricating companies. These special units will, of course, be more expensive than the stock sizes.

War surplus aircraft "blisters" are still around. With a little bit of luck you might find some. They make very fine skylights if you are willing to improvise a frame for these units.

Whether you go this route or any other unconventional route, use butyl-rubber and nothing but butyl-rubber for all sealing purposes. If you don't, don't come complaining to us that your skylight leaks. You brought it on yourself. Use the same butyl-rubber if you are using that translucent colored plastic that comes in flat or corrugated sheets. The kind mostly used for patio or porch roofing.

After all this stalking we finally decided on a couple of Skywindows from Wasco Products, Incorporated, of Sanford, Maine. Their products are well-designed and their local personnel helpful and encouraging. The two units were 46 by 30 inches each, and had clear acrylic venting units.

With this lengthy crash course on skylights out of the way we can finally get down to work.

Installing Leakproof Skylights

Materials: 2 DDRS-RV 4630 clear dome Wasco Skywindows; 1 gallon of butyl-rubber roofing mastic; framing boards; joint compound; nails.
Tools: Measuring tape, carpenter's square, hammer, saber saw, shingle nail puller, tin snips, trowel, plastering or putty knife, ladder, sandpaper, wrecking bar, claw hammer.
Instructions:

1. Measure and mark your ceiling or, more accurately, the underside of your roof.

2. Locate the openings so that only one rafter will have to be cut to accomodate the 30-inch width of the skylight.

3. Drive nails through the roof at all four corners of the interior marked ceiling opening to establish the exterior of said opening.

4. Climb up on the roof.

5. Remove the shingles from the area marked with the help of your shingle nail puller, your claw hammer and your wrecking bar. Also remove two extra layers all around.

6. Mark the roof opening to match the ceiling markings underneath.

7. Make a plunge cut with your saber saw and remove the marked roof section.

8. If necessary, make another plunge cut in ceiling squarely through inside markings.

9. Finish cutting rafter and save, along with roof sheathing, for framing.

10. Frame the opening on the inside with facing boards the thickness of the roof deck plus insulation and drywall.

11. If there's a ceiling, then frame in the distance between the roof and the ceiling as well (Fig. 13-2).

12. Apply butyl-rubber mastic all around the opening of the roof deck.

13. Position skylight unit over the opening and make sure all four corners are aligned with the interior opening.

14. Press the unit's flanges firmly into the mastic.

15. Nail flange to roof.

16. Cover the edges of the flanges and the nail heads with more butyl-rubber mastic.

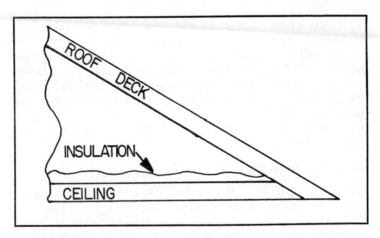

Fig. 13-2. Facing skylight opening in ceiling.

17. Now, replace the shingles, trimming them if necessary with your tin snips to the edge of the built-in curbing on the skylight unit (Fig. 13-3).

18. That's all there is to it. Now you can enjoy a brightly lighted interior as you complete the conversion of your garage to your family room.

Note: When installing a skylight on any roof make sure that the roof has enough pitch for rain water to drain off quickly. Flat roofs are a mess, but fortunately there are very few garages with flat roofs.

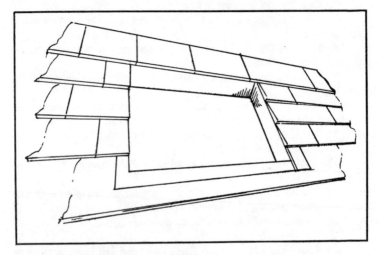

Fig. 13-3. Replacing shingles around skylight.

PROJECT 2: REMOVING GARAGE DOORS.

Follow directions given in Conversion I, Project 1, for the removal of spring powered garage doors. See illustrations in Chapter 12, for greater detail.

PROJECT 3: WALL OPENINGS FOR SLIDING GLASS DOORS

Materials: 13 2 × 4's, 8-foot long each; 1½-inch masonry lag bolts; 8d, 10d, and 16d nails; lockwashers; mending plates; wood preservative.
Tools: Wrecking bar, claw hammer, electric drill with masonry and wood bits, crescent wrench, saber saw, carpenter's apron, slip-stick, paint brush.
Instructions:

1. Remove trim and jambs with wrecking bar and hammer.
2. Go easy so you recycle the lumber you take off.
3. Uncover header and side studs.
4. With your slip-stick measure exact distance from floor to header on both sides of the center post. Record measures.
5. Paint the bottom of four 2×4's with wood preservative for about 3 inches from the bottom. Paint a 3-foot section with wood preservative on another 2 × 4.
6. With masonry nails, nail a treated 2×4 cut to measurement on each side of the post from floor to header (Fig. 13-4).
7. With slip-stick measure along bottom of entire opening. Deduct from that number the size of your new sliding door. Add an extra 2 feet or so to account for the variety of garage doors.
8. From those 2 feet deduct 3 inches (the thickness of the two 2×4's you will install next to the center post on the non-latching side of the door). Deduct another ¼-inch for clearance and you'll have the exact measurement you'll need for your sole plate.
9. Cut this from the 3-foot preservative-treated 2×4.
10. Install with lag bolts.
11. Measure from top of sole plate to header.
12. Cut 2×4 to measurement and nail in place against side of opening (Fig. 13-40).
13. Measure top of opening and cut 2×4 to fit.
14. Nail 2×4 to header and tie to studs with mending plates.
15. Measure with slip-stick from floor to top plate on the inner (post) end of opening. Cut one of the preservative treated 2×4 to measure. Nail in place.
16. Measure from sole plate to top plate at the inner end, 1½ inches in from the inner end, and next to the outer edge (Fig. 13-4).
17. Cut the 2×4's to size and fasten in place with mending plates and corner braces.
18. If you prefer toe-nailing, be our guest, but make darn sure that opening is framed in square or you'll have a hassle when we get to the doors.

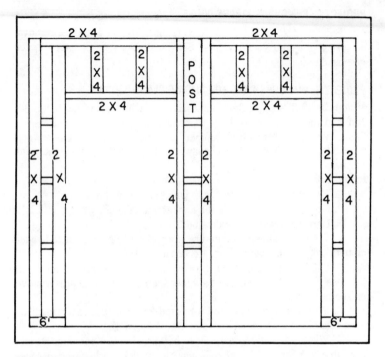

Fig. 13-4. Constructing framing for sliding glass door.

19. Cut three spacers out of scrap 2×4 to fit between the uprights and fasten in with nails (Fig. 13-4).

20. If by some unfortunate coincidence your garage doors were oversized in height and your opening is more than 6-foot 10½-inches tall, you'll have to fill in that space thusly:

21. If you lack another 1½ inches, that's simple, put in one more 2×4 across the top.

22. If you have a considerable difference you'll have to put in a 2×4 top plate at the 6-foot 10½-inch mark and tie that to the header with cripple studs as in (Fig. 13-4).

23. Repeat the entire procedure from step 7 through 22 for the other garage door opening.

24. You are now ready to install your new sliding glass doors.

PROJECT 4: INSTALLING SLIDING GLASS DOORS

Materials: Two sliding glass door sets of your choice, with necessary hardware (doors to be 6-foot wide); screws.
Tools: Carpenters square, level, screwdriver, putty knife.

If you have taken care to build your door frames square and true you will have little problem installing your doors. Don't however, be tempted to over-confidence and attempt to simply slide the units in and screw them down in one easy motion. Take it easy, the step-by-step way, instead—it will save you time in the long run.

Instructions:

1. Slide the door frame in place.

2. Insert several screws *loosely* through the frame into your 2×4 framing studs and header (also top plate in this case).

3. Double check that all is level and true and that the frames slide properly and easily.

4. Make any necessary adjustments with wood shims (thin scrap pieces of wood, or best of all, shingles).

5. Leave a margin of space between the top of the door frame and the header, that ½-inch we spoke about earlier, to allow for possible future deflection of the header on the locking side of the door, so that the door locking mechanism will not jam in case the studs warp a bit.

6. Tighten down all screws holding frame to studs and header.

7. Be careful not to draw the frame out of line since you must leave that ½-inch clearance at the top for the above mentioned header deflection.

8. Check doors for proper rolling once again and make any adjustments suggested by the manufacturer at this step.

9. If the door frames came to you without the glass installed, as is often the case, install said glass according to the manufacturer's directions after step 8 above.

10. As the final step, install all necessary interior molding after you've finished the wall on the inside and all exterior molding after you've finished the wall on the outside (Fig. 13-5).

PROJECT 5:FINISHING THE OUTSIDE WALLS

Since there is such little space to be finished around the sliding glass doors, we didn't bother trying to match siding. Instead, we used panels of marine plywood, trimmed with 1-inch wide corner molding.

Materials: 3×6 (if you can get it that size) marine plywood panel, A-D; 1-inch wide corner molding about 68 feet long; nails.

Tools: Saber saw, hammer, measuring tape, miter box.

Instructions:

1. Rip the plywood panel into two 8-foot strips as wide as your sole plate.

2. Nail these sections in place on the outer edges of your wall.

3. Rip two 8-foot strips 3-inches wide and nail them to the exposed 2×4's at the center post.

4. Cut and miter your molding.

5. Nail molding around all edges of your plywood panels.

6. Sand plywood.

7. Prime and seal.

8. Paint to match house trim.

PROJECT 6: FINISHING THE CEILING

The ceiling and the walls in this garage were unfinished. We opted to keep the beams exposed and finish the ceiling with drywall panels.

Insulating and Finishing Ceiling

Materials: Polystyrene foam boards (enough to cover space between rafters), ½-inch drywall panels; varnish, stain, and clear varnish; foam

Fig. 13-5. View of completed installation of beams and skylight and sliding glass doors, interior.

mastic; large-head, galvanized drywall nails; pressure tape; joint compound; narrow wood trim; caulking compound.

Tools: Saber saw, hammer, miter box, measuring tape, ladder.

Instructions:

1. Make sure your ceiling surface is flat and structurally sound.
2. Get off all dirt.
3. Caulk any cracks you may find.
4. Fasten the insulation board to the underside of your roof with large-head galvanized nails, every 8 inches vertically and horizontally (Fig. 13-6).
5. Make sure you nail into the wood at least 1¼-inch.
6. Don't make holes in the roofing.
7. Cut your drywall panels to fit the spaces between the rafter.
8. Sand rafters. They don't have to be completely smooth but get them so that cobwebs won't easily attach to them.
9. Stain rafters with wipe stain if you like, though in this case we think you can use a varnish-stain combo since it doesn't matter how dark the wood gets or how even the application. Who is going to climb up and inspect?
10. Stain the frames around your skylights at the same time and in the same way.
11. Put a coat of clear satin varnish on top of varnish/stain on rafters as well as frames.
12. Now use your foam mastic and apply ribbons of it to the drywall section you're about to put up. Follow instructions on your mastic cartridge.
13. Place drywall section against the ceiling, press firmly in place all over to get a tight bond.
14. You'll need a helper here. Have the helper hold the drywall section in place while you nail the section down on 16-inch centers in both directions.
15. Make sure you penetrate the roof deck at least 1 inch.
16. Fill in any drywall joints with joint compound, tape, and sand smooth. Fill in over nails, too.
17. Stain wood trim the same color as the rafters.
18. Trim along beams or rafters and around frames of skylights mitering corners of trim (Fig. 13-7).

PROJECT 7: FINISHING INSIDE WALLS

We decided to finish the walls of Garage Conversion II in wood paneling, both for its rich, cozy appearance and its versatility...you can always paint it another color if you decide to change the color scheme of your family room in later years. We'll start from inside the walls and work out: first insulation, then paneling.

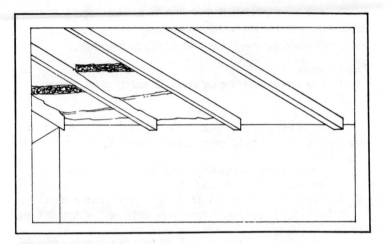

Fig. 13-6. Insulating between the beams.

Insulating Walls

Materials: Enough 48-long insulation bats to cover all surfaces between studs; stables.

Tools: Scissors, staple gun.

Instructions:

1. To figure out the number of insulation bats you'll need count the number of spaces between studs in your walls, including the new wall.

2. Multiply by 2 (for 8-foot ceiling) and there you are.

3. Staple your insulation bats between the studs all around your garage, including the new wall. For the narrow spaces cut the insulation bats to fit before stapling.

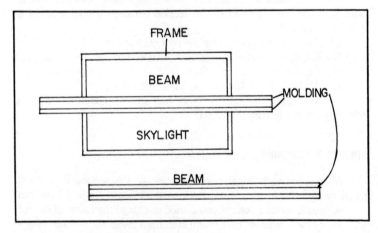

Fig. 13-7. Applying to skylight and beams.

Paneling the Walls

Materials: Hardwood plywood panels or woodgrain hardboard panels, 4×8 feet; panel adhesive; Masonite Brand color coordinated nails (if you can find some to match your paneling); pre-finished Masonite color-coordinated molding; straight inside and outside corners; baseboard.

Tools: Hammer, saber saw or circular saw, adhesive cartridge or caulking gun, level, ruler or measuring tape, electric drill, wood bit, carpenter's square.

Instructions:

1. Clean off the front surface of the studs. Remove any nails or loose splinters, sand and wire brush thoroughly.

2. Measure your walls all around the room along the floor.

3. Measure doorways and large windows, add sliding door measurement to that figure.

4. Now change the number of feet of the perimeter of your room into the number of panels needed to cover by dividing by four (each panel is 4×8 feet and we trust your ceiling or ceiling demarcation will be at 8 feet).

5. For each ordinary doorway you can deduct ⅔ of a panel or, for sliding doors (6-foot each), three panels. The remainder will be the number of panels you need to buy.

6. After you've brought the panels home or they've arrived via delivery truck, stand them up on their long edges inside the room. Let them stay that way for 48 hours so they'll get acclimated to your room's humidity and temperature.

7. Remember, panels have grain and are not always of exactly the same color. So after your 48 hours are up, set the panels upright around the room and match them as to grain and color. Leave them up that way if you can, if not mark the backs in such a way that you'll remember which panel goes where in the color/grain sequence.

8. The time has come to line up a helper. While it is entirely possible, theoretically, to panel a room by yourself, it is also quite a hassle. So why do it the hard way?

9. Measure height of your room in corner and again at a 4-foot distance. (This is not necessarily the same). Deduct ½-inch from total.

10. Mark your panel and cut if necessary.

11. Always cut your panels from the *top* side when using a hand saw or an electric *saber* saw, so mark them on top, too.

12. If you use a *circular* saw, however cut and mark on *back side*.

13. Start paneling in a corner. Tack it up with one nail and test for plumb.

14. Place level along side panel and find the true plumb. This is necessary since you want to have your panels go vertically, not slightly on the slant.

15. A thin piece of wood or a shingle will help hold the panel plumb (Fig. 13-8).

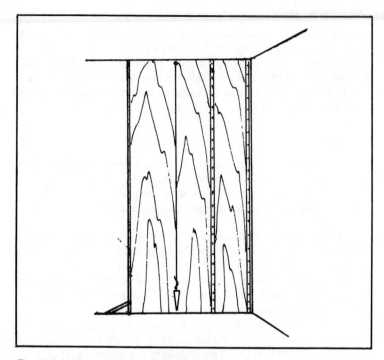

Fig. 13-8. Nailing pattern for installing paneling.

16. Tack at top in another couple of places and mark the edge of the panel on the studs with a pencil or pen.

17. Mark a black line along stud where panels will meet, that will prevent the stud from peeking through.

18. You have your choice in mounting panels: gluing, nailing, or a como of the two. We prefer the combo, (Why be half safe?) But to give you a true choice we'll present all three methods.

Nailing:

1. Start nailing at the corner at the top and move down the stud. Nail down center stud(s), then other edge.

2. Edge nails should be 4 inches apart, nails on the studs in between can be 8 inches apart. Measure paneling to find 16 inch center (Fig. 13-11).

3. If you use those color co-ordinated nails, you won't need to countersink the nails.

4. Measure and put up next full panel alongside first, butting edges together.

5. On unbroken walls continue that way until you run out of room for full panels.

6. When you do, start in corner of next wall and proceed as above.

7. To fill in those bare spots, measure and cut your paneling to fit. Put on wall with cut edge in corner.

8. For door and window openings, measure from your last complete installed panel to the edge of the opening and from the floor to opening (sill for windows, top of door for doors). For windows you'll also need to measure down from the top of the panel to the top of the opening (Fig. 13-9).

9. Measure as accurately as you can, mark on panel, connect lines with straight edge and cut.

10. Check for fit. It had better be correct of you'll have to start over or finagle. Neither alternative is what you had in mind.

Adhesive Application

1. If you want to go the adhesive application route you do it this way: Brush your studs with a wire brush for a better adhesive bond.

2. Use a regular caulking gun and use panel adhesive. Sometimes the adhesive comes in its own cartridge gun.

3. Trim the applying end of the cartridge and put an ⅛-inch continuous strip at the panel joints and at the top and bottom plates.

4. Place 3-inch long beads of the adhesive about 6 inches apart on the studs in between. Be generous, make sure that the beads are at least 3 inches, better longer than too short.

5. Using your level markings which you have made *before* applying the adhesive, put panel in place ¼-inch from the top and tack in place. Double check position of panel.

6. Press the panel down so it will stick. Use firm even pressure so that the adhesive will spread evenly between the studs and the panel.

7. Now take the bottom of the panel by the edges and slooowwly pull the panel out and away from the studs.

8. Freeze for two whole minutes, guaranteed to feel like ten.

9. Press the panel back down onto the studs.

10. After another 20 minutes, go over all the in between studs and the edges again and apply pressure once more. That's to make sure panel sticks firmly and sits evenly on the studs.

Combo Application

1. In general you follow the adhesive route first and then secure the edges of the panel and the top and bottom edges with some of those color co-ordinated nails we talked about earlier. You won't need them in the middle of the panels.

2. Measure and cut baseboards.

3. Stain to match paneling. Finish with coat of clear varnish.

4. Install baseboards except in area where platform will be.

5. Apply inside molding strips to all the inside corners of your room.

6. If you have an outside corner, put a strip of outside corner molding along it.

7. Put straight molding around your window and door openings.

8. If you like you can put strips of molding to form a chair rail or to make some design on your walls, too (Fig. 13-10).

Fig. 13-9. Measuring and cutting window opening into panel.

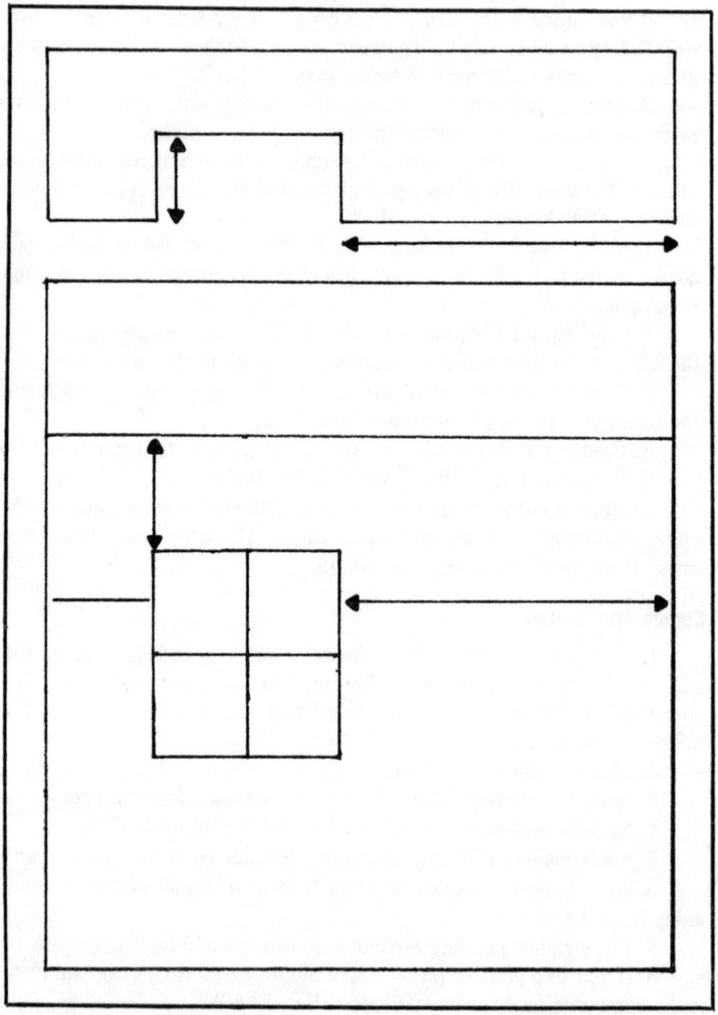

182

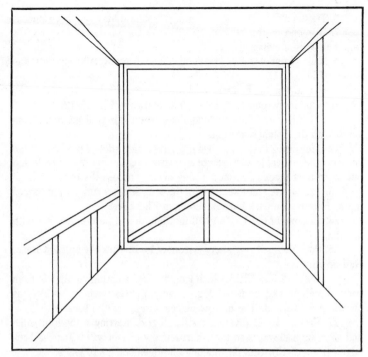

Fig. 13-10. Various ways of applying molding to trim paneled walls.

PROJECT 8: BUILDING A PLATFORM FOR "L" SHAPED NOOK AND MAKING STORAGE DRAWERS

Materials:

5	1×10's	12-foot long;	2	1×10	10-feet long;
4	1×10	14-foot long;	4	1×3	10-feet long;
4	1×2	12-foot long;	3½	4×8	½-inch plywood panels;
4½	4×8	¾-inch panels;	5	1×3	12-foot;

6d nails; 2d finishing nails; corner braces; screws; 21 ornamental drawer pulls; mending plates; ball bearing casters (40); glue; stain and varnish; molding.

Tools: Saber saw, electric drill, wood bit, hammer, carpenter's apron, carpenter's square, measuring tape, sandpaper, miter box.

Instructions:

    1. Cut five lengths of 6-foot 6-inches off your 14 foot 1 × 10's.

    2. Cut one 10-foot 1×10 to 9-foot 6-inches.

    3. Nail the five shorter 1×10's to one of the 12-foot 1×10's as in Fig. 13-11.

    4. Nail 9-foot 6-inch 1×10 at remaining end.

    5. Move entire grid into the L-shaped space.

6. Tie structure into walls by nailing through studs on all three sides.

7. Tie one of the 10-foot 1×10's and one of the 12-foot 1×10's together with mending plates.

8. Nail to front of grid and tie remaining end into wall through studs as above. (Fig. 13-11).

9. Cut 12 lengths of 1×10 to 3-foot length.

10. Notch one end ¾ × 1¼-inch as shown in Fig. 13-12.

11. Attach one of the short lengths on each side wall and to the long 1×10 with the notches in front.

12. Measure 2 feet (24 inches from the inside edge of the 1×10), and lay in another short piece. Measure again from inside edge of this 1×10 and put down next piece. Continue in this manner across the room.

13. Fasten the short sections to the long section with corner braces top and bottom on each side as shown in Fig. 13-12.

14. Cut one of the 1×2's to 10-foot length and tie it to another with mending plates.

15. Put combined 1×2's across front of 1×10's into the notched areas. Nail down.

16. Cut 1×2 into 12 25¾-inch lengths. Use as bridging 3½ feet from back. Bevel short edges at a 45 degree angle, then fasten between 1×10 as shown in Fig. 13-13. The narrow pieces will fall in the back.

17. Fasten ¾-inch plywood panels to grid, starting at the front edge and working backwards so that short narrow pieces will fall at the back edges (Fig. 13-13). Nail down along all edges and 1×10 joists.

Storage Drawers

Materials: Included in list above.
Tools: Ditto.

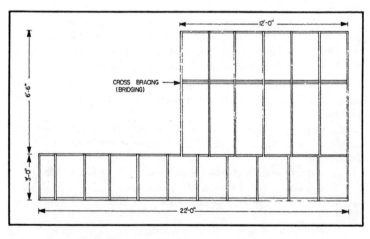

Fig. 13-11. Grid of storage platform frame work.

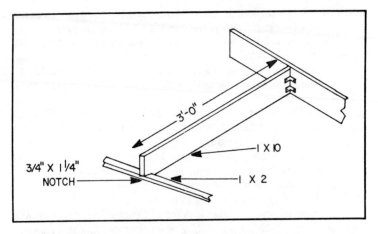

3/4" × 1¼"
NOTCH

I × 2

I × 10

3'-0"

Fig. 13-12. Joining short platform sections with corner braces.

Instructions:

1. There will be 10 drawers in the unit, 11 if you take the option to make a narrow additional one instead of boxing in as in Fig. 12-20. Make and fit one drawer at a time.

2. You may cut all the pieces for the drawers at one time. 10 pieces 8½ × 23½ inches; 10 pieces 10 × 24½ inches; 10 pieces 23½ × 35½ inches; and 20 pieces 8½ × 35½ inches.

3. Next cut your 1 × 3's to 35½-inch length. You'll need 20.

4. Sort out and pile up the pieces for each drawer this way: you'll need one 8½ × 23½ inch piece for the back; two 8½ × 35½ inch for the sides;

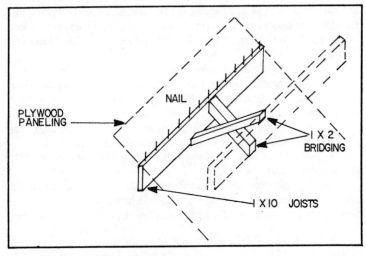

PLYWOOD
PANELING

NAIL

I × 2
BRIDGING

I × 10   JOISTS

Fig. 13-13. Constructing 1 ×2's into bridging.

one 23½ × 35½ inch piece for the bottom and one 10 × 24½ inch piece for the front of the drawer. Two of the 1 × 3's you'll use for cleats.

5. Glue and nail, with finishing nails, the sides, back and front panels to the bottom as in Fig. 13-14.

6. Reinforce with corner braces or chain braces as shown Fig. 13-14.

7. Secure cleats along each side at the outside bottom of the drawer with # 5 screws.

8. Attach small ball bearing casters. One to each corner at the bottom of the cleats and one in the middle of each cleat. Six in all.

9. Sand drawers thoroughly.

10. Stain and varnish to match paneling.

11. Line inside of drawers with quilted contact paper for linens, and plain contact paper for other storage.

12. Stain and varnish molding to match.

13. Measure, cut and miter molding to fit around outside of drawer front as in Fig. 13-15. Attach with color co-ordinated finishing nails.

14. Attach two of the ornamental drawer pulls to each front panel. Drill holes first.

Finishing Platform/Drawer Combo

Materials: 2 12-foot strips of 1¾-inch lattice molding; base boards; varnish; stain; sealer; finishing nails; drawer pull; ½-inch quarter-round plywood scraps; molding; indoor/outdoor rug tiles.
Tools: Saber saw, hammer, measuring tape, brush, rags.
Instructions:

1. Now is the time to decide on your choice of filling in the extra space (in our case it was an extra 15 inches). You can figure your extra measurement out by adding the numbers of drawers, then multiplying the number of 1×10 dividers by ¾-inch, adding the two numbers and subtracting the total from the entire front platform measurement (i.e.) 10 drawers @ 2 feet = 20 feet; 12×¾ = 9 inches; 22 feet − 20 feet 9 inches = 1 foot 3 inches or 15 inches.

2. You can make a fake drawer front by cutting a plywood piece 14½ × 10 inches, and sanding, staining and varnishing it as you did the other drawer fronts. Also trim it with molding to match the rest and affix a single drawer pull.

3. Cut a piece of 1 × 2 15-inches long and set it in the opening of the platform. Fasten to uprights with corner braces as in Fig. 13-16.

4. Nail drawer front to platform with color co-ordinated finishing nails.

5. For a little more work you can have an extra drawer, albeit a narrow one. Cut two pieces of plywood 8½ × 35½ inches; one piece 14½ × 8½ inches; and a piece 14½ × 35½ inches plus two cleats of 1 × 3 35½-inches long.

6. Construct this drawer the same as you did the wide ones and slide in place.

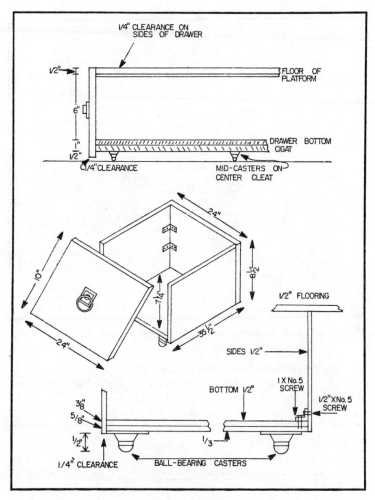

Fig. 13-14. Storage drawer construction in detail.

7. In either case, sand, stain and varnish the ¾-inch side of your 1 × 10 in the front of the platform.

8. Apply two coats of good latex sealer to the plywood.

9. Lay carpet tiles as directed in Conversion I, Project 8, starting tiles even with the front edge of the platform.

10. Stain and varnish lattice strips to match drawers.

11. Glue and nail lattice strips across the front of the platform so that the top edge of the lattice strip is even with the top pile of the rug tiles (Fig. 13-15).

187

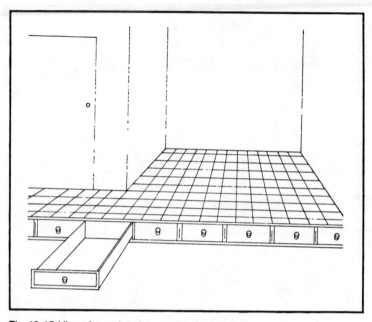

Fig. 13-15. View of completed storage platform and drawers.

12. Put the rest of the baseboards around the platform.

13. Finish platform with stained to match quarter-round along the edges of the walls.

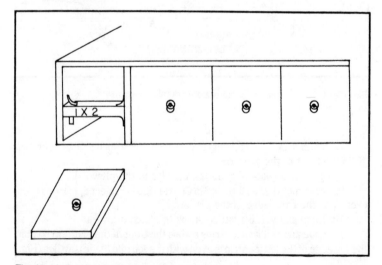

Fig. 13-16. Construction of false drawer front.

PROJECT 9: INSTALLING INDOOR/OUTDOOR CARPET TILES

Materials: Cement sealer; indoor/outdoor carpet tiles; a piece of matching indoor/outdoor carpet for patio; double-faced carpet tape; quarter round.

Tools: Large paint brush, vacuum, broom, measuring tape, pencil, carpenter's square, straight edge, carpet knife, scissors.

Instructions:

1. Clean floor thoroughly (sweep, scrub and rinse well).
2. Seal with two coats of sealer—indoors and out.
3. Lay carpet tiles as directed in Conversion I, Project 8.
4. On patio, measure and mark area to be covered with carpeting. The carpeting should start at the sliding doors and go over to the divider and be as wide as the old garage door openings.
5. Cut and put down strips of double-faced carpet tape around the inside edges of the marked area.
6. Run additional strips of the carpet tape every two feet, running between the doors and the divider.
7. Cut carpeting to fit. First mark on reverse side with felt marker and straight edge. Cut with carpet knife and straight edge or with heavy duty scissors if you prefer.
8. Peel off paper on tapes and gently ease carpet down on the tape along one short side.
9. Unroll the carpet piece and put in place gently, lining up long edge with one tape as you proceed.
10. Press down firmly on all tape joints.
11. If you have to piece the rug, let the seam fall in the middle of two tapes put down side by side.
12. Carpet can be taken up and replaced if necessary.

Note: Remember to put your carpet tiles under your platform, too, in the spaces that will be occupied by the drawers.

13. Finish rug tiling job by putting down quarter-round all around, on the inside, of course, not on the patio.

PROJECT 10: MAKING A PRIVACY SCREEN

Materials: 7 12-foot 1×4's and 1 6-foot 1×4;
54 12-foot 1¾-inch wide lattice moldings; 6d nails, 15 lag bolts, sealer, paint or varnish and stain.

Tools: Electric drill, masonry bit, wood bit, hammer, measuring tape.

Instructions:

1. Cut your seven 12-foot 1×4's in half.
2. Build a 6-foot square frame (Fig. 13-17).
3. Trim 1½ inch off another 6-foot 1×4 and nail it in center of frame.
4. Repeat the above instructions to construct three square frames with a center post each.
5. Cut the 1¾-inch lattice molding into 6-foot long strips.
6. Attach frame to driveway with lag bolts. See step 5, 6 and 7, Conversion I, Project 2.

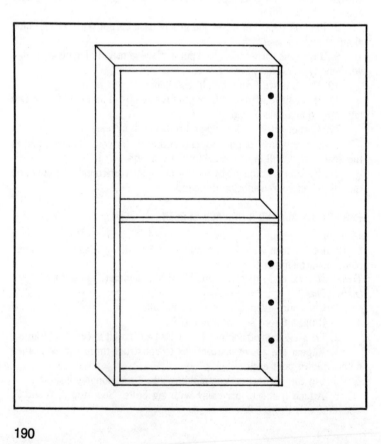

Fig. 13-17. Construction of privacy screen framing.

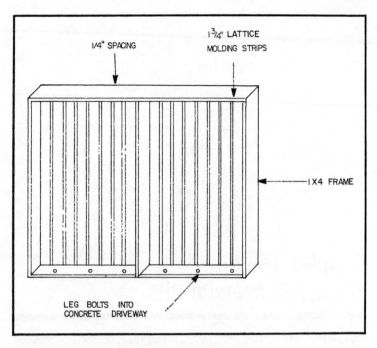

Fig. 13-18. Finishing construction of privacy screen.

7. Tie second and third frame to first and tie down with lag bolts, too. Nail or bolt together.

8. Nail lattice molding to privacy screen on the street side of the frame. Allow ¼-inch spaces between strips of lattice molding.

9. Countersink lag bolts and nails or bolts on sides of frame.

10. Sand well.

11. Seal and paint privacy screen to match trim on house; or stain, and seal; or use varnish stain. If you like the natural look just seal the wood (Fig. 13-18).

Chapter 14
Garage Conversion III

This garage, double-sized and attached to the house, presented somewhat of a problem. The house sat fairly close to the street and the street was quite busy and narrow. Parking on the street was hazardous. The garage did have two small windows along one of the walls—the other long wall was attached to the house—and though we had a bit more space between the garage and the hedge, a bamboo one this time, than we did in Conversion II we felt that even if we enlarged the windows, we needed a lot of extra light.

The conventional solutions of putting windows and/or sliding glass doors into the garage door opening didn't seem too desirable. Since we had to park our two cars in the short drive, this meant that the hoods of the cars would be only a few feet from the window or door. And frankly, neither one of us fancies such close proximity with our cars—at least as far as view is concerned.

However, at the back of the garage was a very nice backyard, not only completely fenced-in but also surrounded by bamboo and a number of lovely shrubs. Both of us longed for easy access to the backyard which at the time could only be reached through the kitchen door. It would be such a blessing not to have the kids tripping through the kitchen on their regular runs to and from their rooms and the bathroom.

So, after much soul searching and figuring, we decided to close up the front entirely and build a storage wall and sewing center in front of it to muffle the street noise. We decided to cut an opening in the back, about equal in area to the garage door opening, and set our sliding glass doors in there.

We chose to use two sliding glass doors instead of only one and some fixed panes of glass because we wanted to take full advantage of the prevailing breezes which, fortunately, came from that direction.

We wanted to finish the walls in sheetrock because we were planning to have a room with a south-of-the-border flavor (we had just returned from a most enjoyable trip to Mexico) and wanted stark white walls, dark woodwork and Saltillo tiles on the floor.

The Saltillo tiles actually started the whole south-of-the-border bit. It was a great solution to the problem of a rather marred garage floor, too cracked to take vinyl tile or rug tiles, but good enough for a base for the Saltillo or De Hanis tiles. In addition, the Saltillo tiles helped raise the garage floor about 2 inches which made the step down from the house lower and therefore more comfortable, particularly for the little kids. Also, it gave us a floor that a swipe with a damp mop would keep neat and clean and one, thank God, that wouldn't show every bit of mud tracked in by the innumerable little feet that trampled on it. See before and after floor plans Fig. 14-1A-B.

PROJECT 1: REMOVING GARAGE DOORS

Follow directions in Conversion I, Project 1, A or B whichever applies in your case. Check the illustrations in Chapter 12 for greater detail of removing spring powered garage doors.

PROJECT 2: WALLING IN GARAGE DOOR OPENING COMPLETELY

Now that our garage doors have been completely removed, we're going to have to wall up the opening they left in order to have a place for any new windows or doors we wish to install. We'll start first with putting up the rough outline or frame of the wall, then go on to finishing both the inside and outside.

Roughing In The Wall

Materials: 2 16-foot 2 × 4s; 13 7-foot 2 × 4s; 4 4 × 8 foot ½-inch thick plywood panels (sheathing);
16 d nails; lag bolts; lockwashers; mending plates; 15-pound felt paper and enough siding to cover.
Tools: Saber saw, hammer, measuring tape, wrecking bar, carpenter's square, pencil, electric drill, slip-stick.
Instructions:

1. For hassle-free construction use a new top plate and build your wall on the floor as suggested in Garage Conversion I, Project 2, then set the whole thing in place.
2. Measure the length of the entire door opening at the top.
3. Cut two 2×4s to this length.
4. One of these is the top plate, the other the sole plate.
5. Set the sole plate aside for now.

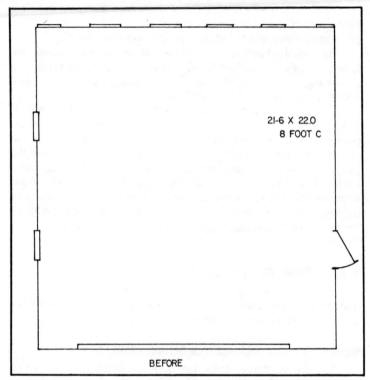

BEFORE

21-6 X 22.0
8 FOOT C

Fig. 14-1A. Scale plan showing before view of Conversion III.

6. Mark the top plate with spaces that are 1½ inches wide and 16 inches distant from center to center of each area, starting at one end of your 2×4. See Fig. 14-2. These markings indicate where your studs will go.

7. Do not change the spacing of studs so you'll come out even at the other end of your 2×4. Instead, mark your last two studs as close together as necessary. Want to know why? Because wallboard panels conform to the 16-inch on-center spacing and you're going to use wallboard on the inside of your wall. So you need to be consistent.

8. Now place your sole plate next to your top plate and transfer all the markings exactly to your sole plate, using your carpenter's square (Fig. 14-2).

9. Treat your sole plate with wood preservative.

10. Remove trim and jambs around garage door with your wrecking bar and hammer.

11. Put sole plate in place and tie down. Details, steps 1-8, Conversion I, Project 2.

12. Measure the exact length of each of the 13 studs with your slip-stick from the sole plate to the existing top plate and cut them each *1½ inches shorter* to allow for your new top plate.

194

13. Set the top plate on its side on the floor and nail in the 13 studs in the places marked, using two 16d nails through the top plate and into the top of each stud to tie them in securely.

14. Brace your work for nailing by inserting 14½-inch lengths of 2×4s between the members to be nailed (Fig. 14-3).

15. Now line up some helpers and with their help raise the frame for your new wall in place.

16. Line up your new and old top plate lines then drive 16d nails through your new side studs and top plate into the old studs and top plate. Use pairs of nails at approximately 16-inch intervals.

17. Tap your studs into place on the positions marked on the sole plate and toe-nail all into place.

18. If you don't like toe-nailing, use angle braces. You are now ready for finishing your exterior wall.

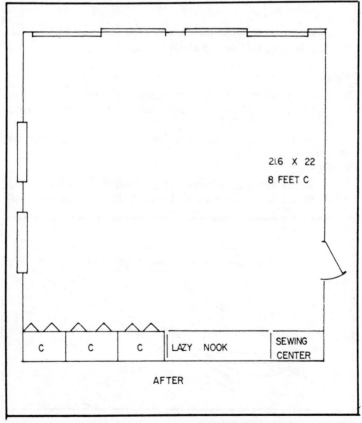

Fig. 14-1B. Scale plan showing after view of Conversion III.

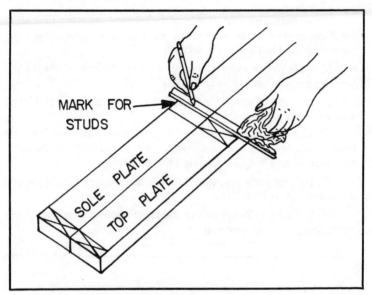

Fig. 14-2. Marking sole and top plates for studs.

Finishing New Wall

Materials: Sheathing, either asphalt-impregnated sheathing or C-D exterior plywood; plus 15-pound felt paper, enough of either to cover entire opening; siding to match; 6d nails, sealer (optional).

Tools: Measuring tape, pencil, calculator, large scissors, saber saw, wrecking bar, claw hammer, hammer.

Instructions:

1. If your siding is horizontal siding, either wood, metal or plastic, follow steps 1-13 in Conversion II, Project 2, Finishing Exterior Wall.

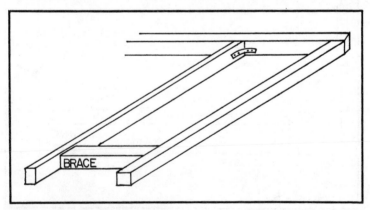

Fig. 14-3. Bracing between studs.

2. If your siding is vertical follow these directions: Instead of the asphalt impregnated sheathing use C-D exterior plywood in the same thickness as your existing sheathing. Nail in place, allowing 1/16-inch between panels.

3. Nail 15-pound felt paper in place over plywood sheathing covering entire surface.

4. Nail vertical siding in place, following nailing pattern of existing siding.

5. Caulk the bottom of the new wall for water proofing.

6. If you're using wood siding seal all new wood.

7. Paint to match rest of siding.

PROJECT 3: ROUGHING IN WIRING

If you want some wiring in the new wall now is the time to do it. A couple of outlets on each side of the wall would be most useful. Follow directions regarding installing receptacles as given in Conversion I, Project 7.

PROJECT 4: CUTTING OPENING IN WALL FOR SLIDING GLASS DOORS

Materials: 4 2×4s of ceiling height (for braces), 1 1×12 for brace.
Tools: Pencil, long straight edge, electric drill with ⅜-inch spade bit, heavy leather or work gloves, claw hammer, wrecking bar, saber saw and multi-purpose saw, tin snips (optional).

Breaking through a garage wall to open up the inside to the outside via sliding glass doors is not nearly as difficult or time consuming as you might think. Even if you encounter stucco walls, which are the worst, it is relatively uncomplicated.

Since demolishing a stucco wall is just a special case of demolition, we are going to include the extra steps it takes to demolish said stucco wall. If yours, you should be so lucky, is not stucco, just ignore the steps outlined for stucco wall demolition.

When you are taking out a section of a garage wall, you're also taking out a section of a load bearing wall. This means that you have to have some special bracing for the wall while demolishing parts of it and before you can install a new header that will carry the load over the new opening safely.

Table 14-1 gives you header sizes for various kinds of openings up to 12 feet wide. Fig. 14-4 gives you the details on making up a header out of 2-inch material which is much more economical to use than the regular 4×6 or 4×8 beams. However, since each 2 ×... is only as we learned much much earlier 1½ ×... you'll need a ½-inch piece of plywood to nail in between to bring the total of your fake "beam" up to 3½ inches, the width of the studs.

On a bearing wall it is a good idea to avoid the use of cripple studs above the door and window openings. Building engineers recommend that

Table 14-1.Recommended Header Sizes.

Width of Opening:	Header size if floor and roof above:	Header size if roof only above:
3'-0"	2-2×4's	2-2×4's
3'-6"	2-2×6's	2-2'4's
4'-0" to 6'-0"	2-2×6's	2-2×6's
6'-0" to 8'-0"	2-2×8's	2-2×8's
8'-0" to 10'-0"	2-2×12's	2-2×10's
10'-0" to 12'-0"	2-2×14's	2-2×14's

you install oversized headers which go from the top of the door or window opening to the top plate. So be it.

Most outside garage walls do not contain any wiring or plumbing. But it's a good idea, just to be on the safe side, to double check yours before you

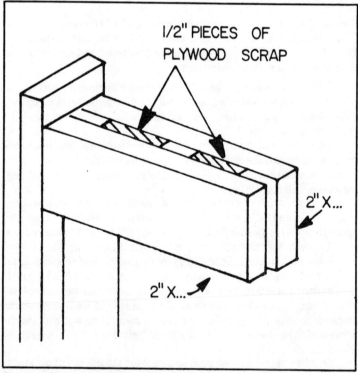

1/2" PIECES OF PLYWOOD SCRAP

2" X...

2" X...

Fig. 14-4. Constructing a header.

wield that saw. Relocating plumbing is quite an expensive proposition. So if there are plumbing outlets in the wall, even an innocuous little outside water faucet or a venting stack coming through the roof above the wall— *beware!* Either bow out and choose another wall for the hatchet job or have a plumber, hopefully a friend or relative who won't charge the current rate, stand by the day you knock out the inside of that wall.

Relocating electrical outlets is not all that complicated. Just be sure the current is off, at the fuse box or circuit breaker, before you run into the "line" wires with your trusty saw.

You can probably move your door or window openings to one side or the other and avoid wiring and/or plumbing complications all together.

Other things to take into consideration are:

1. Avoid extra framing by placing your new door frame about two inches inside an existing stud.

2. Check your wall on the outside, as well as on the inside. Visualize how that new outside wall will look. That sliding glass door centered in the wall may look all right from the inside and really weird from the outside, like the nose of a monster face, or something. Try to find a good solution that will look well outside and inside. And, if at first you don't succeed— back to the drawing board for a second, or even third and fourth try. Don't begrudge time at this point. Better spend a lot of it now: it'll really be only a fraction of the time that the new opening will grace, or mar your wall.

3. Use sliding glass doors of standard height, (i.e.) 6-foot 10-inches to match the other doors you may have in your new family room.

4. Sliding glass doors come in both metal and wood frames. Lately there have been variations on the basic sliding glass door model that most of us grew up with. Pick what you like. Do remember that double or thermo panes are a great help in insulating. The variation between wood and aluminum framing as far as heat conductivity is concerned is real, but not as critical, since there's a lot less frame than glass. So consult the price of each, the state of your pocket book, and your calculator to figure out the rate of saving on the reduced heat loss per decade and see if the present extra outlay is worth it. (Do this if your mind set is in that direction, otherwise go by instinct).

5. Take it slow and easy. Remember, you're not knocking out an entire wall. You're simply cutting an opening. So keep it at that and don't make yourself some extra work when you have to re-finish that wall.

Instructions:

1. Figure out the exact size of your opening, allowing for header and framing studs.

2. Mark exact opening to be cut on the inside wall.

3. Bore holes all the way through the wall.

4. Using the holes as guide, outline opening on outside of wall.

5. You're going to stay outside for some work now.

6a. *Stucco* Your stucco is probably laid on over chicken wire nailed to the sheathing. Chicken wire can be very nasty and tear up your hands in no time. So if you're dealing with stucco wear heavy leather gloves.

b. Divide the exterior opening outline into a grid of approximately 2-foot squares.

c. Smash the stucco with a hammer a 2-foot square at a time, until the chicken wire is exposed.

d. Use tin snips to cut the wire all around the 2-foot square and pull the entire section off the sheathing.

e. Proceed in this way until you've removed the stucco and chicken-wire from the entire area of the proposed door opening.

7. If you're removing shingles or wood siding from an outside wall, use a claw hammer and saw. Same goes for plastic or metal siding.

8. Be very careful to cut your horizontal siding accurately. We know of no good way to patch up a mistake.

9. Returning inside, try to remove the wallboard, if there is any, or the paneling as intact as possible. To do this, pry up gently with your claw hammer or wrecking bar and remove carefully so you can recycle them on the other side.

10. Gypsum board can be sawed to an accurate, neat line. Watch for the taped joints, though and take the panels apart there, that way you'll save yourself a lot of sawing.

11. When you have both the inside and outside wall surfaces removed, you are ready to do the exciting bit, cutting through the sheathing and studs.

12. For this job you'll use the multi-purpose saw you have acquired through purchase, rental or scrounging. Otherwise go with your trusty old saber saw.

13. But before the excitement there's one more step to take; building a temporary support as shown in Fig. 14-5.

14. Use at least three 2×4s wedged between a 2×4 flat on the floor and a 1×12 planted against the ceiling.

15. A blanket can be folded and put between the 1×12 and the ceiling to keep the ceiling finish intact.

16. You'll need a helper to set up this support system. Let the helper hold up the 1×12 (and blanket) while you wedge the 2×4s in as the vertical supports.

17. Measure carefully from the floor up and mark each stud individually before you cut any.

18. Your framing opening needs to be ½-inch larger than the height of the door plus the width of the header.

19. Saw through the studs and pry them off the frame at the sole plate.

20. In our case it wasn't practical to use an oversized header since our garage wall was almost 9 feet high. So we went the cripple stud route. If you have that much wall or almost that much wall left do the same.

21. Leave the top part of the studs you sawed through in place and they can do duty as cripple studs for you.

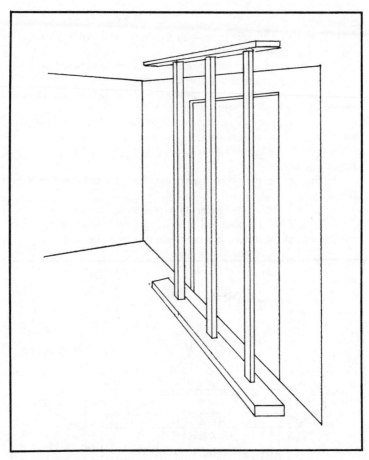

Fig. 14-5.Building a temporary support for newly cut opening.

22. Save your sawed-off studs, too, you can use them as trimmer studs.

23. Cut through the sheathing and remove.

24. Saw through the section of sole plate you need to remove to set in your door or doors.

PROJECT 5: FRAMING AND INSTALLING SLIDING GLASS DOORS

Materials: 2 2×6s, the length of the opening; scrap of 6-inch wide ½-inch plywood or several scraps to piece out to the length of the opening; sliding glass door or doors; thin wood pieces of shingles for shims; hardware for doors; 16d nails.

Tools: Carpenter's square, level, screwdriver.

Instructions:

1. Construct your fake beam—cut the two 2 ×6s to the exact measurement of the top of the opening.

2. Cut plywood strips and make a sandwich of the plywood between two 2×6s. Nail together and use as a unit (Fig. 14-4).

3. Check and recheck your measurements on header and trimmer studs so they will all fit tightly together.

4. Nail the trimmer stud that goes in on the non-locking side of your door (Fig. 14-6) to the outside stud.

5. Inspect your header for bow or warpage so you can install it with its convex side up.

6. Yell for a helper. When he arrives, line up your header with the door opening.

7. Lift one end of the header up to rest on the trimmer stud.

8. Use a piece of scrap metal or plywood to make a temporary rest to hold that end of the header in place while you raise the other.

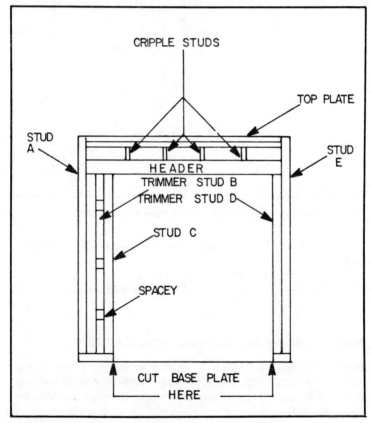

Fig. 14-6. Framing in new opening.

8. Cut a ½-inch triangular wedge off the other end of the header so that the header may be forced into place without binding.

9. Raise the other end of the header into place and force the other trimmer stud (B) into place underneath it.

10. Nail the trimmer stud to its outside stud.

11. Secure header by toe-nailing and/or with mending plates or T-plates.

12. Toe-nail the cripple studs to the header or use mending plates or corner braces.

13. If, by any wild chance or cutting, one or more of the cripple studs do not make contact with the header, force shingle or thin wood wedges into the gap before attaching stud to header.

14. Force under and nail in place the additional trimmer stud (C) and any blocking required to bring door framing to proper width.

15. When you plan to install two doors as we did proceed thusly: When you lay out your opening make it big enough to include the measurement for two doors plus the extra ½-inch all around for each plus an 18-inch section in the center to become the center post (Fig. 14-7).

16. When you start blocking out on the inside wall draw out the two door rectangles with the post in the middle.

17. Make sure that the post includes two studs, one on each side of the proposed post.

18. Cut out each of the rectangles as described.

19. Proceed as above with each opening, adding trimmer studs on each side of post.

20. Unless you have a paved patio, driveway or walk outside your new door openings that is level with the concrete slab floor of your garage, you will need to install flashing. Flashing sometimes comes with your door as you buy it, so check this out before you run out to get more.

21. Install precisely as the manufacturer instructs you to do, butting the vertical flange to the edge of the slab floor and fastening it in place with lag screws.

22. Be sure to form a "dam" by applying a bead of mastic along the length of the flashing and across the two ends.

23. Now you are ready to install the door frame into the door framing. Re-call your helper if he/she has wandered off.

24. Follow instructions for installing sliding glass doors in Conversion II, Project 4.

PROJECT 6: CUTTING BIGGER WINDOW OPENINGS AND INSTALLING NEW WINDOWS

Materials: Two new windows of desired size, sufficient lengths of 2×4s for framing and for headers, 16d nails.

Tools: Multi-purpose saw or saber saw, wrecking bar, claw hammer, long straight edge, drill and bits, pencil, level.

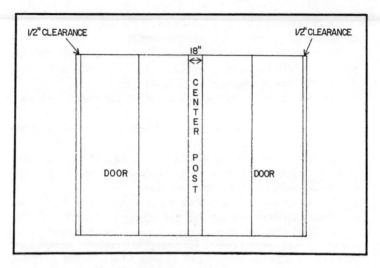

Fig. 14-7. Dimensions of opening and doors.

Instructions:

1. Remove trim from around old window, outside and inside.
2. With wrecking bar gently pry window loose from framing.
3. Remove entire window unit.
4. Enlarge window opening, following procedure for cutting door into wall above.
5. Cut a 2×4 to fit into opening as support for window sill.
6. Nail to studs below and on sides.
7. Use header according to the header size list (Table 13-1).
8. If you are using a wooden window, seal wood, inside and out.

PROJECT 7: FINISHING WALLS AND CEILING

Materials: Gypsum board to cover walls and ceiling; polystyrene foam boards; insulating bats; staples; nails; drywall nails; tape; joint compound; mask; baseboards; quarter-round; wood stain and varnish.
Tools: Saber saw, straight edge, pencil, measuring tape, knife.
Instructions:

1. If you want to install any additional wiring, now is the time to do it. Follow instructions for Conversion I, Project 7.
2. Insulate your walls, old and new, following the steps outlined in Conversion II, Project 7.
3. Your foam boards of insulation will go directly on the underside of your roof sheathing.
4. Nail in with roofing nails on 8-inch centers in both directions.
5. Use nails long enough to penetrate well into the roof sheathing but not so long that they puncture the shingles or other roofing material.
6. Get a helper. Installing a drywall ceiling is not difficult for two.

7. Always cover your ceiling before covering your walls.

8. Measure your ceiling dimensions from top plate to top plate both ways.

9. Make a scale drawing of the ceiling as if you were looking up at it, drawing in your joists.

10. Cut out paper or cardboard panels, in scale with your drawing and place them, long sides at right angles, short sides parallel to the ceiling joists onto your scale drawing.

11. The ends of the wallboard must come out even with the center lines of the joists.

12. Trim your scale wallboard if necessary to get that alignment and stagger the joints so you'll have a minimum of continuous seams on a single joist.

13. Follow the pattern when you lay out your wallboard panels.

14. Place your full sheets of wall board from the walls inwards as in Fig. 14-8, with any necessary filler strips placed in the center of the ceiling.

15. Keep your pattern handy so you can consult it often.

16. Look at the joists that run parallel to two of your walls and see if either are more than 4 inches out from the wall. If not you're in luck.

17. If they are out more than 4 inches you'll need to make some nailing blocks for the ends of your wallboard panels.

18. Make L-shaped blocks from 2×4 scraps and 10d nails and construct as in Fig. 14-9. The short part of the L should be 1½ inches shorter than the width of the joist and the long part as long as the distance between the joist that runs on top of the wall top plate and the next joist over.

19. Nail the L-shaped blocks to the joists and top plate on 16-inch centers and in the corners to provide a nailing surface for the wallboard where the corners join (Fig. 14-9).

20. Mark guidelines for your nails on the plates directly underneath each joist end and nailing blocks to make sight lines for your wallboard nails.

21. With your caulking gun hang a zig-zag bead of wallboard panel adhesive along each joist that will be in contact with the wallboard.

22. This will reduce the number of nails you must drive while practically standing on your head. Keep in mind that you not only have to drive those nails, but you'll also have to cover each and every one of those nail heads with joint compound later on.

23. Make a T-brace from 2×4s the height of your ceiling or a little longer. The cross piece should be from 2 to 3 feet long (Fig. 14-10).

24. Back to your scale drawing and cardboard cut outs. Take another good look and with it as a guide proceed.

25. With your helper, start hutting up a 4×8 wallboard panel in a corner of the room. Put it up with the helper and the T-brace and check to make sure the end cuts across the center line of a joist.

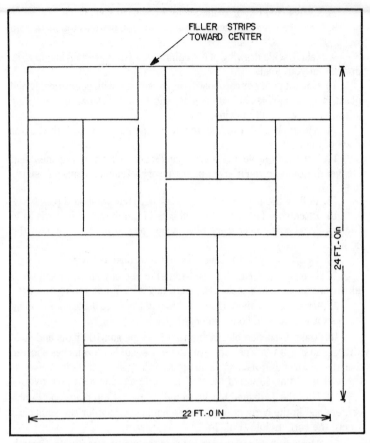

Fig. 14-8. Pattern for applying gypsum board panels to the ceiling.

26. If it doesn't, mark the wallboard on both sides where the center line falls and trim to fit. (See Chapter 9, for detailed directions for scoring and cutting wall board).

27. Drive the first nail at the center of the sheet about ½-inch from one edge. Drywall nails are sharp enough to penetrate into the board with hard pressure and will hang there while you drive them home. So you can use one hand to hold the board against the joist while nailing without worrying about the nails.

28. Here is a trick to help you survive that nasty upside-down nailing position. Hold the hammer directly in front of your face with your thumb against the "underside" of the handle. (Normally you'd hold it with the thumb against the "top" of the handle). Now hit the nails by *rotating* your forearm. Practice makes perfect.

29. Nail at 16-inch intervals along the joist lines you previously marked on the top plates.

30. Nail ½-inch in from all edges.

31. Make sure you "dimple" the surface of the wallboard on the last blow on your nail so that the nail head can be hidden by filling the dimple with joint compound.

32. When you notice that the next sheet will require cuts for light fixtures, air vents or such, measure in from the closest edges already installed to the fixture and use these measurements to locate the opening on your wallboard.

33. Measure the fixture itself and draw the opening onto your wallboard panel.

34. Make a plunge cut and cut out the opening with your saber saw.

35. Spread joint cement with a 4-inch joint knife over all the joints then apply reinforcing tape over the length of the joints.

36. Press tape into place firmly and wipe off any excess compound.

37. Give the joints a 24-hour setting and drying rest, and then apply a second coat.

38. Spread out this coat a bit wider and feather toward the edges.

39. Let dry and set again, then sand lightly with fine sandpaper. *Caution*: It has been discovered that many, if not all, of the joint compound mixtures contain asbestos. Since you breathe in a lot of the dust when you stand there and sand over your head, we advise that you wear a *protective mask* over your mouth and nose.

40. Fill in, let dry and set, and sand all nail hole dimples in the same way.

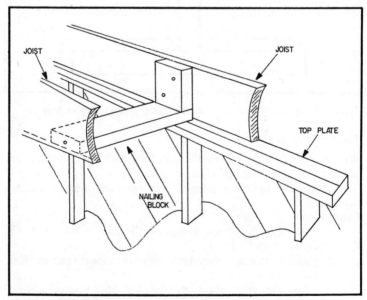

Fig. 14-9. Putting in a nailing block.

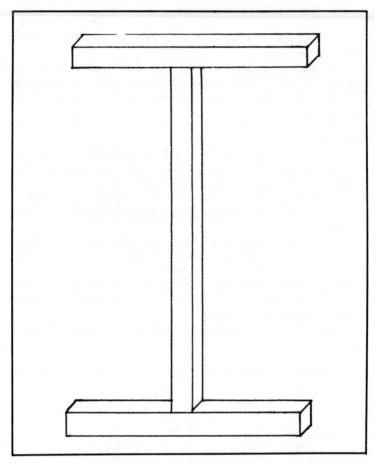

Fig. 14-10. Making a T-brace for installing a gypsum board ceiling.

Finishing The Walls

Materials: Wallboard to cover walls; joint compound; tape; drywall nails; drywall panel adhesive; insulation batts; staples.

Tools: Saber saw, straight edge, pencil, measuring tape, 4-inch joint knife, staple gun.

Instructions:

1. Staple insulating batts between studs all round the room (details in Conversion II, Project 7.)

2. Apply adhesive to studs and plate surfaces as you did on the ceiling installation.

3. In this case, your nails need not be any closer than 24 inches.

4. Measure in to all window, door or other openings from the edges of the mounted wallboard panel to establish the opening location.

5. Draw opening actual size, naturally, on the board and cut with saw as you did for light fixtures.

6. Don't forget to fill in with bits of insulation around your window and outside door openings to complete your insulating job.

7. It is easier and faster to score on both sides and snap the wallboard than it is to saw. So get brave and try that method of fitting wallboard. Once learned you'll use it as often as possible.

8. Scrap pieces of wallboard can be used in sections around doors, windows, and other such small areas.

9. Finish the joints between panels with joint cement and tape as we told you to do in the section about the ceiling, just above. And don't forget to fill in those dimples.

PROJECT 8: STORAGE WALL

As we've said before, the street in front of the house was quite noisy so we decided to put a storage wall against the new wall. Basically we used the same closet design as in Conversion I, Project 3, with a few adaptations that we'll get to shortly. We adapted one of the closet sections for a sewing center but separated it from the rest with open shelves and a pillow nook to disguise the slight discrepancy in depth due to the doors on the sewing center.

Materials: Use material list in Conversion I, Project 3 and add the following: ½-inch sheet of 4×8 plywood, ¾-inch thick; 2 2×4s, 1 4-feet long; 1 2×4 8-feet long; toggle bolts.

Tools: Same as in Conversion I, Project 3.

Instructions:

1. The real difference is that our closets will have to be raised off the slab by about 1½ inches to allow for the Saltillo or DeHanis tile we'll install later.

2. We could possibly lay the tile first and make the closet later but that is a hassle and doesn't work half as well. We'll bring the closet up to the DeHanis floor level by setting it up on a 2×4 frame and providing it with a floor.

3. Locate the studs in your wall.

4. Measure and draw a rough diagram of your storage wall on the cement slab.

5. Lay out one of your long (14-foot) 2×4s and mark for size.

6. Cut it and the other long 2×4 to size.

7. Lay the 2×4, 4-inch side down, along the back wall, tied down with toggle bolts.

8. Cut nine pieces of 2×4 to 14-inch lengths and lay out at right angles to long 2×4 spacing them 18 inches apart with one piece at each end.

9. Lay other long 2×4 in front of short ones to complete grid.

10. Nail together. Toggle bolt to slab along front edge and short edges of grid as well as all the short 2×4s in between.

11. Cut ¾-inch plywood to cover grid completely from wall to front edge of front 2×4.

12. Nail in place.

13. You have now raised the floor level of your closets 1½ inches... the ¾-inch of your plywood plus the ¾-inch of your 2×4.

14. Continue building your closet storage wall by following direction in Conversion I, Project 3 steps 1 through 23.

15. Follow instructions on how to install fold doors in Conversion I, Project 3, steps 1-13.

16. For installation of shelves follow Conversion I, Project 3, steps 1 through 3.

17. If you want hanging space in one of the closets and room for your ironing board follow steps 4 through 10 in the same project. To accommodate the ironing board you should install your pole at 5-feet 6-inches from the closet floor (higher if your ironing board happens to be outsized, so measure first) and raise the shelf above the pole accordingly.

18. Follow Project 3 for finishing the storage wall.

PROJECT 9: SEWING CENTER

Materials: 3 8-foot 2×4s; 6 ceiling height 2×4s; 1 sheet of ¾-inch plywood; 1 sheet of ⅛-inch hardboard; 4 1×4s, ceiling height; 7 1×4s 8-feet high; lattice strips, 8 feet long; lag bolts; nails; two piano hinges, ¾ inches × 20 inches; glue; four pair of butt hinges; corner braces; two pressure catches.

Tools: Saber saw, hammer, measuring tape, carpenter's square, level, pencil, drill and masonry and wood bits, straight edge.

Instructions:

1. Build up closet floor following steps 1 through 14 but cut the back and front 2×4s to 4-foot length.

2. Follow instructions on building closet as given in Conversion I, Project 3, but add the following step:

3. Before applying plywood panels to uprights, put in a 2×4 spacer on each side wall at 27 inches center from the floor.

4. Nail a 2×4, 4-inch side down, 27 inches from floor on center to back wall.

Building doors and fold down-table

1. Cut hardboard into two panels of 48-inch width by ceiling height minus 1 inch.

2. Do the same with your six long 1×4s.

3. Cut the rest of your 1×4s into 21 ¾-inch lengths.

4. Construct a frame work of 1×4s, 2 1×4s on the hinge side, glued and nailed together, with reinforcing corner braces (Fig. 14-11).

5. Nail and glue in five of the short lengths as shelves at regular intervals but make sure that the second shelf from the bottom on one side falls at 28½ inches. Reinforce that shelf with corner bracing to the frame.

6. Nail and glue hardboard front panels to frame.

7. Repeat for other door.

8. Cut lattice strips into 2 ¾-inch strips and nail and glue them on as shelf edges as shown in Fig. 14-11.

210

9. For variations on storage you might want to screw baby food jar lids to the underside of shelves and fill them with buttons, hooks, and other such items (Fig. 14-11).

10. You can hammer in two rows of nails to a shelf, longer ones in back, or staggering your rows for thread storage.

11. You can screw hooks to the underneath side of shelves for hanging scissors and other items.

12. You can omit the shelves on one side all together and construct a pocket system as described in Project 11 and attach it to the inside of one of the doors.

13. Folding table. Cut a piece of ¾-inch plywood to 24 × 60 inch size and another piece to 24 × 28½ inch size.

14. Hinge short piece to long piece along 24-inch edge about 8 inches in from one short edge with one of the 20-inch piano hinges, centering the hinge.

15. Attach the structure to the reinforced shelf at 28½ inches from the floor on one of the doors.

16. Apply a pair of pressure catches, one to each side on the door at a height to receive the folded structure (Fig. 14-11).

17. Apply the butt hinges, four to each door and space them evenly.

18. Sand structure.

19. Seal and paint.

20. If you like, you can apply a piece of pegboard, pre-painted, to the back of closet right above the work table and as wide as the space and high enough to reach to the next shelf. If you do, use screws with sleeves and fasten down the peg board tightly to the wall. Or instead, leave a ½-inch to ¾-inch space so that you have room for hangers.

21. Another option is apply formica to the table top and work surface. Cut to size and apply according to manufacturers' direction.

22. If you like, you could also cover the folding table with canvas or heavy denim for a nice non-slip surface if you prefer that when you sew.

23. As far as the sewing member of our team is concerned a good painted surface is fine. But use a light color so your pins and such won't get "lost." Another alternative is adhesive backed vinyl which works very well.

24. If you like you can add fancy door pulls, but attach them where one of the 1×4 shelves is so that there is something substantial to tie them to. Reinforce that shelf (with the pull behind it) with corner braces for added strength.

PROJECT 10: INSTALLING FLUORESCENT WORK LIGHT

Materials: 1 fluorescent work light (40 watt total = 2 bulbs of 20 watts each).

Tools: Screwdriver, measuring tape, pencil, drill.

Instructions:

1. Measure and mark on underside of third large shelf where you want the hooks for the fixture to fall.

2. Install hooks.

3. Hang fixture using top links of chain, discard rest.

4. In rear corner of sewing center, drill a hole wide enough to accomodate cable from fluorescent light.

5. Take plug off and drop cable through.

6. Replace plug and plug into receptacle in wall.

7. If you like, you can enlarge the hole enough to accomodate two cords and drop your sewing machine cord through it also.

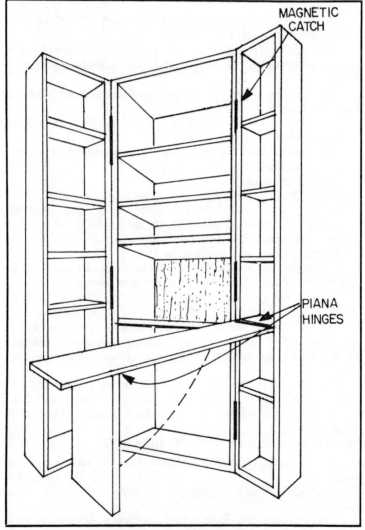

Fig. 14-11. Completed sewing center with fold-down table.

8. There is a catch. This work light is great and inexpensive (around $15.00) but unfortunately it doesn't have a switch. It must be plugged in to turn it on. You can install a plug as we did in Conversion I, Project 7.

PROJECT 11: POCKET STORAGE SYSTEM

To fill in the rest of the storage wall and create room for whatever odds and ends haven't found a home yet, and to provide a space for the kids to lounge around in, we have designed this wall-pocket-storage-and-lazy-nook number.

Materials: Double thickness of canvas, duck or denim, enough to fill in the wall space; heavy eyelets or small wooden curtain rings; two slats about 2 inches wide and as long as the pocket system is wide; thread and needles; hooks.

Tools: Measuring tape or ruler, scissors, saw, eyelet setter (optional); sewing machine; drill.

Instructions:

1. Measure left-over space between the sewing center on the one side and the closets on the other. We had about 6 feet and a few inches left.

2. The next consideration is how high and how low you want the wall pocket piece to go. 5½ feet is the most we can use comfortably at the top and you'll want about ½-foot up from the bottom, so you'll need a piece around 6 feet long which, in fabric, is measured and bought as two yards.

3. If you're happy with a width of 4½ feet you're in luck. 54 inches, which is equivalent in fabric measurements, is a standard width you can get in canvas, denim, or duck.

4. If you want it wider you'll have to use two strips and piece them. Or you can look for 60-inch or 5-foot width canvas which is harder to find and more expensive.

5. To piece denim or canvas: cut two pieces of the length you want. Overlap the long edges, selvage over fabric, about ¾-inch. Stitch down with two rows of stitching ⅛-inch in from the edge and again at ½-inch. That's all.

6. To arrive at the length of your piece; the exact length plus 6 inches is your cutting measurement, so figure and cut.

7. On a sheet of graph paper draw a sketch of how you want your pockets placed and how big you like them. Or follow our general layout adjusted to your measurements (Fig. 14-12).

8. Make a casing at the top and bottom of your piece by turning up a hem, ½ inch then 2½ inches. Stitch twice across, ⅛-inch apart (Fig. 14-13).

9. Cut pockets and pocket strips either by our measurements or by your own, using a scale of one-inch equals ½ square.

10. Lay pockets on background and draw around them with chalk.

11. Narrowly hem (¼-inch and again ¼-inch turn) the tops of your strips and pockets.

12. Press down ½-inch around all other edges.

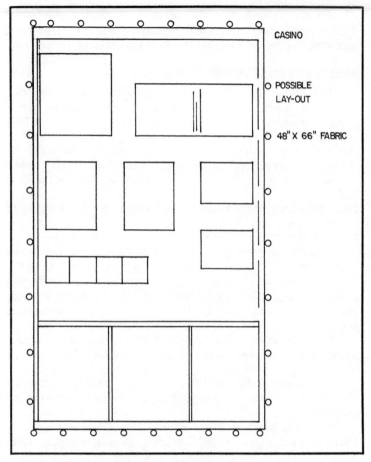

Fig. 14-12. A possible lay-out for a wall pocket system.

13. Draw a second chalk line ¾-inch in from your original chalkline.

14. Pin or tape pockets in place, matching the outer edges of the pockets to the inner chalk line. The pockets will be slightly larger but that is intentional. Stitch in place, twice around.

15. For the pocket strips, stitch at marked intervals up and down twice.

16. Be sure to reinforce stitching at all top edges by going over the row back and forth three or four times for an inch or so.

17. You can either set heavy metal eyelets at 8-inch intervals across the top and bottom and in corners as Fig. 14-14A, or you can hang the system from wooden curtain rings which you will sew on by hand every six inches, top and bottom, starting at the corners as in Fig. 14-14B.

18. It's a good idea to put eyelets into the sides, too, if your system is large or if you plan uneven, large pockets. Just turn under an inch-wide hem on each side edge (one turn is enough because of the selvage) and fasten your eyelets at 8-inch intervals.

19. By the way, those eight inches are approximate. If the spacing doesn't come out even with eight you can use 7½ or 8½ equally well. In fact, you can go up to 9 but not any farther.

29. If you've decided on the wooden or metal curtain rings, you'll need to cut the slats that we mentioned in the material list to the exact length of your pocket system, finished, that is. Then run the slats through the top and bottom hems.

30. You'll need a helper now. Have the helper hold the system exactly where you want to hang it and mark through each eyelet or curtain ring. Mark the eyelet as shown in Fig. 14-14A. Mark curtain rings at the upper edge as shown in Fig. 14-14B. That'll give you the exact spot where you want your hooks.

31. Drill small holes and screws in hooks.

32. Hang your handiwork on the hooks, turning the side hooks slightly to the outside.

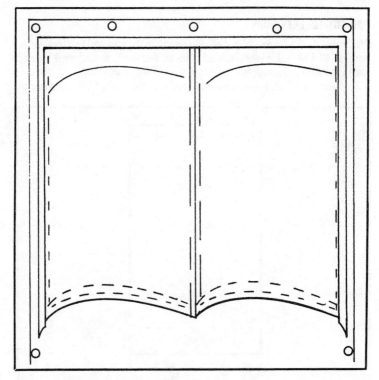

Fig. 14-13. Detail of wall pocket system.

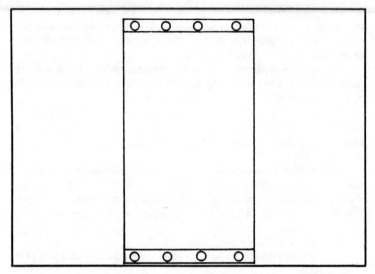

Fig. 14-14A. Wall pocket system with eyelets top and bottom for hanging.

PROJECT 12: LAZY NOOK

Materials: 4-inch foam rubber pad, the length of the area and two feet wide; several 18 ″ 18-inch pieces of foam, two inches thick; and several bags of shredded foam. Enough fabric to cover all of the above. Zippers, thread. Two pieces of 1 ″ 10, 8-feet long each; and one 5½-foot 1 ″ 10; one piece of

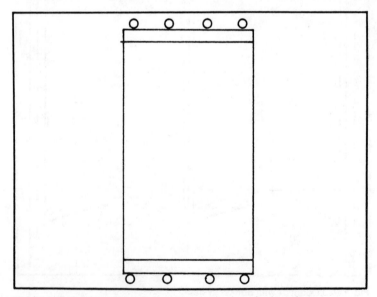

Fig. 14-14B. Wall pocket system with curtain rings for hanging.

¾ inch plywood, 5-foot-6-inches by 24 inches; angle braces; 4d nails.

Tools: Saber saw, measuring tape, scissors, sewing machine, hammer, pencil.

Instructions:

    1. Measure and cut two pieces of 1 × 10 the length of your opening.

    2. Cut the rest of the 1 × 10's into 22½-inch length.

    3. Nail one of the long 1 × 10's to the back wall, tie them into wall studs.

    4. Construct a box using the other long 1 × 10 for the front and two short ones for the sides. Tie into 2 × 4's at sides (the closet floor).

    5. Nail in the rest of the 1 × 10's, spacing evenly.

    6. Reinforce corners of box and joints with corner braces.

    7. Nail ¾-inch plywood to top (Fig. 14-15).

    8. Sand and seal.

    8. Either stain and varnish or paint to match closets.

Mattress and Pillows

    1. Buy a piece of 4-inch foam to fit opening. If necessary trim with an electric knife.

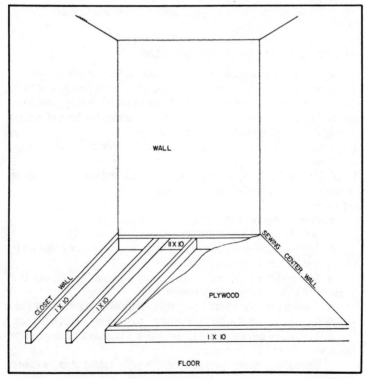

Fig. 14-15. Construction of Lazy Nook.

2. Cut two pieces of material the same size as your mattress plus ½-inch all around. Cut 5-inch strips long enough to go around your mattress plus 1 inch. If you need to piece this strip, allow 1 inch for each time you piece.

3. Sew one of the large pieces to your strip all the way around, inserting zipper into one of the long edges as in Fig. 13-24.

4. Sew up little seam in band.

5. Sew on other large piece all the way around (Fig. 14-16).

6. Do the same with the 18 × 18 inch pillow forms.

7. For large, soft cushions, sew sacks 36 × 24 inches out of some firm material, or use old king size pillow slips.

8. Fill with shredded foam and sew up top.

9. Make covers by cutting two pieces of material to fit the pillows.

10. Sew zipper into one of the short edges, sew up all around.

11. Leave zipper open a bit so you can turn the pillow covers right side out, the same applies to the mattress cover.

Finishing

1. After the floor has been covered with the DeHanis tile and the tile has been sealed, apply strips of pre-finished quarter-round at bottom and up the side to the mattress.

2. If you like, put quarter-round around the plywood top as well (Fig. 14-17).

PROJECT 13: PAINTING WITH TEXTURE PAINT

We decided on texture paint for this conversion for four reasons: 1. we wanted the unevenness characteristic of adobe walls the kind of walls they use in Mexico, 2. we weren't in a hurry to get finished and the taping and sanding got to be quite consuming; and 4. the kids had been clamoring to help this seemed as good as a time as any.

Materials: Texture paint (any good paint with "texture" added, usually sand), sealer.

Tools: Brushes, rollers, screwdriver, hammer, texture tools, such as sponges, brushes, combs, what have you.

Instructions:

1. Seal your walls and ceiling.

2. Wait to install baseboards or trim until the painting is done.

3. Apply texture paint as it comes from the can or mix your own by adding texture mix to ordinary wall paint.

4. Your brush or roller will get pretty heavy so use a smaller one than usual or else don't fill it quite so much.

5. The usual procedure is to apply the texture over an area, fairly thick and then go back over it with your texture tool before the paint is dry.

6. To texture use your sponge or whatever and press it down in the damp paint, over and over again.

7. If you like, you can swirl your tool, or slide it along as in the case of a comb.

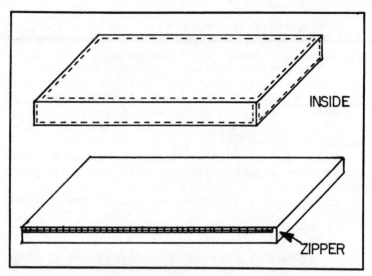

Fig. 14-16.Sewing details for covering mattresses and pillows.

8. Don't try to make an orderly pattern. The texture itself will be the pattern, not the individual units.

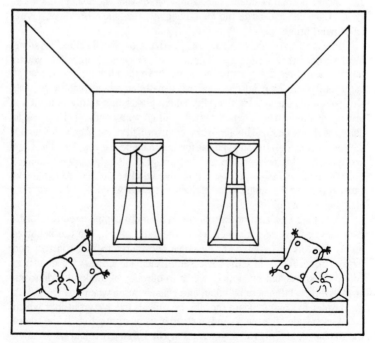

Fig. 14-17.The completed Lazy Nook and wall pocket system.

9. If you like to do two things at one time, you can use a so-called textured roller over your first application and get a reasonable facsimile of a texture though it won't be a very exciting pattern.

10. We got better results by going over the painted area with a heavy paint brush and swirling it as shown in Fig. 14-18. If you're brave and have some kids you might like to try our favorite solution—let the kids swirl their hands in the paint on the wall. It gives a lovely effect. The kids hands are small and the application is so rythmical that it turns out great. And the kids have an absolute ball.

11. If you don't have kids, you can try it yourself. Put on some of your favorite music with a good strong beat and go to it. You'll be surprised how much fun you have and what lovely walls you create.

12. For the ceiling we recommend you stick with a brush or texture roller.

13. Wipe up spills promptly. They get awfully hard after a while.

14. Try to finish one wall at a time.

15. Wash brushes well if you have to stop, they get stone-hard otherwise.

PROJECT 14: LAYING A DEHANIS OR SALTILLO TILE FLOOR

Materials: Enough tiles to cover your floor (the tiles are 11 × 11 or 11½ × 11½ inches portland cement, fine sand, coarse sand, tile sealer, 1 × 4's.
Tools: Carbide saw, large tub for mixing, stirrer, shovel, trowel, level, large paint brush, pencil, carpenter's square.

In case you're not familiar with DeHanis or Saltillo tiles, or some brothers or sisters of same by other names, let us quickly introduce you to them. These tiles are ceramic but do not have the slick glazed surface of bathroom tiles. The Saltillo tiles are usually an adobe pink color, the DeHanis a bit darker. Incidentally, adobe pink is not really pink, it's a lovely earthtone which, when sealed, will go with anything. DeHanis is darker and at times will be almost in the brownish range. Again the sealer darkens it considerably and you can further that effect if you like. The tiles are usually a bit uneven top and bottom, and slightly curved topside. Installed properly they give you a floor that will last and last. And one you can keep clean by going over it lightly with a wet mop. No waxing, stripping or any of that jazz.

Installing DeHanis or Saltillo tile is bit more complicated than ordinary vinyl but we feel it's well worth the extra effort. The tile is not as highly fired as are your bathroom tiles and therefore will contract and expand more. Also, since the tile is semi-handmade it does vary slightly in color, thickness and even size, which to our way of thinking adds to its attractiveness but has to be taken into consideration when you work with it. In order to accommodate the tile the ruler is to have groutlines which are ¾-inch wide all around. And, instead of using mastic to affix the tile to the slab in your family room, you set it in a bed of concrete and sand, called a mud set. So here we go.

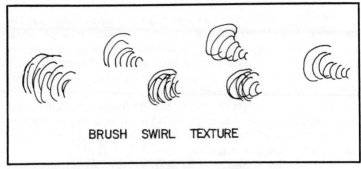

BRUSH   SWIRL   TEXTURE

Fig. 14-18.Example of texture painting, brushing on swirl texture.

Instructions:

1. Figuring out how many tiles you need is a bit tricky because of that wide grout line and the fact that the tiles can vary as much as ½-inch in size. So figure roughly on 1-foot square tiles and go from there.

2. Before you set DeHanis tile, lay them out first and see how they fit. While cutting the tile is not hard, you can avoid unnecessary cuts this way.

3. Try to avoid cuts that take off just a sliver; they are the hardest.

4. Also keep in mind that a DeHanis or Saltillo tile floor will raise the floor level up to two inches. That can make a big-difference in doorways and has to be dealt with. We were lucky that our garage floor was four inches below the floor of the house.

5. You are going to use the ¾-edge of your 1 × 4's as spacers when you set your tile. You can use them as is or you can construct a little grid out of them as follows:

6. You'll need four pieces of 1 × 4, about 14 inches in length each.

7. Nail them together to form an even cross and reinforce the joints with corner braces (Fig. 14-19).

8. You will use the edges for grout lines and you can use the cross to set four tiles at one time. Nifty, isn't it? We invented this one ourselves. There are such things for bathroom tiles made out of plastic, but the 1 × 4 version is ours.

9. Mix your portland cement with *coarse* sand in a mixture of 2 parts sand to 1 part portland cement.

10. Wet the mix and spread directly on slab about 1-inch thick.

11. Level mortar and set in tile.

12. Level tile by checking with level and then pressing down the high part into the mortar until the tile is level.

13. Spread some more mortar, set down your grid and set in three more tiles in the same manner, being sure to level each tile.

14. If your floor is very uneven you may have to use a thicker mud bed up to 1½ inches or more.

15. The same thing holds true if your tile is very uneven on the back side.

16. When you need to cut a tile you'll have to use a carbide saw. You can get a carbide blade sometimes, but we advise you try and rent a carbide saw from either a rental store or an establishment that sets tiles. Sometimes they will cut tile for a fee, which is usually well worth it.

17. Mark your tiles for cutting much like you would a vinyl or rug tile, making a two tile and cardboard sandwich.

18. However, the problem is a bit bigger because your tile is slightly curved and the thickness much greater, so you have to be as accurate as you can, even though you do have a "finagling factor" with your groutline on the outside edges, just in case.

19. When all your tiles are in, let the floor cure for about a month. That time lets the tiles get acclimated to the temperature and humidity in your particular family room. Try not to be hard on the floor during that time, don't drop heavy, sharp objects on it, or dribble grease on it. Light dirt can be mopped off with a slightly damp sponge or mop.

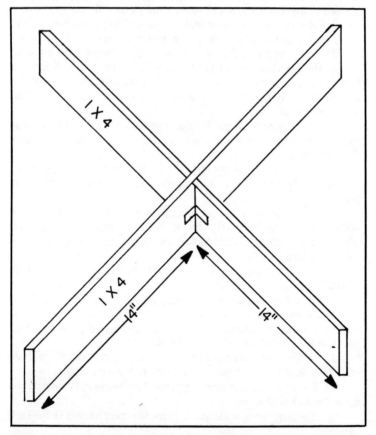

Fig. 14-19.How to construct the Wolverton-Original-Tile-Setter-Helper.

20. When the floor is through curing, we'll need to grout the joints. You can either buy a pre-colored grout product which you'll just wet down and use, or you can mix your own grout thusly:

21. Mix some of that portland cement with some *fine* sand in a 1: 1 proportion (i.e.) half, sand, half portland cement. You can color the mixture by adding manganese oxide, bought for a few pennies at your nearest ceramic supply store. This will give you a blackish grout. Be sure to measure your manganese as you put it in the first batch of mixture, as well as the amount of sand and cement, or your black won't be quite the same each time. Actually the sealer will even out the color quite a bit in any case.

22. After your tile has cured, vacuum and wipe off tiles with a damp sponge or mop.

23. Apply two coats of sealer, drying thoroughly between coats.

24. Mix your grout with water and apply evenly in grouting lines. (The reason we are waiting so long for this is that our colored grout might have stained smudges on the tile if we had applied it before sealing tiles).

25. Fill grout lines well and tamp down with the edge of a 1 × 4.

26. Apply two more coats of sealer over tiles and grout lines.

27. Some people insist on waxing over the whole shebang but we don't.

28. Apply pre-stained and varnished baseboard around the walls.

29. Apply pre-stained and varnished quarter-round.

Chapter 15
Garage Conversion IV

This was a two-car, attached garage; brick exterior; no windows; one door to the outside in the rear of the garage, in an L-shaped nook. The people who lived there needed a large living room to accomodate their large family of children both their own and some foster kids. The house's living room was fairly small and opened directly onto the backyard, which made a convenient through-way for the kids who preferred that route to going in through the garage and kitchen.

It was finally decided to turn the present living room into a family playroom and let the kids trudge in and out all they wanted to. The garage, in turn, was to become the kind of family room in which everyone could assemble for conversation, games and, most important, celebrations and family gatherings. With this in mind, a fireplace was a must. To dead-end the room we decided on large picture windows instead of doors. Also the windows matched the living room and bedroom windows that shared the same facade. A carpet tile floor was chosen because it provided, along with a great bunch of floor cushions, enough extra seating to accommodate a crowd. A solid glass storm window was added to the back door and this added some sorely needed daylight. On the whole, the room remained somewhat on the dark side. Since they intended to use the room mainly in the evenings, this drawback didn't matter. Some pale yellow paint provided a cheerful background.

We built a planter box across the front, in line with the edge of the narrow porch which ran across the front of the house and stopped just short of the garage. This maneuver helped unify the front and made it look as if the house had been planned that way instead of screaming "garage conversion."

Lastly, we added the wood box seat which provided an extra bed if needed, as well as hidden storage for logs and kindling.

The brick of the hearth matched the brick of the house, another unifying detail, while the carpet picked up some of the darker yellows of the fireplace and hearth bricks. See before and after views, Fig. 151 A-B.

PROJECT 1: REMOVING OLD GARAGE DOORS

Follow direction as given in Conversion I, Project 1, for removal of garage doors. Patch drywall ceiling and walls if needed. Go carefully when removing the doors and you shouldn't have too much patching to do later.

PROJECT 2: ENCLOSING OPENING AND
INSTALLING PICTURE WINDOWS IN FRONT FACADE

Materials: 8 2×4's 8-feet long; 4 1×6's 6-foot long
4 1×6's 7½-feet long; 4 1×8-foot, ½-inch thick gypsum board
4 6-inch 1×7-foot strips of ½-inch gypsum board; 4 1×8-foot polystyrene insulating boards; 4 6-inch × 7-foot strips of polystyrene insulat-

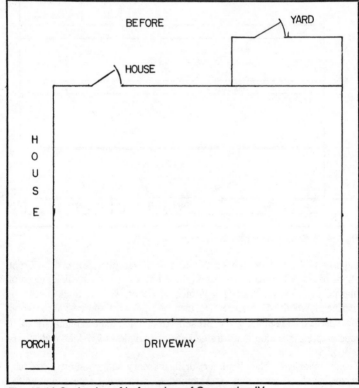

Fig. 15-1A. Scale plan of before view of Conversion IV.

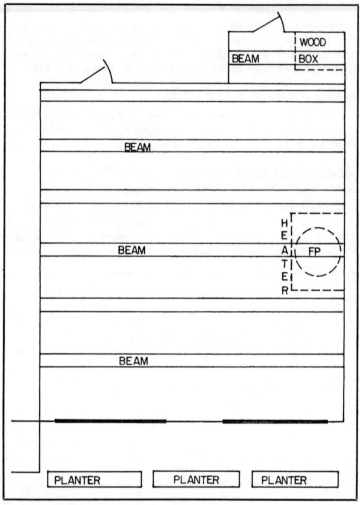

Fig. 15-1 B. Scale plan of after view of Conversion IV.

ing boards; 4 1×8 foot strips of No.15 asphalt-saturated felt; 4 ½″ ×7-foot strips of No. 15 asphalt-saturated felt; 4 1×8-foot, ½-inch thick pieces of marine plywood A-D grade; 4 ½-inch × 7-foot, ½-inch thick pieces of marine plywood A-D grade; 8 1½-inch lag bolts with sleeves; scrap wood for spacers and shims; wood preservative; nails; joint cement and joint tape; staples; two aluminum framed picture windows 7½-feet wide by 6-feet high.

Tools: Saber saw, claw hammer, drill, masonry and wood bits, wrench, screwdriver, scoring awl, straight edge, measuring tape, joint knife, scissors, caulking gun, staple gun, slip-stick.

Instructions:

1. After removing the garage doors you'll have 8-foot wide by 7-foot high openings. The windows in the size given above will, almost by themselves, fill the opening. Framing is done simply as in Fig. 15-2.

2. Coat two of your 8-foot 2×4's with wood preservative, let dry.

3. Lay these 2×4's across each door opening as a sole plate and nail in place with masonry nails. (If they'll hold in your kind of concrete!)

4. If not, go the lag bolt route as in Conversion I, Project 2, steps 5-7.

5. With your slip-stick measure the height of both doors at each side.

6. From each of these measurements deduct 1½ inches and cut four 2×4's that length.

7. Check each stud as you set it in vertically with your carpenter's level. When perfect nail into place.

8. Wedge the remaining 8-foot 2×4's into place as top plates, on top of the studs (Fig. 15-2).

9. Cut ten 7-inch-long cripple studs from the remaining 2×4's.

10. Cut 10 spacers from your 1×6's, 3 inches long each.

11. Nail the 8-foot long 1×6 to the top plate to serve as a window header.

12. Nail it flat with the front edge even with the edge of the 2×4 top plate on the outside of the opening.

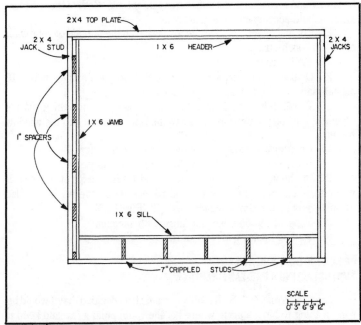

Fig. 15-2. Framing for picture windows.

13. This leaves approximately three inches protruding past the back edge of the top plate on the inside of the room. Before you drive the nails all the way in, tap the header against the top plate and check with carpenters' level. Wedge shims, if necessary, between top plate and header to make header level all the way across.

14. Nail one 6-foot, 8½-inch long 1×6 jamb to the 2×4 jack stud. Check with level and use shims when necessary to square corners and plumb jamb.

15. Nail 1×6 spacers to other jack stud and then nail on another 1×6 jamb, again using your shims to adjust the plumb and the square.

16. Cut a 7-foot 6½-inch sill plate from your 1×6.

17. Nail the crippled studs to that sill plate on 16-inch centers but don't drive the nails all the way in yet.

18. Put sill in place between jambs and toe-nail, or bracket in the crippled studs.

19. Again use your carpenter's square and level, as well as those ever present shims to get your sill perfectly level and your opening perfectly square.

20. Now is the time to drive your nails into the tops of your cripple studs to stay.

21. Double check your sill for level and then tie to each jamb with corner braces below the sill.

22. Lift window frame into place and install with manufacturer's hardware and according to manufacturer's directions. Both of these necessities should accompany your windows.

23. Cut and install polystyrene insulation on the outside of your wall. (6- and 12-inch strips).

24. Caulk around your window.

25. Overlay insulation with 6- and 12-inch strips of single ply No. 15 asphalt saturated felt. Staple felt in place.

26. Cover felt with 6- and 12-inch strips of ½-inch thick marine plywood, butting the plywood between the brick exterior and the window framing.

27. Countersink nails and fill over heads with putty.

28. Sand, seal and paint to match trim of the house.

29. On the inside, finish wall with 6- and 12-inch strips of wall board, butting the strips against the wall board already on the walls and also against the window jambs, header and sill (Fig. 15-3).

30. Tape, fill in dimples and finish with sanding.

31. Seal and paint with rest of room.

PROJECT 3: BUILDING A HEARTH AND INSTALLING A PRE-FAB FIREPLACE

Ever since man (or was it really woman?) first decided that it would be a great thing to have a place where he/she could build a fire and keep it going as long as he/she wanted to, fireplaces have been with us. They have

Fig. 15-3. Fire place and hearth, picture windows and storage seat in completed Conversion IV.

been used as the main source of heat, as the place to cook family meals, and as the focal point to gather around and tell tall tales through the long dark evenings.

Naturally, the job of designing and building fireplaces became important. From a "my fireplace burns better than yours" sort of thing it developed into a highly skilled craft, complete with guilds, apprentices and masterpieces. Then came the turn of this century, the development of central heating and the use of gas and electricity for cooking. Fireplaces became almost obsolete. Only nostalgic souls had fireplaces for purely esthetic reasons.

Now, however, with the energy crunch of the 70's and 80's and 90's and an increased appreciation of all things natural, fireplaces have been restored to their rightful places of great importance. And so has the craft of designing, building and installing them.

If you're planning to install a fireplace, whether from scratch, freestanding or pre-fab, you need to know a bit about fireplace design basics.

First of all, a fireplace is a bit like the sun. It emits heat by radiation, which means that the fire transmits the heat directly to the objects around it. And these objects, in turn, heat the air adjacent to them. And that, friend, is why a fireplace in the center of a room is a good deal more efficient than one placed against an outside wall. And this is also why the New England settlers, thrifty souls that they were, preferred the center fireplace design. They could tell a good thing, for sure.

Even though fireplaces are placed in different locations in houses and come in many shapes and forms, the principles of their function are the same for all. But these principles are not simple. It's taken fireplace builders many centuries to work out the best proportions and other requirements for efficient, safe and smokeless fireplaces. Beginners in these hallowed matters should never, never attempt to design their own fireplaces. They might end up with a great looking design which, alas, will turn their home into an oversized smoke house every time they light the fireplace. So—let someone else experiment. You reap the benefits of tried and true fireplace know-how.

While we truly love the beauty of masonry fireplaces, we have reluctantly desisted from trying our hand at constructing one. (Well, not quite, we built masonry pottery kilns—that's when we found out some of the difficulties mentioned above). The truth is that there is no crash course in becoming a skilled mason. It takes time and practice. Which might be one of the reasons why it is so difficult and at times impossible to find a mason free to do a job for you.

So we settled the problems of fireplace design and construction, at least to our satisfaction, with choices from the wide range of pre-fabricated and free-standing fireplaces available from many good manufacturers. Before we rushed out to buy our first such fireplace we spent some time finding out the mechanics by which fireplaces work. In theory, that is.

How A Fireplace Works

To find out how a fireplace works let's take a fireplace's basic components, the firebox and the chimney, one at a time.

The fire burns in the firebox and this container, of course, receives the most intense heat. Therefore, it is made out of the most heat resistant material, fire brick in the masonry version, and insulated steel in the pre-fab and free-standing units. Most manufacturers of pre-fab and free-standing units claim that the insulating value of their steel walls is enough to make the 2-inch air space requirement between brick and wood framing members required on masonry fireplace units unnecessary.

To help with the radiation of heat, a firebox should have angled walls. Side walls open out toward the room to be heated. The back wall is built vertically up from 12 to 16 inches, and then is sloped forward. It must be angled abruptly, not curved, or the smoke will go out into the room instead of up the chimney.

At the base of the chimney you can find such latter day refinements as dampers, smoke shelves, and smoke chambers. All these refinements are for the purpose of shunting the hot gases and smoke to the outside. Since the hot air in the flue, or chimney, is lighter than the cooler air outside—as we all remember learning in General Science back in 7th grade—it will rise, thus providing a draft, or natural air circulation up the chimney to the outside.

To prevent down drafts—air backing up and coming down the chimney—the chimney must extend at least two feet higher than the highest peak of a sloping roof and three feet higher than a flat roof. This will prevent air currents hitting the roof and bouncing right back down the chimney. Your flues should also run up straight if at all possible.

While all this is great lore to get smoke, soot, and ash up the chimney and to the outside, it's not so good as far as your heat is concerned. A good deal of the heat will go out that same chimney right along with your smoke, soot and so forth. A roaring fire in a well-designed and constructed fireplace can actually cool down a room down several degrees by sucking the warm room air into the firebox and from there up the chimney!

This fact so impressed Ben Franklin that he cogitated on the matter and was later inspired to invent his famous stove—the first free-standing fireplace ever built. It had the capability of being closed up when needed, to prevent loss of warm room air up the chimney and therefore the wood fuel could burn more efficiently. In addition, the Franklin stove had a feature one should look for in today's wood burning free-standers—that is an outside air intake. If you use cold outside air for combustion, then none of the heated air in your room is lost up the flue. Clever, isn't it?

Modern Free-Standing and Pre-fab Fireplaces

When you're out shopping for your free-stander, which is really a hybrid stove-fireplace, look over such units as the Jotul No. 4 Combi-fire which has air-tight doors that you can take off and store underneath whenever you want to convert from stove to open hearth fireplace.

The Provider by Preway is one of the best free-standing fireplace systems we've seen in operation. It can do a serious job of winter heating. What it does is circulate outside air (if you get the optional outside air intake kit, which we highly recommend you do) for combustion, while it forces room air through the heating chamber in high volume and then out again into the room through louvers on each side of its glass doors.

The Coronado by Martin, which some call the updated version of Ben Franklin's stove, has glass bi-fold doors and a fan which forces warmed air out of the top vents.

The model we chose for this family room conversion is a little gem called the Carousel, manufactured by Malm. See Fig. 15-3. It has glass panels all around that absorb and re-radiate heat while blocking heat loss from the room. Combustion air enters the fire box through narrow slits separating the glass panels, then swirls around the fire in a cyclone effect. A long lasting fire and thorough, slow burning rate are insured by a large, flat baffle inside the conical top. The long metal flue pipe radiates most of the heat that rises with the smoke on its way outside, further increasing the efficiency of the Carousel.

It proved to be the least expensive of many free-standing fireplaces we investigated and the easiest to install. Like all free-standers it required no special foundation or framing—only a common brick outer "hearth," and an opening for the chimney.

Materials: 142 common or face bricks; 80 lb bag of mortar mix; free-standing fireplace unit of your choice, with enough chimney sections to clear highest point on roof by two feet (three feet if roof is flat); chimney support box; 2 × 2-foot aluminum flashing; storm collar; chimney cap; common and roofing nails; waterproof mastic.

Tools: Plumb bob, mortar board, trowel, multi-purpose saw, claw hammer, tin snips.

Instructions:

1. Mix mortar according to directions on bag.

2. Mark off 4-foot square on floor where hearth will be located.

3. Lay down thin bed of mortar to cover the four square feet marked off.

4. Nail two 49½-inch 1 × 4's onto two 48-inch 1 × 4's to make a temporary form 48 square inches on inside. True square with corner irons.

5. Lay form over mortar bed.

6. Lay down outside perimeter of bricks against edges of form according to pattern in Fig. 15-4.

7. Lay in next perimeter of bricks inside first and continue working your way into center following pattern shown in Fig. 15-5. "Butter" each brick with mortar, using your trowel, on any side or end that touches another brick. Spacing between bricks should be ⅛-inch.

8. Spread thin layer of mortar on top of first layer when completed and repeat process with second layer of bricks reversing the pattern as indicated in Fig. 15-6. Leave bricks inside form until installation of fireplace and chimney are complete and mortar is firmly set. Allow at least 24 hours before proceeding to step 9, below.

9. Put fireplace unit in place on the brick hearth.

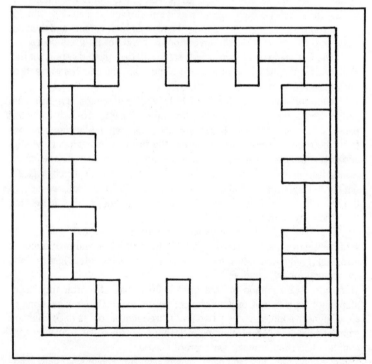

Fig. 15-4. Starting to lay a brick hearth.

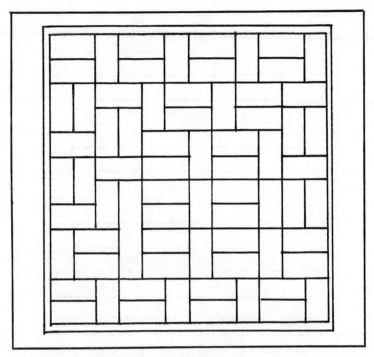

Fig. 15-5. Finished first course of brick hearth.

10. Drop a plumb bob from the ceiling down to the center of the flue opening on your prefab fireplace.

11. Mark the spot on the ceiling that is directly above the center of the flue opening.

12. Draw a circle on the ceiling the diameter of the flue pipe. Square the circle and drive nails through the roof in each corner to mark the opening on the top of the roof.

13. Remove enough shingles to clear the square area marked off by the nail ends. (See Conversion II, Project 1, for how-to on removal of shingles).

14. Cut circular opening in roof from underneath side just large enough for flue pipe to go through.

15. Install the first section of chimney over the fireplace unit and lock it in place according to the manufacturer's instructions.

16. Install each chimney section in the same way, installing the chimney support box where the chimney goes through the roof according to instructions from the manufacturer.

17. Once the chimney is above the roof, close any left over opening with sheathing.

18. Cut flashing to fit tightly over the flue and nail into place.

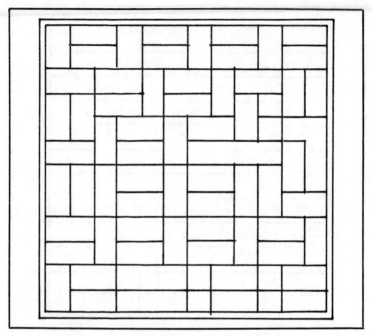

Fig. 15-6.Second course of bricks for brick hearth, reversed pattern.

19. Apply roofing back over flashing, overlapping all but the lower flange, as illustrated in Fig. 15-7.

20. Insert a storm collar in the flue over the flashing.

21. Lock the remaining sections of the chimney together.

22. Seal the joint where the chimney comes through the roof thoroughly with waterproof mastic.

23. Attach chimney cap according to directions that will come with the cap or chimney assemble.

PROJECT 4: INSTALLING A BEAMED CEILING

Somehow, it seems, a room with a fireplace ought to have a beamed ceiling. At least, it might as well have one nowadays when good looking wood-stained beamed ceilings can be installed almost like magic with no weighty and expensive beams to lift and buy.

Synthetic beams made of a rigid polyurethane foam lately out of the chemists cauldron are the magic ingredient. They are available unfinished and will take on any oil-based paint or stain you would like to give them. Or you can get them already finished in sections or in kits.

Materials: two corner beams and three ceiling beams; de-glosser compound; panel adhesive.

Tools: Measuring tape; saber saw; caulking gun.

Instructions:

1. Measure the length the beams are to span and mark their positions on ceiling.

2. Cut beam sections to fit with saber saw.

3. Hold each beam in place on ceiling to make sure it fits and mark its position with light pencil marks.

4. Clean area of ceiling where beams will be glued and apply deglosser to insure good adhesion.

5. Attach corner beams first. Run a ⅛-inch bead of adhesive in a wavy line along the back of the beam.

6. Press the beam against the ceiling in line with the walls. Press firmly to get plenty of adhesive on the ceiling and then remove the beam.

7. Allow the adhesive to cure. When it begins to get tacky, put the beam back into place and press it firmly against the ceiling all along its length.

8. Wedge two or three 2 × 4's between the beam and the floor as a temporary support until the adhesive has had time to set up completely (Fig. 15-8).

9. If installing an odd number of beams, install the center U-shaped ceiling beam first, in the center of the room and work to each side to insure even spacing.

10. Run a ⅛-inch wavy bead of adhesive along each "leg" of the U-shaped ceiling beam and repeat steps 6 through 8 above.

PROJECT 5: BUILDING WOODBOX SEAT

Materials: 1½ sheet of ¾-inch 8 × 4 plywood or particleboard; 2 10-foot 2 × 4's; 18-foot 2 × 4; 16½ feet of 1 × 6; 17½ feet of 1 × 4's; feet of 1-inch

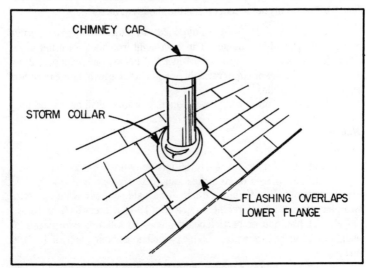

Fig. 15-7. Installation of chimney, exterior view.

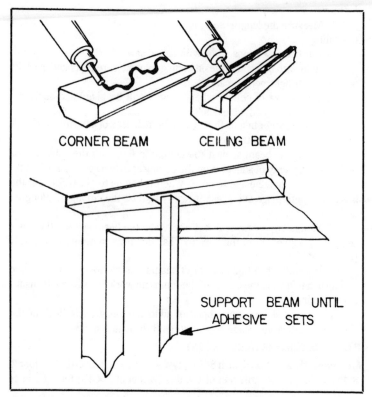

CORNER BEAM   CEILING BEAM

SUPPORT BEAM UNTIL ADHESIVE SETS

Fig. 15-8. Temporary beam support until the adhesive has set.

molding; 16 feet of 1½-inch molding; 2d, 4d nails; wood glue; corner braces; four pair of butt hinges; 1-inch wrought iron hook, or other black chain; four 4-inch eye screws; two 4-inch "S" hooks; one foam pad, 2- by 6-foot; sealer/stain, or stain/varnish; or stain, and varnish; fabric to cover; zipper; thread; glides.

Tools: Saber saw, measuring tape, pencil, scissors, drill and wood bit.

Woodbox

Instructions:

1. Cut two of your 2 × 4's to 65-inch length.

2. Cut four pieces of 20 inches long.

3. Assemble 2 × 4's into a frame, 4-inch side to floor, with the extra two short pieces as reinforcements spaced at 19-inch intervals (Fig. 15-9).

4. Cut plywood or particleboard pieces as follows: two pieces 20 inches by 14 inches, one piece 65 by 14 inches, and one piece 65 by 10½ inches.

5. Notch the two side pieces along the 20-inch edge by cutting out one corner 3½-inches deep by1½ inches wide as in Fig. 15-10.

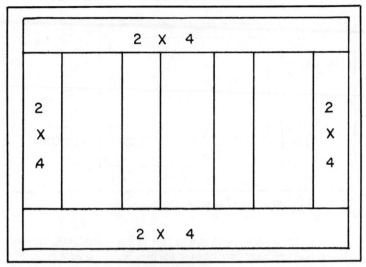

Fig. 15-9. Lay-out for floor frame for woodbox.

6. Cut one piece of plywood or particle board to 65 by 20 inches.

7. Nail the 65 × 20-inch plywood piece to the framing.

8. Cut 1 × 4 into two pieces 14-inches long and two pices 11¾-inches long.

9. Set the 1×4 around the frame, two longer ones in front, the shorter ones in back, wide side facing front and back. Nail in place.

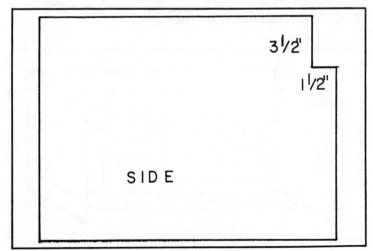

Fig. 15-10. Close-up view of cut out in side of woodbox.

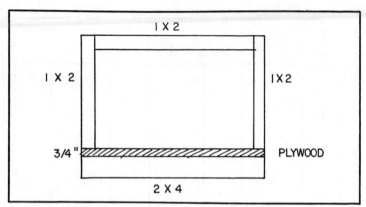

Fig. 15-11.Detailed view of side framing of woodbox.

10. Cut two lengths of 1 × 4 to 18½ inches, and two to 58 inches.

11. Nail long pieces across front and back, short pieces at sides (Fig. 15-11).

12. Cover with plywood sections and reinforce corner at notches in back of box as shown in Fig. 15-12, using corner braces.

13. Attach glides to bottom of box, four in the front, four in the back.

14. Countersink nails, and fill with putty.

15. Sand well, inside and out.

16. Cut molding into strips and apply to box as shown in Fig. 15-13.

17. Fill any remaining nail holes.

18. Stain and varnish to match rafters, inside also if desired.

19. You may wish to just use clear varnish on the inside, in which case we recommend several coats of polyurethane varnish for a really tough finish. Or you might want to use spar varnish.

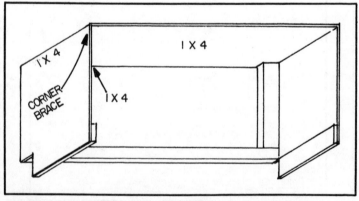

Fig. 15-12.View of inside of woodbox showing corner bracing.

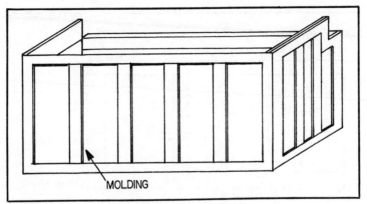

Fig. 15-13.Trimming woodbox with molding strips.

Seat

Materials: Included in material list at beginning of project.
Tools: Ditto.
Instructions:

1. Cut a piece of ¾-inch plywood, 2 feet wide and 6 feet long.
2. Cut two 1 × 6's 6-feet long.
3. Cut four 1 × 6's into 13-inch lengths.
4. Make a frame for the back of the plywood as shown in Fig. 15-14.
5. Locate the studs in the wall where you want your woodbox/seat combo to be.
6. Fasten a 6-foot 2 × 4, wide side against the wall at a height of 10 ¾ inches from the floor, at the lower edge of the 2 × 4 (Fig. 15-15).
7. Edge front and side edges of seat platform with 1½-inch molding strips. Sand, countersink and fill, stain, varnish.
8. Attach butt hinges to 2 × 4 and untrimmed edge of seat.
9. Fasten one of the 4-inch screw eyes into each side of the seat in front.
10. Buy or cut foam mattress to fit. Cover with fabric. For details see Conversion III,Project 12,steps 1-11.
11. Fasten screw eyes to wall at a height of about 6 feet. Make sure you have a stud. Drill holes first.
12. Fasten chain between screw eyes.
13. Place mattress on platform. Your effect should now be as in Fig. 15-16.
14. Attach 2-inch matching "S" hooks to top of chain so you can anchor the box open.

PROJECT 6: PAINTING

Materials: Sealer; matte or semi-gloss latex paint; dark stain varnish. Exterior paint for outside.

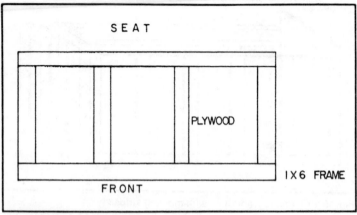

Fig. 15-14. Framing for lid/seat of woodbox.

Tools: Rollers, brushes, hammer, screw driver, drop cloths, paint shields, rags.

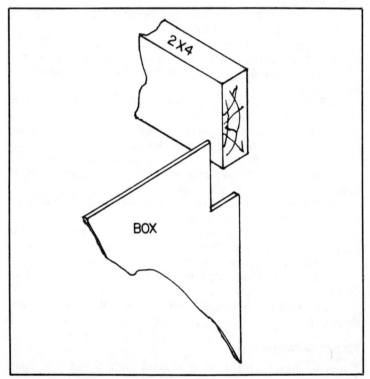

Fig. 15-15. Attaching woodbox to 2×4 wall support.

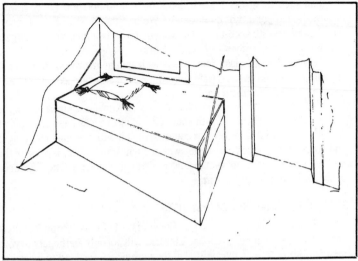

Fig. 15-16. View of completed woodbox/seat.

Instructions:

1. Seal all the walls and the ceiling.

2. Paint with the paint of your choice, (we like yellow in this conversion) using a paler shade on the ceiling. Or if you prefer, you can use white.

3. Start painting on the ceiling. Use a roller. Cut in with a brush around the beams. Use a paint shield to protect the beams.

4. If you are going to stain your woodwork do it now. Follow directions on cans and in Conversion I, Project 6. Finish with varnish.

5. If your existing doors are painted you can either remove the paint with paint and varnish remover, or steel wool the surface after sanding and treat it as you would new wood.

6. Or, if you like, you can paint all the woodwork to match.

7. If you do decide to remove the paint, do this before you do any of the painting in the room and vaccum and wipe every surface thoroughly. Dust is murder when it's varnishing time.

8. Finish your baseboards and quarter-rounds to match the rest of your woodwork, either with stain and varnish or with paint.

9. Install the baseboards after the walls have been painted.

10. Wait to install the quarter-rounds until after the carpet tiles have been laid.

Exterior Painting

Seal all outside wood. Finish to match trim on house.

PROJECT 7: INSTALLING ALL-GLASS DOOR

All-glass storm doors are now readily available. We find these doors a god-send because they let in a lot of light and are easier to keep presentable than such things as French doors or related horrors. (Only from a cleaning stand point, not esthetically. We like the looks of French doors but after living with six 6-foot wide pairs of the darned things one of us gets the hives when it comes to French doors).

Anyway, the all-glass doors come with aluminum or wood frames and are easily installed on the outside of your present exterior door, just like an ordinary screen or storm door.

Since the doors vary somewhat, according to manufacturer, follow the instructions that will come with your door. In most cases it requires only a few minutes for installation, not counting the bit with the chisel for hinges and door catches which can while away an hour or two. Still, it's one of the quickest and showiest project in any conversion. You'll love the difference it makes in your family room.

PROJECT 8: INSTALLING CARPET TILES

Follow instructions given in Conversion I, Project 8 for installing carpet tiles. Remember to choose tiles that will not only add beauty to your new family room, but that will also be appropriate for kind of wear you expect them to receive.

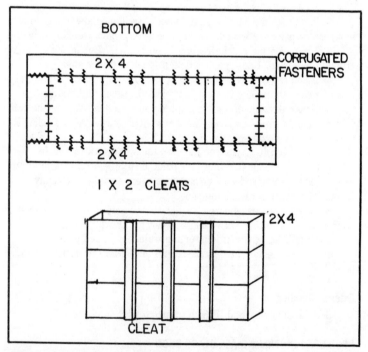

Fig. 15-17. Bottom of planter box, 2×4's held together with corrugated fasteners.

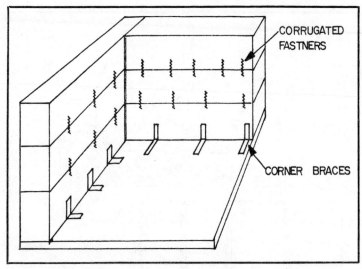

Fig. 15-18. Corner detail of planter showing bracing with corner braces.

PROJECT 9: BUILDING PLANTER ACROSS FRONT

Materials: 36 2 ×1 4's 6-foot; 18 2 × 4's, 9½-inches long, 9 2 × 4's of 65-inch length; 43 feet of 1 × 2's; corrugated fasteners; 4d and 6d nails; wood preservative; stain and varnish; or sealer and paint and marine varnish; corner braces.

Tools: Saber saw, hammer, drill, screwdriver, paintbrush.

Instructions:

    1. Since we had about 18 feet of driveway to set off with a planter box we decided that in this case three would be better than one, because of weight.

    2. To make planter box, cut 2 × 4's to sizes given, (i.e.) 72-inch, 65-inch and 9½-inches.

    3. Lay out 2 × 4's together as in Fig. 15-17.

    4. Fasten together with corrugated fasteners and 1 × 2 cleats as shown.

    5. Pre-fab walls with cleats and corrugated fasteners.

    6. Assembly planter, fastening walls together with corner braces and attaching walls to floor with corner braces about every 4 or 5 inches along the bottom and corners, Fig. 15-18 and Fig. 15-19.

Finishing Planter:

    You have some options here, namely:

    1. Instead of just any 2 × 4's you can buy redwood, in which you'd finish them with a redwood finish.

    2. You can buy pressure-treated douglas fir as lumber and finish with a clear marine varnish.

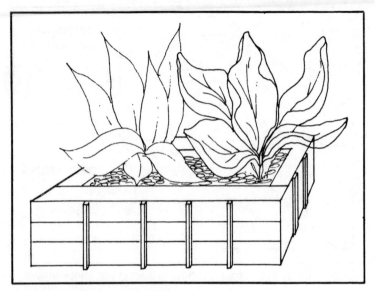
Fig. 15-19. View of finishied planter.

3. You can buy ordinary 2 × 4's, treat each and every one with wood preservative and then, after you've assembled them, paint with exterior paint to match the trim on your house.

4. You can buy the ordinary lumber, treat with wood preservative and stain to whatever color you fancy, and finish with marine or spar varnish.

In any case, be sure to move planter to position in line with edge of porch before you put in the plants and wood or bark chips. Incidentally, we prefer to keep our plants in pots and set in large plastic trays into the bottom of the planters to keep the wood from rotting. That way it's easy to get the plant indoors when it drops to freezing outside. Of course, if you prefer, you can plant directly in these planters. But do it with the planters in place, they are quite heavy to move.

Chapter 16
Garage Conversion V

Again this conversion was a double garage, but it was attached to the rest of the house along both the back wall and one long wall of about 70 feet. This resulted in the garage and the rest of the house forming a U-shaped courtyard or rather what was planned to be such. The street was fairly busy and the view across the street not exactly inspiring. In fact, the house across the street was owned and lived in by a family with six young boys whose hobbies ranged from repairing bicycles, cars, lawn mowers and the like to building "creative structures" out of all kinds of recycled trash. They were all nice kids and occupied their time productively but the esthetics left much to be desired.

It was decided to close off the garage doors and install only two relatively small windows flanked with shutters to match the windows in the bedroom wing which shared the front facade. The long free wall had an excellent view of the neighbor's driveway and assorted vehicles, land and water. Again not exactly what we'd call a pleasing sight. Which made the final solution simple. The U-shaped bit of land embraced by the house and garage was destined to become a manicured courtyard and two large picture windows were installed in the wall facing the courtyard to "frame" the view. We resisted the idea of sliding glass doors which would have made a traffic area out of the courtyard. There was an outside door that led to the fenced back yard in the rear of the garage and that was enough.

The interior design took a bit of thought. The garage belonged to some friends of ours and their wants and needs were varied. Joe wanted a home and also to pursue his hobby, landscape designing. His wife wanted ample storage for her sewing, her rug hooking and braiding; and the two little girls, both of early elementary school age, clamored for storage for their games, collections (were they ever a couple of magpies) and things that they simply had to save for "something."

After a lot of sketching and discussion, the following plan was decided upon. (Fig. 16-1A, the before, and Fig. 16-1B, the after-view). It took care of the home office and storage needs and provided a cozy nook/playhouse for the children and built-in seating arrangement for the adults.

Vinyl tiles were chosen for the floor to make clean-up after all that sewing, collecting, rug making and such easier. Also the shiny tiles provided a great background for those same homemade rugs which, incidentally, were stuck down with double faced tape to keep them in place and prevent mishaps.

Fortunately, the overhead existing light fixture was only a short distance from the new wall so it was easy to tie into the house line for electric current in the new storage wall. There are now outlets on both sides for electric typewriters, sewing machines and lights.

The walls were finished in light colored paneling and the ceiling with acoustical tiles to hold down the noise.

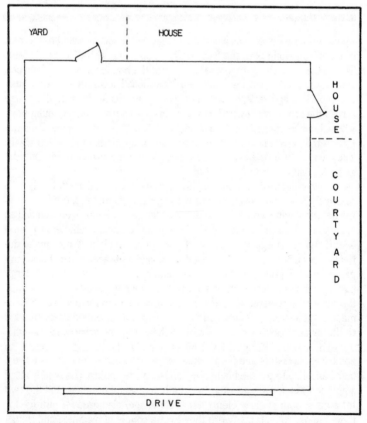

Fig. 16-1 A. Scale plan of before view of Conversion V.

246

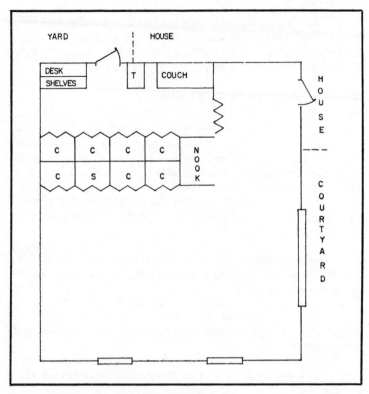

Fig. 16-1 B. Scale plan of after view of Conversion V.

PROJECT 1: REMOVING GARAGE DOORS

Follow instructions in Conversion I, Project 1, for removing spring powered garage doors. Be sure to use extreme caution when unwinding springs. See illustrations in Chapter 12 for further details.

PROJECT 2: BUILDING ENCLOSURE FOR
GARAGE DOOR AND INSTALLING TWO WINDOWS

Follow instructions in Conversion I, Project 2. Substitute a second matching window for the door. Ignore all instructions pertaining to door. Wire wall for receptacles. You won't need an outside light and switch. Finish outside wall with siding to match rest of house or with plywood panels if that matches the rest of the decor.

PROJECT 3: CUTTING OPENING AND INSTALLING DOUBLE PICTURE WINDOW

For cutting the opening, follow the instructions given in Conversion III, Project 4 to the letter, allowing enough space to install two 4-foot or there abouts picture windows side by side.

For installing the windows follow the instructions in Conversion IV, Project 2, and the directions which come with your windows on how to tie the two windows together. If you prefer you can cut two openings and leave some space in between and install your windows separately.

PROJECT 4: FREE STANDING CLOSET WALL

Materials: 4 17-foot 2×4's; 2 14-foot long 2×4's; 43 8-foot 2×4's; 2 17-foot 1×4's; 1 4-foot long 1×4; 12 8-foot 1×4's; 19 panels of ½-inch plywood C-D interior; enough acoustical material to cover backs of closet walls and nook enclosure; 6d and 8d nails; lag screws; eight bifold doors; wood putty; glue; 2×8's as long as room is wide (optional); dowel rod, 1-inch thick; drapery hardware; fabric; thread.

Tools: Drill with masonry bit, saber saw, hammer, screwdriver, measuring tape, pencil, carpenter's square, level, scissors, slip stick, plumb line, straight edge, miter box (optional).

Instructions:

1. Basically you follow the same plan as in Conversion I, Project 3, so consult that section for details. We are going to concentrate on the differences in this section.

2. Our closet wall will differ from the one in Conversion I in two important ways: our new closet wall is free standing, and also double-faced (Fig. 16-2). So we'll build the closet wall as a hybrid between a closet and a partition or wall.

3. Measure and find your joist nearest to the location of your new closet wall. If your garage is unfinished, as this one was, that's easy. Just look up.

4. If you do have a ceiling, measure in from the end wall. Joists usually fall every 12, 16 or 24 inches. Tap and listen. The spaces in between should sound hollow, the joist itself will not.

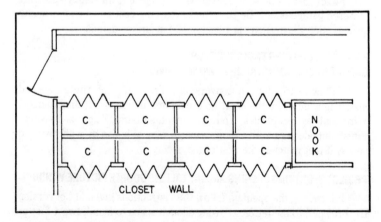

Fig. 16-2. View of proposed storage wall and nook at rear of garage.

248

5. If your ears aren't that finely tuned, proceed as above with measuring in from the wall and gently poke a nail through at 12, 16 and 24 inches. Sooner or later you'll meet resistance and that's the joist. (You'll have to fill in those nail holes later, don't forget.)

6. Once you've located the distance between joists in your particular structure it's time to re-group. If your joists are 12- or 24-inch on center as ours were, you're home free. Skip next steps down to step 12.

7. If you end up with a 16-inch on center distance you have two possibilities: A) you'll build a closet wall of the same outside dimensions as the one in the conversion before you but instead of dividing the space half and half, you can build shallow, 16-inch closets on the office side and deep 32-inch closets on the family room side, or vice versa (Fig. 16-3).

8. Or you can follow course B which is to put in two extra joists between two existing ones so that you'll have three joists with 24-inch or rather 16-plus-8 inch intervals between them (Fig. 16-4). This is not hard to do, but only feasible if you do not have a finished ceiling or are willing to tear out that particular section.

9. To make new joists, cut 2×8's to fit width of room.

10. Install between existing joists and nail to top of top plate.

11. Drop a plumb line from the center of your joist down to the floor. Mark the spot. Repeat this three times.

12. With pencil and straight edge draw the outline of your sole plate on the floor. It will be 13-feet 7½-inches long.

13. Repeat the performance in back of the sole plate at the next joist (if you have a 24-inch center) and at the joist in front. These should be 16-feet, 7½-inches long.

14. If you have joists that are 12-inch on center, simply skip one joist in each direction and mark your sole plate under the second one, front and back (Fig. 16-5).

15. If your joists are 16-inch on center and you've decided to go the uneven route, skip one joist and mark under the next on one side (wherever you want the deeper closets) and directly under the next joist on the other side. You'll end up with two rectangles, one double the width of the other (Fig. 16-6).

16. Install your sole plate in the middle marks using lag screws to tie the 2×4 into the slab.

17. Cut 2×4's to 16-feet 7½-inches. Lay in place on marks. *Don't tie in*.

18. Measure the distance from the sole plate of your wall to the top plate with your slip-stick right to where your center 2×4 is situated. Cut a 2×4 stud to this exact measurement.

19. Put this stud between the other wall studs directly beside the sole plate. If there's a stud already there omit this step.

20. Repeat step 18 and 19 for each of the other sole plates so that there will be a stud alongside each joist in the wall. If your joists and studs by some miracle coincide ignore the above (Fig. 16-7).

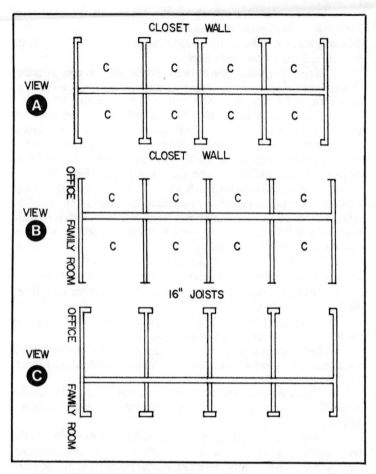

Fig. 16-3. A. Closet space divided evenly between family room and office. B. Closet space arrangement with shallow closets on the office side. C. Closet space arrangement with the shallow closet space on the family room side.

21. With your slip-stick, measure from your tied-down sole plate to the joist above, deduct 1½ inches from the measurement. Cut two 2×4's to fit.

22. Proceed in this way across the sole plate, measuring at 18-inch intervals, using two studs every other time (i.e.) every 3 feet. Mark studs with numbers so you won't mix them up.

23. Mark your remaining 13-foot 7½-inch 2×4 at 18-inch on center intervals. Draw in outline of 2×4s.

24. Cut 2×4 to 13-foot, 7½-inches, lay on end on floor and nail in 2×4 studs.

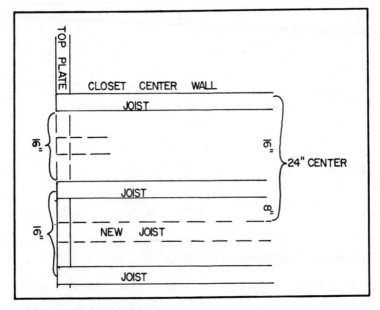

Fig. 16-4. Closet walls need joists.

25. Yell for help. When helper arrives the two of you lift the framing in plate on top of the sole plate and nail inn place against header joist.

26. Cut 10 2×4s to 22¼-inch length.

27. Lay out on floor as shown in Fig. 16-8.

28. Nail to back sole plate and tie to floor with lag screws.

29. Now measure and cut your front studs, by measuring up from your 15-foot 2×4 on the floor, starting at the wall and proceeding along at 3 foot intervals (on center) four times. *Deduct 1 ½-inch from each stud measure*.

30. This will leave a 3-foot length at one end. Don't panic we intended that all along. Measure your last two studs from end of the 16-foot, 7½-inch 2×4, (they'll be back to back).

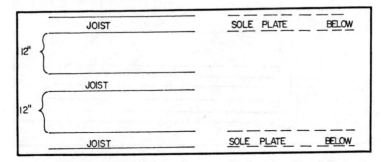

Fig. 16-5. Joist and sole plate layout.

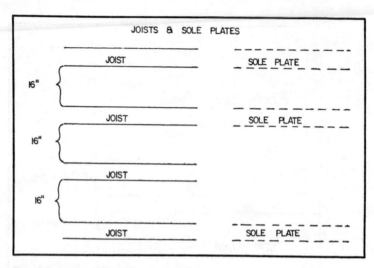

Fig. 16-6. Joist and different sole playe layout.

31. Place the long 2×4 on end and attach the studs where you marked them.

32. Cut four 2×4 pieces to 3-foot lengths.

33. Nail these short pieces between the studs you just attached to the long 2×4, 6-foot 10-inches from the bottom of the stud and 10 inches down from the bottom of your plate.

34. Cut four cripple studs, 10-inch long 2×4's, and nail them at 18-inch centers between the studs in the 3-foot space.

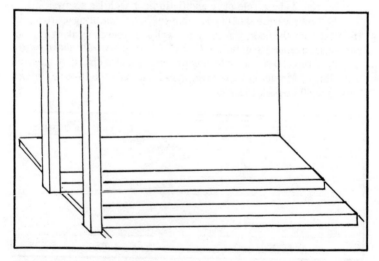

Fig. 16-7. Attaching studs to joists.

252

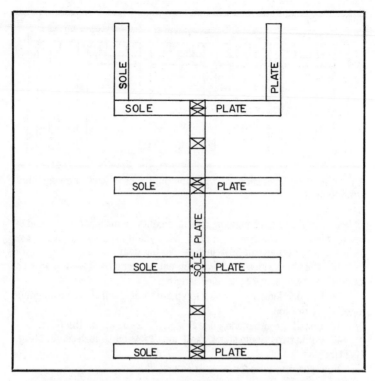

Fig. 16-8. Sole plate layout for the entire double closet wall and nook.

35. Cut two 2×4 studs (floor to joist minus 3½ inches) attach in 3-foot space. See Fig. 16-9.

36. Now cut five 2×4's to 22½-inch lengths.

37. Attach to top plate of frame at right angles as shown in Fig. 15-10.

38. Cut 3 feet of 2×4. Attach it to the last short sole plate at right angles and use lag bolts to tie to floor.

39. Get a crew of three or four people together. Lift the frame in place, short ends toward partition, studs resting on sole plates, top plate against joist.

40. Tie in place against the new wall stud, then attach top plate to joist and short pieces to rear top plate.

41. Tie studs into sole plates.

42. Relax, have a beer, admire your handiwork. Half the job is done. Yes, half, because now you're going to repeat the whole thing.

43. Follow the steps from 27 through 41 for the other side of the closet enclosures.

44. If you follow a different model for your closets, that is if you have the 16-inch joists and go the 16-inch and 32-inch closet route, you can follow the instructions as given except when you cut the short sole and top

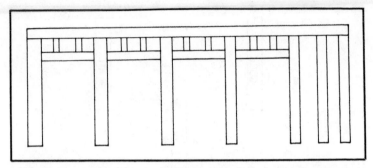

Fig. 16-9. Front elevation of free standing closet wall showing stud arrangement.

plates. You'll have to change the measurements in this manner: instead of having plates of 22¼-inches on each side, you'll have half of them 14¼ inches and the other half 30¼ inches. No big deal.

45. After both sides are framed in, cut two lengths of 2×4 to 45-inch lengths and two pieces to 10-inch lengths.

46. Use one longer piece as a top plate to tie the front of the opening together at the top.

47. Install the other long one 6 feet, 10 inches from the floor.

48. Put in two cripple studs, the 1-inch 2×4s on 16-inch centers (Fig. 16-11).

Now you may rest for as long as you like.

Finishing Closet Wall

Materials: Included in material list for project.
Tools: Ditto.
Instructions:

1. From your plywood, cut panels to fit the wall sections for your closet backs. You'll need eight 3×8-foot panels.

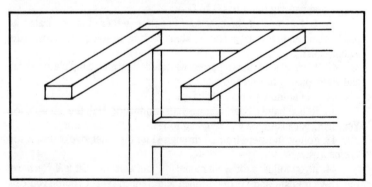

Fig. 16-10. Attaching top plates to front wall of free standing closet.

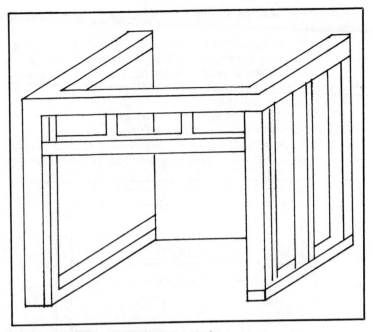

Fig. 16-11. Framing in the playhouse nook.

2. Cut 16 panels to fit the side walls, 22¼ inches by 8 feet.

3. Cut 2×4 sections to fit between the front studs and the wall in back (Fig. 16-12). Five for each wall section, and 20¾ inches long. Nail between studs.

4. Repeat this for each wall.

5. Panel the inside of your closet sections by gluing and nailing your pre-cut plywood panels in place.

5. Cut two 3×8 panels and one 4×8 panel to wall in the nook.

6. Finish ceiling in closets and nook as the rest of ceiling with acoustical material. See ceiling, Project 6, this conversion.

7. Finish closet back walls on the office side with acoustical material, glued or stapled to plywood.

8. Finish inside of nook with acoustical material in the same way.

9. This should give pretty good noise shielding to your home office. If that much shielding is not necessary, simply finish closet walls inside with paint or varnish. You might also consider adhesive-backed vinyl as closet interior finishes.

10. If sound proofing isn't that important, finish the inside of the nook/playhouse with the same paneling you're going to use on the rest of the walls in the room.

11. In any case, finish the area above the doors and the walls on the outside of the nook with the same paneling.

12. Finish front opening of nook with 1×4 frame. Miter if desired (Fig. 16-13).

13. To finish off nook, install wooden dwell across top of opening with curtain rod hardware. Hang draperies. Hold back on each side with cord.

14. To make draperies, cut fairly heavy fabric to 76-inch length using 48-inch wide fabric. (You can also use 45- or 42-inch width. 36-inch would be a bit skimpy, 54-inch very full).

15. Turn a top hem of 1 inch and then 1½ inches and a bottom hem of ½-inch and then 1-inch. Sew or clip curtain rings to top hem.

16. You can use whatever you like for curtains to match or contrast with your decor. Printed bed sheets are a good, inexpensive alternative.

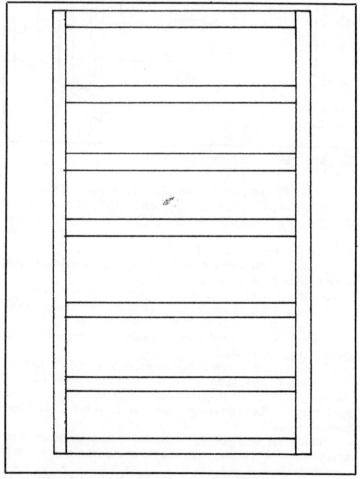

Fig. 16-12. Detail of side wall showing bracing for shelves.

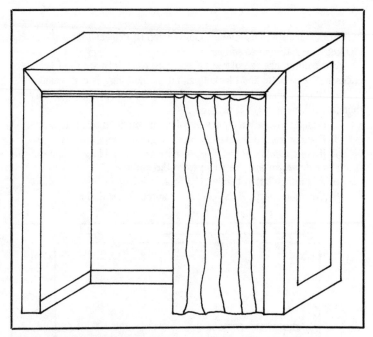

Fig. 16-13. Completed playhouse.

17. As a variation on the curtain theme, you might like to use heavy canvas in 48-inch widths and 73 inches long.

18. Hem top and bottom one inch, by simply turning up an inch on the wrong side and stitching or fusing it in place with iron-on fusing material.

19. Sketch the facade of a house on the canvas as in Fig. 16-14.

20. Fill in details with magic markers or acrylic or oil paints.

21. Cut out window and door openings. Paint along edges with clear nail polish to prevent raveling.

22. Use clip on or sewn on curtain rings to hang.

Installing Fold-Doors On Closet Wall

Materials: Eight Fold doors and hardware; 1×4's listed at beginning of project.
Tools: Listed under tools at beginning of project.
Instructions:
Follow instructions on installing fold doors given in Conversion I, Project 3.

PROJECT 5: INSULATING WALLS AND CEILING

Materials: Enough insulation blanket material to cover ceiling and walls.
Tools: Scissors, tape measure, staple gun, pencil, straight edge.

Instructions:

Follow instructions given in Conversion II, Project 7 for walls, using blanket material instead of batts.

For ceiling, use the blanket insulation, too. Here are the few differences between batts and blankets as far as installing is concerned:

1. Blanket insulation comes with a foil or kraft paper vapor barrier, though you can also get it unfaced.

2. Blanket insulation comes in rolls, so you need to cut it to length.

3. Blanket insulation usually has a stapling flange.

4. If your insulation has a vapor barrier it should face inside of the room—or down toward the room from the ceiling.

5. Staple insulation blankets to tops of joists.

6. For more particulars, consult chapter on insulation.

Fig. 16-14. A novel playhouse curtain door.

PROJECT 6: FINISHING CEILING WITH ACOUSTICAL TILE

Materials: Enough ceiling tile to cover ceiling; enough 1×3 furring strips to cover ceiling; nails; staples; corner molding, 1½-inch wide.

Tools: Saber saw, ladder, carpenter's level, measuring tape, chalk, fine-toothed blade, hammer, chalk line, staple gun.

Instructions:

1. Figure out how many tiles you'll need. The tiles are 12×12 inches, which is convenient. But it isn't as simple as multiplying the length of your room by the width of your room (a solution one of us thought perfect until told otherwise). There's the matter of the border. So—

2. Measure your walls, a long one and a shorter one. We came out with 22 feet and 5 inches and 24 feet and 6 inches. Disregard the feet for the time being. What's important right now are the inches. To the five inches over 22 feet on the short wall, add 12. Then divide by 2. (5+12=17, 17÷2=8½).

3. The magic number is 8½ inches for the border on that wall and the wall of the same length opposite.

4. The other wall had a 6-inch remainder which meant that 6+12=18, 18÷2=9 and so would have a 9-inch border.

5. Now back to how many tiles—we'll need one tile for every square foot plus a tile for any fraction of a square foot so—22 × 24=528, and 22 (for that extra 5 inches) and 24 (for the extra 6 inches) =46. 528+46=574. You'll need 574 tiles at least. A couple or so more won't hurt in case you make a mistake.

6. To find out the number of furring strips you'll need, you must find the middle of your first joist. From that point mark at 12-inch intervals out to the walls. Count the number of marks and add 2. This will be the number of furring strips you'll need.

7. To put up the furring strips level, first check the joists with a level. Probably they'll be fine. If not you'll have to shim up low spots.

8. Nail your furring strips at right angles to your joists between those chalk marks, 1-foot apart and against the walls (Fig. 16-15).

9. Now is the time for a last minute check to see if you've forgotten any major wiring job that needs to be done. Fixtures you can put in place later. But you do need your connections ready.

10. If one of the existing fixtures is in the way of one of your furring strips proceed thusly:

11. Turn off the current at the fuse box or circuit breaker box, leaving the switch in the *on* position on your fixture so you'll be sure the current is off.

12. Remove the screws or nuts that hold the fixture in place.

13. Pull it away from the box and disconnect the wires.

14. Now take the box from its post or hanger and slide it along the cable out of the way of your furring strip.

15. Fasten the box on again. You might have to lower it a bit to make it come flush with the ceiling tiles once they are in (Fig. 16-16).

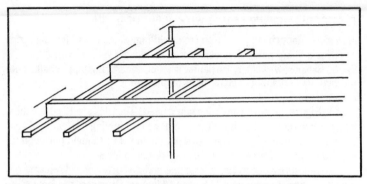

Fig. 16-15. Putting in furring strips for an acoustical tile ceiling.

16. Now pick out a corner to start putting up the tiles.

17. Measure out the width of your borders and snap a chalk line each way. Snap one in the center of the room, too, both ways, for good measure (Fig. 16-17).

18. Cut the corner tile first, with the staple tabs toward the center.

19. For cutting the tile use the fine-toothed saw blade on your saber saw or a fiberboard knife. If you pick the latter, make sure it's sharp or it's a disaster.

20. Always cut your tiles face up.

21. Now put the corner tile on the chalk lines, line it up and staple it in place. You can nail in the back sides because they'll be covered by the molding you'll install after the ceiling and the paneling on the walls is finished.

22. Don't worry about the staple flange, that is covered when the next tiles are interlocked with this one.

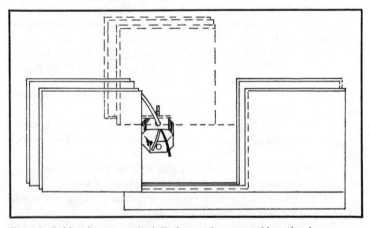

Fig. 16-16. Marking acoustical tile for cutting around junction box.

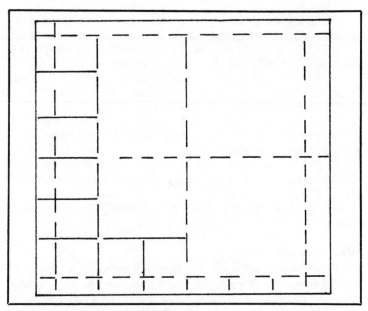
Fig. 16-17. Installing acoustical tiles.

23. When you attach the next tile, you'll get into the matter of the interlock. Align your tile tongue-to-groove with the one already in place (the groove will be on the stapled one) and slide the new tile in place.

24. Now staple the edges in place again. Nail where there is no flange along the wall. That's all there is to attaching one tile to the next.

25. Now cut a complete course of border tiles for one wall and install them, nailing their back sides in place against the last furring strips on the wall.

26. Now do the same for the other wall which adjoins your corner tile.

27. Next comes the good part. Set in rows of whole tiles stapling them in as you go. That's fun because you make such great progress and it's so visible!

28. Before you get to the point where you're about to tile over the outlet box of a ceiling fixture, you want to retain, pause. Then go through the steps 10 through 15 if you haven't done so.

29. When you re-attach the box to the joist, do it so that the box will be in the center of a tile—more or less—and its lower rim flush with the ceiling.

30. Tile as close as you can to two adjacent sides of the fixture box.

31. Slide a loose tile into the groove and bring it up as close to the box as possible. Mark the point where the tongue touches the midpoint of the rim of the box.

32. Don't mark on the face of the tile, just on the tongue.

33. Slide in the tile from the other side and mark the midpoint of the rim where it touches the other tongue.

34. This sounds very complicated but it's really quite simple when you look closely at Fig. 16-16.

35. Use your carpenter's square and extend the lines across the back of your tile. Where they cross will be the center of your outlet box.

36. Now measure the outlet box from rim to rim.

37. With a compass draw a circle of a radius slightly less than half of the rim-to-rim measurement, the center of the circle being that intersecting point you marked before.

38. Transfer marking to right side of tile and cut out circle with your saw. If you want to be really fancy hold your saw at an angle and bevel the edge slightly.

39. Apply 1½-inch wide cove molding all around after your walls are finished.

PROJECT 7: PANELING WALLS

Follow directions for paneling given in Conversion II, Project 7. Remember that the color and pattern of the paneling you choose is very important. Be careful of very dark colors or very grainy patterns. Try to keep in mind the color scheme of rugs, furniture and drapery when choosing paneling.

PROJECT 8: HOME OFFICE

When we first started to research home offices we came upon a very strange fact. All those lovely home offices you see in remodeling magazines and how-to books are made for show—not for actual work by normal people. Now it may be that we are somewhat fanatical on the subject of working comfort—at least one of us admits to this. But it stands to reason that if you have to do work at home, most likely after a long day at the job, you should at least be comfortable. Comfort and efficiency go hand in hand. How in the world can you be comfortable, even if your desk and chair fit you by some miracle of clever aforethought, if you have to jump up every few minutes to consult your dictionary which is across the room, or get stuff out of your files, ten feet away, or reach to that 6-foot high shelf for a needed book? Maybe those statistically average people can cope with that kind of set-up, but we can't. And neither, we think, should you. Not if we have anything to do with it.

The first thing to consider is desk height. You have no idea what a difference a couple of inches can make in terms of aching shoulders, stiff necks and even roaring headaches. From tension, naturally. Maybe it is because one of us is a bit shorter than the hallowed average, just 5-foot, 3-inches, that made us so aware of the importance of such measurements.

A good way to find out the appropriate height of a desk surface is to sit down in the chair you're going to be using (having previously made certain that it is, indeed, comfortable—we'll tell you how to do this in just a minute), with your feet flat on the floor, your back straight and your shoulders relaxed. Now put your forearms on your desk. If your elbows are at a right angle the desk is fine. If your arms curve up from the elbow, your desk is too high, if they curve down too low. This is usually just a matter of an inch or two up or down. But it's also a matter of immense difference in comfort ratio.

As to finding the right chair, the same technique applies. Sit down in the chair, feet flat on the ground (for shorties that is often impossible and also for those of us taller than the "average." When you sit like this your thighs should be straight, your knees not jutting up. Whatever back support there is should be in the small of your back. For an office chair a tilting back is a godsend.

Thirdly, we want to clue you in on the matter of the typewriter table. On this we are experts. After all, our typewriters are almost an extension of ourselves, at least at those times when we aren't sawing, hammering, painting or otherwise occupying ourselves. Here we must tell you what we saw in one very respectable volume on furniture design. It was a typewriter table which very cleverly slid under a desk in company with a second unit to make something that looked like a large chest. The catch was that said typewriter table provided a lot of under-top storage space but, believe it or not, no knee-room whatsoever. We speculated for a while as to how to use this wonder. Did the designer expect you to kneel in front of it, Chinese fashion, or stand up while typing, though there really wasn't enough toe room, or most likely, lie on your stomach on a bench in front of it and type that way?

Most home office designs ignore typewriter tables and plunk the typewriter right down on the desk. Which is fine if you have your desk lowered to typewriter height which makes it hard to write by hand on the same desk without getting a mightly crick in your neck, or, if the desk height is normal, you'll get the same crick, though in a different vertebra, from having to reach up constantly.

Again there's no hard and fast rule—which is probably the reason why the whole subject is ignored or, in some cases, handled as if everyone would be comfortable with the same height desk and typewriter table. To find out what height you need as far as your typewriter table is concerned, you need to take into consideration not only your height but the type of machine you're using and how high it sits off the desk, the way the keyboard slants and how you're used to holding your hands and fingers.

Here are some of the ways we found to measure these variables to come up with the proper height. In the home offices you are going to build, there is no reason why you shouldn't have everything really customized.

How to Arrive at Proper Desk Heights

Materials: Chair you're going to use, typewriter.
Tools: Ruler, pencil, pad and a helper.

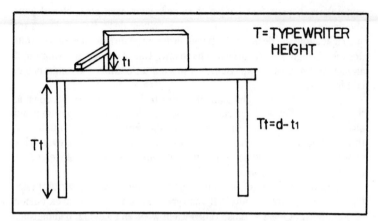

Fig. 16-18. Establishing correct typewriter height.

Instructions:

1. For desk, sit down on chair and have helper measure from floor to your elbow. That's all—that's the height for your writing desk.

2. To measure for the correct typewriter table height, you need to measure from the table on which the typewriter is sitting up to the keyboard. This can be as much as 4 or 5 inches for office machines, less for those extra flat streamlined portable jobs. Measure the typewriter in front and again at the rear of the keyboard. Again there's a difference anywhere from ½-inch to an inch depending on the camber of the keyboard. Now deduct that height from your writing desk height and you'll end up with a truly comfortable typing height (Fig. 16-18).

4. One more important thing to consider is knee room. Not only do you have to remember to leave some in your zest for utilizing every inch for storage, but you'll need more than you think. To figure that out take the width of your chair seat plus at least 6 inches, preferably 8 or 10 if you want to keep from barking your shins or hitting your knees when you move. And the height of the knee room has to be chair seat height plus at least 8 inches for you and some clearance. Add 9 or more if your thighs are particularly muscular, thick, or heavy (Fig. 16-19).

5. The last thing to consider on a typewriter table is elbow room. That's where most of those slide out-of-the-desk-at-right-angles jobs fall down in the expensive office furniture as well as home made desks.

6. Recall that your writing desk is anywhere from 1½ to 5 inches higher than your typewriter table. If you have your typewriter sitting smack up against it, as is the case in many such unfortunate combos, sooner or later you'll be hitting your crazy bone against the desk. Also, if your machine happens to be the flat kind your carriage may get hung up or jam into the desk. Measure from your elbow to the tip of your middle finger and multiply by 2. That's the distance that will keep your crazy bones forever safe and also the carriage of your typewriter. Follow Fig. 16-20 for

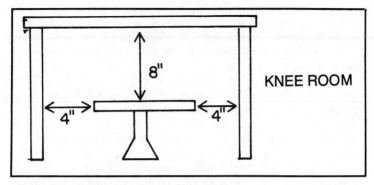

Fig. 16-19. Considering the knee room question.

2. Construct 2×2 bracing as we did for desk.
3. Mount plywood on top,

an ideal typing set-up. You'll be surprised how long you can work without fatigue.

7. If you are going to type more than just letters and such, you'll need space for reference books, a typing stand, and other necessary equipment. That's why our typewriter tables are even wider than the measurements given above.

Fitting Out the Home Office

As you know we have four closet openings on the office side of our home office, each 36 inches wide and about 24 inches deep. (If you have opted for the 16-inch depth you'll have to add a fold-down or pull-up addition to the shelf that will serve as your desk.) You can add to that if you like but on the whole we find that a 24-inch depth is plenty. Otherwise, all kinds of junk accumulate in the corners.

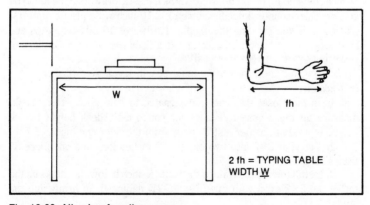

Fig. 16-20. Allowing for elbow room.

In Conversion V, we fitted out two adjacent closets for writing and typing desks respectively. The third closet became a supply closet and number four held Joe's camera and other photographic equipment as well as such things as old bank statements, records and whatever else Joe felt like keeping.

For projects that needed more space, such as some of the landscape plans that Joe likes to do, and also to serve as a cutting table for his wife, we rigged up file cabinets and a slab door across the room from the desks. As you will see if you consult the plans for the room—across the room was only a matter of 4 feet, easily transversed by a scoot and a turn on the desk chair.

We believe that secretary chairs are the thing to have. They are superb for comfort once they are adjusted properly, rugged, and you can wheel around on them easily. We recommend them for sewing chairs and drawing chairs as well. (You can get good secretary chairs in a used office furniture outlet. The upholstery might be a bit scuffed, but usually it's a matter of the entire office suite having been refurnished as a tax write-off).

To round-out the room, we designated a seat/table combination in one corner on which to flop when the income tax return or the checkbook balancing becomes too much. It also can serve as a guest bed. In fact, Joe was so intrigued with the double use idea that he decided to get a hide-a-way bed instead to make a neat guest room whenever his or her folks came to visit.

With this double use in mind we designed the other partition and specified that a 3-foot fold door be installed or that if preferred, a 6-foot accordion door be hung to close off the office.

Fitting Out the Closets for Home Office Use

Materials: 2 pieces of ¾-inch plywood, 22×36 inches for desk tops; 14 feet of 2×2's for supports; 6 feet of 1-inch corner molding for desk fronts; 6 feet of 1×6; 12 20×36 inch shelves; particle board or plywood ½-inch thick or ¾-inch, depending on shelf load; 6 12-inch plastic drawers, (the kind you get for under-counter kitchen cabinets); 2 10-inch wide plastic drawers, (narrower if you can find them), plus hardware; 16 pilaster strips and hardware; sealer; paint; formica or extra floor tiles (optional); piece of carpeting or carpet tiles (optional).

Tools: Saw, hammer, measuring tape, pencil, level, screwdriver.

Instructions:

1. In the closet that you've designated to hold your writing desk, measure up the required distance for comfortable desk height (which you've figured out as per instructions) from the floor and mark.

2. Cut your 2×2 into two pieces, 22 inches long and one piece 33 inches long.

3. Install these pieces along the walls ¾-inch below the marks on the top of the 2×2 even with this (Fig. 16-21) nailing them firmly into the studs.

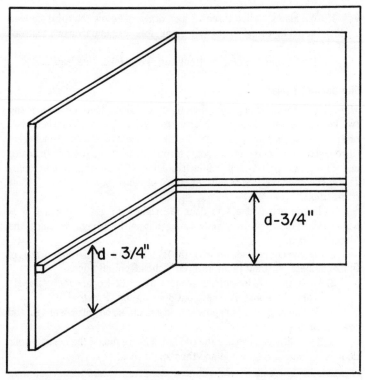

Fig. 16-21. Installing supports for build-in desk or typewriter table.

4. Nail plywood on top of 2×2 supports.

5. Install pilaster strips, two to a wall, on all side walls.

7. Finish shelves by painting or varnishing.

8. Install narrow shelves (1×6) above the desk then follow by full width shelves.

10. Install 10-inch or narrower, drawer on right side under desk if you're right-handed, on left if left-handed, following instructions that come with drawers.

11. Repeat instructions for typewriter desk changing only the measurement for the desk top height.

12. To finish desk top, apply a piece of formica or, better yet, use your leftover floor tiles. Be sure to seal the wood well, two coats at least— three are better. Follow instructions for laying vinyl tiles in the next project.

13. For the supply and hobby closets install the pilaster strips along the side walls.

14. We have figured six shelves (22×36-inch or narrower if you like) per closet.

15. We also installed three 12-inch drawers below the third shelves for little items that tend to get lost. Again follow manufacturer's instructions.

16. Put corner molding on front edges of desks. See Fig. 16-22.

File Cabinet Table

Materials: 2 18-inch deep file cabinets, or 1 18-inch deep file cabinet and two legs of the same height with hardware; one slab door, 60 inches long, or a piece of ¾-inch plywood, 60×24 inches, 15 feet of molding 1-inch wide (if you go the plywood route); epoxy; formica or floor tile (optional); sealer and stain; or paint; 1¾-inch or 2-inch molding if tile is used, 15 feet long.
Tools: Hammer, saw, screwdriver, paint brush.
Instructions:

1. If you can find a slab door the right size get it. Even if it is waterstained or otherwise visibly damaged it will be all right as long as the frame is intact.

2. Lay the door upside down on the floor and draw in outlines of tops of filing cabinets, settling them in three inches from all edges.

3. Apply epoxy to tops of file cabinets, about 12 drops, evenly spaced.

4. When the epoxy is tacky, put door on top. Presto—table!

5. To finish, if door is in good condition, stain and varnish or seal and paint with enamel.

6. If you like you can use the tile finish as we did on the desks if your door is damaged. Seal wood and then apply tiles.

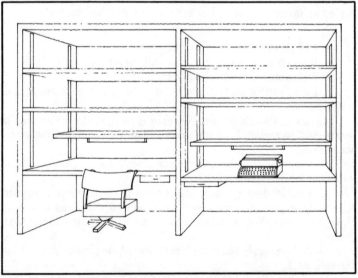

Fig. 16-22. Free standing closet in home office furnished with shelves, desk, and typewriter table.

268

7. Edge slab door with 1¾-inch or 2-inch molding to hide edges of tiles.

8. If you want to use formica, cut to size and cut two strips 60 inches long and two 24 inches long the exact thickness of the door (usually 1½ inches plus the thickness of the formica ¼-inch to ⅜-inch). Glue in place (Fig. 16-23).

9. If you want to use only one file cabinet, measure the exact height of what you have and get a pair of ready made table legs to match. In case you can't get the exact same size, buy some longer ones and cut to measure.

10. Install legs along one end of table before applying epoxy.

11. If you want to use plywood, follow either the instructions for two file cabinets or one file cabinet plus legs as given above.

12. Finish plywood as you choose, then put 1-inch molding all the way around even if you choose a stain and varnish or paint finish. If you choose tile, make sure your tile is only ¼-inch thick. Take 1¼-inch molding if thicker.

13. Your handiwork should resemble Fig. 16-24.

Build-In Seat/Bed

Materials: 90×28 inch piece of ¾-inch plywood; 20 feet of 1×4; 5 2×12's, 28 inches long (11 foot 8 inches in all); 1 1×10 90 inches long; nails; one foam mattress pad 4 or 5 inches thick and 6 feet long by 28 inches wide: four 4-inch thick 18×18 inch foam cushions; or three 4-inch thick foam cushions 24×24 inch; fabric to cover cushions and mattress; thread; zippers; stain and varnish; nails.

Tools: Saber saw, hammer, measuring tape, pencil, carpenter's square, sewing machine, scissors.

Instructions:

1. Cut your 2×12's into five pieces, 28 inches long.

2. Notch each 2×12 with a notch, 7 inches deep and 5 inches high (Fig. 16-25).

3. Space your 2×12's 22 inches apart, one on each end to make a base for your plywood. Put them notched side down.

4. Nail top to 2×12's.

5. Nail a 90-inch piece of 1×4 across the notches for toe space.

6. Nail the 90-inch 1×10 across the front, raising it up so that the top edge is about ¾-inch above the plywood so you'll have a lip to prevent the cushions from sliding off.

7. Nail a strip of 1×4 flat along the back of the plywood. Nail two strips, 23¼ inches long of the 1×4, along the sides of the top. Miter corners if you are really finicky, we don't feel it's necessary.

8. Cover cushions and mattress as instructed in Conversion III, Project 12.

9. Sand base and top and finish with stain and varnish.

10. You will now have a 6-foot couch plus an 18-inch space for a table.

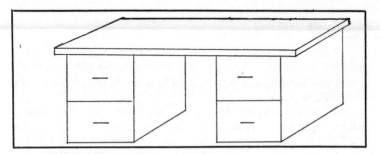

Fig. 16-23. Double file cabinet desk marvel.

You can either give that space an extra coat or two of varnish, put in a piece of formica, or some more floor tiles. Take your choice (Fig. 16-26).

PROJECT 9: SEWING CENTER IN CLOSET

One of the closets on the family room side of the closet wall was outfitted to become a sewing center. Basically the procedure was the same as in the home office closets.

Materials: ¾-inch thick plywood for table top; 2×2's for supports; two plywood or particle board shelves; 1×6 for narrow shelf; three large 12-inch plastic drawers; drawer dividers; nails; one 10-inch drawer; four cork tiles, (self-stick); small wall pocket storage system; 3 feet of 1-inch molding pilaster strips (4).

Tools: Hammer, saber saw, screwdriver, measuring tape, pencil, level.

Instructions:

1. To measure for proper table height proceed as we did for typewriter table, substituting your sewing machine for the typewriter. Measure from the pressure foot down. Again, make sure that forearms can be held level or with very little upward tilt.

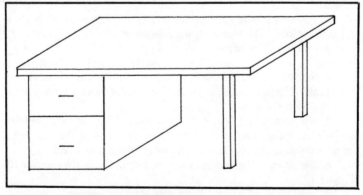

Fig. 16-24. Single file cabinet desk with lots of room at the top.

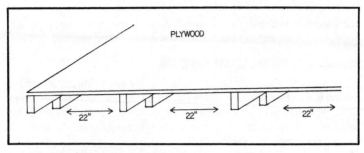

Fig. 16-25. Building base for build-in bed/seat combo.

4. Install pilaster strips on side walls.

5. Install 10-inch drawer on one side below table top.

6. Put in shelves, narrow one first, large ones on top.

7. Finish table top as desired, trim with molding.

8. Mount four self-stick cork tiles on one of the side walls.

9. Sew small wall pocket systems, see Conversion III, Project II, and hang on back and/or side wall as desired.

10. Install three large drawers underneath first large shelf divide with drawer dividers, use for notions.

PROJECT 10: CUSTOMIZING OTHER CLOSETS

There are three closets left on the family room side of the closet wall. One of these became a general storage closet for fabric and needle work supplies. It was outfitted with six large shelves and four plastic drawers.

Each of the little girls was allocated one of the remaining closets. The first shelf in each was placed 14 inches from the floor to allow scooting in of bulky toys such as block boxes, Lite-brites and such. The next two shelves were spaced 18 inches apart and each had two drawers attached. While

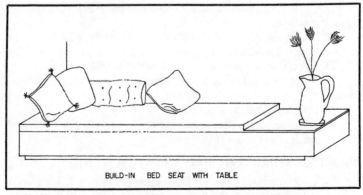

Fig. 16-26. Nifty build-in bed/seat combo with attached table.

there were two more shelves in each of these closets they were up too high to be of much use and so were delegated to out-of-season toys and clothing.

PROJECT 11: BUILDING SHORT PARTITION

If you like, this partition can be built at the same time, or just after, you put in the closet wall and before you install the ceiling. This will mean a bit of additional tile cutting when it's time to put in the ceiling. It can also be installed at this point and treated as an independent project. Just don't put in your floor until you think of it.

Materials: 5 2×4's, 8-feet long; 2 pieces of 2×4, 3-feet long; 1½ panel of the paneling you're using in the room; 1 2×4, 6-feet long and 1 piece of 2×4, 10 inches long; nails; baseboard; quarter-round; glue; lag screws.

Tools: Drill and masonry bit, screwdriver, hammer, measuring tape, pencil, carpenter's square, slip-stick.

Instructions:

1. Exactly across from the corner of your playhouse-cozy nook and in line with the front edge of it, install a 3-foot 2×4 as a base plate, using lag screws to tie it into the slab.

2. With your slip-stick measure the distance from the sole plate to the ceiling or header, whichever is nearest.

3. Deduct 1½ inches from that measurement and cut two studs.

4. Measure again in the middle of the sole plate and do the same. Cut one stud.

5. At the other end, cut two studs again to the same measurement.

6. Mark the studs on your sole plate.

7. Lay the 9-foot 2×4 alongside and transfer markings to it, starting at the wall side. There will be a 3-foot section left over (Fig. 16-27).

8. 6-foot 10-inches from the floor, attach another of the 3-foot long 2×4's parallel to the top plate.

10. At 18 inches from the last stud fasten a 10-inch cripple stud between the top plate and the parallel 2×4.

11. Call for help. With your helper lift up the frame and set in place on top of the sole plate.

12. Tie in top plate and tie into wall. Use molly bolts if you are between studs. Toe-nail to sole plate.

13. Tie end of top plate to corner 2×4's of playhouse/nook.

14. Panel walls and opening, use corner molding on corners to reinforce.

15. Install baseboards if desired.

16. Install accordion door in opening or, if you prefer, install bi-fold door to match closet doors (Fig. 16-28).

PROJECT 12: INSTALLING ALL GLASS STORM DOOR IN OFFICE

Follow instructions given for Conversion IV, Project 7. It's a good idea to paste decals on both all-glass storm and sliding glass doors to remind children not to run up against them.

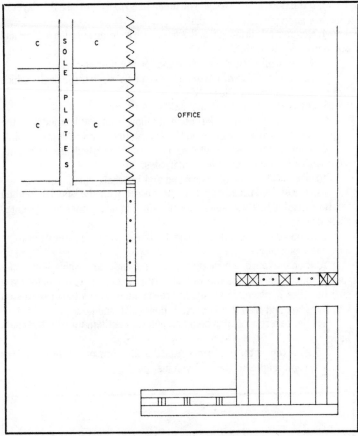

Fig. 16-27. Putting down sole plate for short partition to divide home office from family room.

PROJECT 13: LAYING A VINYL TILE FLOOR

Laying vinyl tile is quite similar to laying carpet tile. Re-read the instructions for that venture. Here we will only emphasize those aspects that are different.

Materials: Vinyl tile (vinyl-asbestos, or any hard floor tile other than ceramic) self sticking variety; cement sealer; chalk line; mastic, if tiles without self-stick feature are used; TSP (trisodium phosphate); hot water.

Tools: Mastic spreader (optional); wire brush, scrub brush, tub, straight edge, scissors, pencil, measuring tape, trowel.

Instructions:

1. Inspect floor. If there are cracks and holes patch with sand-mix concrete. (Sakrete brand comes in small bags).

2. Wire brush all over the concrete.

3. If the floor is very rough you might need to trowel on a thin layer of concrete and smooth it thoroughly.

4. Remove all surface oil and grease with a strong solution of TSP and hot water. Scrub well.

5. Rinse well with clear water and let dry thoroughly.

6. Seal thoroughly with two coats of sealer. Ask your tile dealer which works best under your tiles.

7. Make the decision to buy self-stick or not.

8. If you go the self-stick route just follow what you learned with the carpet tiles and review section on tiles in the first section of this book.

9. If you go the mastic route, again consult your tile dealer to find out what works best with your particular tiles.

10. Find the center of your room and lay chalk lines.

11. Carefully spread some of the mastic with the special toothed mastic spreader that you get at the tile store in one corner of the center chalk cross.

12. Spread it out evenly, enough for one row, being careful not to go over the chalk line.

13. Some experts advise putting down mastic on a whole fourth of a room. But unless yours is the kind of mastic that needs to dry before you put your tiles in place, we would not recommend it. It's too easy to step into the gook and trail it all over the floor, slab and new tiles.

14. Set in a row of tiles being careful to line them up with the chalk line.

15. Now repeat the performance on the other arm of the corner and lay a row at right angles to the one you just put in.

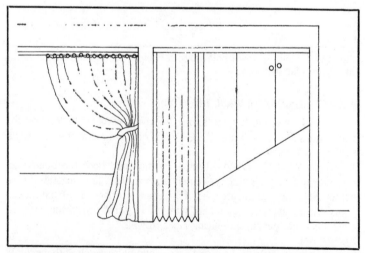

Fig. 16-28. Completed partition, new door and glimpse of playhouse nook.

16. Continue that way until that quarter of the room is tiled, except for the border where you will have to cut tiles.

17. Now repeat all this for the other three corners.

18. Lastly cut your tiles to fit the border. Most tiles can be easily cut with scissors.

19. Use the old trick of laying a loose tile on top of your last set in one. Then put another on top of that and slide it out to butt against the wall.

20. Now mark the tile for trimming along the back edge of the measuring tile. (The waste piece is the one covered by the loose tile).

21. Butt your tiles as you lay them.

22. Snap the tiles in place, don't slide them in.

23. Adhesives vary in drying time so consult your can very closely.

23. Use a rolling pin to roll over your tiles to be sure they bond well. Roll each time you've put down three rows.

23. If you have trouble cutting a tile with scissors, warm it slightly. That usually helps.

24. Of course, you can cut tiles with a knife and a straight edge but we prefer scissors. The heating to make cutting easier applies to that method, too.

25. Don't spread adhesive so thickly that it will ooze out between the tiles.

26. Clean up specks and spots of adhesive that are on the tiles with water. Use steel wool if you have to. If you wipe as you go you shouldn't have much trouble.

27. Don't wash your new tile floor for about a week.

28. Now we both know why people prefer ready-stick, don't we? But it isn't as bad as it sounds. We've lived through it several times, and so can you. The question one of us asked at this point was "why suffer?"

PROJECT 14: FINISHING UP

This conversion takes a lot of work and there are usually a lot loose ends left after the individual projects are completed. Here are some of them:

1. Stain or otherwise finish baseboards and quarter-round and put in place around your walls.

2. Put up corner molding between walls and ceiling.

3. Install fixtures in your home office cubicles. You can either use a fluorescent work light over each desk as in Conversion III, Project 10, or you can put up some fluorescent strip lights under the shelves.

4. Install fluorescent under-the-counter lights along the sidewalls of your sewing center, two to a side. These lights are inexpensive and can be wall mounted or hung.

Chapter 17
Garage Conversion VI

This was the conversion of a single, attached garage in an older home. The garage was attached to the house on one long side. The other long side faced the back yard, as did one short end. The other short end was the original garage opening, which faced a busy intersection. There were no windows in the garage and only one exterior door in the short wall opposite the garage doors. Since the lot sloped toward the back, the garage was several steps below the floor level of the house. Concrete stairs led from the garage floor close to the rear door up to a landing and the kitchen door. Incidentally, this was the only exterior door in the house that led out to the back yard. In fact, it was the only other outside door beside the front door.

What the family, parents, a boy, 13, and a girl, 10, really wanted was a room in which they could pursue their varied interests and hobbies. They also needed scads of storage space to accomodate the materials and where-with-all required by their myriad interests.

In addition, the family wanted to have a view of their lovely, secluded back yard, lots of natural light, and floors and walls that could be cleaned easily.

The most difficult requirement, and one that was of special concern to all of them, was their wish to divide the new family room from the back door/kitchen door hallway. As the mother of the family succinctly put it—"We really don't want to have the trash carried out through our family room, or the dirty cat boxes, for that matter."

It was decided to close up the garage door opening completely. That still left the driveway intact, but out of sight from the family room. Instead, two big picture windows were cut into the long wall to over-look the back yard and bring in lots of beautiful daylight. The former garage door wall was selected to become a very unique storage wall guaranteed to have room for all the millions of odd bits and pieces the family found indispensible to their hobbies and interests.

The problem of the back door was solved by building a divider closet, which served to store coats, boots and like accouterments for forays outdoors. A new short flight of steps that led from the landing into the family room was also installed.

The walls were finished with plastic coated paneling and the floor, after long and heated arguments, with DeHanis tile.

The back entry floor also got some DeHanis tile and the concrete steps, landing and new steps painted to match the color of the tile. Strips of indoor/outdoor carpeting, gold color to match the gold tones of the paneling were used on both stairways and landing.

The divider closet was finished in matching paneling and the doors stained and varnished in a related darker shade. See before and after floor plans, Fig. 17-1A and B.

PROJECT 1: REMOVING GARAGE DOORS

Follow instructions given in Conversion I, Project 1.

PROJECT 2: ENCLOSING GARAGE DOOR OPENING

Follow instruction given in Conversion III, Project 2.

PROJECT 3: CUTTING OPENINGS AND INSTALLING PICTURE WINDOWS

Follow directions given in Conversion IV, Project 2.

PROJECT 4: BUILDING UNIQUE STORAGE WALL

Materials: 6 6-foot long standards; 30 16-inch brackets; 35 1¾-inch #6 flat-head screws; 12 1×6's 14-foot long; 78 beer boxes; 1 gallon paint sealer; 3 gallons high gloss oil based enamel; 1 quart wood stain; varnish; two dozen 4d masonry nails.
Tools: Drill, small bit for starting screw holes, screwdriver or screwdriver attachment on drill, carpenter's level, measuring tape, pencil, level.
Instructions:

1. Beginning at corner stud, mount standards to studs, 32-inch on center (every other stud) ending at opposite corner stud.

2. To install, hold standard up to wall, 12 inches above floor and mark the first screw hole.

3. Drill hole and fasten standard to wall with screw.

4. Check standard with level to make sure it's perfectly vertical before marking bottom screw hole.

5. Drill hole and tighten screw.

6. Drive home the rest of the screws on the standard.

7. Mount the other five standards in the same way.

8. Put in the six bottom brackets so the bottom shelves will be 16 inches from the floor.

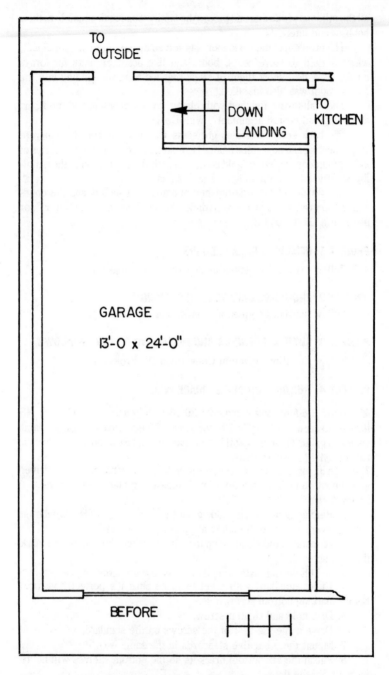

TO
OUTSIDE

DOWN

TO
KITCHEN

LANDING

GARAGE

13'-0 x 24'-0"

BEFORE

Fig. 17-1A. Scale plan showing before view of Conversion VI.

278

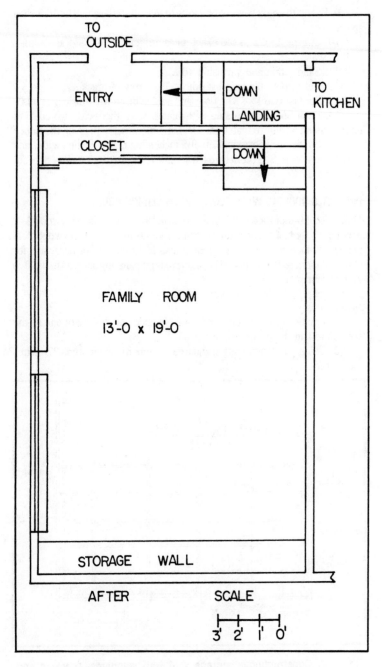

TO
OUTSIDE

ENTRY

DOWN

TO
KITCHEN

LANDING

CLOSET

DOWN

FAMILY ROOM

13'-0 x 19'-0

STORAGE WALL

AFTER SCALE

3' 2' 1' 0'

Fig. 17-1B. Scale plan showing the after view of Conversion VI.

279

9. Put up the next rows of brackets to that all shelves will be 16 inches apart.

10. Cut the 1×6's to the exact measurement of your storage wall— wall to wall.

11. Sand, stain and varnish 1×6's.

12. Put two 1×6's side by side on each row of brackets.

13. Put last two 1×6's on floor and hold in place with masonry nails.

14. Paint boxes on outside with sealer, first, then with two coats of enamel using a color to match the DeHanis tile which will go on the floor.

15. Boxes are approximately 9½ inches high, 10½ inches wide, and 16½ inches deep. See them on each shelf level, endwise, one box per foot as in Fig. 17-2.

PROJECT 5:DIVIDING WALL CLOSET WITH SLIDING DOORS

Materials: 4 9-foot 2×4's; 8 7-foot 2×4's; 4 2×8-foot, ¼-inch plywood A-D panels; 42 foot of corner molding; 4 2-foot×6 foot 8 inch plywood A-D panels, ¾-inch for doors; 2 4-foot tracks and two sets of hardware for sliding doors; 16 foot of inside corner molding; paneling and 10d nails; two sets of four pilasters.

Tools: Saber saw, hammer, screwdriver, caulking gun.

Instructions:

1. Lay two of the 9-foot 2×4's side by side and designate one as the sole plate and the other, top plate #1.

2. Using your combination square mark positions for studs 27-inches on centers.

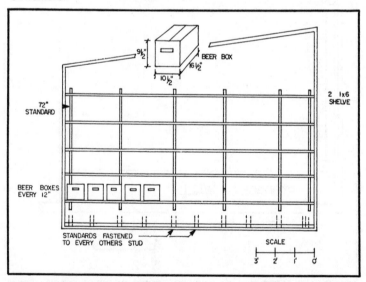

Fig. 17-2. Constructing a storage wall with standards, brackets and enameled beer cartons.

3. Pull top and bottom plates about seven feet apart and insert five of the 7-foot 2×4's at the positions marked.

4. Nailing through the top of the top plate and the bottom of the sole plate, nail the five 2×4 studs into place (Fig. 17-3).

5. Cut one of the 9-foot 2×4's into 17 inch lengths (six are needed).

6. Fasten one on each corner of the wall frame and two in the center with corner braces as illustrated in Fig. 16-5.

7. Lay the remaining 9-foot 2×4 onto the three 17-inch spacers fastened to top plate #1 and secure to the spacers with T-plates. This is top plate #2.

8. The remaining three 7-foot 2×4's are now nailed into place between top plate #2 and the 17-inch spacers extending from the sole plate. (Fig. 17-4).

This completes the frame for your dividing wall closet. While it is still "on its back" on the floor, install the tracks for the sliding doors.

9. Secure the 4-foot door tracks to the underside of top plate #2 with screws provided in sliding door hardware kit. Note. the tracks go on the underside when the frame is in its normal upright position, not the position it is in now, on the floor. (Fig. 17-5).

10. Nail one of the ¼-inch 2×7-foot plywood panels on each end of the frame to close in the sides of the closet wall.

11. Lift the frame up to its normal position and place one end against a wall so that the frame is occupying its final space as a dividing wall.

12. The end against the wall will span two studs (it's 24 inches deep). Your wall studs are likely 16 inches on center. Find the two studs and nail that end of the divider closet to the wall studs.

13. Since you just tied one end of the closet into the wall of the garage, you can tie down your sole plate with masonry nails the 8d size.

14. Use a heavy hammer, at least a 2-pounder and check the point of each nail before you drive it to make sure it is sharp.

15. Use two nails every foot or so along the sole plate.

16. Use six nails in each of the 17-inch spacer 2×4's that are on the floor.

17. Cut four plywood panels to 2×7-foot size (the ¼-inch kind).

18. Nail these panels to the inside ends and both sides of the middle partition in the closet.

19. Cut plywood pieces to fit across the top of the structure.

20. Nail in place.

21. Finish outside of closet with paneling to match rest of room.

22. Stain and finish molding to match paneling unless you have brought color matched molding.

23. Mount the eight pilasters on the inside ends and center divider with the screws that some with the pilaster sets.

24. Cover the back side of the frame by nailing and glueing paneling to the 7×9-foot space.

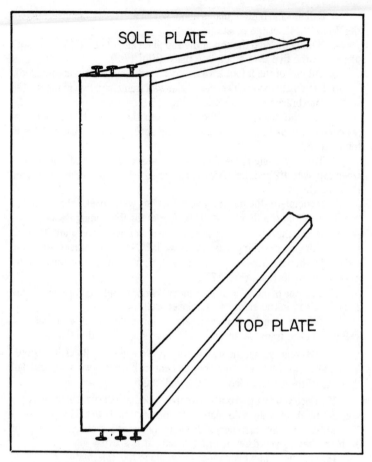

Fig. 17-3. Constructing divider closet, nailing detail.

25. Sand, stain and varnish the four 2×6-foot, 8-inch, ¾-inch thick plywood panels which are going to be your closet door.

26. Attach wheels to tops of panels according to the instructions that came with the closet door hardware.

27. Hang doors in tracks and install guide tracks on floor.

28. You should use lead shields to hold screws (Fig. 17-6).

29. Fit out your closet to suit yourself. Use 1-inch plywood or particle board for shelves. Cut any width you like providing it is less than 21 inches.

30. If you use particle board, support your shelf in the middle by mounting a utility bracket directly underneath and anchor it with screws to the center stud in each closet.

31. Do the same even if you use plywood or other material if the shelf will bear a heavy load.

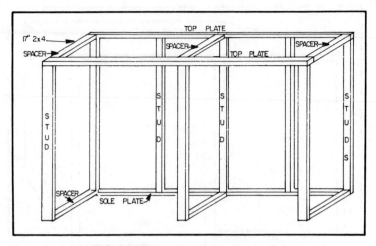

Fig. 17-4. Framing in the divider closet.

32. If you like you can use utility brackets to support one end of a half shelf.

33. You can install hardware for a hanging pole at any height.

34. Finish your divider closet with corner molding on all edges.

PROJECT 6: STAIRS FROM LANDING TO ROOM

Materials: 1 10-foot 2×12-inch lumber for three stringers; 1 16-foot 1×10-inch lumber for risers and header joist; 1 12-foot 2×12-inch lumber for treads; 8d & 16d nails; masking tape; plastic wood; lag screws.

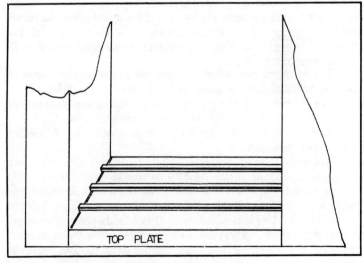

Fig. 17-5. Putting down the track for the sliding doors.

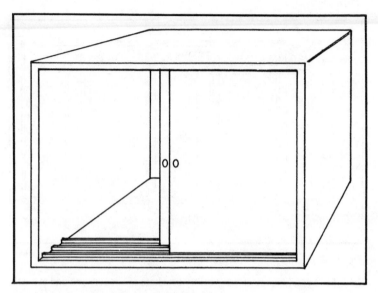

Fig. 17-6. The completed divider closet.

Tools: Saber saw, hammer, framing square, story pole (see below).

A story pole is any pole (a 2×4 does nicely) which is longer than the difference in elevation between floors and on which you can inscribe evenly spaced markings.

Instructions:

1. Place your story pole beside the landing with one end resting on the garage floor and mark off the location of the landing floor on it. In our conversion it measured 29 inches (Fig. 17-7).

2. Divide this measurement into something around seven that comes out to an even number. In our case 7.25 gives us 4 which is the number of risers 7¼-inches high that we will need for our stairway, raising it by 29 inches from floor to floor.

3. Mark off the riser height as evenly spaced markings on your story pole and hold it against the landing to double check your arithmetic. If the last riser does not come out *exactly* right, re-calculate and re-space on your story pole until it does. All the riser spaces must be equal.

4. Saw the 10-foot 2×12 lumber into three equal lengths of 40 inches each to form stringers.

5. On your framing square, tape off the riser height on its short leg. We put a piece of masking tape at the 7¼-inch mark.

6. A good way to determine your tread length for inside residential stairways is to subtract the riser height from 17½ inches. This will give us a tread length of 10¼ inches. Subtracting 1 inch for the nosing (that part of the tread that overhangs the riser) we arrive at 9¼-inch as the length of the tread cut on the stringer. Mark this distance off on the long leg of the framing square.

284

7. Begin an inch or so from what will be the top of one of the 40×2-inch stringers, position the framing square as shown in Fig. 17-8 and trace the outline of the triangle onto the stringer.

8. Move the framing square down the stringer and repeat the triangular outline until the required number of risers and treads have been measured off. In our stairway up to the landing we have three risers and three treads.

9. The last riser, the one at the bottom of the staircase, will be shorter than the rest since there is no tread thickness below. So you'll have to cut it off to 5¾-inches.

10. When you add to this the 1½-inch thickness of the first tread you'll come up with the required riser height of 7¼ inches. See Fig. 17-8.

11. When you get to the top riser, on your stringer you must increase it by the amount you took away at the bottom riser.

12. Remember, though, that you are using the header joist as your top riser so it is not marked on your stringer. (Sounds like "Catch-22" doesn't it?)

13. But it isn't. Ultimately you'll align your stringers so that the top step cut will be 8¾ inches below the top of the landing. Clever?

14. Carefully saw out the stringer on the lines you have drawn, cutting away everything in the shaded area shown on Fig. 17-9.

15. Make a right angle cut underneath the lowest riser and another at the end of the lowest riser.

16. Make a similar right angle cut at the end of the uppermost tread.

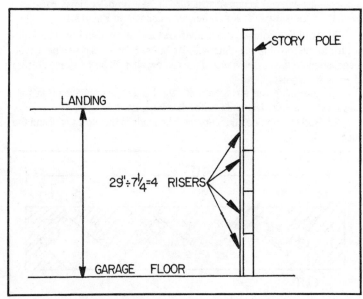

Fig. 17-7. Using a story pole.

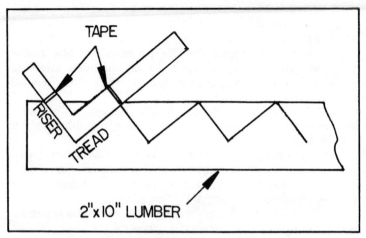

Fig. 17-8. Measuring stringers for stairway.

17. Trace the pattern of treads and risers onto the other two stringers by laying the cut-out stringer over them.

18. Carefully saw out the other two stringers and lay all three aside for the moment.

19. Cut 48 inches, or exactly enough for a tight fit between the closet wall and the room wall, off the 16-foot 1×10 lumber to use as a header joist. Since our landing was a cement structure there was no floor joist to use as a header for the stairway. Notch header as shown in Fig. 17-10.

20. Drill five holes in the header joist as indicated in Fig. 16-14 and secure to the top of the landing with lag bolts. 8d nails can also be driven diagonally into the closet wall and the room wall from both top and bottom of the header joist.

21. Assemble the stringers onto the header joist as shown in Fig. 17-11 and nail with 16d nails to the header joist.

22. Nail the outside stringers into the studs in the closet wall and the room wall.

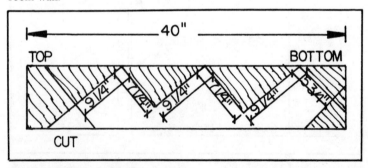

Fig. 17-9. Cutting stringers for stairway.

286

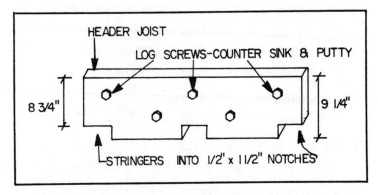

Fig. 17-10. Preparing header joist for stairway.

23. Secure all three stringers to the garage floor with 16d masonry nails, or lag screws if your brand of cement floor will not take nails.

24. Cut the threads from the 2-inch lumber, three threads, 4 feet wide in our version. Remember that the width of the tread includes the nosing, minus the thickness of the riser material, so we cut three 10¼-inch treads—(11 inches—¾-inch=10¼ inch).

25. Cut risers from remainder of 1×10 lumber: Two 7¼-inch and one 5¾-inch in 4-foot lengths.

26. Nail risers and treads into place across the stringers with 8d nails.

27. Countersink and putty over all nail heads so that stairway is ready for carpeting.

28. Sand and seal wood.

29. Paint with deck enamel to match DeHanis tile or stain and varnish to match paneling.

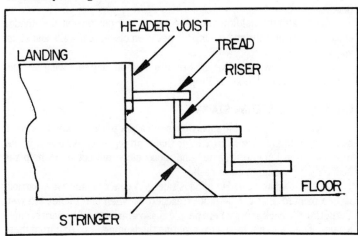

Fig. 17-11. Stairway after header joist is installed.

30. For carpeting see Project 11, this section. For finished view, see Fig. 17-12.

PROJECT 7: INSTALLING ACOUSTICAL TILE CEILING

Follow directions given in Conversion V, Project 6.

PROJECT 8: FINISH WALLS WITH PANELING

Follow directions given in Conversion II, Project 7.

PROJECT 9: LAYING DEHANIS TILE FLOOR

Follow instructions given in Conversion III, Project 14.

PROJECT 10: FINISHING THE JOBS

Materials: Color-coordinated baseboards, quarter-round and nails; or baseboard and quarter-round stained to match paneling; enough for the family room and the new back entry. Paint for the back steps and landing to match the DeHanis tile on the floor. Sealer for concrete, a glass storm door for the back door, new fixture for landing.
Tools: Saw, hammer, pencil, paint brush, knife.
Instructions:

1. First, finish the back hall stairway by installing a glass stormdoor in the back door following instruction that come with the door.

2. Either before you have put down your DeHanis tile or after you've finished sealing it (a month after installation) seal your stairs and landing.

3. Paint to match DeHanis tile.

4. Install your baseboards and quarter-rounds in this area.

5. Second, finish the family room walls by installing prefinished (by the factory or you) baseboards and quarter-rounds around the DeHanis tile floor.

6. Install any molding you have not as yet put up—at the divider closet, between walls and ceiling, or between closet and walls and stairways.

7. Install new attractive light fixture over landing following instructions given in Conversion I, Project 7.

PROJECT 11: CARPETING STAIRS

Though it seems a bit superfluous to carpet perfectly good concrete stairs, or a brand new staircase for that matter, there is reason in our madness, not just the urge for one more more project or to help the economy by spending more cash.

Actually what we had in mind is safety. A concrete stairway, particularly a painted one, can be quite treacherous when one's soles are wet. Carpeting the back stairs where people chase in and out of the yard seemed a must. That, inevitably, led to carpeting the landing, too. And from there it was obvious that the other flight of stairs needed its bit of carpeting to

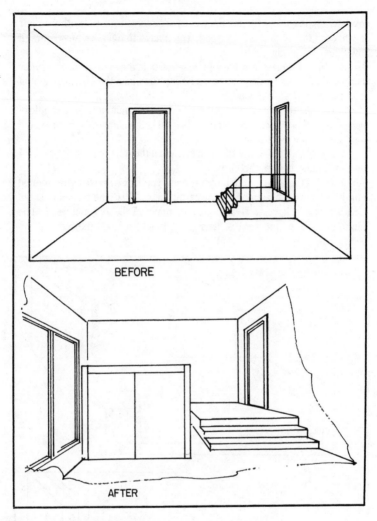

BEFORE

AFTER

Fig. 17-12. Before and after views of stairway conversion.

keep equal status. We used indoor/outdoor carpeting for easy cleaning and installation and because of its low cost. We used double-faced tape so that the carpeting could be taken up and hosed off outdoors.

Materials: Enough carpeting to cover the staircase, double-faced carpet tape.

Tools: Measuring tape, straight edge, pencil, scissors, chalk.

Instructions:

1. Decide how you want your stairway covered. There are several options: see Fig. 17-13. You can have all of the stairway treads and risers

covered or you can opt for just the treads. You can start level with the floor or you can start with the first tread. You'll have to figure out for yourself how much carpeting you'll need.

2. This, of course, is quite simple—you take the measurement of your risers and multiply by the number of risers, then take the measurement of your treads and do likewise.

3. Add the thickness of your treads times their number plus a couple of inches to tie down bottom and top. This total is the number of inches you'll need for carpet length.

4. As to width, 3 feet will do nicely, even though the front stairs are 4 feet wide. Just center the carpet.

5. Using the total length measurement you'll also arrive at the needed length of your double-faced rug or carpet tape. This tape comes in small reels and you'll have to figure out how many of those you'll need. The length of the tape per reel is usually marked clearly on the box.

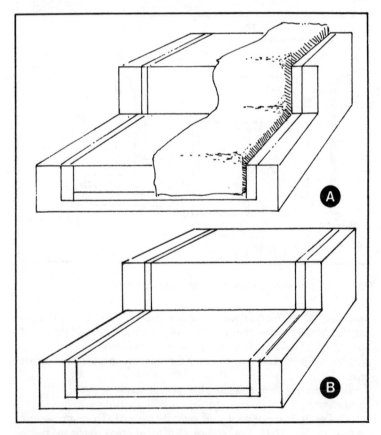

Fig. 17-13. Various ways of carpeting of stairway.

6. Make sure your stairs are clean and dust-free and your paint or varnish completely and utterly dry and cured.

7. On your 3-foot stairway, attach tape along the outside edges, following the contours of the stairs exactly.

8. Be sure not to pull the tape too taut. Bring it around the edge of the treads carefully, making sure it adheres well. Now take off top paper.

9. Put your rug piece on the stairs, lining up the edge with the tape and gently let it fall down over the steps, pressing it down with your hands so that it sticks to the tapes.

10. If you don't do it right at first, don't worry. That's the beauty of the double-faced tape, you can take the rug off without harm. So try agin.

11. Anchor bottom of carpet with a piece of tape running along the bottom of the bottom riser.

12. Glue a piece of quarter-round over it if you like, but remember that if you do that you won't be able to take up your rug and hose it off outside.

13. Bring the top piece up over the edge of the landing and anchor there with a long piece (3 feet of double-faced tape).

14. On the front stairs you proceed likewise with one difference. Put the strips of tape in 6½-inches from the edge of your stairway.

15. To cover the landing you'll need a 4-foot long strip of 3-foot wide carpeting.

16. Cut three strips of double-faced tape 4 feet long and two strips 3 feet long.

17. Place double-faced tape all over landing in the pattern illustrated in Fig. 17-13.

18. Start the strips along the stairs ½-inch in from the edge.

19. Trim off that ½-inch from the two corresponding edges of your carpet piece.

20. Lay down carpet on tapes and press in place.

21. You'll notice that you'll have a double thickness of carpet and tape at the edges of the stairway. Since the carpeting is thin, we can get away with this overlap and at the same time, reinforce the edge of the landing.

22. If you want, you can tie the carpet down at the edge of the landing with stair nosing from the hardware store. But again, this will prevent you from taking up the carpet for hosing down or other methods of thorough cleaning.

Chapter 18
Garage Conversion VII

This conversion is one that started as a single, attached garage. The garage itself was wood. The house, to which it belonged, was a 2-story with brick veneer on the first floor and wood siding above. A short driveway led to the street. Though the street was not busy, the view, with two cars nuzzling at the front so to speak, was not terrific. The family of five; two little girls, one boy and parents, needed a room in which to work and play. Though the house itself was larger than usual, it didn't provide space for the activities the family wanted and needed to do. The father repaired small appliances as a sideline, the mother did all of the family's dressmaking and often earned extra money by making clothing or slipcovers for friends and neighbors. The two little girls adored making collages out of the bits and pieces left over from their parent's efforts plus anything else they could find. And the boy's great passion was collecting rocks of all kinds. He collected, sorted, and displayed them, and spent hours and hours tumbling and polishing them.

The mother requested a really good place for her plants, because the house, in spite of her acknowledged green thumb, had made it difficult to raise and display plants.

The garage had finished, sheetrock walls and ceiling and a smooth concrete floor that had been painted. There were two 3-foot square windows in one long wall and an outside door in the center of the rear garage wall. The other long wall, the exterior wall of the house was brick, and there was one door leading from the garage into the dining room of the house.

Since the garage was a single, it was a bit hard to come up with all the space needed for all that activity, particularily because this family was one of those about which you read in kids' books but rarely hope to meet: they really enjoyed each other and loved to be in the same room all together. They literally thrived on togetherness, in spite of all the bad publicity togetherness has had in recent years.

Finally it was decided to enclose the garage door opening and set in a large, 6×4-foot window. Two storage areas flanked the window and the space directly in front of the window was designated as the plant bench.

On the opposite end of the room two work areas were designed one on each side of the door in the rear wall. A third work area, identical to the other two, was placed between the two smaller windows in the long wall.

The brick wall was painted white and became the featured background for the family's favorite posters. A 7½-foot homemade sofa and a couple of comfortable work chairs for the grown-ups completed the furnishings. The little girls were still in the floor-sprawling stage, but three stools with back rests were on hand to provide the kids with comfortable seating when they wanted it.

As an afterthought it was decided to build a screen across the driveway from the corner of the house to the fence, put a gate in the fence and treat the area as a patio where the plants could be protected from the heavy summer wind storms that were common in the area. Also an all-glass storm door was installed in the rear door for more light. See before and after views, Fig. 18-1A-B.

PROJECT 1: REMOVING GARAGE DOOR

Follow directions in Conversion I, Project 1.

PROJECT 2: ENCLOSING FRONT OF GARAGE DOOR AND INSTALLING WINDOW

Follow directions in Conversion I, Project 2 disregarding the installation of door.

PROJECT 3: STORAGE UNITS

Materials: 20 pieces of 2×3 cut to 77½-inch length ⎫
    20 pieces of 2×3 cut to 33-inch length ⎬ = 305 Foot
    64 pieces of 2×3 cut to 22½-inch length ⎭
    2 sheets of 4×8-foot, ¾-inch thick plywood; 8d finishing nails;
    22 feet of 1-inch molding or veneer tape; glue.
Tools: Saw, hammer, measuring tape, pencil, carpenter's square.
Instructions:

1. Lay five of the long (77½-inch) pieces on the floor, spacing them 2½ inches apart.

2. Use pieces of 2×3 as a spacer to make the layout perfect.

3. Now lay the 22½-inch pieces across your layout to form a grid.

4. Start 2½ inches in from the end of your long pieces and space the cross pieces 2½ inches apart, just like you did before (Fig. 18-2).

5. You should end up with a 2½-inch space at the top end.

6. Nail and glue cross pieces in place.

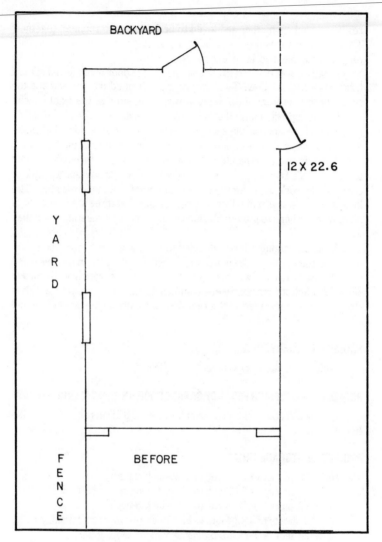

BACKYARD

Y
A
R
D

12 X 22.6

F
E
N
C
E

BEFORE

Fig. 18-1A. Scale plan for before view of Conversion VII.

7. Repeat procedure for the other side of your storage unit.

8. Now put both sides on end along the long sides and glue and nail the 33-inch long pieces to each of the uprights or long pieces on both sides, forming a four-sided frame (Fig. 18-3).

9. Sand and finish with clear varnish after countersinking nails.

10. You may stain it if you wish, but clear is easiest and airiest.

11. Cut four shelves from the ¾-inch plywood. If you are going to use molding to finish off your shelves in front cut your shelves to 33×21

¾-inches of whatever length will include the thickness of your molding plus the width of your shelf and equal 22½ inches.

12. If you are planning to use the veneer tape you can save yourself all that figuring and simply cut your boards to the required 22½ inches.

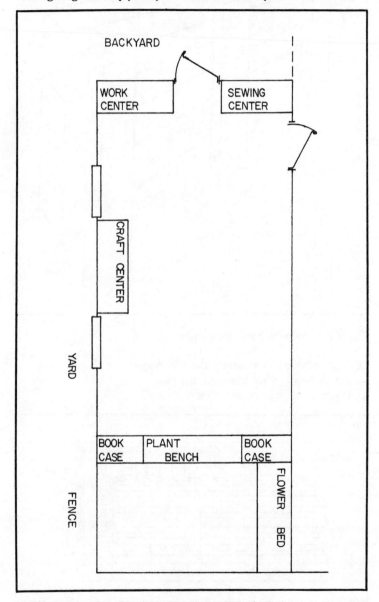

Fig. 18-1B. Scale plan for after view of Conversion VII.

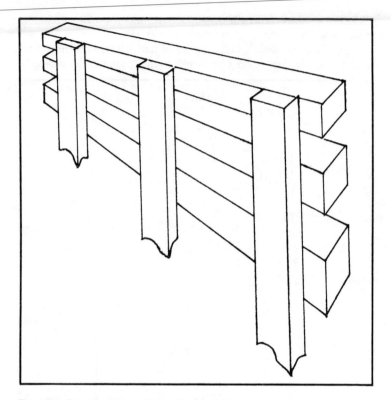

Fig. 18-2. Constructing wall for storage unit.

13. Sand and finish shelves as you did for frame.
14. Put shelves in place wherever you like.
15. If you want, you may add more shelves.

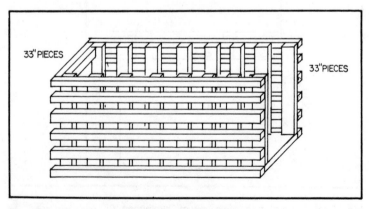

Fig. 18-3. Attaching top and bottom to storage unit.

16. You can also use half shelves or one/fourth shelves if you like; the system is quite versatile (Fig. 18-4).

17. Now repeat steps 1 through 14 for the second unit.

PROJECT 4: PLANT BENCH

Materials: 1 piece of ¾-inch plywood, 20¼ × 72 inches; 1 piece of ¾-inch plywood, 15 × 72 inches; 7 pieces of 1×3, 72 inches long; 5 2×12's, 20¼ inches long; 8 d finishing nails, glue, marine varnish, 6 feet of veneer tape, wood putty.

Tools: Saw, hammer, measuring tape, pencil, carpenter's square, paint brush, sandpaper.

Instructions:

1. Lay out your 2×12's on end, 14½-inch on center.

2. Nail on large plywood sheet across the top of the 2×12's.

3. Nail strip of plywood across the long front edge so that one edge extends up over the plywood top (Fig. 18-5).

4. Nail the 2×3 strips across the plywood front, 2½ inches apart, ending with a 2×3 strip at the top edge.

5. Countersink nails; putty and sand.

6. Finish with marine varnish on platform floor, two or three coats.

7. Finish the rest to match your storage units. You may use the marine varnish on the entire unit if you like.

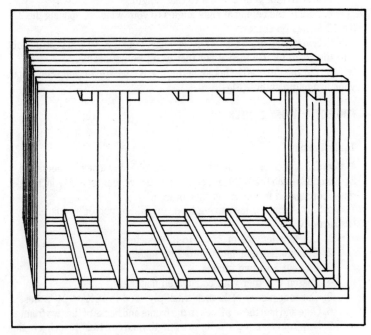

Fig. 18-4. Completed storage unit with shelf.

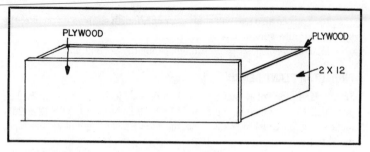

Fig. 18-5. Plant bench with front panel in place.

PROJECT 5: HANGING PLANTER ANCHORS

Materials: Prefinished, (i.e.) varnished 2 × 3's; nails; decorative hooks.
Tools: Saw, tape measure, ladder, hammer, drill.
Instructions:

1. Locate your ceiling joists.
2. If they are 16-inch on center cut the 2 × 3's to that length.
3. If they are 12-inch on center, either cut them to that length or to 24 inches.
4. If they are 24-inches you've got no choice but to cut them to that length.
5. Cut five of your 2 × 3's to that length.
6. Nail to the ceiling at right angles to your window, spacing the 2 × 3's 12 inches on center.
7. If you have that 24-inch joist spacing, your 2 × 3's will protrude out into the room for 1½ inches but that won't be noticeable.
8. Put the decorative hooks in the 2 × 3's wherever you want to put your hanging planters (Fig.18-6).

PROJECT 6: WORK CENTER

Table/Counter

Materials: 1 piece of ¾-inch thick plywood, 24 × 54 inches; 2 sheets of 4 × 8 plywood ¼-inch thick; 29 feet of 2 × 2; nails; veneer tape, 2¼-inch wide; glue; corrugated fasteners; corner braces.
Tools: Saw, hammer, measuring tape, pencil, carpenter's square.
Instructions:

1. Cut four lengths of 2 × 2 to 27¾ inches.
2. Cut another four lengths to 22½ inches.
3. Lay out into two frames.
4. Fasten together with corrugated fasteners.
5. Cut four pieces of ½-inch thick plywood to 29½ × 24 inches.
6. Glue and nail these pieces to the fronts and backs of the two frames.
7. Now cut two 2 × 2's to 50-inch lengths and two to 27¾-inch length.
8. Construct frame as in Fig. 17-8.

9. Cut two pieces of ¼-inch plywood to 50 × 27¾ inches and nail and glue to both side of frame.

10. Fasten the three "universal boxes" together by nailing through the 2 × 2's.

11. Cut another 2 × 2 to 50-inch length and nail across the front top as in Fig. 18-7.

12. Nail ¾-inch plywood sheet across top.

13. Turn upside down and fasten corner braces to the front 2 × 2 to tie it into the sides (Fig. 18-8).

14. Countersink nails. Putty and sand.

15. Finish with clear varnish if your plywood is top quality. If not, and it will save you a bundle if it isn't, stain and varnish.

16. If it's not good enough for that, seal and paint with two coats of enamel or use two coats of latex paint and two coats of clear varnish on top.

Table/cart

Materials: 1½ sheet of 4 × 8-foot ¾-inch plywood; 40 feet of 2 × 2; 4 22 × 25-inch pieces of ¼-inch plywood; veneer tape, 2½-inch wide; 4 2-inch casters (at least one of which has a lock) with soft rubber wheels and plate tops; or the more expensive metal ball-type casters; nails; glue; two large ornamental drawer pulls (optional); four table braces (small size).

Tools: Saw, hammer, screwdriver, drill, measuring tape, pencil, carpenter's square, drill.

Instructions:

1. Cut four pieces of 2 × 2 to 23-inch size.

2. Cut four pieces of 2 × 4 to 20½-inch size.

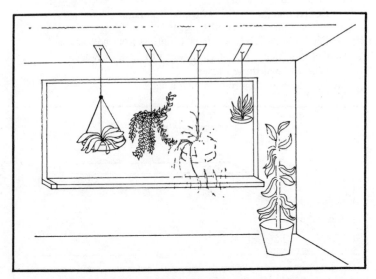

Fig. 18-6. Plant bench and hanging plants' anchors installed.

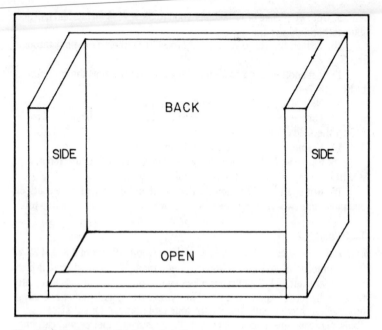

Fig. 18-7. Putting on the back panel.

   3. Cut two pieces to 17½-inch size.
   4. Lay out two of the 23-inch pieces and two of the 20½-inch as shown in Fig. 17-8 (Table/counter).
   5. Fasten together with corrugated fasteners.
   6. Repeat for the rest of the pieces.
   7. Fasten 17½-inch 2 × 2 in at 13 inches from bottom.
   8. Cut four pieces of ¼-inch plywood to 22 × 24½ inches.
   9. Glue and nail these frames.
   10. Cut four 2 × 2's to 47½-inch length.

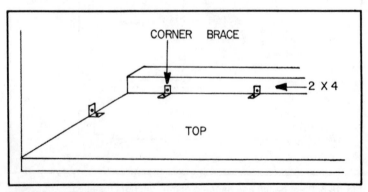

Fig. 18-8. Installing bracing.

11. Nail and glue these 2 × 2's between the two universal boxes: two on the top and two on the bottom as in Fig. 18-9.

13. Cut one piece of ¾-inch plywood to 47½ × 24½ inches.

14. Nail this on the frame as a back as in Fig. 18-9.

15. Cut two pieces out of the ¾-inch plywood 44½ × 22 inches.

16. Cut one piece of ¾-inch plywood to 47½ × 22 inches.

17. Cut one piece of 2 × 2 44½-inches long and two pieces 21½-inches.

18. Nail the 44½-inch 2 × 2 across the back plywood piece 13 inches from the bottom.

19. Nail the two 21½-inch 2 × 2's along the sides at 13 inches from the bottom.

20. Nail one of the 44½ × 22-inch plywood panels on the inside frame as a bottom as in Fig. 18-10.

21. Nail the 47½ × 22-inch plywood piece across the top of the frame as the top.

22. Nail the remaining 44½ × 22-inch piece to the 2 × 2 frame on the inside middle of the box as a shelf.

23. Attach four 2-inch casters, one to each corner, at the bottom of the cart.

24. Cut one piece of ¾-inch plywood 22 × 24½ inches.

25. Attach table braces, two to each side of the cart. (Fig. 18-10).

26. Attach the 22 × 24½-inch pieces, one to a side to the table braces.

27. Countersink nails, fill and sand.

28. Stain and varnish, use clear varnish and leave natural or paint, just as long as it matches the table counter.

29. If you feel in the mood you can paint a graphic on it.

30. Fasten two large (at least four or five inches each) drawer pulls on the back panel with screws going into the rail that supports the shelf (Fig. 18-11).

31. If you prefer two shelves, you may put in another. It depends on what kind of things you want to store.

32. You may also use some of those handy plastic drawers and dividers. Cutlery trays are excellent for zippers knitting needles and other such long items, for instance.

Wall Shelf Unit

Materials: 1½ sheet of ¾-inch plywood; 26 feet of 2 × 2' 15 feet of 1-inch molding or veneer tape; nails; glue; screws.
Tools: Saw, hammer, carpenters' square, drill, screwdriver.
Instructions:

1. Cut two pieces of plywood into 54 × 12-inch lengths.
2. Cut two pieces of plywood into 12 × 36-inch lengths.
3. Cut one piece of plywood to 54 × 36-inches.
4. Cut two pieces to 12 × 54½-inch lengths.

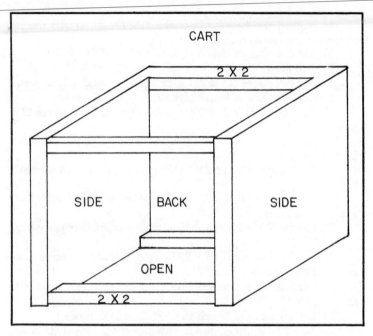

CART

2 X 2

SIDE   BACK   SIDE

OPEN

2 X 2

Fig. 18-9. Joining sides with 2×4s and attaching back panel.

5. Glue and nail a frame out of the two 54 × 12 pieces and the 36 × 12 pieces.

6. Glue and nail back onto frame using the 54 × 36-inch piece.

7. Cut the 2 × 2 into two 52½-inch pieces and four 10½-inch pieces.

8. Nail and glue 2 × 2's to inside of cabinet, one row at 12 inches above the floor of the cabinet, the next at 10 inches.

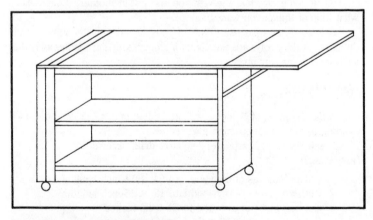

Fig. 18-10. Attaching folding shelf.

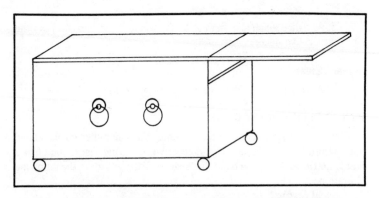

Fig. 18-11. Completed cart with casters, shelf and folding shelves.

9. Glue and nail the remaining plywood pieces onto the 2 × 2's as shelves.

10. If you prefer you can vary the spacing of the shelves or add extra shelves.

11. Cut molding to fit outside of cabinet and attach.

12. Finish to match table/counter and cart.

13. Screw cabinet back to wall studs above the counter/table allowing at least 2 feet clearance between table and bottom of unit.

14. We chose to use bamboo blinds to close off the cabinets because we've been hit in the head with too many cabinet doors. Attach them at the top of your cabinet (Fig. 18-12).

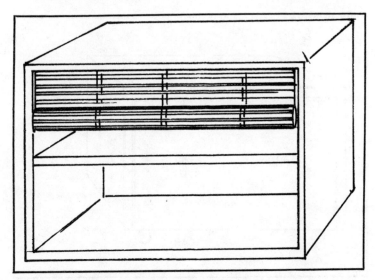

Fig. 18-12. The finished wall shelf unit with a match stick blind.

15. As a nice touch use them on all the windows, too, to carry out the airy, garden-like decor.

Sewing Center

Follow instructions for work center (Fig. 18-13).

PROJECT 7: KIDS' HOBBY CENTER

This is a variation on the basic theme. You can either go ahead and build a third 54-inch unit as we've done or you can build a larger unit 6 or 7 feet long. However, if you build that size you'll have to make the following alterations:

Adjustment Instructions:

1. Anything much larger than our 54-inch module must have a center support (Fig. 18-14).

2. This addition, however, as you can clearly see, gives rise to another. You need two carts instead of one. This actually works very nicely if two or more people are going to use the craft center at the same time.

3. If you make the wall storage unit to match, that is, the same length as the table/counter, you will also need divisions, or you can build two separate units and hang them side by side.

4. To start you off on your very own designing, we'll give you the dimensions for a deluxe 7-footer and you can make your adjustments from there.

5. *Important:* Always remember to allow for clearances of at least ¼-to ½-inch.

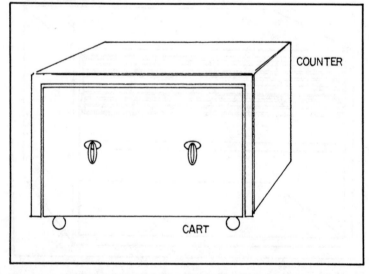

Fig. 18-13. Table counter with cart in place.

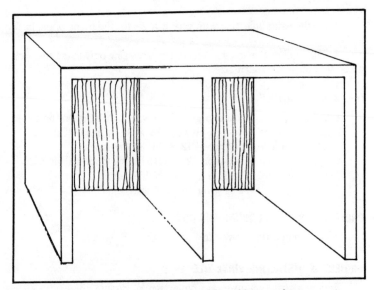

Fig. 18-14. 7-foot hobby center table counter with room for two carts.

6. *Ditto*: Remember to allow for the thickness of your lumber.

7. Use 2 × 4's as framing members instead of 2 × 2's on table/counter.

8. Good luck.

Double 7-Foot Hobby Center

Instructions for Table/Counter

1. Follow instructions for previous Table/Counter, steps 1-6 using 2 × 4's instead of 2 × 2's.

2. Build another frame exactly the same way.

3. Cut two 2 × 4's to 80-inch length, two to 27¾-inch length.

4. Construct frame as in Fig. 17-8 but add a 23½-inch 2 × 4 in center.

5. Cut two pieces of ¼-inch plywood to 84 × 27¾-inch size and nail and glue to both sides of the frame.

6. Nail and glue your four universal boxes together into an "E" shape as shown in Fig. 18-14.

7. Cut two 39¾-inch pieces of 2 × 4 and fasten them into the frame across the front.

8. Nail the 84 × 24-foot ¾ inch plywood sheet to the top.

9. Follow steps 13-18.

Instructions for carts:

1. You can follow the instructions as given in Project 4-B, steps 1-11, but you'll have to change the measurements of your ¾-inch plywood pieces to conform to a 39 × 22 inch top. The bottom piece will be 36 ″ 22 inches and the shelves will be the same.

2. Do the same adjusting with your 2 × 2's for the frame of the back and front.

3. Then follow the steps as given, remembering only to cut the back piece to a 39 × 24½-inch size.

4. Proceed as in steps 12-32.

Instructions For Wall Unit

1. Cut two pieces of ¾-inch plywood, 84 × 12 inches (top and bottom).
2. Cut one piece of ¾-inch plywood 84 × 36 inches (back)
3. Cut two pieces of plywood 12 × 36 inches (sides).
4. Cut one piece of plywood 12 × 34½ inches (center divider).
5. Cut eight pieces to 39½ inches (shelves).
6. Follow steps 6-14 as given for wall shelf unit.

PROJECT 8: PAINTING INSIDE AND OUT

Follow instructions given in Conversion I, Project 6.

PROJECT 9: INSTALLING VINYL TILE

Follow instruction given in Conversion V, Project 13.

PROJECT 10: INSTALLING GLASS STORM DOORS

Follow instructions given in Conversion IV, Project 7.

PROJECT 11: BUILDING PRIVACY SCREEN ACROSS DRIVEWAY

Materials: 7 12-foot 2 × 4's; 4 36-inch wide and 6-foot long bamboo matchstick blinds that can be used outdoors; 16 corner braces; staples; 10d nails; masonry nails; lag screws; wood preservative, stain and spar or marine varnish.

Tools: Saw, electric drill with masonry and wood bit, measuring tape, pencil, screwdriver, staple gun, slip-stick, paint brush.

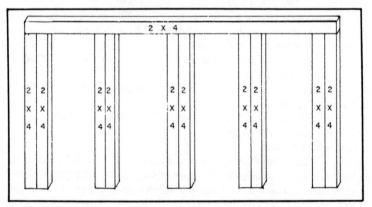

Fig. 18-15. Framing in a privacy screen.

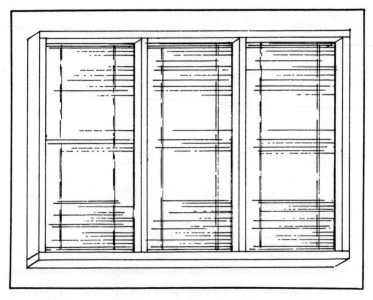

Fig. 18-16. Completed privacy screen with match stick blind insets.

Instructions:

1. Treat 1 of the 2 × 4's with wood preservative.

2. Line the short end up with the corner of the house or the exterior wall and lay the 2 × 4 across the driveway at right angles to the house.

3. Make sure the angle is square. Then tie the 2 × 4 to the driveway with lag bolts.

4. Measure and cut 10 2 × 4's to 69 inches.

5. Set one of these on the sole plate and tie it into wall of house with masonry nails (if you have a brick or stucco house that is). Use ordinary nails if yours happens to be frame.

6. Lay the remaining 2 × 4 on the floor and arrange the short ones as shown in Fig. 18-15.

7. Nail together, reinforcing corners with corner braces.

8. Get a helper. Put the frame up on the sole plate and tie in one of the 2 × 4's to the one already attached to the house wall.

9. Toe-nail in the rest of the 2 × 4's making sure they are plumb.

10. Reinforce corners with corner braces.

11. If there's a fence post on the other side of your screen tie into that, too.

12. Sand and stain the frame, finish with two or three coats of marine or spar varnish.

13. Staple bamboo matchstick blinds to the frame work across top, sides and bottom (Fig. 18-16).

Chapter 19
Garage Conversion VIII

This was a hard one though it didn't seem that way at the start. On the contrary, we thought it would be a cinch. The garage was, in a sense, already converted. The house had been a model home and the garage used as the office for the realtor. It had finished and painted walls and ceiling and the de rigeur sliding glass doors across the front. Sounds good doesn't it? But—It also had washer and dryer connections and a hot water heater in the rear wall, naked and exposed. The kitchen door and the outside door made a hallway off that end of the room which was also rather dark. The sliding glass doors slid out onto the driveway via a narrow covered porch. And these same sliding glass doors were only a few feet away from the front door and shared the facade.

There was a large attic above the garage which housed a good deal of ducting from the heat pump system and eliminated the possibility of skylights. The garage was connected to the house along one long side. It was a brick house, to make matters more complicated.

The room obviously had to serve as laundry and rear entrance as well as family room. In addition, the family clamored for more eating area. The only hope lay in the old "divide and conquer" strategy.

We designed enclosures for the washer and dryer and a screen for the water heater. It had to be a screen, because some state building codes forbid water heaters to be enclosed in closets in the inside of the house. That took care of some of the problems.

After a lot of argument of the "... if you have sliding glass doors, for God's sake use them..." and "... with a door in the middle of each of the short walls the room's like a super hallway" kind, we finally settled the issue by building a brick planter across the front of the room. This in effect closed off the sliding doors for casual running in and out, but it allowed the easy transport of plants out to the porch in the summer and back into the house in the winter. It also allowed access to the family room with bulkier items such as furniture if the need arose. After all, one only had to step over a 1-foot partition.

A super table/counter across the laundry end of the room served two or even three purposes. It provided the much needed extra eating and serving space, it was an excellent place to fold laundry and stash ironing temporarily, and it could be used for all kinds of craft and model building activities. Furthermore, by going crosswise, it visually made the room more attractive.

We added the ladder across one short side later. We not only found the idea intriguing and practical—it also provided space to hang pocket systems that could be changed for the occasion, a place to hang up clothes as they came off the ironing board, and a sort of mini-art gallery—but it also effectively prevented chairs and stools being left in the middle of the passage-way between kitchen, back door and laundry and the family room. This had been the case on so many previous occasions that we came to regard bruised shins as normal until confronted by a suspicious school nurse.

The light banks helped a lot in the evenings and provided fill light on dreary days. The all-glass storm door in the rear entrance was quite successful on sunny ones.

The room had been half-paneled in a dark and dreary but good wood paneling which added to the "super-hall" look. We decided to retain the paneling after painting it to match the walls and to use the same kind of paneling for our closets and enclosures, for a unified look.

It was decided to use carpet samples for the floor, for several reasons: we happened to luck into a sale of same, we liked the thick lush texture which we couldn't have afforded otherwise at that time, and we also loved the idea that if one of the kids spilled something fatal to rugs, like india ink or airplane glue (both of which had on other occasions found their way to the floor) it wouldn't be a horrid disaster. All we'd have to do would be replace that one piece of rug, which could be done quite simply.

Outside the sliding glass doors was a 4-foot roofed porch and directly beyond that a long paved driveway. Since the room was already darkish, designing a screen which would shield the room from the street was tricky. We finally settled on a white canvas and wood combo that seemed to reflect more light than any other and wasn't glary. See Fig. 19-1 for before and after views.

PROJECT 1: BUILDING WASHER/DRYER CLOSET

It was decided to house the washer and dryer in a common closet for several reasons: a wall to ceiling closet would provide some extra storage space above the appliances; full bi-fold doors gave easy access to the washer and dryer and made any pulling out of the appliance for service

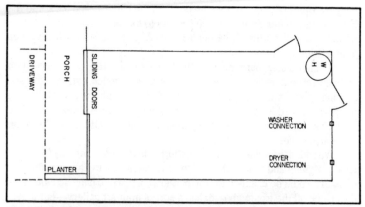

Fig. 19-1A. Scale plan of before view of Conversion VIII.

relatively simple; closed, the appearance would be that of any storage wall.

The closet was designed to the 79-inch size because that happened to be the space available and also because it was excellent for installing two sets of bifold doors. Since there was some extra space available in the closet it also became home for the ironing board, the vacuum sweeper and a host of brooms, mops and other such cleaning tools.

Materials: 2 2×6's 6 feet long; 1 2×4 79 inches long; 8 2×4's 8 feet long; 4 2×4's 32 inches long; 5 2×4's 6½ inches; nails; lag bolts; two sheets of 4×8 paneling; 49 feet of 1×4; two bifold doors; hardware; brackets; corner braces; pegboard; standards.

Tools: Saber saw, hammer, drill and masonry bit, screwdriver attachment, level, carpenter's square, slip-stick, miter box.

Instructions:

1. Measure your space and mark the dimensions of your closet on the slab.

2. Lay one of your 32-inch 2×4s along one short end of your outline against the wall and the other short one at the other end of your outline.

3. Tie them down with lag bolts.

4. With your slip-stick measure from sole plate to ceiling and deduct 1½ inches from that measurement.

5. Cut one 8-foot 2×4 to that length, set it on your sole plate against the back wall and nail into the wall.

6. Repeat on the other end of the closet.

7. Measure again from the middle of your sole plate and cut a stud to fit.

8. Measure in once more 1½ inches in from the end of your sole plate, cut to fit.

9. Measure in 1½ inches from the end of one of your remaining 32-inch 2×4's and mark. Measure again. 16 inches on center and put down another mark.

10. Nail the long studs to the short 2×4 on the marks.
11. Repeat for other side.
12. Call a helper and lift up frame and set on sole plate.
13. Tie in back stud with T-plates, nail into joists.
14. Toe-nail into sole plate.
15. Measure from the front edge of your sole plate and cut a stud 1½ inches shorter than that measurement.

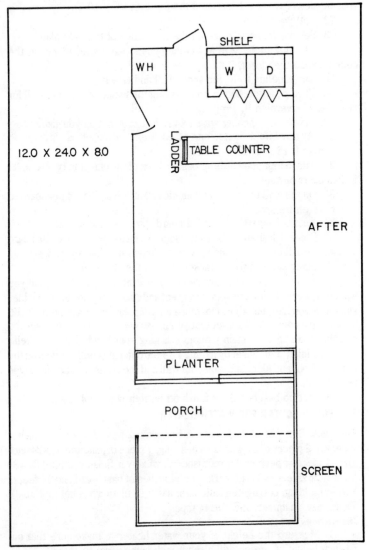

Fig. 19-1B. Scale plan of after view of Conversion VIII.

16. Repeat on other side.

17. Lay your 79-inch 2×4 across the floor.

18. Nail a stud to each end of the 2×4.

19. Manufacture a beam out of your 2 2×6's and plywood scraps as explained in Conversion III, Project 3.

20. Attach your new beam between the 2×4 studs, 6 feet 10 inches from bottom of stud. Reinforce with corner braces.

21. Nail in your 6½-inch cripple studs at 14-inch on center between your header (your new beam) and the top 2×4 (Fig. 19-2).

22. Call your helper.

23. Set the frame in place on the front edge of the sole plate.

24. Tie into studs, wall and ceiling joist. Use corner braces at the ceiling inside the closet.

25. Cut paneling to fit the short wall and attach.

26. Then panel the top in front, saving the inside of the side wall for last. See Conversion II, Project 7, for particulars.

27. Frame the opening with 1×4's. Miter or not as you like.

28. Attach bifold doors, one at each end of closet as directed in Conversion I, Project 3.

29. Attach four standards across the back of the closet in two sets, 32 inches apart per set.

30. On the wall (old) side of your closet, attach a piece of pegboard to cover the entire space.

31. Put on hangers for ironing board, brooms, and so on.

32. Pre-finish shelves, 36 inches long, 12 inches wide, (particle board is fine) according to directions given in Conversion I, Project 6.

33. Hang shelves from brackets across the standards.

34. It's up to you how many shelves you want. It depends on what you want to store in addition to your detergent and such. You can also use wider shelves if you like, but allow clearance for your washing machine lid if you have a top loader. Don't forget that you'll also need room to bend over the machine and come up again without cracking your head against a shelf.

35. Finish your closet by nailing 1×4's around the ceiling edges on the outside, front and side, and along the wall and the corner on the short side (Fig. 19-3).

36. Put up baseboard, or finish off bottom with 1×4, too.

PROJECT 2: SCREEN FOR WATER HEATER

Materials: 3 pieces of 2×4, 52½ inches long; 2 pieces of 2×4 30 inches long; and 2 pieces of 2×4 21½ inches long; 1 piece of paneling 54×24-inch size; 1 piece of pegboard (prefinished to whatever finish you like) 24×30 inches; 26½ feet of 1×4 for trim; or 54 inches of baseboard and 14 feet of corner molding; corrugated fasteners; nails; insulation blanket (optional).
Tools: Saw, hammer, measuring tape.
Instructions:

1. Measure the height of your water heater to make sure that our 54-inch height of screen will clear it with some room to spare.

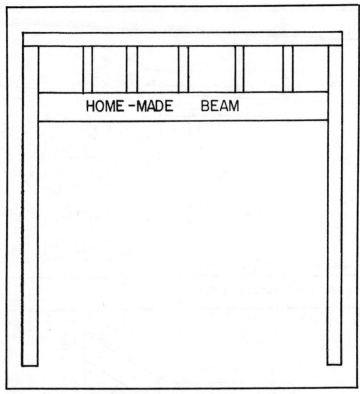

HOME –MADE   BEAM

Fig. 19-2. Constructing the front frame for the laundry closet.

2. If it doesn't, simply add to the height of your screen allowing at least 3 inches of clearance above.

3. If you have a gas water heater you will have to use an insulation blanket around it so there won't be so much heat. This is a good thing anyway because it saves you money on your gas bill.

4. Apply insulation blanket to gas water heater according to directions that come with the blanket.

5. You can put around the electric kind, too, if you like. It simply isn't necessary as far as the screen is concerned.

6. Cut 3 2×4's to 52 inches; 2 to 30 inches; and 2 to 21½ inches.

7. Make a box frame out of your 30-inch ones and your 52½-inch ones.

8. Now make a U-shape out of your remaining 52½-inch 2×4 and your 2 21½-inch 2×4's.

9. Use nails and corrugated fasteners.

10. Connect the two frames as shown in Fig. 19-4.

11. Cover with paneling.

12. Nail on pegboard top.

13. Trim with 1×4's or molding and baseboards (Fig. 19-5).

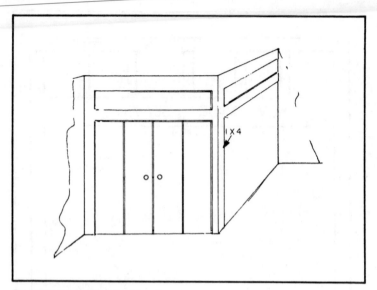

Fig. 19-3. Completed laundry closet.

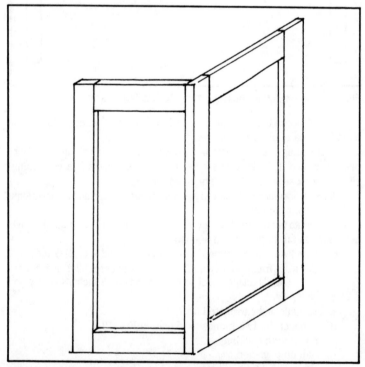

Fig. 19-4. Making a box frame for water heater screen.

314

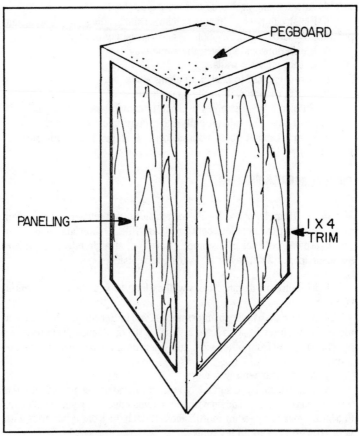

Fig. 19-5. Completed water heater screen with pegboard top and 1×4 trim.

PROJECT 3: WALL-HUNG CABINET

Materials: 2 pieces of ¾-inch plywood, 30×23½ inches; 2 pieces of the same plywood 28½×23¼ inches, for sides; 13 feet of 1×2; 2 pieces of 28¼×23-inch plywood for shelves; and 1 piece 30×30-inch plywood for doors; 30×30-inch piece of plywood for back; one cabinet door pull; screws; four decorative hinges; nails; finishing materials.

Tools: Saber saw, hammer, carpenter's square, level, measuring tape, pencil, ladder.

Instructions:

1. Construct a box frame out of the 28½×23¼-inch pieces and 20×23¼-inch pieces.

2. Attach 30×30 piece across as back.

3. Nail in 1×2 strips at 1-foot and 2-foot distances from the bottom of the box.

4. Attach along each side and across the back.

5. Finish cabinet by filling in nail holes and sanding, then sealing and painting to match walls, or staining and varnishing to match paneling.

6. Finish door and shelves the same way.

7. Locate studs in walls.

8. Screw cabinet to back wall along studs.

9. Attach to side wall in the same manner.

10. Put prefinished shelves in place in cabinet and nail down.

11. Drill holes for cabinet pulls and mount on cabinet door.

12. Mount cabinet doors with decorative hinges flush with cabinet (Fig. 19-6).

PROJECT 4: BRICK PLANTER

Materials: 70 bricks of the 8×2½-inch variety, whatever color you like; mortar; metal ties; pebbles, bark or other "filler" materials; nails.

Tools: Trowel, cold chisel, hammer, chalk line, straight edge, or straight 8-foot or longer 2×4; level; measuring tape; bucket.

Instructions:

1. Measure off distance from wall as long as you want your planter deep.

2. If you want hanging planters above, you better make it 16 inches or more. Most larger baskets have at least a 10- or 12-inch diameter.

3. Measure from other side, too, then drop a chalk line across the room.

4. Mix mortar with water.

5. 'Butter' one large surface of your brick and one short end with the mortar and set the brick down with the outside edge along your chalk line. (To butter means spreading mortar about ½-inch thick onto your brick with your trowel). Try to do it evenly.

6. Line up your 2×4 or straight edge along your chalkline to the outside and continue buttering your bricks and setting them down deeping your mortar coat even and your line straight.

7. When you come to the end of a row, you might have to cut the brick to fit. To cut bricks safely and easily, follow these directions:

● With a nail, scratch your cutting line the entire way around the brick.

● Using a cold chisel and light hammer blows, hit the cutting line the entire way around the brick. Repeat this several times.

● When you have scored the brick to a depth of about ⅛-inch, position your cold chisel in the center of one wide side and give the chisel a heavy blow. The brick should break apart evenly. If it does not, repeat the above steps.

8. Now you're ready for the next course. Make sure the tops are level and sides plumb.

9. Now mark and cut a brick so it will go half-way across your first brick, that is 3¾ inches (not counting the ½-inch mortar line which will fill in that extra ¼-inch).

10. Cut a piece of the metal tie and nail it into each wall level with your first course of bricks so that the end extends over your bricks as in Fig. 19-7.

11. Butter your cut brick and set on top of metal tie.

12. Continue across the room making sure your row stays level and plumb. It should look like Fig. 19-8.

13. When it comes to row three, repeat step 10 again, then start with a whole brick across that row.

14. Now lay one more row, metal ties and all, starting with a 3¾-inch brick.

15. Let it set in peace then fill with pebbles, bark chips or other such and set your plants in place.

PROJECT 5: INSTALLING PLATES FOR HANGING PLANTERS

Follow instructions given in Conversion VII, Project 5.

PROJECT 6: ADJUSTABLE TABLE COUNTER

This adjustable table/counter combo is actually a compromise between those factions who voted for a counter, which would also be the right height for folding clothes, and the ones who wanted to use the table/counter for craft work and who hated to balance on stools at any time. (ok, so it was a minority of one, but a very vociferous one as you can see). With the adjustable feature the table can be raised and lowered easily, so everyone wins.

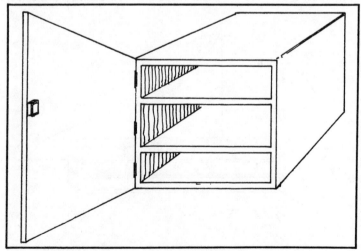

Fig. 19-6. View of wall hung cabinet showing shelves and door.

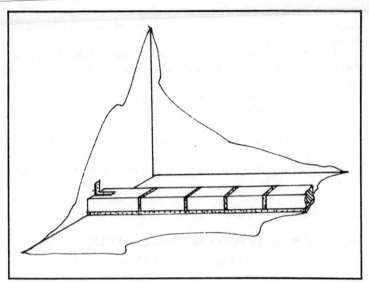

Fig. 19-7. Laying first course of bricks for planter and putting in metal tie.

Materials: 1 solid core door 7-foot × 30 inches or so; or 2 sheets of ¾-inch plywood to the same measurements; 2 adjustable steel support posts, (short length); 4 pieces of 1-inch plywood, 1-foot square; screws; 1½-inch molding, 19 feet long (if you use plywood); wood glue; nails.
Tools: Drill and wood bit, screwdriver attachment, hammer, c-clamps.

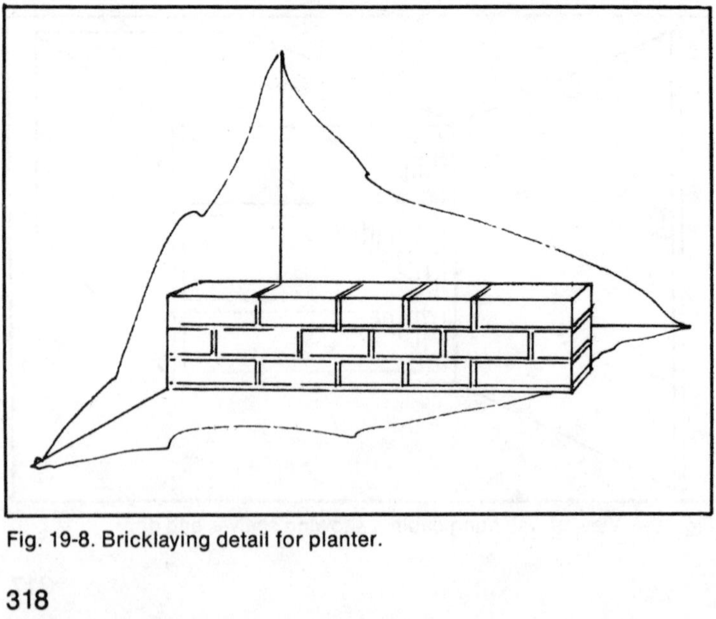

Fig. 19-8. Bricklaying detail for planter.

Instructions:

1. Buy two of those adjustable steel support posts that people use in basements to jack up sagging floors.

2. Before you bring them home, stop at a machine shop and have them drill one hole into each corner of the top or lifting plate, and one hole each into each corner of the base plate.

3. Now go home and bolt one of those 1-foot square plywood pieces to the top and one to the bottom of each of the posts.

4. If you have a solid core door, finish the door's surface with stain and varnish, or clear varnish. Use several coats to make a good hard surface.

5. If you're using the two sheets of plywood, spread wood glue liberally on one surface then put the second sheet on top.

6. Use a rolling pin and roll smoothly and evenly over every inch of the surface, first the long way then across.

7. C-clamp together with three clamps on each end and five on each side.

8. If you go that route, it would be a good idea if you glued before you made your planter and used all those bricks evenly distributed for ballast to get a good bond (Fig. 19-9).

9. Follow the directions on the glue for amount to use and also drying time.

10. In the meantime, finish your plywood squares to match the top of the table.

11. If you prefer, paint the steel support posts white, black, or red, or whatever else pleases you.

12. Finish plywood top by putting 1½-inch or 1¾-inch molding of your choice around the edges.

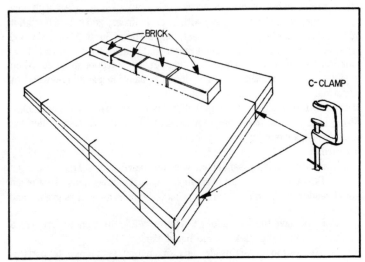

Fig. 19-9. Gluing and clamping table/counter top.

13. Then finish by either using clear varnish, stain and varnish or enamel paint.

14. If you prefer, you can have a laminated top by applying formica. In this case do the application of the formica first and then apply your molding which will need to be at least 1¾ inches wide to accommodate the thickness of the formica.

15. You can also use strips of formica instead of molding along the edges.

16. Use a similar technique to glue the formica on as you did in making your plywood sandwich. Check with your formica dealer about the glue to use on his product.

17. On the underneath side of your table mark the 18-inch measurement in from each end.

18. Now divide the width of your table in half and snap a chalkline. The two lines will cross at the center of your steel support.

19. Measure 6 inches along each line and draw a square (Fig. 19-10).

20. Line up the square on the post to make sure everything fits together.

21. Pre-drill screw holes, one in each corner and two at equal distances in the sides. All the holes should be one inch in from the edge of the plywood.

22. Screw steel supports to table.

23. Set right side up. See finished table, Fig. 19-11.

PROJECT 7: PAINTING THE PANELING

Most people shudder in disbelief when we mention painting paneling. There seems to be something sacrosanct about paneling once it's up on a wall and you have to learn to live with it, dark, dreary and horrid though it may be. Well, we beg to differ. In fact, may we point out that painted wood paneling was de rigeur in colonial times, and before that time, and after, too. So what's good enough for our forefathers is good enough for us. When it suits us, that is. But let's get down to painting paneling—wood or imitation.

Materials: Liquid sander (a lot of that); sealer; latex paint; clear varnish.

Tools: Lots of rags, one brand new paint brush for the varnish, roller and small brush, or one larger paint brush.

Instructions:

1. Soak rag in liquid sander and wipe down every inch of the paneling.

2. Be sure to have a lot of fresh air, open windows, fans. That much liquid sander can be quite overpowering to humans as well as grease and gloss.

3. If you have the fortitude, go over the whole thing once more with a fresh rag and another dose of the liquid sander.

4. The reason for all this cleaning, or sanding, is that people, particularly those good housekeeping kinds that get dark paneling in the first place, tend to keep the paneling glossy and shiny with tons and tons of oily

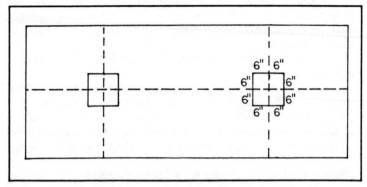

Fig. 19-10. Marking table/counter top for legs.

paneling polish. And, as you well know, grease and paint are deadly enemies. They won't get along for anybody.

5. After you've done your bit with the sander, it's sealing time. One coat will do.

6. By this time you have probably noticed that while a roller will make short shrift of all that surface, there will remain the original dark lines in the grooves. Those you can only get out with a small, thin paint brush.

7. We have found, at times, that it is even quicker to use a fairly wide brush for the whole job of painting paneling that's grooved. As you brush up and down you can get one corner of your brush to ride in the groove. This way there's less chance of paint bubbles and drips.

8. If you are a roller addict, as one of us is, then the best solution we've found is to take your paint brush to those grooves first, before you ever touch the wall with a roller, about a half a wall at a time, and then go over the surface with your roller, smoothing out any bubbles or drips.

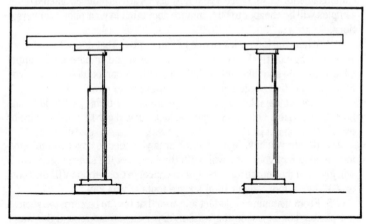

Fig. 19-11. Side elevation of table/counter with jack legs in place.

321

9. After the sealer has dried thoroughly, apply a coat of good latex semi-gloss paint to match your walls, or, if you like, in a slightly darker shade. The operant word here is *slightly*. If you go to dark, you're right back where you started.

10. Sometimes you won't need a second coat, but most of the time it's a good idea.

11. Lastly, we like to put a coat of clear varnish over the whole thing. This gives a very durable surface, much like a good antique job.

12. And that's all folks. If you have brand new paneling that you want to match to your painted one, follow the same directions, but you needn't be quite so generous with the liquid sander. Once over will do nicely.

PROJECT 8: COVERING A FLOOR WITH CARPET SAMPLES

The first time we saw this unique method of floor covering was when our sister-in-law Betty found tons of carpet samples on a super-duper sale at J. C. Penney's and used them to cover the floor of her garage conversion. They were different shades of yellow, gold, burnt orange and soft green and the effect was scrumptuous. While we do admit that it takes more time and planning than working with plain carpet tile, it's also much more creative and the result is more distinctive and individual. Three cheers for our creative relative, Betty K. Wolverton. And here's how you can do the job yourself:

Materials: Carpet samples (obtainable in stores which carry carpeting, discount carpet stores and outlets); double faced carpet tape, graph paper.

Tools: Chalk line, long straight edge, pencil, heavy utility scissors or carpet knife, block for cutting, crayons.

Instructions:

1. In order to find the carpet tiles in the first place, your best bet is the yellow page part of your phone book. Spend an hour or two finding out who has what and at what price. The prices fluctuate tremendously between establishments. Also, twice a year new styles are introduced and the older samples will be cheaper to buy. Inquire about that in your phone conversations.

2. When you buy, stick to one height of pile. That doesn't mean they all have to be exactly the same pattern or even brand or material. It simply means that you shouldn't mix deep shag with indoor/outdoor, unless you like the sensation of stepping into holes every so often.

3. Carpet samples usually come in 12×18-inch, 12×24-inch and 36×12-inch sizes. Often, too, you can luck out and get 18×24-inch size or even 18×36-inch size.

4. Before you buy, figure out the area you need to cover by multiplying the length of your long wall with the length of the shorter wall which will give you the square footage. For instance, in Conversion VIII the room was 12 by 24 foot, so out total square footage was 288.

5. From that number deduct any area that isn't to be carpeted such as the planter box or inside the washer/dryer closet and around the water

heater. In this case that was 51 square feet. Take this figure from your total (i.e.) 288—51=*237 square feet*. This is the amount you need to buy.

6. But—and there is a but—this is not quite as simple as it sounds. You have to figure out how many samples of what size it will take to do the job. Figure out the area of the samples this time; a 12×18-inch sample equals 1½ square feet; a 12×24-inch piece equals 2 square feet; a 12×36-inch piece is 3 square feet; an 18×24-inch piece equals 2½ square feet and an 18×36-inch piece equals 3½ square feet.

7. The easiest way to proceed from here is via graph paper. Draw out the shape of your family room on a piece of graph paper including such things as closets, planters and what have you, using a scale of two squares to a foot.

8. On another piece of graph paper, draw a number of carpet sizes in the various sizes available.

9. Remember that the biggest bargain is the most square footage per dollar. Take out your trusty calculator while you work with this project at this point.

10. Color samples with your kids' crayons and cut them out. Make sure you have enough of each size to cover the area of your floor plan.

11. Now comes the fun. Lay out your tiles, trying different patterns until you find a size and pattern that you like. Carefully glue down your "tiles" on your plan. If you like more than one design and have trouble deciding, make two plans.

12. Look at it again the next day and make your decision.

13. Now trot over to the carpet place and see what colors are available in your size and how many of each.

14. There usually is no problem with pile, they are mostly higher pile.

15. Don't overlook the patterned samples, they can make a very interesting border or center for your handiwork.

16. Try to stick to related colors, for instance a pale yellow, gold, and orange mixture would be nice, or a beige, rust, and brown, or two shades of green with a green and brown tweed or print, or a brown and yellow with a brown and yellow tweed or print. You get the picture.

17. Ask your rug dealer to let you take them home on approval (you've carefully counted your pieces and noted how many of what size and color on a piece of paper). Give him a deposit or even pay him if you must, just make sure he'll let you exchange some colors if need be.

18. If he lets you take them home with option to exchange some, do so, it's a lot easier that way even if it involves lugging carpet tiles back and forth.

19. If you have the actual samples, clear your room of everything movable and lay out the samples following the pattern on your plan.

20. You may notice that the colors, or the colors and patterns, don't go together quite as well in quantity as they seemed to at the store.

21. You might notice further that it would look better if you had more of the pattern, or less of it, or limited yourself to colors only, or other such alternatives. In any case work out your final design on the floor.

22. Write down what you need to exchange.

23. On some fresh graph paper and with your crayons, using the same two squares to a foot scale, note down the design you ended up with, by coloring in the squares on the graph.

24· Now back to the store to do your exchanging if any.

25. Buy a few extra carpet samples to match your design to have on hand in case of need (remember the india ink!)

26. Now you can finally get to work on the floor. Clean it, wash and scrub with detergent and heavy cleaning solution in greater consentration than the directions suggest. Seal with two coats of sealer.

27. If your carpet samples are 1-foot wide, drop a chalk line every foot, parallel to the long wall in your room. If the sample is 1½- or 2-feet wide, then drop the chalk line at 1½ or 2 feet respectively.

28. Now put your double-faced tape inside these lines, two tapes back to back as shown in Fig. 19-12. Be sure you leave the top paper on the tape or you'll have a sticky mess.

29. Now drop chalk lines the other way, spacing them the length of each carpet sample, (1½, 2, or 3 feet).

30. Cut short pieces of tape and put them down just inside these lines.

31. Starting in a corner, peel back the tapes for one carpet piece and put down the piece according to the pattern on your graph paper.

32. Continue to work, one row at a time.

33. Leave any cutting till you come to the end of the row. You can't precut because those samples aren't always exactly what they claim to be and the pile has something to do with the size, too.

34. Start on the corner which has no build-ins or other obstructions, in the case of this conversion at the planter end of the room at either side. That way all your cutting will be where you'll have to cut in any case, around your closets and screens.

35. If you want to carpet your closet, too, that's fine. It will cut down on the vibration and noise from the appliances. It will, however, make it difficult to pull them out for repair, you'll need helpers if it comes to that.

36. You needn't worry about water damage if the washer should leak, since you can replace that section in a jiff.

37. You might, though, consider putting indoor/outdoor carpeting in a matching color inside the enclosures.

38. If you have a gas water heater, we would recommend that you leave the area directly underneath the tank bare concrete. It's even a good idea with an electric one.

39. To cut carpet samples mark on the back side with a piece of sharpened chalk or a crayon.

40. Lay across a block, a piece of 2×4 will do fine, and cut with your knife against the straight edge.

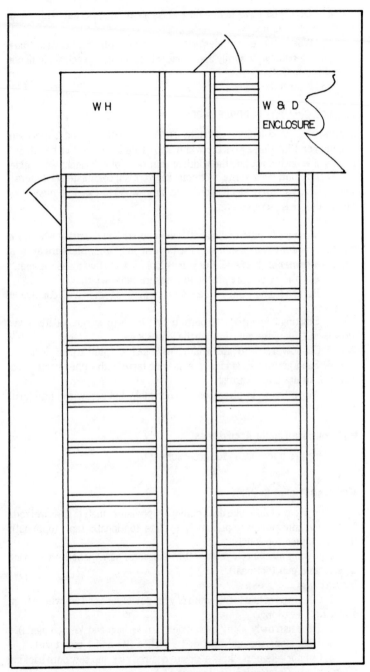

Fig. 19-12. Example of tape layout for carpet sample floor.

41. Or if you have heavy duty scissors or shears, cut with them, always back-side-up.

42. When all your samples are down, run or roll or otherwise transport yourself and your family and friendly helpers along each seam line in both directions.

43. Finished—enjoy.

PROJECT 9: MULTI-PURPOSE LADDER

Materials: 2 good-looking, straight 2×4's, 8 feet long; and 2 pieces of equally good-looking 2×4's the width of your table minus 3 inches; 6 or 7 pieces of ¾-inch doweling the width of your table plus ½-inch; wood glue; sealer and paint; clear varnish; or stain and varnish; corrugated fasteners.

Tools: Saw, hammer, electric drill and large wood bit, pencil, measuring tape, slip-stick, screwdriver.

Instructions:

1. Measure floor to ceiling with your slip-stick in the place where you want the ladder to be, just beside the table at short end. Measure again at the other corner of short end. Cut your 8-foot 2×4's to that measurement.

2. Cut the two short pieces to measure table width.

3. Build a frame from your 2×4's fastening together with corrugated fasteners.

4. Starting 2 feet from the bottom, drill holes to accommodate ¾-inch dowels at 1-foot intervals through the long 2 × 4's.

5. Cut dowel rods to table width plus ½ inch and glue in place in holes.

6. Sand and finish ladder to suit your taste with either paint, clear varnish, or stain and varnish.

7. Move frame in place beside your table and screw top into joists (Fig. 19-13).

Multi-Purpose Ladder Accessories

Here are a few ideas for accessories:

Mini-Wall Pocket Systems

Materials: Heavy fabric like duck denim or upholstery material; dowel rods of narrow lathe strips (optional); eyelets (optional); tape (optional); thread; staples (optional).

Tools: Sewing machine, eyelet setter, scissors, saw, pencil, measuring tape, staple gun (optional).

Instructions:

1. Cut strips of fabric the width of your dowel rods and anywhere from a foot to 2 feet long.

2. Hem narrowly along each side (turn ½-inch and ½-inch again).

3. Hem along top and bottom 1½ inches (½- and 1-inch turn).

4. Cut pockets or pockets strips to desired size and sew onto backing (Details: see Conversion III, Project 11.)

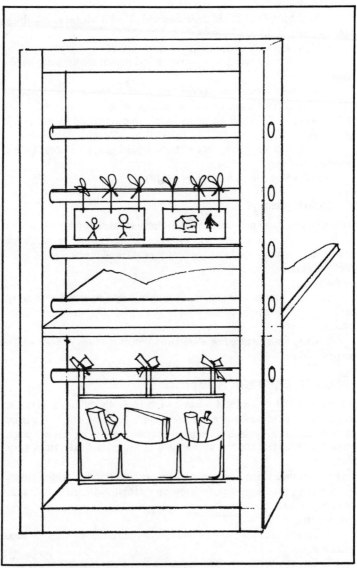

Fig. 19-13. View of multi-purpose ladder.

5. Set four eyelets at equal distance into top hem or make self ties or tape ties and sew in those spots instead.

6. Cut lathe strip or dowel to the finished size of your pocket system and insert in bottom hem. If you are not using eyelets (and it's better not to if you're going to use this system a lot), run another piece of lathe or dowel through the top hem.

7. Now hang from any of the rungs and fill with whatever you think best.

8. Here are a few suggestions to start you off:

—a system for napkins, silverware and placemats for party and/or every day use.

—a system for current pocket books, magazines and newspapers.

—a system for mail, in-coming and outgoing.

—a catch-all system for items found lying about and for projects in progress.

—a system for emergency clothes repairs (i.e.) scissors, thread, needles, buttons.

—and so on and so forth (Fig. 19-13).

Mini-Gallery System

Materials: Fillers for photo albums (the double sided clear plastic kind with the sticky layer in between); prints, photos, kids' drawings, etcs.; twist-ties or short white shoe laces (or brown or colored if you prefer).
Tools: Measuring tape.
Instructions:

1. Insert your prints, photos, or drawings as you would for a scrap book or photo album except that you are going to arrange them lengthwise instead of across.

2. Hang with twisties or shoe laces onto the rungs of your multi-purpose ladder.

PROJECT 10: A DIFFERENT PRIVACY SCREEN

Materials: 2 12-foot 2×4's; 4 6-foot 2×4's; 14 2×4's, 5-foot, 9-inches in length; 15 yards of canvas or extra heavy duck; large eyelets; fusing tape; nylon cord; screw-eyelets; corrugated fasteners; nails, lag screws, wood preservatives, stain and marine varnish, or sealer and exterior or deck paint.
Tools: Saw, measuring tape, pencil, hammer, electric drill with masonry bit, scissors, iron, eyelet-setter, sewing machine (optional), chalk line, carpenter's square.
Instructions:

1. Treat one of your 12-foot and two of your 6-foot 2×4's with wood preservative.

2. On your driveway, measure out 6 feet from your porch posts.

3. Snap a chalk line along these lines and one across from the two end marks so you'll end up with U-shape.

4. Lay out two 2×4's that have been treated with the wood preservative on the inside of those lines and fasten down with lag bolts.

5. Make sure your corners are square.

6. Lay the other long 2×4 on the ground and attach two of the 5-foot 9-inch 2×4's to each end, as you did when building a wall. This is your top plate.

7. Mark the center of the inside distance and attach two more 2×4's side by side; one on each side of the center mark.

8. Again divide the remaining distance on each side of double center post and put a 2×4 centered on that mark.

9. Transfer marks to long sole plate.

10. Get helper and toe-nail structure in place.

11. Now lay out your two remaining 6-foot 2×4s alongside the 6-foot sole plates.

13. Attach a 5-foot 9-inch 2×4 to each end of the free 2×4's and attach one 2×4 in the center.

14. Mark sole plate to match.

15. Put top plate with studs in place.

16. With corrugated fasteners, fasten side section top plate to front section top plate (Fig. 19-14).

17. Nail into the rest of front frame and into porch pillars.

18. If you don't happen to have any handy porch pillars, make this change: Use two 2×4's as the open end as you did in the front section and use a couple of fair sized corner braces lag bolted to the slab on each side.

19. You can also tie the fence into the house walls if possible.

20. Finish your frame as desired.

21. Cut four panels of fabric, 32½ inches wide and 67 inches long. Cut four other panels 32 inches long. (If you're not a fiend for accuracy, cut all of them 32 inches, it won't really show unless you go out and measure).

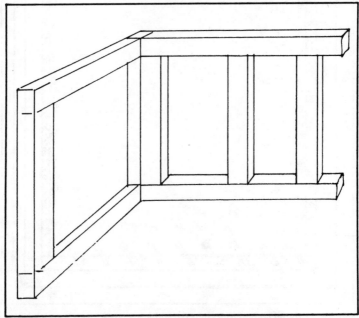

Fig. 19-14. Constructing corner of different privacy screen.

22. Mark a 1-inch hem all around the panel and press it down with your iron.

23. Cut fusing tape, like Stitch Witchery, to size and insert in hem.

24. Press and fuse according to directions.

25. If you like, you can put a row of machine stitching at the edge of the hem, about ⅞-inch in from turned up edge.

26. With your eyelet-setter, set eyelets, centered on the hem, on the right side of the fabric. Put one in each corner and the others 4 inches apart (Fig. 19-15).

27. You'll have to fudge that 4-inch bit a little on your short sides because the panels will be only 30 or 30½-inch respectively, which doesn't divide properly.

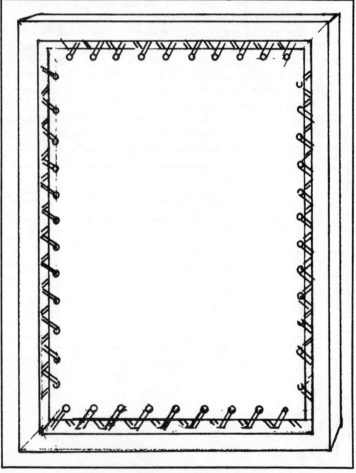

Fig. 19-15. Panel lashed to framing of different privacy screen.

28. To fudge successfully, use a measure of 3⅞-inch for spacing across and set the corner eyelets in 4-inch as on the side (which you have to do anyway since there is only one eyelet in each corner).

29. Now take your measuring tape and pencil and mark a point 2 inches from the corner onto each post.

30. Now measure off 4 inches all the way to your next corner.

31. Continue that way all around the frame.

32. Pre-drill holes on your marks.

33. Screw in eyelet screws on the marks.

34. Lash canvas to frame as shown in Fig. 19-15.

Variations On The Theme

Materials: Same as above except: 4 sheets of 4×8-foot, ¼-inch pegboard instead of canvas; molding.

Tools: Same as above.

Instructions:

1. Follow steps 1-20 as above.

2. Cut your pegboard to 66×31½ inches.

3. Put molding around pegboard to hide the unfinished edges.

4. Since your screen is visible both from the house and the street, you'll need to do this on both sides.

5. Seal and paint brightly.

6. Mark off spacing on the peg board with pencil.

7. Follow steps 30 through 37.

PROJECT 11: A WALL-TO-WALL "LIGHT BEAM"

Materials: 3 12-foot 1×6s; Sears brand strip fluorescent lighting fixture, 96×4¼×3¾ inch size; 2 75-watt bulbs; mounting hardware; 4d casing nails; white glue; 12 1½ inch #10 flathead screws; 3 wire nuts; 4 corner braces.

Tools: Saber saw, hammer, c-clamps, drill and wood bits, screwdriver, 12-foot story pole.

Instructions:

1. Turn on overhead light in fixture to be removed.

2. Turn off current at fuse box or circuit breaker box. Be sure light has gone out.

3. Remove fixture and expose outlet box affixed to ceiling joist.

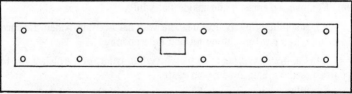

Fig. 19-16. Drilling holes in joists on each side of outlet box hole for Wall-to-wall light beam.

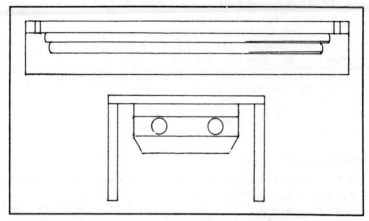

Fig. 19-17. Making U-shaped "beam container for light fixture.

4. Measure 16-inch intervals out from each side of exposed joist and mark approximate location of other ceiling joists on ceiling. Push finishing nails through ceiling to pinpoint exact location of ceiling joists.

5. Lay story pole along ceiling and mark exact intervals of centers of ceiling joists on pole, as well as location of outlet box.

6. Lay story pole along one of the 12-foot 1×6's and transfer markings to 1×6.

7. With saber saw cut out square hole at outlet box location.

8. Drill holes to accomodate screws at location of three joists on each side of outlet box hole. Drill two holes at each joist location about ¼-inch in from edge of 1×6 (Fig. 19-16).

9. Place 1×6 in place against ceiling and make sure wires from outlet box will come through opening at center.

10. With pencil, mark through screw holes onto ceiling where screw starter holes will need to be drilled into joists.

11. With 4d casing nails and white glue, glue and nail the other two 12-foot 1×6's, one on each side of cut, and the drilled 1×6 to make u-shaped "beam" container for light fixture (Fig. 19-17).

12. Apply four c-clamps along beam and allow a few hours for glue to set. Remove c-clamps. Paint inside flat white.

13. Install lighting fixture in beam, with hardware provided. Be sure to bring wires out through outlet box hole opening.

14. Paint sides of beam to match ceiling paint, or varnish wood to contrast with ceiling to suit your taste.

15. With two helpers holding each end, lift beam into place and connect fixture wires coming from outlet box: white to white; black to black. Secure to ceiling with screws.

Chapter 20
Conversion IX

This is one of the most unusual conversions. It was designed to meet some rather special needs. See Fig. 20-1 for before and after views.

The house was located on a quite street in a fairly new, fairly expensive subdivision. The garage was set back and off to the side of the house. There was ample space for a carport to be built later without interfering with any of the windows of the house.

The adults in the house wanted a retreat, a place for some peace and serious stereo listening, in contrast to the blaring of the smaller versions that could be heard from each of the rooms of the three children, usually counterpointed by one or the other of the TV's and some friendly argument among the siblings. The three children; two girls and a boy, ranged in age from 6 to 16. Each had a bevy of friends and interests and ideas that were seldom geared to the participation of the rest of the family. Therefore, the whole house, though rather large, was always, or seemed always, to be overflowing with youngsters with little space left for adult conversation and activities.

One condition was important in designing the new family room. The garage front elevation was supposed to be maintained intact until a carport would be built. In the meantime there was necessity for storage space: the brand new Moped, the 10-speed bikes, the lawnmower, and other garden tools. There was no room on the relatively small lot for a storage building of any kind.

This problem was solved by retaining the front section of the garage as a storage area, complete with garage doors and locks. If, and when, the carport was added, the storage area could continue to function just as well.

The garage lent itself well to the function of an adult hide-away. There already was a roofed area-way connecting the house to the garage, from the back door to a separate garage door. Enclosing this area-way with sliding glass doors connected the house to the new family room in all weather.

Inside the new family room there was need of light and air. The rear of the garage overlooked the youngest child's narrow play area, which backed up to a similar strip and a garage. Not an inspiring view. Clerestory windows were a good solution for bringing in light and keeping out the view. One of the side walls overlooked the yard and windows were cut in it.

The new family room also got a closet, a built-in seat and a wall shelf system. The floor was carpet-tiled and the breezeway was outfitted with indoor/outdoor carpeting.

PROJECT 1: INSTALLING CLERESTORY WINDOWS

Materials: 6 Andersen Flexivent #318 awning windows; 8-foot 2 × 4 studs; 4 10-foot 2×4's for headers and sills; 8d and 16d nails; caulking compound; exterior redwood trim.

Tools: Combination saw, saber saw, hammer, drill, caulking gun, carpenter's square, carpenter's level.

Instructions:

(*Note*: "before" and "after" floor plans, Fig. 20-1).

1. You will need to make the following calculations: Multiply the maximum number of windows you can use in your clerestory by the width of each individual window and subract from the inside length of the wall.

2. Convert to inches and divide by the number of spaces between windows (this will be one less than the number of windows. Yes—for sure).

3. Subtract 4½ from this figure.

4. The result is the width of the spacers you'll need to cut.

5. You'll need the spacers so you can place the trimmer stud to frame the individual window openings accurately. For effect see Fig. 20-2.

6. Here are the calculations for this conversion: using 2×3-foot 5 inch awning windows:

● The maximum number of windows you can install in a 23-foot 10-inch long wall is six. We arrive at that number like this:

● 6×3-foot 5-inches =18-feet 30-inches =20-feet 6 inches

● Subtracting 20-feet 6-inches from 23-feet 10 inches= 3-foot 4-inches.

● Converting this into inches: 3-foot 4-inches = 40 inches.

● Dividing by the number of spaces between windows—5— 40÷5=8. You will have a space of 8 inches between windows.

● Subtracting 4½ from 8 = 3½ inches.

● 3½ inches is the width of the spacer we need.

7. Now you can cut your spacers—you can use a 2×4 on the 3½ inch side; at least 4 for each window.

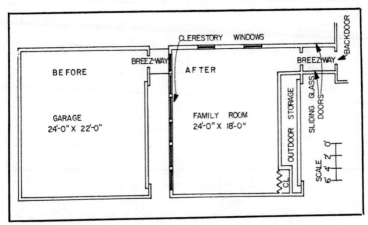

Fig. 20-1A. Scale floor plan showing before view of garage Conversion IX.

8. Nail them on to every fourth wall stud, evenly spaced up and down the stud (Fig. 20-3).

9. Place trimmer stud against spacer blocks and nail into blocks.

10. Toe-nail into top and sole plates or use T-plates to secure.

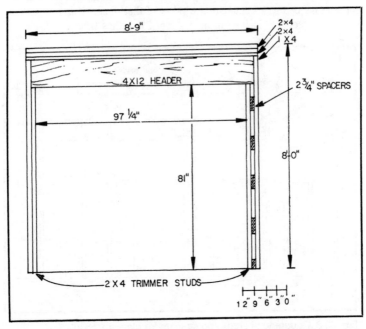

Fig. 20-1B. Scale floor plan showing after view of Conversion IX.

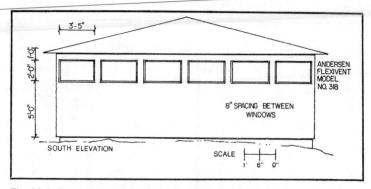

SOUTH ELEVATION

ANDERSEN
FLEXIVENT
MODEL
NO. 318

8" SPACING BETWEEN
WINDOWS

SCALE

1'   6"   0"

Fig. 20-2. South elevation showing clerestory window wall.

11. Be sure to check with your carpenter's level several times as you nail into place, to make sure it goes in vertically and at the right distance from the other studs which will frame the window.

12. Use shims where and when necessary.

13. Check the old stud and if it needs to be adjusted pry and shim where needed.

14. Repeat steps above for each window in the clerestory.

15. Measure your window vertically. Add ½-inch for the top or header clearance and 3 inches for width of header and sill. This will be the amount of stud needed to accomodate a window of that dimension:

2-feet +½-inch+3-inches=2-foot 3½ inches (Fig. 20-3).

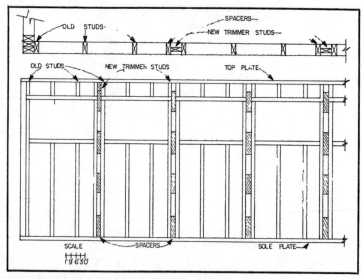

Fig. 20-3. Roughing in studs and spacers for clerestory wall.

16. Since we are dropping our ceiling nearly one foot, we measure down 12-inches and mark our studs for the top cut. Measure on down the additional distance arrived at in step 15 and mark for the bottom cut.

17. Cut studs and remove from sheathing.

18. Cut sill and header to fit snugly and pound into place.

19. Using your carpenter's square and level, nail down header and sill true and square. Use shingle shims and take your time with this fine tuning.

20. Repeat steps 6 through 9 for each window.

21. Drill tiny holes through the sheathing and siding from the inside at the corners of the window frames.

22. Using the tiny holes as guides on the outside, remove the necessary siding (see Conversion I, Project 2, for how to do it) to accommodate the clerestory windows.

23. With the sheathing exposed take a straight edge and connect the tiny holes you have drilled with pencil lines, making a rectangle the exact size and location of each window opening.

24. Using the combination saw, carefully cut out each opening flush with its 2x4 framing.

25. Lift each window into place and install with the hardware and instructions that came from the manufacturer.

26. Cut and replace siding between and around windows.

27. Caulk around the exterior of all windows.

28. Trim each window individually with narrow redwood trim.

PROJECT 2: INSTALLING FIXED AND AWNING WINDOW COMBINATIONS

Materials: 2 Andersen Flexivent awning #318 windows; 2 Andersen fixed model #349 windows; 2 8-foot 2×4 studs; 2 14-foot 2×4's; caulking compound; exterior redwood trim.

Tools: Combination saw, saber saw, hammer, drill, caulking gun.

Instructions:

These floor to ceiling windows should be located about four feet in from the corner of the wall. Assuming that the studs you are working with are 16-inches on centers, count seven studs in from the corner on each side and mark that as the stud on which to place your spacers for locating the trimmer studs. See Fig. 20-4 for final effect.

1. Cut 3½-inch spacers (use width of 2×4) and nail to the marked studs. Consult Fig. 20-5.

2. Nail trimmer stud into place against the spacer blocks checking with your carpenter's level to make sure it goes in vertically. Use shims for any corrections needed.

3. Repeat step 2 above, for second window.

4. Measure 12 inches down from top plate on the two adjacent studs that will come out for window openings and mark for cuts.

5. Cut studs and pull out from sole plate.

6. Cut headers and sills to fit snugly and pound into place.

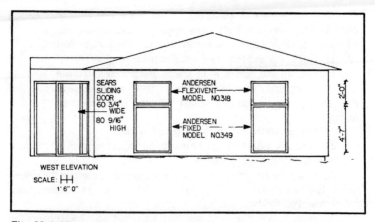

Fig. 20-4. West elevation showing fixed and awning window combinations.

7. With carpenter's square, level and shims, square and true top window frames, then bottom frames. Make sure dimensions are exact with ½-inch clearance all around.

8. Repeat steps 21 through 28 of Project 1 to finish installation.

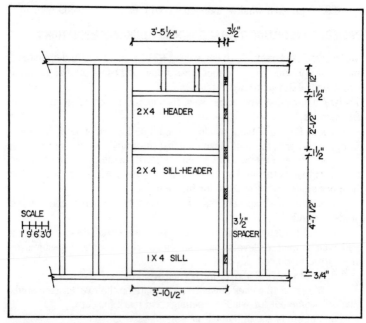

Fig. 20-5. Spacers and header details in combo window wall.

PROJECT 3: INTERIOR PARTITION FOR
OUTDOOR STORAGE AREA AND INSIDE CLOSET

Materials: 27 8-foot 2×4 studs; 2 16-foot 2×4's; 2 10-foot 2×4's; 8 4×8-foot panels of ¼-inch masonite pegboard; 20 lag screws and sleeves; 8d, 4d and 16d nails; 1 4-foot 1×4; 1 2×4-foot panel of ¼-inch C-D plywood.

Tools: Saber saw, hammer, drill and masonry bit; wrench; screwdriver, carpenter's square; level.

Note:

To enclose the outdoor storage area behind the overhead garage door, and the family room closet as well, a staggered wall is built in one 2-foot, two 4-foot, and two 8-foot sections. The 8-foot sections are tied together to make one continuous 16-foot wall. The other sections are angled 90 degrees to one another and tied together with a 2×4 corner brace as illustrated in Fig. 20-6. Figure 20-1, "after" shows the plan of the walls. The closet opening is closed by a 48-inch accordian folding door. Pegboard is used to line this closet as well as the outside storage area in order to give complete versatility in the use of pegboard hangers for holding shelves, bottles, tools, hooks, etc.

The wall should be built at least 7 feet high plus a few inches—as high as clearance for the overhead door will allow—so as to extend slightly above the 7-foot high suspended ceiling you will install over the family room later on. A 2×4-foot ¼-inch plywood "ceiling" should be nail-glued to the top of the closet to seal out dirt and dust from the outdoor storage area.

Instructions:

1. Build the first 4-foot section of wall that forms the back of the closet according to instructions for wall building given in Conversion I, Project 2.

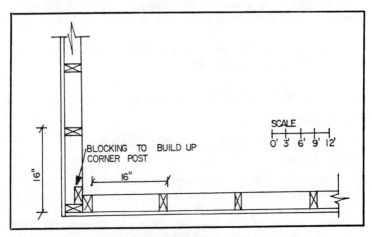

Fig. 20-6. Detail of turning a corner with two walls.

2. Erect the wall exactly 24 inches inside the overhead door opening. Tie together the new and old sole plates and nail the end stud of the new wall into a stud in the old wall. If there is no old stud where you connect, put one into the old wall exactly where needed (Fig. 20-7).

3. Construct the 2-foot wall section and erect it at right angles to the previous section, projecting toward the family room area (Fig. 20-8).

4. Place a 2×4 stud as a blocking post in the corner where the two walls meet as indicated in Fig. 20-9.

5. Nail the blocking post securely to the end studs of both walls with 16d nails.

6. Tie top plates together with a flat corner iron.

7. Assemble the first 8-foot wall section.

8. Erect at right angle to 2-foot section and tie together with blocking post and flat corner iron (Fig. 20-10).

9. Assemble the second 8-foot wall section, erect and fasten to other 8-foot section. Nail end studs together with 8d nails and top plates and sole plates with T-plates.

10. Construct the final 4-foot section of the wall and erect at right angles running back toward front of garage structure (Fig. 20-11).

11. Position blocking post and nail securely to both wall sections. Use corner iron on top plates.

12. At the front of the garage, where your new wall meets the old garage structure, tie the new wall in firmly by nailing old and new sole plates together and tie end stud of new wall to stud in old wall. Again, if there is no stud already there to nail into, put one in yourself.

13. Cut pegboard panels to wall height and nail in place with 4d nails inside storage area and closet.

14. Using corner brackets, place 1×4×48-inch board across closet opening on family room side at the tope of the wall 81 inches from floor. This will give one inch clearance for the 80-inch folding door you will be installing. Track for the folding door goes on underneath the edge of the 1×4.

15. Install accordian type folding door with its own hardware according to manufacturer's instructions.

PROJECT 4: BUILD STORAGE SHELVES AND BUILT-IN COUCH

Built-In Couch

Follow directions given in Conversion IV, Project 5.

Storage Shelves

Follow directions for book shelves in Conversion I, Project 5, for mounting of standards. For a new look in shelves follow instructions below.

Materials: Shelving of your choice (pine, plywood, particle board); 1-inch or 1¼-inch molding; 1×4, enough for 2 strips as long as short side of

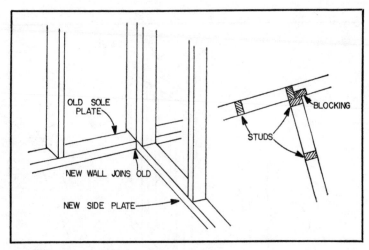

Fig. 20-7. Tying into old sole plate with detail of stud arrangement.

shelving boards; glue, finishing nails, bright enamel paint and sealer, filler.

Tools: Saw, measuring tape, pencil, hammer, screwdriver, drill, paint brush, countersink tool.

Instructions:

1. Mount standards, following directions in Conversion I, Project 5, spacing them between 28 and 30 inches apart at regular intervals all over the wall on which you want the shelves to hang.

2. Buy or cut your shelving to length of 36 inches, 42 inches and 48 inches.

3. Keep the width of the shelves uniform at 10 or 12 inches.

4. Cut the 1×4 into lengths to fit at the short edges of the shelves plus the thickness of the molding, usually ½-inch.

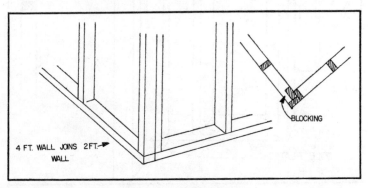

Fig. 20-8. Turning a corner with detail of blocking.

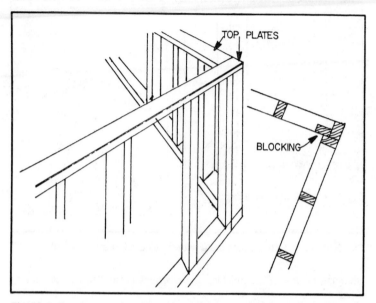

Fig. 20-9. Turning and outside corner showing top plates and blocking.

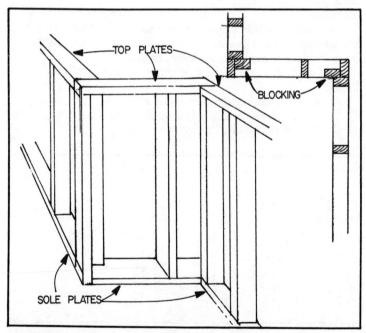

Fig. 20-10. Putting on the top plates with detail of blocking on inside and outside corners.

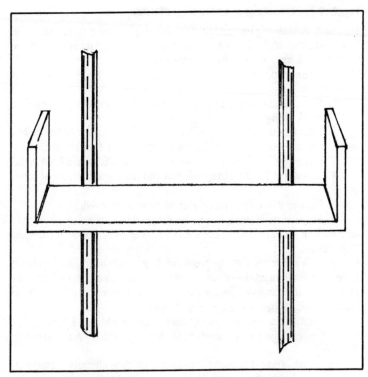

Fig. 20-11. Storage shelf hung with standards and brackets.

5. Nail and glue in place.

6. Cut molding to the length of the shelf and nail and glue in place between 1×4 along one side of the shelf.

7. Countersink nails and fill. Sand.

8. Seal and paint in the dominant colors of your decorating for the room.

9. If your room is monochromatic, use three shades. Bright clear colors are most effective, but muted shades work well, too.

10. Hang on standards.

PROJECT 5: INSULATE

See Conversion II, Project 7 for how-to on insulating.

PROJECT 6: FINISH INTERIOR WITH
SHEETROCK OR GYPSUM WALLBOARD AND PAINT

See Conversion III, Project 7 and follow directions for covering walls with drywall and making "invisible" joints. See Conversion I, Project 6 for instructions on painting and finishing drywalls.

PROJECT 7: INSTALLING A SUSPENDED CEILING

Materials: Armstrong Integrid System suspended ceiling components: 86 feet of wall molding; 112 1×4-foot ceiling tiles; enough main runners and cross tees to install; 2d nails, 25 screw eyes.

Tools: Hammer, pliers.

Instructions:

1. Nail molding to all four walls and into entry alcove at 7-foot height with 2d nails going into studs (Fig. 20-12).

2. Starting on one of the walls that run perpendicular to the ceiling joists, measure out exactly 26 inches for location of first runner.

3. Place row of screw eyes every other joist 26 inches from wall.

4. Measure 48 inches from this row and place another row of screw eyes.

5. Repeat above until other side of room is reached.

6. Suspend main runners on wire dropped from rows of screw eyes with ends of runners resting just above molding on each side of the room (Fig. 20-13).

7. Pick any corner of the room and begin installing tiles by simply laying the first ceiling tile on the molding and then snapping a 4-foot cross tee onto the main runner. Then slide the tee into the special concealed slot on the leading edge of the tile (Fig. 20-14).

8. Continue across the room, inserting tiles and cross tees.

9. To finish out a row, cut tile to fit and *use the leftover piece to start the next row!*

When this type of suspended ceiling is finished all metal suspension members are hidden from view. There is no visible grid work (Fig. 20-15).

PROJECT 8: ENCLOSING BREEZEWAY WITH SLIDING GLASS DOORS

Materials: 2 Sears Double-Pane Sliding Patio Doors, size 80½×96¾-inch, 8 8-foot 2×4 studs; 4 9-foot 2×4's; 2 9-foot 1×4; 4 9-foot 2×12's; 4 8-foot

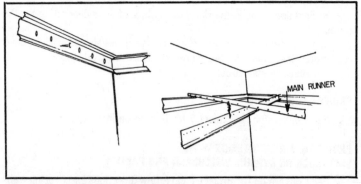

Fig. 20-12. Suspending main runners on wire dropped from rows of screw eyes with ends of runners resting just above molding.

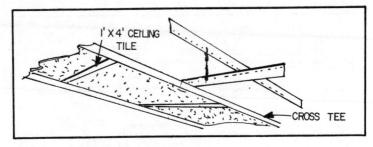

Fig. 20-13. Installing the ceiling tile.

1×4 facing boards; 4 1×6 facing boards; 4 8-foot strips of ¼-inch molding; 8d and 16d nails; 1 dozen screw sleeves.

Tools: Saber saw; hammer, drill and masonry bit; screwdriver; carpenter's square; carpenter's level.

Instructions:

Consult instructions on Conversion III, Project 5, for details on framing in and installing a sliding glass door. Here is how you adapt those instructions to closing in an 8-foot 9-inch × 4-foot cement floor and roofed breezeway, which measures 8 feet from cement floor to underside of the top plates spaning the space between house and garage. The top plates support the rafters of the gabled roof.

1. Measure dimensions of breezeway.

2. Measure dimensions of doors.

3. As illustrated in Fig. 19-18, work out framing members to enclose a space equal to dimensions of door plus ½-inch clearance. The header for the slightly larger than 8-foot span will need to be at least 4 inches wide and 10 feet long. Use an oversized header rather than crippled studs of only a few inches in length.

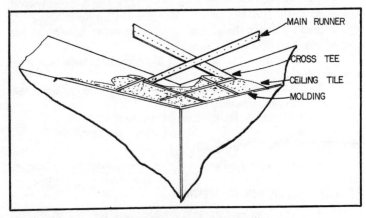

Fig. 20-14. All suspension members are hidden by tiles.

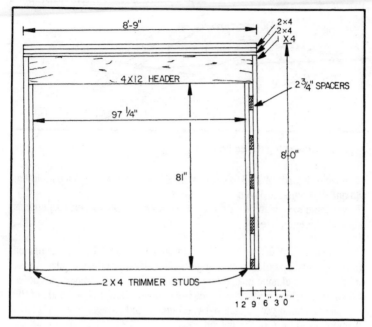

Fig. 20-15. Roughing in the breezeway enclosure.

4. Beginning on either side, nail two 2×4's and one 1×4 under the top plate of the breezeway structure.

5. Cut end studs and nail in place on edge of breezeway structure or onto house and garage. Remove enough siding to accomodate flush fit of 2×4's to house and garage if necessary.

6. Construct header beam from two 2×12's and ½-inch plywood spacers as detailed and illustrated in Conversion III, Project 5.

7. Install trimmer studs, raise header and square opening as per instructions, Conversion III, Project 5.

8. Assemble door, install and test according to manufacturer's instructions.

9. Drill holes in concrete "floor" of breezeway to accomodate screw sleeves for securing bottom of door.

10. Repeat steps 4 through 9 on other side of structure.

PROJECT 9: LAYING CARPET TILES

See Conversion I, Project 8 for how-to on laying carpet tiles.

PROJECT 10: CARPETING BREEZEWAY

Materials: Indoor/Outdoor carpeting, double-faced tape, sealer.
Tools: Scissors, measuring tape, scrub brush, drill with masonry bit.

Instructions:

1. Scour breezeway floor with heavy duty cleanser, rinse thoroughly.

2. Let dry. Seal.

3. Lay a row of tape on either side of the breezeway along the new doors and one row down the center.

4. Every 2 feet fill in with short strip between the long strips going crosswise.

5. Place a crosswise strip in front of the house and garage entrances.

6. Cut and fit carpet.

7. Lay in place.

8. If you like, you can tie down the carpet by the entrances with plastic or metal strips.

9. Pre-drill holes with your masonry bit and use sleeved screws.

10. Remember, though, that if you use the strips you won't be able to take up the carpeting to hose off outside.

Chapter 21
Garage Conversion X

This garage sat at the very end of a small city lot and opened out into an alley. The house itself towered 12 feet in front of it. There was a strip of yard to one side and a hedge almost abutted it on the other. There was a terrace at the side of the house and a small front yard.

The garage itself was in good condition, finished with real plaster on the inside. Both the house and garage were pretty old. The neighborhood had been designated as a historical district and was centrally located. A nice place to live, but no place for someone who wanted to have a lot of plants. The terrace was too shady and so was the strip of garden. There was no front porch and the house itself was rather full of furniture and a bit on the dark side.

The greatest need was for a room that was big enough to entertain informally. The owners belonged to a number of groups and clubs which took turns meeting at each others' homes. Also, the husband and his father who lived with them were avid plant lovers whose idea of heaven were miles and miles of shelves full of every conceivable kind of house plant.

After some soul searching and brainstorming the conservatory addition to the garage was conceived. From there on the room practically designed itself. There was, of course, a potting bench and a DeHanis tiled floor.

Obviously there was need for a lot of light in the large room so strip lighting was chosen as the answer. A heatpump was decided upon to be the most economical and efficient heating and cooling system.

A couple of built-in storage seats provide bulk storage for supplies and provided seating for guests.

A deck was constructed to connect the house with the new family room which provided additional entertaining space during the summer months and kept one's feet dry during the rainy season. See the before and after floor plans in Fig. 21-1.

PROJECT 1: BUILDING A CONSERVATORY
WELL AND SOLAR ENERGY COLLECTOR

Materials: 27 8-foot 2 × 4 studs; 2 8-foot 2 × 4's; 4 9-foot 2 × 4's; 2 16-foot 1 × 4's; 2 4 × 8-foot 1 × 4's; 12 4-foot C-D grade ½-inch plywood panels for sheathing; 6 4- × 8-foot B-D grade ½-inch plywood panels for exterior siding; 50 feet of Kraft building paper; 1 roll (25 × 4-foot) .037-inch

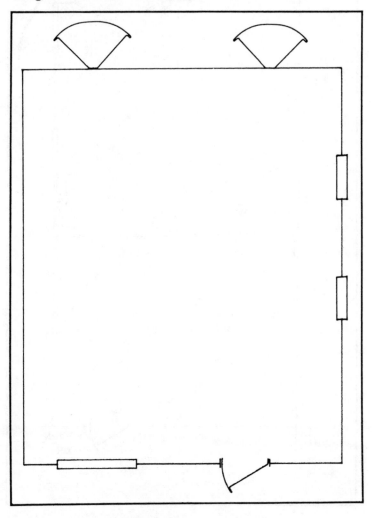

Fig. 21-1A. Scale plan of before view of Conversion X.

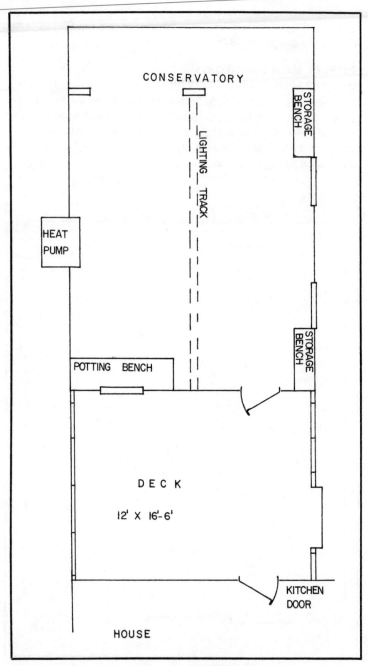

Fig. 21-1B. Scale plan of after view of Conversion X.

colorless, translucent fiberglass; 40 packages of 30 5/16-inch wallboard bricks; 13 gallons adhesive; If alternate real brick is chosen for walls of conservatory, you'll need: 1200 common antique white bricks and sufficient mortar for ½-inch beds; 1 gallon sand or other textured exterior paint; 3 gallons textured interior paint; 6d, 8d, and 16d nails, one dozen lag screws with sleeves.

Tools: Saber saw; hammer; drill with wood and masonry bits; trowel; mortar board; putty knife; tin snips; wrench.

Instructions:

1. Pre-fabricate four wall sections as described in Conversion IV, Project 3. Two of the walls will be 8 feet high and 8 feet wide, and the other two 8 feet high and 46 inches wide. Refer to Conversion I, Project 2, if necessary, for basics of wall construction and fastening sole plates to cement floor or driveway.

2. Fasten 46-inch walls to garage structure as described in Conversion IV, Project 3, except that the connection is to the exterior, as in Fig. 21-1 ("after" floor plan), and sole plates attach to concrete driveway rather than garage floor.

3. Attach 8-foot sections with 2 × 4 corner post and tie together as per instructions in Conversion IV, Project 3.

3A. Mark stud positions on floor.

4. Remove and dismantle old garage doors. If gate type, as shown in Fig. 21-1 "before" floor plan, salvage boards to frame openings.

5. Nail 1 × 6's or 1 × 8's salvaged from old garage doors to sides of trimmer studs and underside of header to frame door openings as in Fig. 21-2. Align boards flush with wall on conservatory side of opening and allow projection into family room side.

6. Trim 4 × 8-foot plywood sheathing panels to exact fit and nail to studs in walls to sheath in interior wall.

6A. Attach metal tie strips if you're going to use real brick.

7. With tin snips, cut fiberglass material to length to fit length of top of conservatory and install as illustrated in Fig. 21-3.

8. Tuck one inch along long edge of fiberglass under the 1 × 4 facing board, nail to front of garage just above conservatory wall height.

9. Pull fiberglass material tight and tack down at edge of conservatory "roof" with one foot lengths of half-round spaced three inches apart, with one inch of the 48-inch wide material lapping down the top of the long wall of the conservatory and the two side walls.

10. Tuck the 1-inch overlap behind the 1 × 4 facing board and nail along the tops of the conservatory walls.

11. The fiberglass "roof" you have just constructed is shatter resistant, water and rot proof, and will transmit 92 percent of the light and solar thermal energy that reaches it. Water will drain off this fiberglass roof due to the slight pitch of the driveway to which it is anchored.

12. If you like you can "cheat" and construct your side walls so that they are slightly higher where they attach to the garage to get a bit more slope.

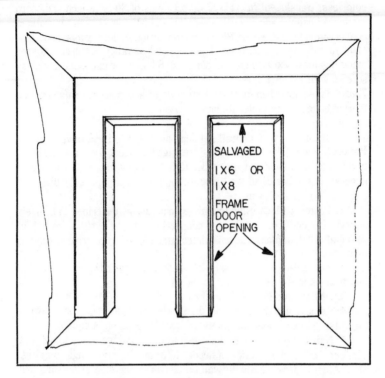

Fig. 21-2. Trimming the conservatory doors, detail.

13. Install 5/16-inch brick wallcovering according to instructions that come with the installation kit. Be sure to "butter" both wall and brick with adhesive and work each one firmly into place.

14. This so called "Realbrick" wallcovering is made from kiln-dried shale clay and will be fireproof, but since they are only a little more than ¼-inch thick they will store *some* but not very much heat energy.

15. The alternative, if you wish to make your conservatory an efficient solar energy collector, is to build the walls from full dimensional common brick which will store up lots of heat energy during the day and release it into the family room at night (Fig. 21-4).

16. Building brick walls on the inside of your conservatory is not difficult since the walls are all solid with no openings. In fact, if you have never laid brick before this is a good project on which to learn. If you are game, following steps 18 through 36 will see you through.

17. If not, go with step 14 and then skip onward to step 41.

18. Mix a small quantity of mortar according to instructions on the bag.

19. Put some mortar on the mortar board and position it at a convenient working height.

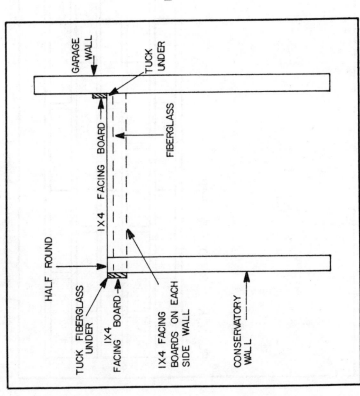

Fig. 21-3. Installing fiberglass roof over conservatory.

353

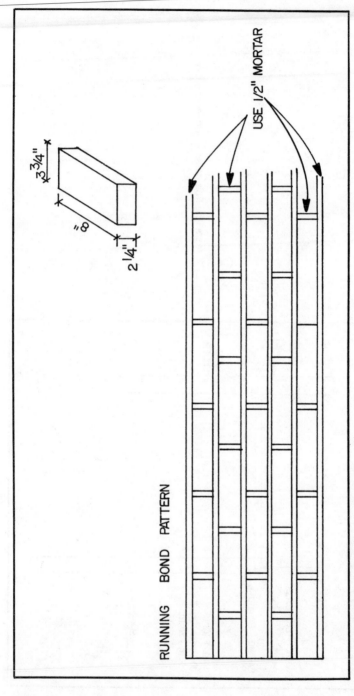

RUNNING BOND PATTERN

USE 1/2" MORTAR

Fig. 21-4. Scale drawing of a section of the brick wall.

20. Put together a small supply of bricks close to the corner of one of your new short walls and the garage structure.

21. Grasp the trowel firmly with the palm and thumb of your hand up. It's the muscles of your forearm that you use to spread the mortar and butter your bricks. After a few hours of brick laying, if your forearm is sore you know you are holding your trowel properly.

22. Troweling mortar off your mortar board, lay a bed ½-inch deep and a brick width in each corner, about the length of three bricks.

23. Lay the corner bricks for your first course, as in Fig. 21-5. Butter one end of each brick and set it in the mortar bed always working from the corners out.

24. To keep your bricks level, place a level over the brick and tap it lightly with the handle of your trowel until the level's bubble is centered.

25. Make sure each brick is butted tightly against the wall sheathing.

26. After the first course of corner bricks have been laid, lay metal ties on top of each brick that is in front of a wall stud as determined by your markings made on the floor in step 3.

27. Nail ties into studs. This needs to be done about every six courses as you lay the wall (Fig. 21-6).

28. Lay a ½-inch mortar bed on top of the first course of corner bricks and lay down two to four more in half lap pattern taking care to keep them all level and straight and butted firmly against the wall.

29. Now top your corners with a third course of two bricks and check to see that all corner top bricks are the same distance from the floor—exactly. If they are not, adjust bricks with more or less mortar until a string line run across the top bricks in each corner will run parallel with the floor (Fig. 21-5).

30. Make sure that the corners are plumb, level and aligned smack against the plywood wall. Use your level constantly and making up a story pole with regular markings corresponding to brick thickness and mortar thickness (2¼-inch and ½-inch). This is handy for checking to see if the top of your course comes out as planned.

31. If the top courses of your corner guides do not line up it is probably because your mortar mixture is too thick or too thin. A little more experience will solve the problem Meanwhile make your corrections on that third course by making the mortar bed underneath thinner or thicker than the ½-inch "norm."

32. Secure a thin cord line across the tops of the corner bricks by laying a brick on top of it at each corner (Fig. 21-5).

33. Lay the side walls, now, between the corner bricks, leveling each brick as you go and working up to the "mason's line," where, if your third course does not top exactly at the string's height, you make corrections, leveling that third course exactly before building any higher.

34. Be sure to lay your metal ties on the first course bricks at each stud and nail to the stud before laying the mortar bed on top of it.

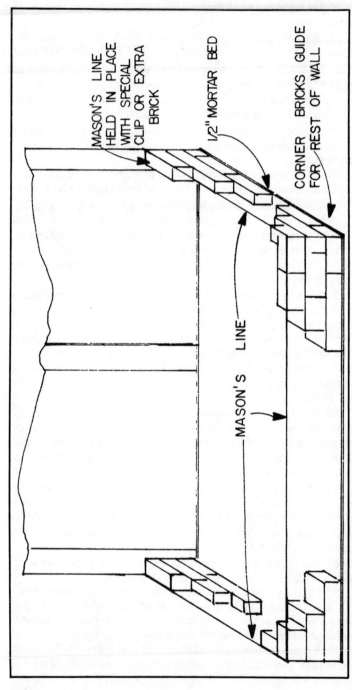

MASON'S LINE
HELD IN PLACE
WITH SPECIAL
CLIP OR EXTRA
BRICK

1/2" MORTAR BED

CORNER BRICKS GUIDE
FOR REST OF WALL

MASON'S LINE

Fig. 21-5. Laying the corners of the brick wall first.

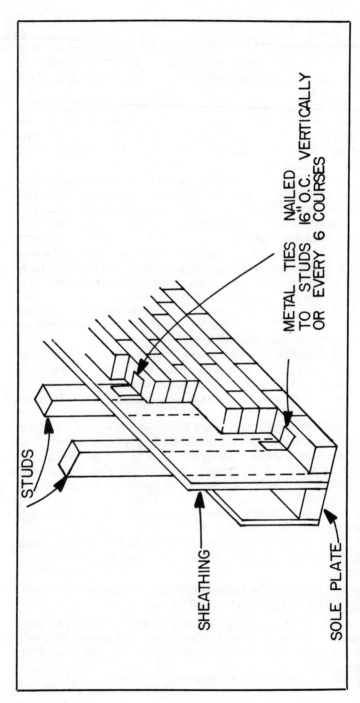

STUDS

METAL TIES NAILED TO STUDS 16" O.C. VERTICALLY OR EVERY 6 COURSES

SHEATHING

SOLE PLATE

Fig. 21-6. Tying brick wall to sheathing.

35. Repeat steps 21 through 33 every three courses until the 8-foot high walls are completed.

36. For instructions on cutting bricks in half, which you will need to do every other course on the bricks that end the walls abutting against the front of the old garage, see Conversion VIII, Project 4, on building a brick planter box.

37. With 1200 or so bricks to store the sun's heat for night time and cloudy days, you will not want all that free energy escaping out the fiberglass top on your conservatory. You will also want some control over the input of all that solar energy on days and in seasons when cooling, not heating, is called for.

38. Ideally, your conservatory should be on the south side of your garage (if you live in the northern hemisphere) and shaded to keep the summer sun from ever shining directly in, but with the southern winter sun pouring directly in from November thru April. However, it is not likely that a garage you might want to convert would be so ideally oriented.

39. The solution is to "hang" three Sears brand 1-inch steel fashion blinds horizontally across the fiberglass opening. Three 64-inch long by 42¾-inch wide blinds cover the opening perfectly and the louvers can be controlled to admit or bounce back sunlight from any angle.

40. They are also easy to install since their hardware secures them on all four corners. There is little sag on the 1-inch versions if they are stretched tight when installed (Fig. 21-7).

41. Insulating the walls of the conservatory is done from the outside, stapling insulating bats onto the inner sheathing between the wall studs. See Conversion II, Project 7 for details on insulating inside walls.

42. Trim remaining 4 × 8-foot plywood sheathing panels to fit and nail to studs.

43. Apply Kraft building paper in horizontal layers from its 48-inch wide rolls. Use the white line as a guide for overlapping layers.

44. Starting at one of the corners, apply the bottom layer of paper. While your helper unrolls the paper, staple or nail it down approximately every 8 inches. Always make sure that the paper is going on straight (Fig. 21-8).

45. Trim and nail plywood siding panels over Kraft paper with corrosion resistant box nails.

46. Paint siding with an exterior texture paint to match stucco finish of the rest of the building. Your finished conservatory well should resemble Fig. 21-9.

PROJECT 2: TRACK LIGHTING FOR ARTIFICIAL MOONLIGHT AND CONVENTIONAL LIGHTING

Materials: Mounting plate; 2 8-foot sections of track; 1 2-foot track extension; 1 T-connector; 2 4-foot track sections; 3 flood-light fixtures; 1 framing projector with blue gel; hardware that comes with above; 3 wire nuts.

Tools: Screwdriver and wire strippers.

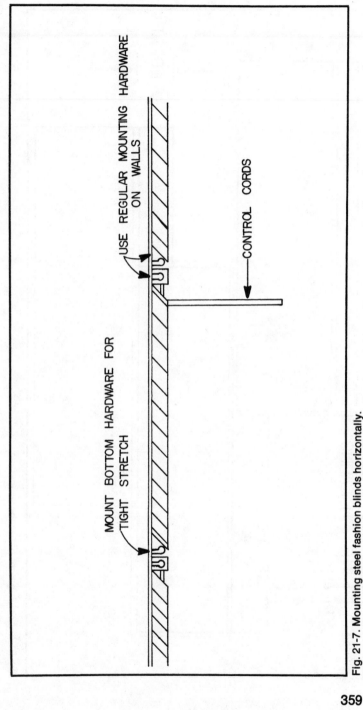

MOUNT BOTTOM HARDWARE FOR TIGHT STRETCH

USE REGULAR MOUNTING HARDWARE ON WALLS

CONTROL CORDS

Fig. 21-7. Mounting steel fashion blinds horizontally.

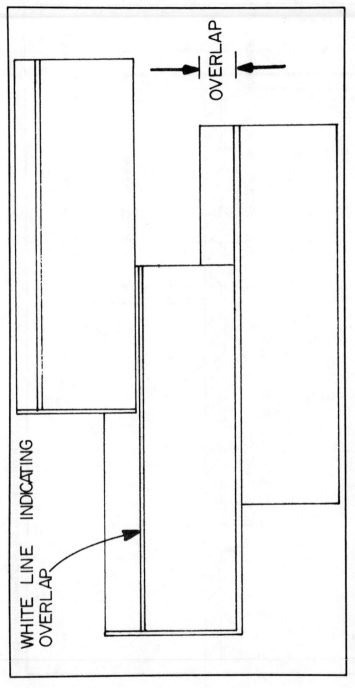

WHITE LINE INDICATING
OVERLAP

OVERLAP

Fig. 21-8. Applying kraft paper the proper way.

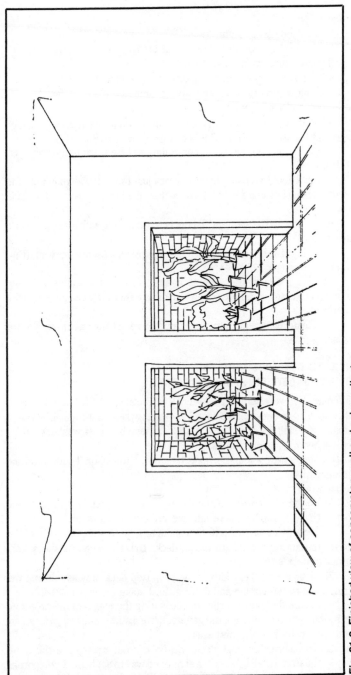

Fig. 21-9. Finished view of conservatory wall and solar collector.

361

Instructions:

1. Turn on garage light.

2. Turn off garage circuit at circuit breaker or fuse box.

3. Make sure garage light is out.

4. Unfasten garage ceiling fixture from ceiling outlet box.

5. Follow directions accompanying mounting plate for fastening to outlet box and wiring it.

6. Plug two 8-foot sections of track into mounting plate, one on each side, and secure to ceiling with hardware provided (Fig. 21-10).

7. Bore small hole in wall near ceiling to take track extension (Fig. 21-10).

8. Cut 2-foot extension track to reach just through wall plug in to the 8-foot track on one end and the T-connector on other end just on other side of wall.

9. Tie down extension and T-connector to ceiling with manufacturer's hardware.

10. Plug 4-foot tracks into T-connector and secure to wall (Fig. 21-11).

11. Set fixtures in tracks as desired for most effective lighting. Framing projector with blue gel on track in conservatory can give effect of moonlight.

12. Restore current to garage circuit by re-setting circuit-breaker or replacing fuse.

PROJECT 3: CONSTRUCTING DECK CONNECTION BETWEEN HOUSE AND GARAGE

Materials: Redwood lumber: 4 16-foot 2 × 6 beams; 9 12-foot 2 × 10 joists; 39 16-foot 2 × 4 decking; 6 3-foot 2 × 4 railing posts; 1 12-foot 1 ″ 4 rail; 1 6-foot 1 × 4 rail; 1 3-foot 1 × 4 rail; 12 carriage bolts; 24 washers; 16 lag screws and expansion shields.

Tools: Saber saw, combination saw, hammer, wrench, drill with wood and masonry bits.

Instructions:

1. Locate one corner of the deck site where deck will tie onto the house. Drive a wooden stake into the ground at that point.

2. Tie a piece of string to this stake and run it along the side of the house, measuring the length of the deck. Drive a second stake at that corner of deck site.

3. Measure off the width of the proposed deck now as you run the string over to the garage and drive a third stake (as in Fig. 21-12).

4. Locate the fourth corner by measuring the length of the proposed deck along the foundation of the garage, drive a stake, and bring the string around it on back to the first stake.

5. To insure that your deck will be laid out square use the 3-4-5 system illustrated in Fig. 21-12, a simplified way to apply the Pythagorean theorem. Any multiple of 3-4-5, such as 9-12-15, may be used to square off

362

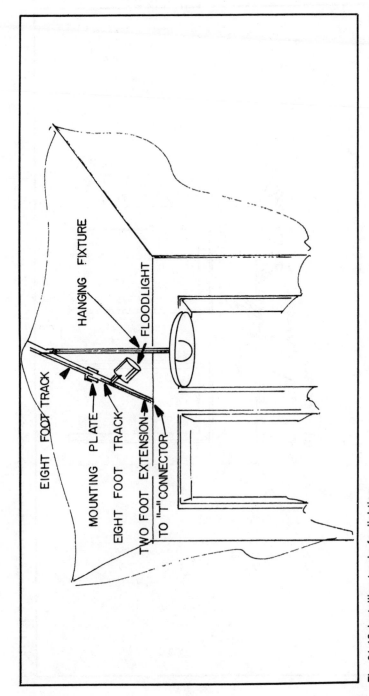

EIGHT FOOT TRACK

HANGING FIXTURE

FLOODLIGHT

MOUNTING PLATE

EIGHT FOOT TRACK

TWO FOOT EXTENSION

TO "T" CONNECTOR

Fig. 21-10. Installing tracks for lighting.

363

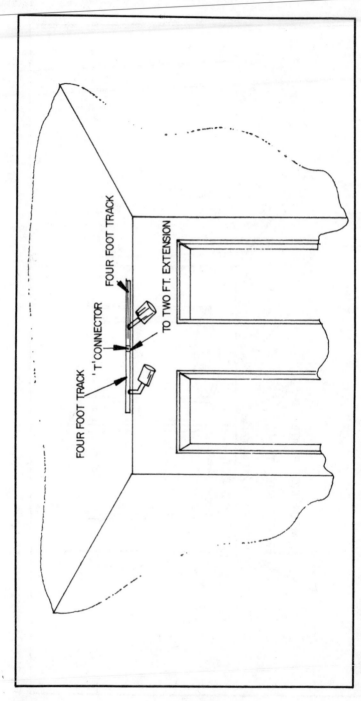

FOUR FOOT TRACK

'T' CONNECTOR

FOUR FOOT TRACK

TO TWO FT. EXTENSION

Fig. 21-11. Extending lighting track into conservatory.

a corner. From one corner we measure 9 feet along the line parallel with the house, and 12 feet across to the garage. If the layout is square the diagonal, or hypotenuse will be 15 feet. If it isn't you simply adjust stake C until it is (Fig. 21-12).

6. Double-check the squareness of your rectangle by measuring the full diagonal distance between opposite corner stakes. Both diagonals should be the same. In other words, line AC equals line DB (Fig. 21-12).

7. Once your layout is squared, construct your L-shaped header beams and anchor one each to house and garage foundations, along lines AB and CD, with lag screws as shown in Fig. 21-13.

8. Make up a story pole with 16 inch intervals marked and lay it along the header beams and mark the position for the center of each joist.

9. Lay the 2×10 joists into position across the header beams (Fig. 21-4) and toe-nail into place.

10. Lay 2 × 4 deck boards across joists, bark side up as in Fig. 21-14.

11. Use 16d galvanized casing nails for spacers and to nail the decking to the joists. Drive two nails into each joist through each decking board. Use nails as spacers to keep boards parallel.

12. Snap a chalk line at edges of deck, or use a straight board to guide saw and trim decking even, with combination saw.

13. Bolt railing posts to outside joists as shows in Fig. 21-15, then nail 1 × 4 rails onto top of posts.

14. Skirt exposed sides of deck with 2 12-foot 1 × 10's if it suits your fancy.

PROJECT 4: INSTALLING HEAT PUMP OR AIR CONDITIONER

Materials: 1 8-foot 2 × 4; 1 16-foot 1 × 4; 8d & 16d nails; metal bracket and support frame; single unit heat pump or air conditioner.

Tools: Combination saw, saber saw, hammer, carpenter's square, level, screwdriver.

Instructions:

1. Locate stud nearest center of planned wall opening by tapping wall for solid sound. Push finishing nails into wall to locate edges of stud exactly.

2. Measure 14½ inches out from each side of the stud and locate edge of next studs exactly by piercing wall with finishing nails.

3. Connect nail holes vertically with pencil marks using a straight edge to establish edges of opening between studs.

4. Measure height of unit, add 3½ inches and mark off on vertical lines.

5. Using carpenter's square finish drawing rectangular hole area on wall.

6. With combination saw cut opening along outline of rectangle.

7. If saw will not penetrate studs and sheathing all the way to the outside, drive nails through the wall from the inside, in each corner of the rectangle to indicate dimensions on outside wall. Connect nail holes with penciled line and finish cut from outside wall.

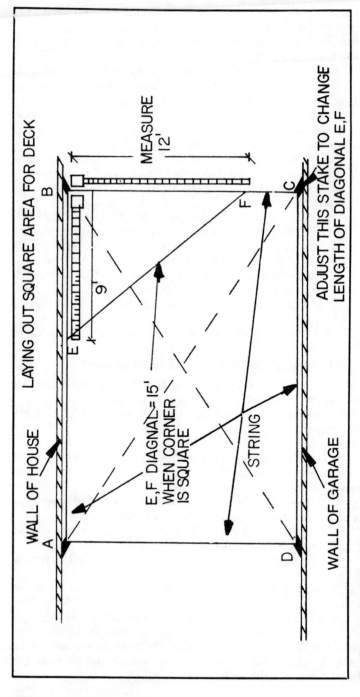

Fig. 21-12. Laying out square area for deck.

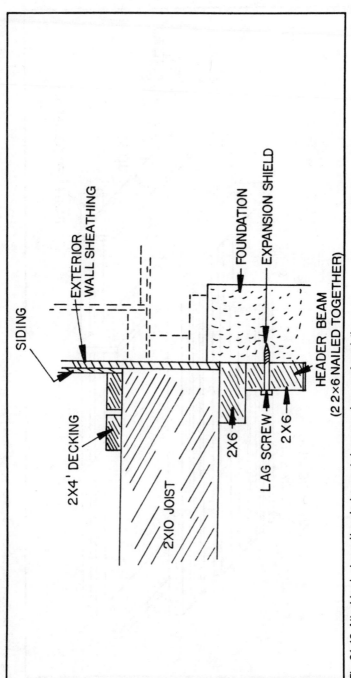

SIDING

EXTERIOR
WALL SHEATHING

FOUNDATION

EXPANSION SHIELD

2×4' DECKING

2×6

LAG SCREW

2×6

HEADER BEAM
(2 2×6 NAILED TOGETHER)

2×10 JOIST

Fig. 21-13. Attaching L-shaped header beams to house and garage foundation.

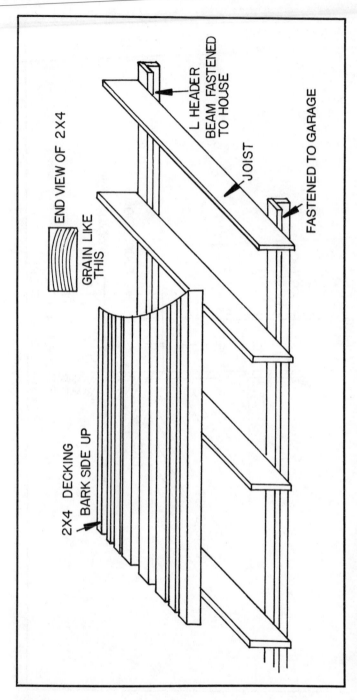

END VIEW OF 2X4

GRAIN LIKE
THIS

L HEADER

BEAM FASTENED
TO HOUSE

JOIST

FASTENED TO GARAGE

2X4 DECKING
BARK SIDE UP

Fig. 21-14. Deck construction details showing headers, joists and decking.

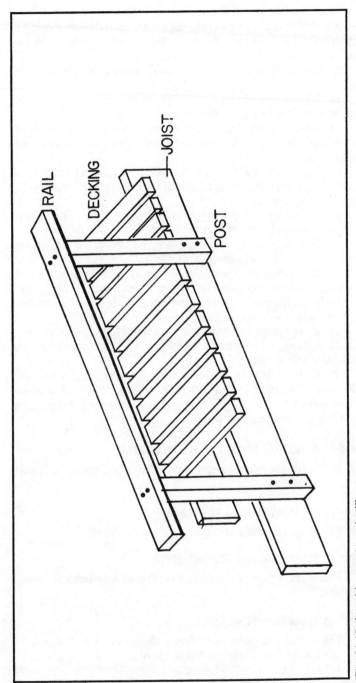

Fig. 21-15. Attaching posts and railing.

8. Cut sill from 2 × 4 lumber and nail in place across bottom of opening with 8d nails. Use level and shim if necessary to make certain sill goes in level.

9. Cut two side jambs from 2 × 4 lumber, ½-inch longer than height of unit.

10. Nail one of the jambs into stud at side of opening with 16d nails. Use carpenter's square to make sure corner is square.

11. Measure width of unit and add ½-inch. Measure off this distance on sill from side jamb just installed and nail other side jamb to sill at that distance with 8d nails.

12. Using carpenter's square to check corner, insert scrap wood spacers as needed between jamb and stud and nail in place to make solid, squared jamb. (Fig. 21-16).

13. Cut header from 2 × 4 lumber to fit snugly between studs and between jambs and crippled stud and nail into place with 8d nails.

14. From outside, lift unit into place, supporting rear end of unit temporarily with 2 × 4 props (Fig. 21-17).

15. Place carpenter's square on top of unit and adjust props so that unit is slightly lower at very back than at front of unit which is in the wall.

16. Install supporting bracket between wall and bottom of unit according to manufacturer's instructions.

17. Remove props from under unit when firmly supported by bracket.

18. Measure, cut and miter 1 × 4 lumber for trim around unit opening both inside and outside.

19. If electrical work is needed other than just plugging unit into 220-240 volt receptical hire a qualifled electrician for the job. Heat pumps can be especially tricky, so try to get someone who has had experience installing and servicing heat pumps.

PROJECT 5: TEXTURE PAINTING WALLS AND CEILING

Follow texture painting instructions given in Conversion III, Project 13.

PROJECT 6: LAYING DEHANIS TILE FLOOR

Follow instructions given in Conversion VI, Project 9.

PROJECT 7: BUILDING TWO STORAGE SEATS

Follow instructions of Conversion IV, Project 5, for building a woodbox seat.

PROJECT 8: SUPER POTTING BENCH

Follow instructions for Plant Bench, Conversion VII, Project 4.
You can also use following modifications:

1. You may want to attach some plastic drawers to the shelves on your carts to hold smaller items.

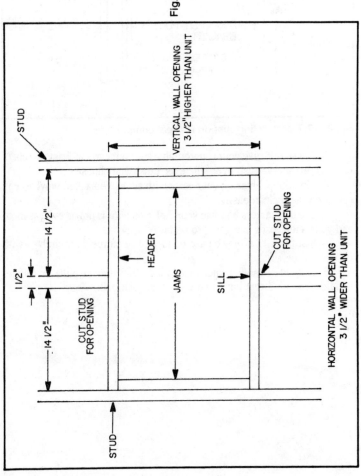

STUD

VERTICAL WALL OPENING
3 1/2" HIGHER THAN UNIT

14 1/2"

1 1/2"

CUT STUD
FOR OPENING

14 1/2"

HEADER

JAMS

SILL

CUT STUD
FOR OPENING

HORIZONTAL WALL OPENING
3 1/2" WIDER THAN UNIT

STUD

Fig. 21-16. Building framing for heat pump.

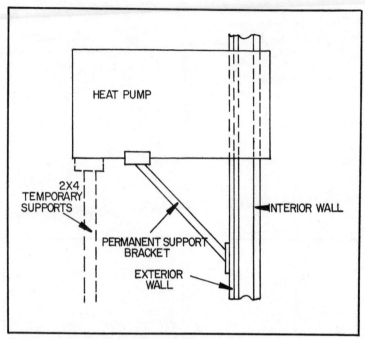

Fig. 21-17. Constructing support for heat pump.

2. You should give your counter table and your carts at least two coats of polyurethane varnish over whatever finish you choose.

3. Line the shelves on your carts with adhesive backed vinyl so you can keep them clean easily.

4. Use ball casters because your DeHanis floor is not as even as most and your shelf loads are going to be fairly heavy.

5. Just in case, it may be a good idea to reinforce your shelves with corner braces.

6. Instead of cabinet knobs use good sized drawer pulls or cabinet handles, the kind that have two screws in each pull.

Chapter 22
Garage Conversion XI

This was the garage of a friend of ours. It, too, sat almost flush against the alley with its back wall. In this case though, the alley was quiet and fringed by lovely old trees and blooming shrubs on both sides. There was little traffic except in the early morning and before supper time. Only the garbage collector made a twice weekly foray down its length during the day. Otherwise it was deserted.

The garage was connected to the main house by a roofed and floored (concrete slab) breezeway. The question was how to put the space to maximum use without bankrupting the family. Money was tight and the family was bursting out of the smallish three bedroom, living room-with-dining-L, post World War II model. They loved the location and the neighbors, and, of course, with today's prices they couldn't even hope to replace what room they did have in a newer home, much less think in terms of all their very real space needs. Converting the garage and the breezeway to real useful space seemed the best answer.

The man of the house wanted, and needed, his own space—room to pursue his ham radio hobby and other electronic pas-times, was well as adequate storage for his equipment away from the clamor of three youngsters under eight years of age.

The woman was in need of storage also, all her books, records and tapes needed a safe place to survive the youngest's terrible two's, and so did her collection of turtles from all over the land. (Handcrafted—not live).

The clerestory window-hobby-entertainment unit which recycled the old garage doors was a veritable stroke of genius (Mike's). In one swoop it took care of enclosing the garage, providing light in that area, giving the effect of clerestory windows to make lemonade out of the lemon, and lastly provided miles of storage for stereo components, television set and whatever other gadgets might join the crowd. And for the books, tapes, and turtles, too, of course.

The guest sleeping loft/storage/room divider was to be the man's own space. Here he could house his ham equipment, his hobby computer and all the other electronics his heart ached for. The guest bed loft, in addition to serving as just that for a favorite younger brother who dropped in regularly from school, was most convenient to stretch out on for that long wait until one in the morning when the bloke in Adelaide, Australia was ready for a bit of a chat. The wardrobe held out-of-season clothing and also provided room for kids' clothes that were between owners, (i.e.) too small for number one and too big for number two or three.

The walls and ceiling were insulated with insulation blankets and covered with acoustical tile to provide the best acoustics possible on a limited budget.

The hobby/entertainment unit and the guest sleeping loft were finished with semigloss latex paint, the best finish for economy grade lumber which was specified throughout for obvious reasons.

The floor was a miracle of scrounging. Someone, somewhere, had wanted to get rid of yards and yards of fine quality second-hand carpeting in a tolarable shade of brown. The catch was the was the carpet was really extra long runners—each 3 feet wide. It would be had dirt cheap—or as cheap as anything can be in this economy.

With the garage thus provided for, the attention could be turned to the former breezeway.

This 16×18 room was designated to take care of double and fortunately compatible purposes. The family needed an area for practicing their physical and spiritual rituals—yoga, rope skipping, jogging-in-place and other aerobics as well as a place to meditate alone or in a group. In addition, the three youngsters needed a play area for those times when the outdoors was too wet, too cold or too hot. As an added bonus, the woman wanted an area for her plants which would thrive in the room, with all that lovely light and would, at the same time provide a beautiful addition for the meditators to focus on.

The walls were painted a soft green to blend with the outdoors. The floor was covered in terra cotta indoor/outdoor carpeting. The exercise mats and other small physical culture paraphernalia were stored in one of two identical storage seats while the other housed the children's larger toys. Several large floor cushions and a cluster of small cushions completed the furnishing of the new room. For the before and after floor plans of Conversion XI, see Fig. 22-1.

PROJECT 1: CLERESTORY WINDOW-HOBBY UNIT FROM OLD GARAGE DOOR

Materials: 5 7-foot 1×10's, 1-16 foot 1×10; 16 4-foot 1×10's; 5 2-foot 1×10's; 48 corner irons; 8d casing nails; white glue; 1 16×7-foot wood frame garage door with 8 tempered glass windows, corner braces.
Tools: Saber saw, hammer, wrench.

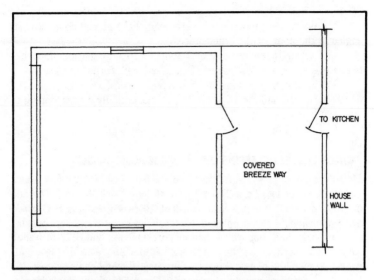

Fig. 22-1A. Scale plan showing before view of Conversion XI.

Instructions:

1. Remove lifting mechanism on garage door according to instructions in Conversion I, Project 1.

2. With door in its normal closed position nail it into its opened as a permanent fixture and remove any extraneous hardware, including tracks, etc.

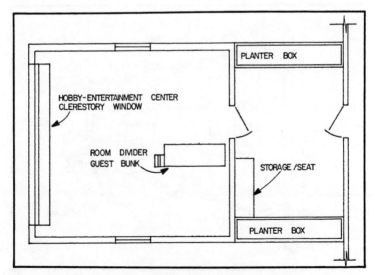

Fig. 22-1B. Scale plan showing after view of Conversion XI.

3. Fasten one 7-foot 1×10 to each end of the garage door, at right angles to the door, with corner braces.

4. Fasten three remaining 7-foot 1×10's to garage door between every two window panels (Fig. 22-2), with corner braces.

5. Glue and nail 16-foot 1×10 to top of vertical 1×10's.

6. Glue and nail the 16 4-foot 1×10's horizontally corresponding to door sections as in Fig. 22-3.

7. Glue and nail the 5 2-foot 1×10 verticals in place as shown in Fig. 22-3.

PROJECT 2: GUEST SLEEPING LOFT-STORAGE-ROOM DIVIDER

Materials: 4 5-foot 2×12's; 2 5-foot 2×8's; 8 5-foot 1×12's; 2 6-foot 3-inch 1×8's; 11 3-foot 1×12's; 1 2-foot 6-inch ×6-foot 3-inch ¾ inch B-D grade plywood panel; 2 3-foot 2-inch × 4-foot 10½-inch, ¾-inch B-C grade plywood panels; 2 closet poles with associated hardware; 2 sets pilaster standards and shelf supports; 4 shelf support standards and 12 12-inch shelf supports; 1 overhead sliding door track, bottom guides and hardware for doors; 26 mending plates; 12 corner braces; 18 metal chair braces; 250 ½-inch flathead screws; 4d casing nails; 5-foot household stepladder.
Tools: Saber saw, drill and wood bit, screwdriver, hammer, carpenter's level.
Instructions:

1. Fasten 2×12's and 2×8's together with mending plates to make two solid "walls" 29¾ inches wide and 60 inches high as shown in Fig. 22-4.

2. Fasten six 1×12's together with mending plates to make one 60×72-inch wide "wall."

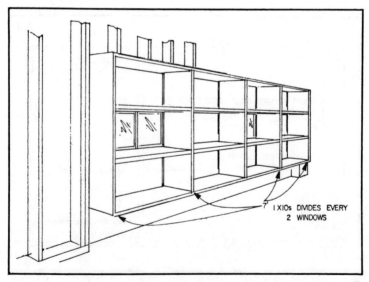

Fig. 22-2. The original garage door/clerestory window/storage unit.

376

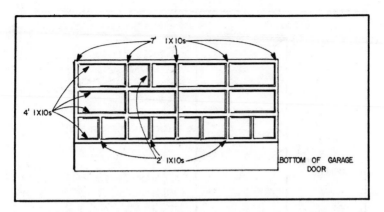

Fig. 22-3. Placements for the dividers of the garage door storage unit.

3. Tie all three "walls" together into an "I" pattern (Fig. 22-5) with corner braces.

4. Nail the 2-foot 6-inch × 6-foot 3-inch plywood panel to top of structure with 4d casing nails and countersink.

5. Insert a 5-foot 1×12 *vertically* into each side at exact center of structure and secure with casing nails through the top. Use carpenter's level to make sure the divider is plumb and secure further with corner braces.

6. Install closet poles in one quarter of the structure as illustrated in Fig. 22-6.

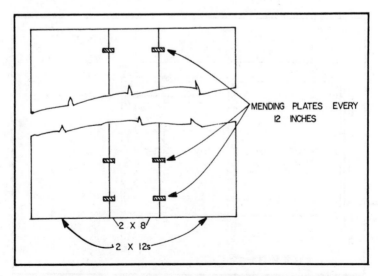

Fig. 22-4. Making a solid wall out of 2×12s and 2×8s fastened together with mending plates.

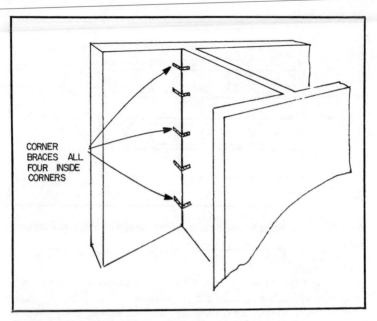

Fig. 22-5. Tying three walls together with corner braces.

7. Adjacent to the closet quarter install pilasters, shelf supports, and 5 3-foot 1×12 shelves as indicated in Fig. 22-7.

8. Fasten sliding door track across the top on the underneath side.

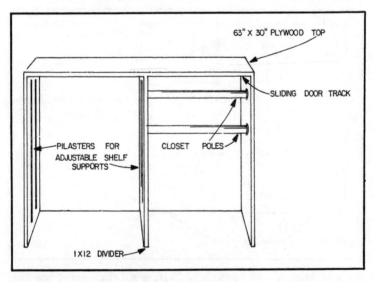

Fig. 22-6. Installing pilasters and closet poles.

378

9. The 2 3-foot 2-inch × 4-foot 10-inch panels of ¾-inch plywood panels will be the doors.

10. Sand, seal and prefinish them, either with varnish if you have a natural finish in mind or with paint if you go the economy route.

11. Put hardware on doors according to manufacturer's instructions.

12. Hang doors and put bottom guides in place.

13. On the other side of structure, install shelf standards, one pair in each side, and shelf supports for the 6 remaining 3-foot 1×12 shelves.

14. Arrange shelves to accommodate your stereo, TV, games, collections, etc.

15. Put the 6-foot 3-inch long 1×8 bed rails in place with chair braces to complete sleeping loft. Loft will take a 29½×72-inch cot sized mattress (Fig. 22-7).

16. Strip a 5-foot household ladder to steps and rails by removing back braces, bucket shelf, and top shelf.

17. Fasten steps and rails to foot end of sleeping loft (head end goes against wall) with chair braces—two under each step. (Fig. 22-7).

PROJECT 3: CONVERTING CONNECTING BREEZEWAY INTO SOLAR HEATED SOLARIUM

Materials: 8 aluminum storm doors minus hinges and handles; 48 feet of F-channel; 42 feet of H-channel; ½-inch wood screws or masonry pin-grip fasteners; sheet metal screws.
Tools: Hammer, screwdriver, drill with metal working bit; plumb bob; chalk line.
Instructions:

1. If floor to ceiling height at edges of breezeway is more than 81 install headers across top of opening to bring height down to this figure, or order oversized doors to fit (Fig. 22-8).

2. Mark the underneath side of the top beam (header) by tacking one end of a chalk line to the garage, flush with the outer edge. Hold the other end of the line the same distance from the edge on the house side.

3. Snap the line.

4. The F-channel, which will support the top of your new storm door walls, will run along this line.

5. At several points along the top chalk line hold a plumb bob and mark where the plumb bob just touches the floor.

6. Stretch a chalk line through the points you have marked on the floor and snap a line to establish the route of the horizontal F-channels along the floor.

7. Measure the top and bottom lines and cut two sections of F-channel to fit.

8. Measure the floor to ceiling height and subtract 4 inches.

9. Now cut two sections of F-channel to this length to run vertically up the garage and house walls.

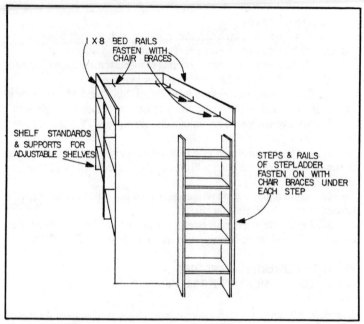

Fig. 22-7. Finishing the sleeping loft with details of bed rails, steps and rails, shelves.

10. Subtract 3 inches from the floor to ceiling measurement and cut 3 H-channels to this length.

11. Take one of your lengths of F-channel and lay along the chalk line on the floor between house and garage (Fig. 22-9).

12. With the flange facing out, drill holes every 2 feet through the flange into the floor.

13. Screw the channel down with ½-inch screws. Or if the floor is stubborn concrete, use pin-grip fasteners, a combination of masonry nail and lag screw that can be hammered in.

14. Remove the glass panels from your storm doors and lay them down on the floor of the breezeway side by side in the order of their appearance in the wall you are about to assemble.

15. Slip the vertical F-channels onto each side of each door (first and fourth doors) in the assembly.

16. Slip the edges of each door into its proper H-channels (Fig. 22-10)

17. Adjust all channels so that the doors extend 2 inches below the bottoms of the channels.

18. Slip the upper horizontal F-channel over the top of the entire wall assembly, making sure it goes over the *outsides* of the H-channels.

19. Yell for your trusty helper and raise the entire wall, after slipping the bottoms of the door panels into the base F-channel you previously secured to the foor.

20. With the wall now standing in its final resting place, fasten the flanges of the F-channels to the house, garage and breezeway roof structures by drilling and placing screws in place every 2 feet, up, around, and down.

21. Line up your wall panels now (they used to be storm doors, remember?) by pushing the first panel all the way down into the bottom F-channel.

22. Align the kick plates on each wall panel with your first panel's kick plate by pushing them down into the bottom F-channel, then raising or lowering it a bit for exact alignment. See Fig. 22-11.

23. With your helper holding each panel into perfect alignment, drill pilot holes every 2 feet along the H-channels and secure with sheet metal screws.

24. For good measure, insert two screws through the top and bottom F-channels on each panel.

25. Replace glass panels in each former door.

26. Repeat instructions 2 through 22 on the other side of your breezeway.

27. Vertical blinds that rotate almost 180 degrees may be installed floor to ceiling to achieve perfect control of sunlight, and to some degree, heat.

PROJECT 4: FINISHING CEILING WITH ACOUSTICAL TILES

Follow directions for installing acoustical tile ceiling in Conversion V, Project 6.

PROJECT 5: FINISHING WALLS WITH ACOUSTICAL TILE

Walls can be finished with acoustical tiles as easily as a ceiling. If you have finished walls of any kind—drywall, shabby paneling, particle board or plaster, you can attach your tiles directly to the wall surface.

As far as technique is concerned, we believe in the staple gun route, for walls as well as ceilings.

If your walls aren't finished, you'll have to put up furring strips just as we did on the ceiling in Conversion V, Project 6. The only difference is that you'll nail your furring strips to the studs instead of the joists. In fact if you can just think of the job as a ceiling put on its side that would do the converting for you. If you're not up to such mental gymnastics forget them and just follow directions.

Start the tiling at the top, trimming away one flange as you did for the ceiling and work across the wall and down. That will leave all your trimming and tile cutting at the floor level where it is a lot less noticeable.

Trim the joint at the ceiling and floor with pre-finished molding and put in corner moldings, too. By the way, treat corners like you did the joint between wall and ceiling. Cut your flange and start a fresh. The molding will cover the ragged edges. Be sure it is pretty wide, so that it can hide a multitude of sins. Besides, it is a lot better looking that way.

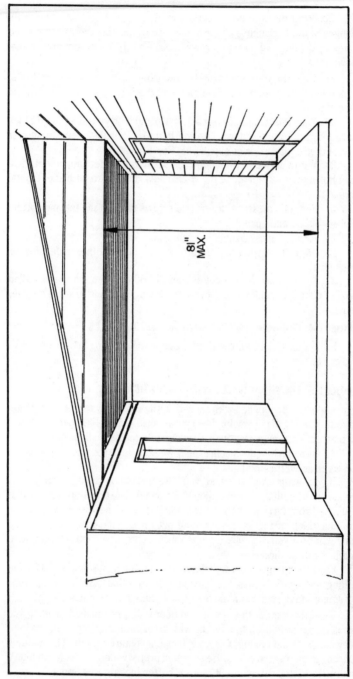

81"
MAX.

Fig. 22-8. Breezeway height adjusted to 81-inch maximum with headers.

382

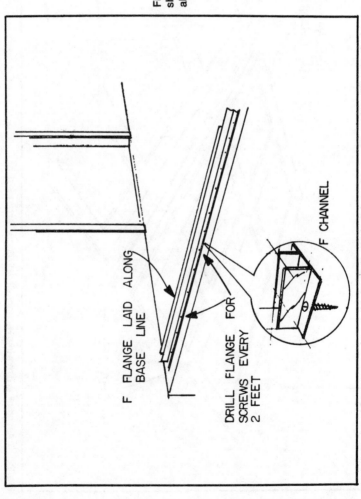

Fig. 22-9. Assembling the F- channels showing the laying of the F-flange along the base line.

F FLANGE LAID ALONG
BASE LINE

DRILL FLANGE FOR
SCREWS EVERY
2 FEET

F CHANNEL

θ

383

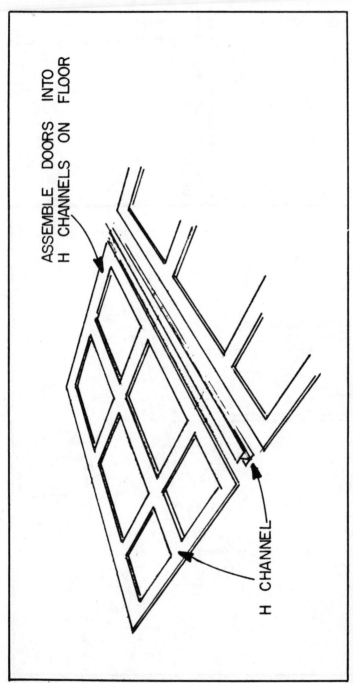

ASSEMBLE DOORS INTO
H CHANNELS ON FLOOR

H CHANNEL

Fig. 22-10. Assembling doors into H-channels with doors flat on the floor.

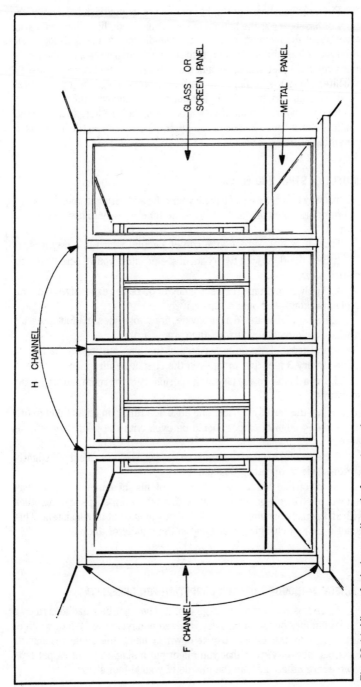

GLASS OR SCREEN PANEL

METAL PANEL

H CHANNEL

F CHANNEL

Fig. 22-11. View of windows, all made from storm doors.

Put your baseboard at the bottom or not as you like.

Put baseboard at the bottom of your walls if you like. You could also forget about the molding which costs a bundle and do the finishing work with 1×4's either mitered or not, in the corners. In that case, run the 1×4's which you have prefinished—stained in this case a dark brown or finished in white, along the ceiling, the bottom of your walls, and two vertical boards at each corner, around your doors and windows, too.

If you think that's a lot of 1×4 it is—so if you'd rather, stick with the molding. But it has to be one or the other. The acoustical tile has to have something to finish it off.

PROJECT 6: STRIP RUG FLOOR

In a way this is a case of having your cake and eating it, too. The strip rug offers nice deep pile and, at the same time, is easy to handle and put down.

Treat it as if it were a large carpet sample, which in a way it is.

1. Seal the floor with two coats of sealer, after you've scrubbed it to pristine cleanliness.

2. Apply carpet tape. (This is going to be rather expensive comparatively speaking—but only comparatively).

3. If your pieces are 36 inches wide, draw your lines at 3-foot intervals in whatever direction you want the carpet to run.

4. Put tapes down on either side of the line, butting on the line.

5. Every 3 feet, put in tapes in the crosswise direction.

6. Put a double row of tape at the periphery of the room and across any doorways.

7. Lay the carpet in place, one strip at a time and trim at end to fit.

8. Long edge of carpet should be even with the joint between the tapes.

9. Be careful to match your pile unless you want the effect of a slightly darker shade in one strip than another.

10. If you like you can take advantage of this phenomenon and use it as you would stripes—going one way with all the even strips and the other with all the uneven number ones. Do what you like but be consistent. This is not a case of changing your mind in the middle of the pile.

PROJECT 7: INDOOR/OUTDOOR CARPETING FOR BREEZEWAY

Since this room is fairly large too, it might not be a bad idea to do a similar number on the breezeway. Instead of buying the 12-foot width of carpeting, but the 6-foot. Lay it down in much the same manner as described above, except that you might put a single row of carpet tape down every other time, in the middle of your 6-foot strip.

PROJECT 8:STORAGE SEAT

Follow directions given in Conversion IV, Project 5, on how to build a woodbox seat.

PROJECT 9: PLANTER BOX

Follow directions for planter given in Conversion VIII, Project 4. Build two, one along each bank of windows.

Note: Put in the planter before you lay the carpet—please! Ditto with the painting.

Chapter 23
Garage Conversion XII

This garage was attached to an ordinary, run-of-the-mill three bedroom, two bath, small living room, kitchen-breakfast-type house which, however, had a beautiful large yard and an excellent location in a charming subdivision on a ridge above a small university town.

The house sat on a corner lot. The garage, attached along one of its shorter ends, shared the brick veneer facade of the front of the house. The back, or garden side, however, was siding and so was the short wall of the house and the area around the garage door. There were two long, high windows in the front wall and a door almost at the corner in the other long wall. An interior door led into the breakfast-kitchen area.

The family needs were somewhat unusual. Since the owner taught piano at the university and also had a few private students, one of the prime requirements for the new room was that it would hold a grand piano and serve as a music studio. Secondly, since the house proper was so cramped, the family needed room for entertaining. Thirdly, the lady of the house was also a college teacher. Her field was English and she desperately needed a place to grade papers and pursue other such teacherly activities. And a place to continue her hobbies of making banners and Christmas decorations, too.

The first big problem was the grand piano. Not because of its size, (the garage was huge), but because of the requirements of temperature, humidity and sound quality. It would have been proved impossible. It would have been to make do without an exterior door, but that made the kitchen a thoroughfare for company, music students and the family.

Instead, it was decided to create a foyer at the outside door end which would   keep any stray drafts off the piano and, at the same time, provide closet space for wraps and a place to pull off boots and galoshes.

To help the sound quality, the garage door end of the room was enclosed completely and swathed in carpeting. The outside of the new foyer closet wall was carpeted, the inside lined with acoustical tiles.

The home office and craft center were designed to share a wall at the kitchen end of the room. The home office section was provided with a mobile cart that provided work space for typewriter and sewing machine. And, joy of joy, it could double as a good-sized serving counter for parties and recitals.

In fact, the idea was so splendid, that it was incorporated in one of the two-faced closets at the foyer end. The closet facing to the inside of the room was fitted out with shelves and a cart. The cart, pulled out with the drop leaves flipped up, became a quite respectable bar.

A picture window was added on the garden side of the room and a divider designed to screen off the foyer, and most particularly the drafts, from that side. See Fig. 23-1 for before and after floor plans.

PROJECT 1: ENCLOSING GARAGE DOOR OPENING

Follow instructions Conversion I, Project 2, for enclosing the garage door opening.

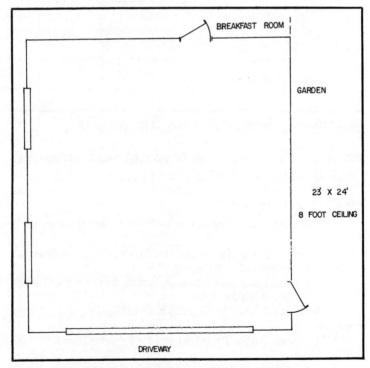

Fig. 23-1A. Scale plan of before view of Conversion XII.

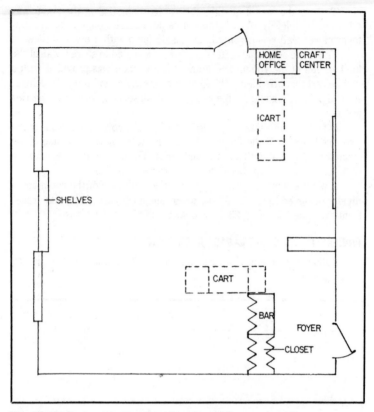

Fig. 23-1B. Scale plan showing after view of Conversion XII.

PROJECT 2: INSTALLING PICTURE WINDOW IN LONG WALL ON GARDEN SIDE

Follow instructions Conversion IV, Project 2.

PROJECT 3: BUILD FOYER CLOSET WALL

Follow instructions in Conversion V, Project 4, with these modifications:

1. You'll be building only one-fourth of the closet complex described so you'll need only one-fourth the materials.

2. One part of your closet is going to face the foyer but it will have a solid wall on the family room side.

3. The other one will face the family room and have a solid wall on the foyer side.

4. This means that you'll need an extra 4 × 8 sheet of ½-inch plywood for these walls.

5. Get the C-D, because you're going to cover it with carpeting anyway.

6. Use louvered bi-fold doors on the foyer side if you have to hang dampish coats a lot of the time.

7. Use plain ones elsewhere.

Materials: 18 8-foot 2 × 4's; 3 7-foot 2 " 4's; 6 2-foot 2 × 4's; 4 11-inch 2 × 4's; 4 panels of ½-inch 4 × 8-foot C-D plywood; 8 8-foot 1 × 4; 2 6-foot 1 × 4's; 4 3-foot 1 × 4's; 4 2-foot 1 × 4's; acoustical material to cover inside of closet walls, 6d and 8d nails, lag screws, 2 bi-fold doors, wood putty, glue, 36-inch dowel rod 1 inch diameter, shelves, pilaster strips.

Tools: Drill with masonry bit, saber saw, hammer, screwdriver, measuring tape, pencil, carpenter's square, level, scissors, slip-stick, straight edge, plumb line, miter box (optional).

Instructions:

1. Sound wall and find stud nearest to where you want your closet to go, either front or back. Mark.

2. Mark next stud which will fall within the closet.

3. Lay down sole plates as shown in Fig. 23-2.

4. Lay down long 2 " 4 cut to 8½-inch length on the floor.

5. Measure from the longer sole plate to the ceiling at points indicated on Fig. 23-2.

6. Cut 8-foot 2 × 4's to measure and fashion two frames as shown on Fig. 23-3. For details see Conversion V, Project 4.

7. Repeat for other side.

8. With helper, install on top of longer sole plates, tie into short sole at open side of frame.

9. Construct side walls as in Fig. 23-4.

10. Install in place between front and back walls.

11. Cut ½-inch plywood to sheath outside and inside of both closet sections.

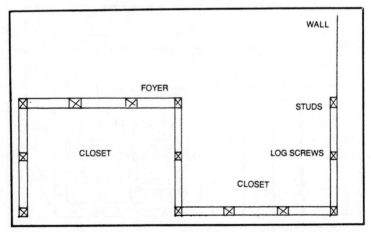

Fig. 23-2. Putting down the sole plates for the foyer wall closets and marking for studs.

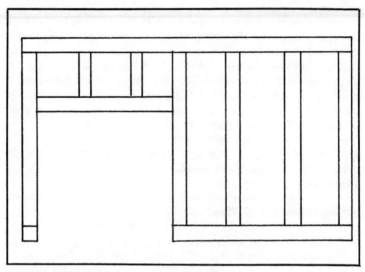

Fig. 23-3. Front framing for foyer closet wall.

12. Finish inside of closets with acoustical material.

13. Trim outside of closets with 1 × 4's.

14. Hang bi-fold doors.

15. Install clothes pole and one shelf in foyer closet.

16. Install pilaster strips in family room closet starting 32 inches from the floor.

17. Install shelves and wine rack.

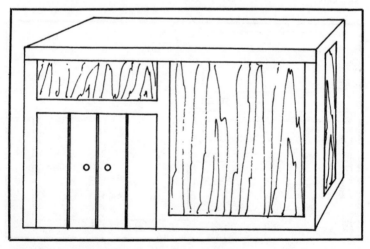

Fig. 23-4. View of completed foyer closet wall.

18. Mobile cart goes under first shelf.

19. Countersink nails, putty and sand.

20. Seal structure.

21. Paint trim to match walls of room.

22. Cover outside closet walls with carpeting to match wall when you work on that project.

PROJECT 4: BUILDING HOME OFFICE AND CRAFT CENTER

Follow directions for building storage wall in Conversion I, Project 3, but build only two units, each with a 36-inch opening.

For finishing home office section follow Conversion V, Project 8, steps 1-10 and 12 (Fig. 23-5).

PROJECT 5: CRAFT CENTER

To finish the other closet as a craft center, you will follow basically the same steps as in the home office project, except that you lower the desk shelf to typewriter or sewing machine height. To customize, use any or all of the following items to help store those odds and ends that craft work involves:

1. Plastic drawers of all sizes and widths.

2. Those marvelous plastic boxes with the umpteen drawers.

3. Plastic double-totes (actually sold for cleaning supplies and other under-the-sink goodies) are great for small jars, bottles, and boxes as well as larger paint brushes rulers and such.

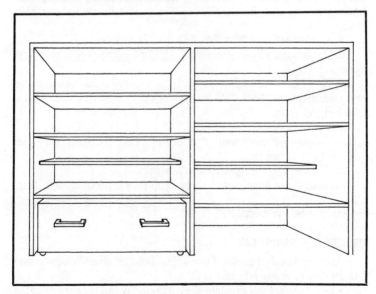

Fig. 23-5. Home office craft center combo.

4. Turn-tables—double, single, the kind you get for sewing supplies and the one for tools.

5. Cutlery trays—superb (and cheap) for knitting needles, paint brushes, felt pens, and so on.

6. Wall pocket systems you can make to fit your needs as in Conversion III, Project 11. See also under multipurpose ladder, Conversion VIII, Project 9.

Incidentally, do invest in one good comfortable secretary chair which you can use for the home office and the craft center.

PROJECT 6: WORK TABLE/SERVER CART WITH ELECTRICAL OUTLETS

Follow directions for Conversion VII, Project 6. Build your cart to a 34 " 28 inch module.

Instructions for modified cart (Conversion VII, Project 6).

1. Change the measurements of the ¾-inch plywood top to 22 × 34 inches.

2. The bottom, then, will be 22 × 31 inches.

3. The shelf also 22 × 31 inches.

4. Use the same height for your cart if the desk shelf in your home office closet is at 30 inches.

5. If the shelf is lower, you will have to make the cart lower. Deduct 1 inch from shelf height to arrive at cart height.

6. For instance—shelf is 28½ inches high, you need 1 inch clearance, so your cart will be 27½ inches high total. Deduct 2 inches for the casters; that leaves 25½ inches. Now deduct ¾-inch, the thickness of your top; that leaves you with 22¾ inches. This will be your measure for your side pieces.

7. Cut the sides to 22 inches wide and 22 ¾ long.

8. Do the same adjusting with the 2 ×2's for the frame and the back and front.

9. Now follow the steps as given, remember to cut the back to fit the new measurements: 34 × 24½ for a 30-inch desk top or 34 × 22¾ for a 28½-inch desk top.

10. Follow steps 1-11 and 12-32.

11. On the right inside wall above the shelf, install an electrical power outlet strip 8 inches long.

12. Follow direction given with the strip.

13. Install two small hooks above strip to wind cord around (Fig. 23-6).

14. Use heavy, metal, ball casters.

PROJECT 7: ROLL-OUT BAR

Another modified friend. Follow directions as given in Conversion VII, Project 6. Steps 1-11 and 12-32.

Use measurements as established in Project 6, this conversion and to get them follow steps 1-4 and 8-9.

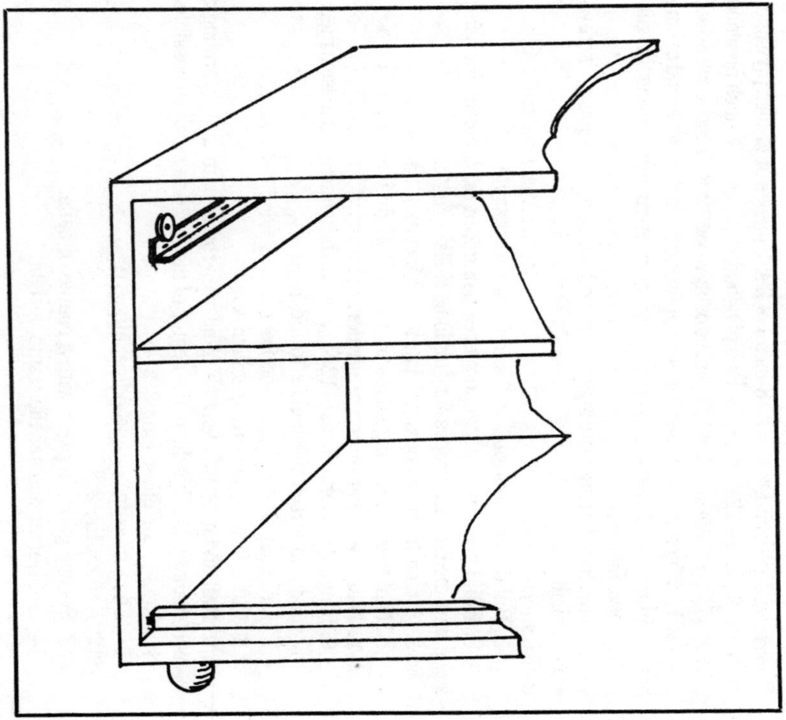

Fig. 23-6. Work table/server cart with electrical outlets showing hooks to wind up cord.

This will give you the basic cart. To transform it into a roll-out bar you'll need to do the following:

Materials: 17 foot of ll × 4's; enough cork squares to line bottom of cart; 2 shallow pull out drawers of the plastic kind, about 10 inches wide each, hardware for them; heavy drawer pulls for cart; and metal ball casters. Glue, nails.

Tools: Hammer, screwdriver, measuring tape, scissors, pencil.

Instructions:

1. Build your cart as indicated above but raise the shelf so it is at least 19 inches above the bottom shelf.

2. Before you install the shelf and casters, turn the cart on its side and install a strip of 1 × 4 on top of the front as shown in Fig. 23-7.

3. Next cut 5 1 × 4 strips to 20½ inches and glue and nail them onto the bottom shelf at 5-inch intervals.

4. This will give you five 5-inch compartments and one larger one.

5. Line the compartments with self adhesive cork tiles.

6. Install the shallow drawers, 1 at each side under the top.

7. Install heavy drawer pulls in front of cart (Fig. 23-8 and Fig. 23-9.)

PROJECT 8: BENCH/PLANTER/DIVIDER

Materials: 2 18-inch 1 × 2's; 2 48-inch 1 × 2's; 2 pieces of ¾-inch plywood; 54 × 18; 2 pieces 22½ × 18, ¾-inch plywood; 1 piece of ¾-inch plywood 52½ × 17¼; 1 52½-inch 1 × 3; 2 pieces of plywood 12 × 27 inches; 2 8-foot 2 × 4's; 1 54-inch 2 × 4, 1 piece ½-inch plywood 54 inches wide and ceiling height minus 19½ inches, 4 pieces of quarter-round; ceiling height-minus-19½ inches.

Tools: Saw, hammer, measuring tape, pencil, carpenter's square, screwdriver, drill.

Instructions:

1. Build frame out of 1 × 2's to form receptangle.

2. Build box out of plywood pieces using 22½-inch pieces for short sides and the 54-inch pieces for the long sides.

3. Attach frame to box, setting it in 3 inches all around.

4. Nail remaining long strips of plywood as divider into box.

5. Nail 1 × 3 flat on top of divider.

6. Hinge the short pieces—12 × 27 on the butt hinges, 2 to each piece of plywood and attach the hinges to the 1 ″ 3.

7. Lay your 2 × 4 flat on the floor.

8. Cut quarter-round to specified length.

9. Nail and glue two lengths of quarter-round onto 2 × 4 forming a ⅝-inch channel. Do this down the center of the 2 × 4 as much as possible.

10. Repeat for other long 2 × 4.

11. Slide in ½-inch plywood panel.

12. Nail on top 2 × 4.

13. Secure panel in place with a couple of nails.

14. Get helper and set the frame upright.

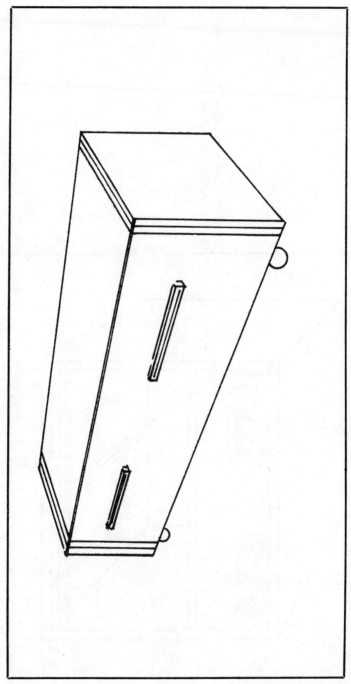

Fig. 23-7. Complete roll-out bar, front view, showing large drawer pull hardware.

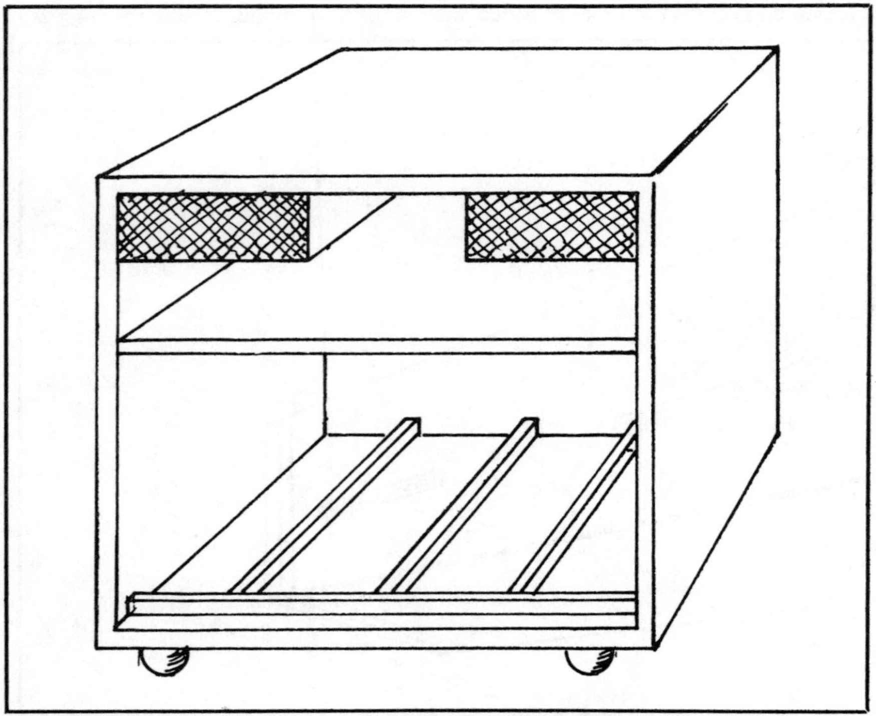

Fig. 23-8. Roll-out bar showing bottom with divider strips to keep bottles up right.

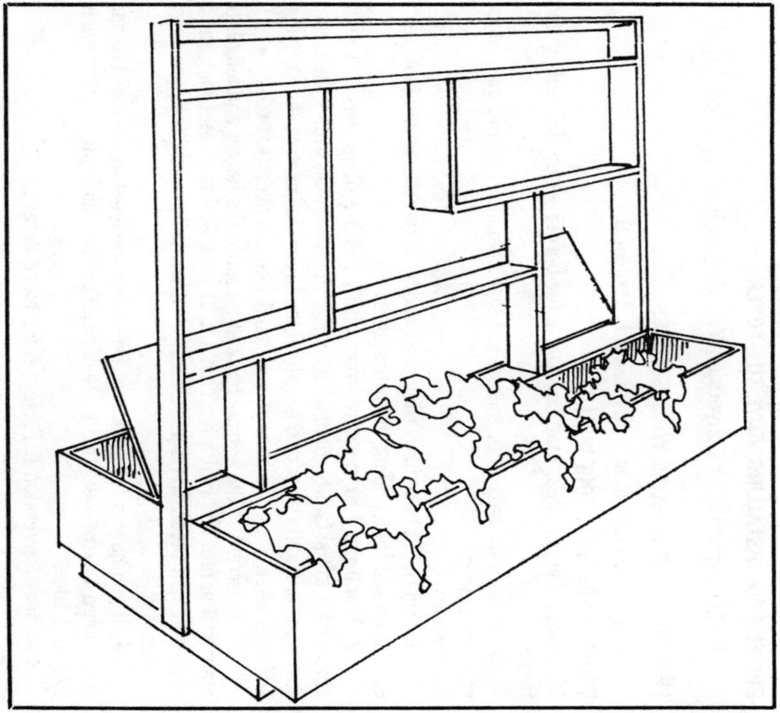

Fig. 23-9. Bench/planter/divider trimmed with molding in a geometric pattern.

15. Attach to box so that 2 × 4 rests on floor (Fig. 23-10).

16. Countersink nails, fill and sand.

17. Seal wood and paint to match walls.

18. If desired use narrow molding strips to outline a geometric pattern as shown on Fig. 23-10. Paint to match.

19. Fill rectangles with cork tiles on the foyer side.

20. Paint stripes on the other side of a contrasting color and hang photos or prints in the spaces.

21. Paint inside of open and lidded box with coats of marine or spar varnish.

22. Fill open box with bark or pebbles and set in potted plants.

23. If desired, make cushions to fit lids of boxes as in Conversion III, Project 12.

24. Cut Velcro strips and attach one side to back of lid the other to cushion.

PROJECT 9: PAINTING WALLS.

Follow directions in Conversion I, Project 6. Don't paint the new wall or the closets.

PROJECT 10: INSTALLING VINYL TILE FOYER

Follow direction in Conversion VII, Project 9.

PROJECT 11: INSTALLING WALL SHELVES

Follow directions in Conversion I, Project 5.

PROJECT 12: CARPETING WALLS

Materials: Carpet tiles, staples, 1 × 4 for border along the ceiling and floor.

Tools: Scissors, chalk line, measuring tape, hammer, staple gun, stepstool or ladder.

Instructions:

1. Figure out how many tiles you need by taking the square footage of each area and then adding them together.

2. You'll need to measure your family room wall as area # 1 your closet back in the family room as area # 2, the short side wall of the closet as area # 3, and the rest of the wall on the foyer side as area # 4. You can add the other closet as area # 5 if you'd like to cover that too.

3. To arrive at the square footage measure the height and length of your wall in feet and multiply. That's it. If your wall is 23 feet long and 8 high that will mean 184 square feet or tiles. Allow extra tiles for extra inches.

4. If you have a room 22-foot 6-inches, you'll get an area of 176 and you'll need 4 extra tiles, that is, ½ of a tile per row multiplied by 8 rows is 8/2 or 4 tiles.

5. See Conversion I, Project 8 for more details.

6. Seal your wall and other areas where you are going to apply tiles.

7. Proceed just as you would on a floor except that you will be working up-right on a ladder, instead of hunched over on the floor.

8. When you have a quarter of a wall tiled, use your staple gun loaded with large staples to staple the corners of each tile to the wall. The nap will hide the staples.

9. Continue in this fashion until all the surfaces are tiled.

10. Nail pre-finished (to match the walls and ceiling) 1 × 4's to the ceiling and floor edge of the walls and closets.

PROJECT 13: CARPET TILING FLOOR

Follow direction in Conversion I, Project 8 for details.

Appendix:
Additional Reading

Brann, Donald, R. Wall to Wall Cabinets . Briarcliff, N. Y. Directions' Simplified, Inc., 1975.

Browne, Dan. Multiply Your Living Space. New York: McGraw Hill Book Co., 1979.

Davidson, Margaret. Successful Studios and Work Centers. Farmington MI: Structures Publishing Co., 1977.

Day, Richard. Remodeling Rooms. New York: Arco Publishing Co., 1977.

Galvin, Patrick J. Successful Space Saving at Home. Farmington, MI: Structures Publishing Co., 1976.

Green, Floyd and Susan E. Meyer. You Can Renovate Your Own Home. Garden City, NJ: Doubleday & Co., 1978.

Hedden, J.W. Successful Shelves and Built-Ins. Farmington, MI: Structures Publishing Co., 1979.

Hennesey, James and V. Papanek. Nomad Furniture. New York: Random House, 1973.

Nomad Furniture II. New York: Random House, 1974.

Kinney C. and Barry Roberts. Don't Move, Improve. New York: Thomas and Crowell Publishers, 1979.

Philbin, Tom. The Encyclopedia of Hardware. New York: Hawthorne Books, Inc. 1978.

Scharff, Robert. The Complete Book of Home Workshop Tools. New York: McGraw Hill Book Co., 1979.

Watkins, A.M. The Complete Book of Home Remodeling, Improvement and Repair. New York: Charles Scribners Sons, 1979.

Zarkas, Spiro. Furniture in Twenty-four Hours . New York: St. Martin's Press, 1978.

Index